"Dr. Poythress's book walks the
This volume invites the reader to
God's personal presence in the whole canon of Scripture. Those who look in faith
will be rewarded and encouraged in their walk with Christ."

David Wenkel, Adjunct Faculty, Trinity Evangelical Divinity School;
author, *Shining Like the Sun: A Biblical Theology of Meeting God
Face to Face*

"This work is broader than any I have seen in its coverage of the biblical theology
of theophany. I appreciate the many explanations of how each Old Testament
aspect of theophany is fulfilled in Christ. The many chapters provide a spiritually
uplifting study that is well organized and carefully written in terms any layman
can understand, but also stimulating for advanced students."

James A. Borland, Professor Emeritus of New Testament and Theology,
Liberty University

"Poythress is a master at pulling together various strands of Scripture and
showing their coherence. This book on the multifaceted aspects of God's presence is no exception. *Theophany* fills a real void in evangelical theology—in-
formative for the scholar but accessible to the layman. Students often ask
me about the various senses of God's presence discussed in Scripture, and I
typically give a vague answer. But now, after reading Poythress, my answers
will be much more informed; and I have a first-class resource to share with
my students."

Robert J. Cara, Provost, Chief Academic Officer, and Hugh and Sallie
Reaves Professor of New Testament, Reformed Theological Seminary;
author, *Cracking the Foundation of the New Perspective on Paul*;
contributor, *A Biblical-Theological Introduction to the New Testament*

"In biblical times, God appeared visibly to people in many different ways,
and divinely inspired authors reflected on his appearances throughout the
Scriptures. Yet the modern Christian experience is so different that we are
often left wondering what significance biblical appearances of God have for
us today. Poythress explores this theme within its ancient historical context
and explains how Christ fulfills its significance in himself and in his followers' lives. Poythress's discussions are rooted in sound biblical scholarship, but
clearly express how this facet of Scripture should enhance every Christian's
daily service to God."

Richard L. Pratt Jr., President, Third Millennium Ministries

"Vern Poythress's *Theophany* is a theologically rich, spiritually edifying exploration of all that the Bible says about an awe-striking reality that fills the pages of Scripture: our infinite, personal Creator 'who dwells in unapproachable light, whom no one has ever seen or can see' delights to make himself known through the senses he has given us, the universe he made and sustains, and his redemptive deeds in history, culminating in Jesus Christ. This biblical theology of God's appearing will expand your thoughts and nourish your heart."

Dennis E. Johnson, Professor of Practical Theology, Westminster Seminary California; author, *Triumph of the Lamb*; *Him We Proclaim*; and *Walking with Jesus through His Word*

Theophany

Theophany

A Biblical Theology of God's Appearing

Vern S. Poythress

:: CROSSWAY®

WHEATON, ILLINOIS

Theophany: A Biblical Theology of God's Appearing

Copyright © 2018 by Vern S. Poythress

Published by Crossway
          1300 Crescent Street
          Wheaton, Illinois 60187

Cover design: Crystal Courtney

Cover image: Lightstock / Brenton Clarke

First printing 2018

Printed in the United States of America

Scripture quotations are from the ESV® Bible (The Holy Bible, English Standard Version®), copyright © 2001 by Crossway, a publishing ministry of Good News Publishers. Used by permission. All rights reserved.

Scripture quotations marked NASB are from *The New American Standard Bible*®. Copyright © The Lockman Foundation 1960, 1962, 1963, 1968, 1971, 1972, 1973, 1975, 1977, 1995. Used by permission.

Scripture quotations marked KJV are from the *King James Version* of the Bible.

The Scripture reference marked ASV is from the *American Standard Version* of the Bible.

All emphases in Scripture quotations have been added by the author.

Trade paperback ISBN: 978-1-4335-5437-7
ePub ISBN: 978-1-4335-5440-7
PDF ISBN: 978-1-4335-5438-4
Mobipocket ISBN: 978-1-4335-5439-1

Library of Congress Cataloging-in-Publication Data

Names: Poythress, Vern S., author.
Title: Theophany : a biblical theology of God's appearing / Vern S. Poythress.
Description: Wheaton : Crossway, 2018. | Includes bibliographical references and index.
Identifiers: LCCN 2017025804 (print) | LCCN 2017033112 (ebook) | ISBN 9781433554384 (pdf) | ISBN 9781433554391 (mobi) | ISBN 9781433554407 (epub) | ISBN 9781433554377 (tp)
Subjects: LCSH: Theophanies in the Bible.
Classification: LCC BS680.T45 (ebook) | LCC BS680.T45 P69 2018 (print) | DDC 231.7/4—dc23
LC record available at https://lccn.loc.gov/2017025804

Crossway is a publishing ministry of Good News Publishers.

VP   28   27   26   25   24   23   22   21   20   19   18
15   14   13   12   11   10   9   8   7   6   5   4   3   2

To my wife, Diane

Contents

**PART III: A HISTORY OF GOD APPEARING:
THE OLD TESTAMENT**

**PART IV: A HISTORY OF GOD APPEARING:
THE NEW TESTAMENT**

APPENDICES

Tables and Illustrations

PART I

THE BIBLICAL THEME OF GOD APPEARING

1

God Coming

In the Western world, we live in a time of doubt. People ask, "Does God exist? If he does, where is he? How can we find him?" To some people, the words of Job may seem appropriate: "Oh, that I knew where I might find him" (Job 23:3).

The Experience of Job

To many, it seems that God cannot be found. But what if God actually came and met you? What if he spoke to you? According to the Bible, just such a thing happened to Job (Job 38–41), and it was overwhelming. We should not be surprised that it was. It would be overwhelming for us, if we were to meet the God of infinity, who made the galaxies and the stars, and who also made you and me. Meeting God turns out to be an earthshaking experience that may change you forever.

When God met Job, he not only spoke; he *appeared* to Job in a whirlwind: "Then the LORD answered Job out of the whirlwind" (Job 38:1). Job knew that he had met God. There was no mistaking it. Not only did God speak words with divine authority and wisdom, but the visible accompaniment in the whirlwind reinforced the solemnity of the occasion. Job knew that he was meeting the all-powerful God.

Job was changed by the experience. He says,

"I know that you can do all things,
    and that no purpose of yours can be thwarted." (Job 42:2)

Even before this point in time, Job would have said that God was all-powerful. But when God met him, the truth became new and living for Job—it took on fresh depth. Job had a deep change, a change of heart.

Meeting God Today

Job's experience was unique. Why does God not give the same experience to everyone else? We cannot say. God decides when and how he will meet us, when and how he will come to us. God deals with each one of us according to his wisdom. He takes into account everything that we are; he treats each person in his individuality and uniqueness (Psalm 139). If we think we want to have an experience like Job's, we might first think about whether we really want the "full package," so to speak. For example, do we want to go through the suffering that Job experienced that led up to the climactic encounter with God? And even if we could avoid the suffering of Job, do we really want to be overwhelmed by encountering the infinite God as Job did? In reality, it is frightening.

But God can and does come to meet people in a real and deep way today. For one thing, he does it when they hear how he met Job and how he met other people in cases recorded in the Bible. The Bible is not just a record of past works of God. God had it written so that we might still learn about him *today*. The Bible is the very word of God, and he still speaks what it says *today*. The word of God is alive and active (Heb. 4:12). So meeting God happens when we listen to the Bible.

We can learn more by focusing on the places in the Bible that describe God as coming and meeting with people. Among these, we will focus especially on the cases where God *appears* to people, like the whirlwind in which God came to Job. These cases are among the most intense instances when God comes. We can learn from them the meaning of who God is and how he comes to us today.

Does God Appear?

According to the Bible, God is invisible. But the Bible also describes incidents in which God makes himself visible, by appearing to human beings. How do we fit these two sides together?[1]

Answering this question helps us understand God, ourselves, and our place in the world. God has made us as creatures, to whom he

---

1. See Andrew Malone, *Knowing Jesus in the Old Testament? A Fresh Look at Christophanies* (Nottingham, UK: Inter-Varsity, 2015), 44–79, and the further discussion in appendix A of the present work.

makes himself known. To know God is all-important. Many people have questions about God. We can receive satisfactory answers only if we come to know him. And we come to know him when he comes to us and shows himself to us. He manifests himself. How?

Seeing God in Christ

The issue gains in depth because the supreme instance of God becoming visible is found in Christ. God makes himself known supremely in Christ. And when Christ was on earth, he was visible. What does it mean to see Christ? And do we see God through him? Christ himself gives an answer in a dialogue with the apostle Philip:

> Philip said to him, "Lord, show us the Father, and it is enough for us." Jesus said to him, "Have I been with you so long, and you still do not know me, Philip? *Whoever has seen me has seen the Father.* How can you say, 'Show us the Father'?" (John 14:8–9)

Jesus indicates that it *is* possible to see God. "*Whoever has seen me has seen the Father*" (John 14:9); that is, the person he describes has seen God the Father.

What does it mean, then, to have "seen the Father"? In the next verses Jesus explains more fully how this seeing takes place:

> "Do you not believe that I am in the Father and the Father *is in me*? The words that I say to you I do not speak on my own authority, but the Father who *dwells in me* does *his works*. Believe me that I am in the Father and the Father is in me, or else believe on account of *the works* themselves." (John 14:10–11)

Seeing in the right sense goes together with believing—believing that "I am in the Father and the Father is in me." And that in turn goes together with understanding the meaning of Jesus's works. Jesus's opponents saw him with their physical eyes. But they opposed him. They did not accept his claims. It was not enough merely to see him physically. The opponents did not rightly understand the significance of his works. They did not understand who he was, nor the reality that the Father was in him.

Understanding the Works

Jesus more than once points to the significance of his works, if people will only take to heart that significance:

But Jesus answered them, "My Father is *working* until now, and I am *working*." This was why the Jews were seeking all the more to kill him, because not only was he breaking the Sabbath, but he was even calling God his own Father, making himself equal with God. So Jesus said to them, "Truly, truly, I say to you, the Son can do nothing of his own accord, but only what he sees the Father doing. For whatever the Father *does*, that the Son *does* likewise. For the Father loves the Son and shows him all that he himself is doing. And greater *works* than these will he show him, so that you may marvel. For as the Father raises the dead and *gives them life*, so also the Son *gives life* to whom he will. (John 5:17–21)

Jesus answered them, "I have shown you many good *works* from the Father; for which of them are you going to stone me?" The Jews answered him, "It is not for a good *work* that we are going to stone you but for blasphemy, because you, being a man, make yourself God." (John 10:32–33)

God appears to human beings in Jesus, as Jesus himself affirms to Philip. But people must interpret what they see. They must see God the Father's works in the works of Jesus, and God the Father's words in the words of Jesus:

"For I have not spoken on my own authority, but the Father who sent me has himself given me a *commandment*—what to *say* and what to *speak*. And I know that his commandment is eternal life. What I *say*, therefore, I *say* as the Father has *told* me." (John 12:49–50)

"The words that I *say* to you I do not speak on my own authority, but the Father who dwells in me *does his works*." (John 14:10; also 17:8)

In sum, the "seeing" is not merely a physical seeing but a spiritual seeing. This kind of seeing takes place through believing in Jesus. It is enabled by the words of the Father and the Son, which the Son gives to his disciples. The words are received and understood by the people whom the Father gave to the Son:

"you [God the Father] have given him [God the Son] authority over all flesh, to give eternal life to *all whom you have given him*." (John 17:2)

"I have manifested your name to the people *whom you gave me* out of the world. Yours they were, and you *gave them to me*, and they have kept your word." (v. 6)

Seeing and Not Seeing

So there is more than one *kind* of seeing in the Bible. A person can "see" and yet not understand:

> And he [God] said, "Go, and say to this people: 'Keep on hearing, but do not understand; keep on *seeing*, but do not perceive.' Make the heart of this people dull, and their ears heavy, and *blind their eyes*; lest they *see* with their eyes, and hear with their ears, and understand with their hearts, and turn and be healed." (Isa. 6:9–10)

To "see" the Father, in the way that Jesus described to Philip, is possible only when a person *understands*.

In addition, there is a sense in which even believers who have divinely been given understanding do not "see," because it is never possible to master God or to grasp him the way one grasps a leaf or an apple within one's vision. The Bible in this sense says that God is invisible and will remain invisible:

> To the King of the ages, immortal, *invisible*, the only God, be honor and glory forever and ever. Amen. (1 Tim. 1:17)

> He who is the blessed and only Sovereign, the King of kings and Lord of lords, who alone has immortality, who dwells in unapproachable light, whom no one has ever *seen or can see*. To him be honor and eternal dominion. Amen. (1 Tim. 6:15–16)

Other passages, however, combine invisibility and visibility, reminding us that this invisible and unmasterable God does make himself known. He makes himself known through the works of creation:

> For his *invisible* attributes, namely, his eternal power and divine nature, have been clearly *perceived*, ever since the creation of the world, in the things that have been made. (Rom. 1:20)

Supremely, God makes himself known in Christ, who is the "image of the *invisible* God" (Col. 1:15). Moses in his day knew God, as described in Hebrews 11:27: "By faith he left Egypt, not being afraid of the anger of the king, for he endured as *seeing him who is invisible*."

Old Testament Anticipations

The Old Testament contains many anticipations of the time when Christ would come to earth and would accomplish salvation. These anticipations or "shadows" of what was to come include instances where human beings experience visible manifestations of God. Some experiences take place in dreams, some in broad daylight. These manifestations look forward to the day when God will appear in a climactic and final way, in Christ:

> And the Word [Christ] became flesh and dwelt among us, and we have seen his *glory*, glory as of the only Son from the Father, full of grace and truth. (John 1:14)

John 1:14 uses the word *glory* in a way that evokes the Old Testament instances where God appears in glory. By using this word, John is indicating that Christ brings to fulfillment the Old Testament instances when the glory of God appeared (e.g., Ex. 16:10; Num. 16:19).

A few verses later, after John 1:14, the Gospel indicates how Jesus answers the desire to see God:

> No one has ever *seen* God; the only God,[2] who is at the Father's side, he has *made him known*. (John 1:18)

The verse begins by observing that "no one has ever seen God." But the rest of the verse indicates that we come to know him intimately through Jesus, who is "the only God, who is at the Father's side." The implication is that this intimate knowledge is a kind of seeing.

The Word *Theophany*

Theologians have a specialized word to describe the instances when God appears to human beings. A visible manifestation of God within the Old Testament is called a *theophany*. The word *theophany* derives from two Greek words, the word for God (*theos*) and the word for appearing

---

2. Some New Testament manuscripts have "only Son" instead of "only God." Since the Son is God (John 1:1), the overall thrust is similar if this is the original reading.

(*phainō*, which in the passive means *appear*). That is, a theophany is an appearance of God.

We can use this word *theophany* more narrowly or more broadly. In a broader use, it would encompass not only obvious instances describing an appearance of God, but also appearances that are more veiled, as when God appears in a cloud and no one can see inside the cloud. A broad use would also include appearances of God in the New Testament, including the appearing of Christ himself. In his incarnation, Christ is the *permanent* "theophany" of God.

The Significance of Theophany

The theme of theophany—the theme of God appearing—is important for several reasons. First, as we just observed, the theme has at its center the person of Christ, who is the permanent theophany anticipated by the temporary theophanies in the Old Testament. Second, the theme finds its culmination in the final vision of God described in the book of Revelation: "They [the saints] will *see his face*, and his name will be on their foreheads" (Rev. 22:4). Thus, theophany is central to Christian hope. The final destiny of redeemed mankind is to experience the final theophany, when we "see his face."

It helps to remember the larger plot of history. God's purpose in history is to establish communion with mankind. That communion comes to consummation in the new heavens and the new earth (Rev. 21:1–22:5). At that time, the consummate communion takes place in a final theophany. God comes. God appears, and the Lamb appears on the throne (22:1). God's promise is that his servants "will *see* his face" (v. 4). This purpose of God is behind the whole history leading up to the consummation. It drives all of history. So it is important to reckon with it.

The purpose of God also has practical implications for us. It is God's purpose for the church, for each one of *us* who belong to Jesus Christ. It defines who we are by showing what God's plan is for us. Even now, in this life, we can experience communion with God through Jesus Christ. In the Bible, theophanies show us this same God. They show us that God comes to us and establishes communion with us in Christ. Understanding God's appearing reorients the meaning of our lives and enables us to know the purpose of our life by knowing God.

Third, a focus on this theme of God appearing reminds us and encourages us concerning the God-centered character of the Bible and of the Christian faith. We should seek communion with God, not just enjoy his benefits or focus on ourselves as beneficiaries of salvation.

Theophany is also an important theme within the Old Testament. Theophanies occur in the Old Testament more often than most people realize. It is easy for modern people quickly to pass by the descriptions of theophany when they are trying to find out what happens to the human recipients. Theophanies include symbolism that needs to be appreciated, rather than passed over as a puzzle. Moreover, theophany in a narrow sense has connections with the broader theme of God's presence, a theme that runs through the whole Old Testament.

Favorite Themes: Promise, Covenant, Kingdom, and Presence

It is helpful for us to see how the theme of God's presence integrates with other themes in the Old Testament. Several themes are important in understanding the Old Testament. Among the prominent ones are the theme of promise and fulfillment, the theme of covenant, the theme of kingdom, and the theme of God's presence. Any one of the themes offers a powerful way of understanding the entire record of God's dealings with his people, in the Old Testament and New Testament alike. Let us consider them briefly, one by one.

First, God makes *promises*. From very early, he promises to send a redeemer to undo sin and its effects (Gen. 3:15), to save people from their rebellion against God. God's promises include long-range promises about the coming of Christ, as well as short-range promises about acts of redemption within the Old Testament period. The promises include the central promise that God will *be God* to his people (e.g., Gen. 17:7). He will have a personal, intimate relation with them. Since the promises of God are trustworthy, they imply that God is able and willing to fulfill what he has promised. The promises imply that God rules all of history and will surely accomplish his purposes, including the final purpose of dwelling with mankind in the new heaven and the new earth (Rev. 21:1–3). The promises of God give us, in summary form, the plan of God for all of history. History moves forward in harmony with God's promises, and moves toward the goal of fulfilling his promises.

The second theme is the theme of *covenant*. God makes *covenants* with mankind. A covenant is a solemn agreement that involves personal commitments and a personal relation between the parties to the covenant. The whole of biblical history can be viewed as the outworking of two covenants: the covenant of works that God made with Adam before the fall, and the covenant of grace after the fall.[3] In the Old Testament we find a record of a number of distinct covenants: the covenants with Noah, Abraham, Moses, and David. All these are particular expressions of the covenant of grace. They express God's plan for salvation, which comes to culmination in the work of Christ.

The use of the concept of the covenant of grace does not imply that we would ignore the differences between different historical covenants, with Noah, Abraham, Moses, and David, or Jeremiah's promise of the new covenant (Jer. 31:31–34). Rather, the covenant of grace is a theological category expressing the unity of *one* way of salvation throughout the course of biblical history. Salvation is by grace through faith, on the basis of Christ's work. The concept of the covenant of grace encourages us to focus on this one salvation expressed in the various historical covenants.

Third, consider the theme of *kingdom*. God rules over all of history as *king* (Ps. 103:19; Dan. 4:34–35). God exerted his kingly power and authority when he created the world. The world is his kingdom. He made mankind in his image with the purpose that mankind would exercise *dominion* over the world, in imitation of God's dominion (Gen. 1:28–30).

Even after the fall, God continues to rule over all history. At the climax of history, in the coming of Christ, God exerts his power and his rule to bring salvation through the work of Christ. In the Gospels, the expression *the kingdom of God* is used in a focused way to designate God's presence in bringing *salvation*, not just his rule in providence. God's kingly rule achieves its final realization in the new heaven and the new earth, in which the central reality is the rule of God on his throne (Rev. 22:1).

Fourth, consider the theme of God's *presence*. From creation onward, God expresses his presence in the things that he has made, but especially in the ways in which he establishes a personal relation with human beings. God's personal relation with mankind was disrupted when Adam

---

3. See the Westminster Confession of Faith, 7.

fell into sin. But God renews the relation in preliminary forms in the Old Testament, especially with Abraham and his descendants. Then he opens the way to intimate fellowship with himself through Christ, who bore the penalty for sins and purified the people of God to make them fit to come into his presence. The final enjoyment of the presence of God comes in the new heaven and the new earth, when his saints "will see his face" (Rev. 22:4).

These four themes—promise, covenant, kingdom, and presence— intertwine with each other. They reinforce one another, and any one of them can be used as a perspective on all of history. The promises of God, as we have noted, express in summary form an outline of all of history. The high points of history occur in the fulfillment of God's promises. The promises of God come in the context of covenants, and are integrated into the covenant relation between God and his people. So promise-and-fulfillment can be seen as a subordinate theme within the theme of covenant. The promises are *covenantal* promises, so covenant serves as a perspective on promise. The events of fulfillment express God's faithfulness to his covenant.

The covenants that God makes involve the expression of God's power and authority as king. Because he is the great king, his covenants are binding on us. So covenant is an expression of kingship. Since God's kingly rule is always in harmony with his covenantal words, kingship itself can be seen as an expression of covenant.

We can see the significance of the theme of the presence of God by observing its coherence with the themes of promise, covenant, and kingship. God's promises are forms of his presence, where he commits himself to fulfilling his words. Fulfillments of promises take place by God coming to bring about the fulfillment. When God comes, whether in the visible appearance of a theophany or in another way, he is intensely present. So fulfillment manifests the presence of God. At the heart of God's covenantal relationship with mankind is the promise, I "will be your God, and you shall be my people" (Lev. 26:12; Jer. 7:23; etc.), a promise that includes the *presence* of God with his people. This presence finds its New Testament fulfillment in the indwelling of the Holy Spirit in believers.

Similarly, God's kingly rule over his people and over all the world involves his presence in power, to actually exert and make manifest his rule. So the kingdom of God always involves the *presence* of God.

Thus, there is coherence among four themes: (1) promise and fulfillment; (2) covenant; (3) kingdom; and (4) presence (see fig. 1.1).

Fig. 1.1: Interlocking Themes in the Bible

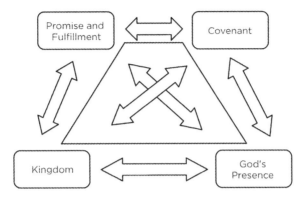

If we treat promise-and-fulfillment as a subtheme under covenant, we can say that there is coherence among three themes: covenant, kingdom, and presence (see fig. 1.2).

Fig. 1.2: Interlocking of the Themes of Covenant, Kingdom, and Presence

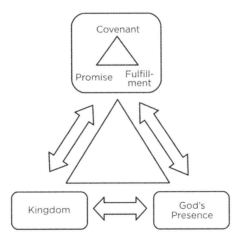

Each of the three themes runs through the entire Bible. Each gives us a perspective on all of history. (See fig. 1.3.)

Fig. 1.3: Three Perspectives on History

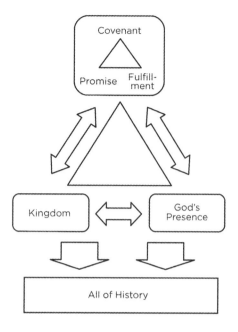

In this book, we are especially focusing on the theme of God's presence. Like the themes of covenant and kingdom, the theme of the presence of God encompasses all of biblical history. It gives us a comprehensive picture of God's purposes. It is important for us to reckon with the presence of God, because it illumines the meaning of all of history. It also illumines the meaning of each person's life, each person's individuality. Within history, God chooses to come and establish a personal relation with each one of us who belong to Christ. He comes in person, and in intimacy.

God also has a personal relation with people who do not belong to Christ. This relation is broken, because of sin. But no one escapes God; all of us are accountable to him. And from time to time even unbelievers may have intense encounters with God, as happened several times in the Bible: Cain (Gen. 4:9–15); the dreams of Pharaoh's cupbearer and baker (Gen. 40:1–23); Pharaoh himself (Gen. 41:1–36); Balaam (Numbers 22–24); Nebuchadnezzar (Daniel 4); and Belshazzar (Daniel 5).

Understanding the presence of God illuminates not only the broad sweep of history but also the smallest bits of history, including the story of each one of our lives, and the details in these stories, because God is present in the details. God is present in every verse of the Bible, because it is his word—it is what he speaks. But in addition, God has included in the Bible the specific *theme* of his presence, and he teaches us about this theme in order that we may grow in understanding him, in understanding his purposes, and in understanding ourselves as included in his purposes. God comes to be present with us and even *in* us, through the indwelling of the Holy Spirit. (See fig. 1.4.)

Fig. 1.4: God's Presence as a Perspective

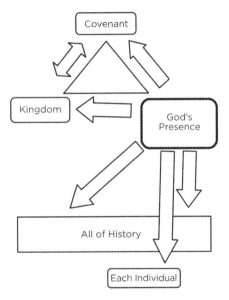

Theophany and the Presence of God

Now what is the relation of the presence of God to the theme of theophany? Theophany represents an intensive form of the presence of God. So theophany is like a subtheme within the broad theme of God's presence. At the same time, the intensive forms of God's presence show us a lot about the meaning of God's presence in the broadest sense. (See fig. 1.5.)

Fig. 1.5: Theophany and Presence

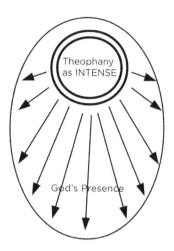

The intensive presence of God in theophany offers a key for understanding more deeply the broader instances of God's presence. As we shall see, theophanies of the most spectacular kind have a significant relationship to other forms of God's presence. For example, poetic language that evokes memories of theophany can be used to describe God's presence in a broad sense. And more spectacular theophanies can be compared to less spectacular theophanies and then to instances of God's presence that may not clearly have a special visible component. All these expressions of the presence of God receive illumination from what we find with the more spectacular theophanies. (See fig. 1.6.)

So let us use a definition of theophany that has some flexibility built into it:

> A *theophany* is a manifestation of divine presence accompanied by
> an extraordinary display *mediating* that presence.[4]

The word *display* focuses on *visual* phenomena. The visual phenomena may be more or less "extraordinary," so there is flexibility in this defini-

---

4. I am not sure where this definition came from, but I suspect that it did not originate with me. I have made my own modifications. I am sorry that I can no longer remember and cannot credit the author. Also, readers may note that my definition does not directly distinguish temporary from permanent manifestations. Other definitions may choose to make distinctions in other ways. For example, if we wish, we may highlight the uniqueness of the incarnation by building an explicit distinction in terminology between the incarnate Christ and Old Testament theophanies that foreshadow it.

Fig. 1.6: Theophany as a Perspective

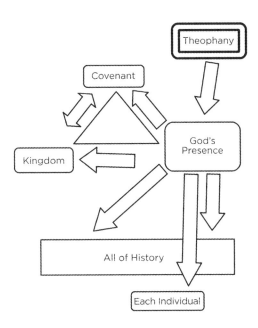

tion. The flexibility increases if we extend our definition beyond visual phenomena to phenomena in sound—that is, divine speech. The Bible contains quite a few instances describing God speaking to a human being, where the text does not specifically indicate whether there was an unusual visual display. God is present in his speech, and manifests his character by speaking, as well as in instances with an unusual visual display. In a broad sense, any speech of God to man is theophanic in nature. God could also express his presence internally to someone's spirit, without either a special visual or a special auditory display (Job 32:8). The indwelling of the Holy Spirit in believers is a special expression of God's presence (Rom. 8:9–10; 1 Cor. 6:19).

What are the implications? When we want to consider how the Bible applies to us, we should pay close attention to what it teaches about theophany and about God's presence. The God who reveals himself intensively in theophany is the same God who comes to each one of us as an individual. He establishes and maintains his presence with individuals through the work of Christ, who is the permanent theophany of God. And Christ sends the Holy Spirit, who brings new birth and establishes his dwelling in each person who believes in Christ. The narrow theme of theophany and the broader theme of God's presence both have pointed lessons for us, because they show us what it means to enjoy God's presence in blessing—or, alternatively, to experience his presence in wrath against sin. Because there is only one way of salvation, the way of Christ (John 14:6), God's presence with each of us as an individual reflects the same principles that we see intensively in the records in the Bible. These principles have a climactic manifestation when Christ accomplishes his work on earth.

2

God Appearing with
a Thunderstorm

The appearing of God in a theophany takes a variety of forms. We will devote a chapter to each of the main kinds of theophanies found in the Old Testament. (The New Testament also contains some theophanies, but the situation is different at that point, because Christ has come into the world!) In each chapter, we consider some representative examples of theophany, but we will not try to list them all. Once we understand a pattern in theophanies, we can see how still other passages fit into and confirm the pattern.

The first kind of theophany is a *thunderstorm* theophany or thunderstorm appearance. These appearances may or may not take the form of a literal thunderstorm. The point is that there is a cluster of characteristics—a dark cloud, lightning, thunder, wind.

In all theophanies, a clear distinction is in place between God the Creator and the phenomena of creation. God the Creator is absolute; everything in creation is dependent. There is never any mixing of the two; there is no confusion between the Creator and his creation. Thunderstorms, clouds, lightning, and wind are all part of the created world. They are not God. But in special cases of theophany, God *uses* these created things as media through which he manifests himself as the Creator.

Mount Sinai Theophany

In the whole Old Testament, the most prominent of these thunderstorm appearances is the appearance of God at Mount Sinai, after the people of Israel have come out of Egypt.[1] Here is the heart of the description:

> And the Lord said to Moses, "Behold, I am coming to you in a thick cloud, that the people may hear when I speak with you, and may also believe you forever."
>
> When Moses told the words of the people to the Lord, the Lord said to Moses, "Go to the people and consecrate them today and tomorrow, and let them wash their garments and be ready for the third day. For on the third day the Lord will come down on Mount Sinai in the sight of all the people. . . ."
>
> On the morning of the third day there were thunders and lightnings and a thick cloud on the mountain and a very loud trumpet blast, so that all the people in the camp trembled. Then Moses brought the people out of the camp to meet God, and they took their stand at the foot of the mountain. Now Mount Sinai was wrapped in smoke because the Lord had descended on it in fire. The smoke of it went up like the smoke of a kiln, and the whole mountain trembled greatly. And as the sound of the trumpet grew louder and louder, Moses spoke, and God answered him in thunder. The Lord came down on Mount Sinai, to the top of the mountain. And the Lord called Moses to the top of the mountain, and Moses went up.
>
> And the Lord said to Moses, "Go down and warn the people, lest they break through to the Lord to look and many of them perish. Also let the priests who come near to the Lord consecrate themselves, lest the Lord break out against them." (Ex. 19:9–11, 16–22)

Prominent in the description is not only the awesome display but the warning against coming near. The Lord is a holy God, and the people are not qualified to draw near to his presence without a mediator. Moses functions as a mediator, but he too is an imperfect shadow of the final perfect mediation through Christ (1 Tim. 2:5).

The appearance of God goes together with God speaking. He speaks to the people of Israel in an audible voice, and gives them the Ten Commandments (Ex. 20:1–21; Deut. 5:23–27). Other theophanies in the Old Testament include divine messages. The awesome character of the visual appearance underlines the authority and authenticity of God's message.

---

1. A thorough study of the theophany at Mount Sinai, and its relation to the rest of the Bible, can be found in Jeffrey Jay Niehaus, *God at Sinai: Covenant and Theophany in the Bible and the Ancient Near East* (Grand Rapids, MI: Zondervan, 1995).

Other Thunderstorm Appearances

There are also other thunderstorm appearances. It is worthwhile looking at some of the passages, in order to appreciate the number of times that such descriptions come up. Here is one from David:

> "Then the earth reeled and rocked;
>> the foundations of the heavens trembled
>> and quaked, because he was angry.
> Smoke went up from his nostrils,
>> and devouring fire from his mouth;
>> glowing coals flamed forth from him.
> He bowed the heavens and came down;
>> thick *darkness* was under his feet.
> He rode on a cherub and flew;
>> he was seen on the wings of the *wind*.
> He made *darkness* around him his canopy,
>> thick *clouds*, a gathering of water.
> Out of the brightness before him
>> coals of fire flamed forth.
> The LORD *thundered* from heaven,
>> and the Most High uttered his voice.
> And he sent out arrows and scattered them;
>> *lightning*, and routed them." (2 Sam. 22:8–15; cf. Ps. 18:7–14)

This extended description comes to us as part of "A Psalm of David" (Psalm 18 title). As 2 Samuel 22:1 indicates, "David spoke to the LORD the words of this song." As far as we know from the historical records in Samuel and 1 Chronicles, there was no literal thunderstorm that delivered David from his enemies. Moreover, the description is poetic and invites us to think of many instances of escaping enemies. In 2 Samuel it occurs near the end of the life of David, and it includes in its introduction a generalizing expression, "on the day when the LORD delivered him from the hand of *all* his enemies, and from the hand of Saul" (2 Sam. 22:1).

This song by David uses the language of theophany or the appearing of God in order to depict God's presence and power, working on behalf of David through providential events. This use of language is important, because it shows that God's presence in providence can be viewed as very much analogous to a theophany in the narrow sense of the word (as in fig. 1.5). The description also shows the association of fire and earthquake with phenomena of a thunderstorm.

Here are more instances that have features of a thunderstorm:

> The voice of the LORD is over the waters;
>> the God of glory *thunders*,
>> the LORD, over many waters. . . .

> The voice of the LORD *flashes* forth flames of *fire*. (Ps. 29:3, 7)

> Our God comes; he does not keep silence;
>> before him is a devouring *fire*,
>> around him a mighty *tempest*. (Ps. 50:3)

> O God, when you went out before your people,
>> when you marched through the wilderness, *Selah*
> the earth quaked, the heavens poured down *rain*,
>> before God, the One of Sinai,
>> before God, the God of Israel. (Ps. 68:7–8)

See also Psalms 97:2–5; 144:5–6; Zephaniah 1:15; and Zechariah 9:14.

We also find an instance of earthquake with no mention of thunder or lightning, but with the inclusion of fire:

> Oh that you would rend the heavens and come down,
>> that the mountains might *quake* at your presence—
> as when *fire* kindles brushwood
>> and the *fire* causes water to boil—
> to make your name known to your adversaries,
>> and that the nations might *tremble* at your presence!
> When you did awesome things that we did not look for,
>> you came down, the mountains *quaked* at your presence.
>> (Isa. 64:1–3)

Significance

Many of these instances may be invoking the remembrance of Mount Sinai. Thunderstorms and earthquakes vividly exhibit the power of God and are fitting accompaniments of the appearance of God in power. They also remind us of the threat of God's anger against sin. The appearance of God at Mount Sinai pointedly stresses the holiness of God and the threat of death if anyone approaches the mountain. Some of the passages explicitly mention God's *anger*. Others mention the overthrow of God's enemies. The appearance of God in a *dark* cloud can easily suggest his anger. Even an ordinary thunderstorm can be terrifying in its power. How much more when the phenomena accompany a special, intense appearance of the presence of God!

These theophanies underline the power and authority of God's promises, his covenants, and his kingship. The thunder in a thunderstorm theophany depicts the thunderous character of God's voice, a voice that "breaks the cedars" (Ps. 29:5) and shakes the nations. Thus, theophany manifests the power of God's promises and God's covenantal words. God is the Creator and ruler, who makes the thunderstorm. So a thunderstorm is a massive display of God's power; a thunderstorm manifests his kingship. (See fig. 2.1.)

Fig. 2.1: Thunderstorm Theophany Manifesting God's Character

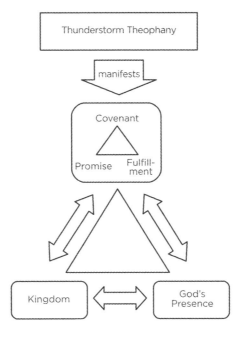

The Relation to Christ

How do thunderstorm appearances relate forward to Christ? Thunderstorm appearances remind us of the seriousness of God's anger

Fig. 2.2: Fulfillment of Thunderstorm Theophany in Christ

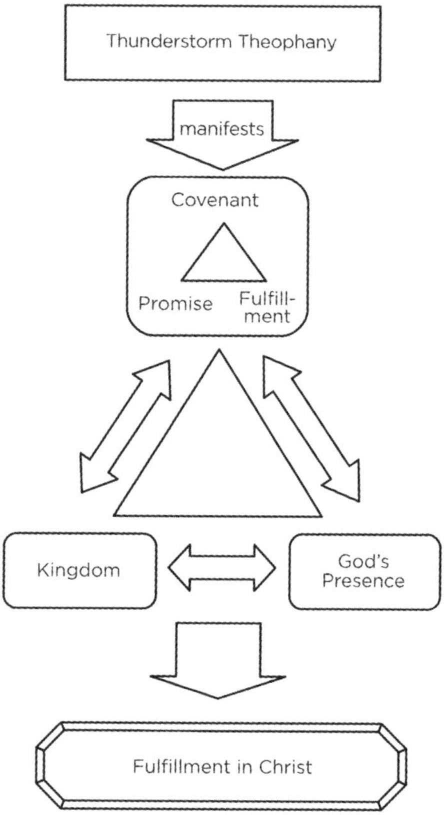

and his zeal for justice. This justice was fulfilled on the cross, when Christ became a sin-bearer for us: "He himself bore our sins in his body on the tree, that we might die to sin and live to righteousness. By his wounds you have been healed" (1 Pet. 2:24). It was fitting, then, that darkness accompanied the last hours of the crucifixion: "Now from the sixth hour there was *darkness* over all the land until the ninth hour" (Matt. 27:45). An earthquake accompanied Christ's death: "And behold, the curtain of the temple was torn in two, from top to bottom. And *the earth shook*, and the rocks were split" (v. 51).

Old Testament thunderstorm appearances foreshadow the first coming of Christ, when Christ bore God's judgment as our sin-bearer. They also foreshadow his second coming, when God will execute judgment against the wicked on the final day of judgment. In addition, thunder accompanies some of the descriptions of God's presence in the book of Revelation, a book that focuses on God's judgment.

The theme of judgment intertwines with promises, covenant, and kingship. Judgment and salvation both take place in accord with God's character, his promises, and his covenantal commitments to justice. Judgment belongs to kings, and God as supreme king manifests his kingship when he judges the world and all people in it.

These themes all come to their culmination in Christ, in his first coming and also in his second coming. (1a) First, consider the theme of promise. All the promises of God are "Yes" in Christ (2 Cor. 1:20)—they come to fulfillment in him. (1b) Next, consider the theme of covenant. Christ is himself the heart of God's covenant with man. Isaiah 42:6 and 49:8 identify the "covenant" with the coming messianic servant. (2) Consider the theme of kingdom. Christ is the king of Israel and the king of the world. In him God's own kingship is manifested. (3) Finally, consider the theme of presence. God is climactically *present* in the coming of Christ (John 1:14–18). (See fig. 2.2.)

3

Appearing in Fire

We have seen the mention of fire in connection with several of the thunderstorm appearances of God (Ex. 19:18; Pss. 18:8, 12, 13; 29:7; 50:3; 97:3; Isa. 64:2; Zeph. 1:18). Fire also occurs in instances where there is no obvious connection with a thunderstorm. Let us look at some of these instances.

Instances of God Appearing with Fire

One of the famous instances with fire is the episode with the burning bush:

> And the angel of the Lord appeared to him in a flame of *fire* out of the midst of a bush. He looked, and behold, the bush was *burning*, yet it was not consumed. (Ex. 3:2)

Next, let us consider the cloud that accompanied the people of Israel in the wilderness. The cloud represented the Lord's presence. It was a cloud by day and a pillar of *fire* by night:

> And the Lord went before them by day in a pillar of cloud to lead them along the way, and by night in a pillar of *fire* to give them light, that they might travel by day and by night. The pillar of cloud by day and the pillar of *fire* by night did not depart from before the people. (Ex. 13:21–22; cf. Ex. 14:19; Num. 9:15–23)

The presence of the Lord at the top of Mount Sinai is described as being like "a devouring fire":

Now the appearance of the glory of the LORD was like a devouring *fire* on the top of the mountain in the sight of the people of Israel. Moses entered the cloud and went up on the mountain. (Ex. 24:17–18)

The Holy Spirit's presence is represented at Pentecost by tongues of *fire*:

And suddenly there came from heaven a sound like a mighty rushing wind, and it filled the entire house where they were sitting. And divided tongues as of *fire* appeared to them and rested on each one of them. And they were all filled with the Holy Spirit and began to speak in other tongues as the Spirit gave them utterance. (Acts 2:2–4)

Note the accompanying "mighty rushing wind," which is reminiscent of the wind in some of the thunderstorm appearances of God.

In the light of these clear instances we can add an appearance of fire to Abram as another instance:

When the sun had gone down and it was dark, behold, a smoking *fire* pot and a *flaming* torch passed between these pieces. On that day the LORD made a covenant with Abram. (Gen. 15:17–18)

The fire represents the presence of God in intensive form.

As with the thunderstorm theophanies, a clear distinction exists between God and created things. Fire is not the Creator. Through fire, God manifests who he is as Creator, in distinction from all created things.

Further Instances

In some instances in the Old Testament, fire comes from the Lord to destroy or consume, without an obvious indication as to whether the fire is directly an appearance of God or a more indirect manifestation of his judgment:

Then the LORD rained on Sodom and Gomorrah sulfur and *fire* from the LORD out of heaven. (Gen. 19:24)

Then Moses stretched out his staff toward heaven, and the LORD sent thunder and hail, and *fire* ran down to the earth. And the LORD rained hail upon the land of Egypt. There was hail and *fire* flashing continually in the midst of the hail, very heavy hail, such as had never been in all the land of Egypt since it became a nation. (Ex. 9:23–24)

And *fire* came out from before the LORD and consumed the burnt offering and the pieces of fat on the altar, and when all the people saw it, they shouted and fell on their faces. (Lev. 9:24)

"And you call upon the name of your god, and I will call upon the name of the LORD, and the God who answers by *fire*, he is God." And all the people answered, "It is well spoken." (1 Kings 18:24)

See also Leviticus 10:2; Numbers 11:1–3; 16:35; Deuteronomy 32:22; Judges 6:21; 1 Kings 18:38–39; 2 Kings 1:10, 12, 14; 1 Chronicles 21:26; 2 Chronicles 7:1, 3; Job 1:16; Psalms 21:9; 78:21.

Significance

What is the significance of fire? In the Old Testament, fire can symbolize either purification or destruction. More often than not, it is destructive fire. The two sides are not incompatible, since purification comes by removal or destruction of what is impure.

Fire has ties with the themes of promise, covenant, and king-dom, as well as manifesting the presence of God. Fire fulfills God's promises to bring judgment and consume wickedness. Fire as an expression of God's holiness also shows that God is faithful to his own character. So it underlines God's commitment to his promises. Fire expresses God's covenantal presence as the holy God. In covenant he draws near to human beings. But if those human beings are unholy, the fire of God breaks out as an expression of his holiness and the holiness of his covenantal commitments. Fire also appears in some instances where God is establishing a covenant. The fire in the burning bush is one of the events leading to the establishment of the Mosaic covenant. And the Mosaic covenant established at Mount Sinai is accompanied by fire on the mountain. The fire in the pillar of cloud accompanies the people of Israel as a sign of God's covenantal presence. Fire expresses the fierceness of God's commitment to his covenant. Finally, fire expresses God's kingship—it shows that he acts in power to purify his people and destroy the king's enemies. (See fig. 3.1.)

Fig. 3.1: Fire Manifesting God's Character

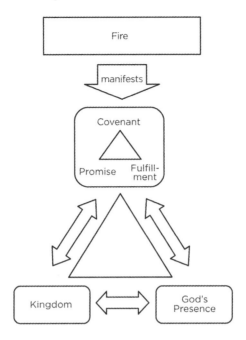

Fulfillment in Christ

How does the symbolism of fire in the Old Testament point forward to Christ? Christ is introduced by John the Baptist using the symbolism of fire:

> "I baptize you with water for repentance, but he who is coming after me is mightier than I, whose sandals I am not worthy to carry. He will baptize you with the Holy Spirit and *fire*. His winnowing fork is in his hand, and he will clear his threshing floor and gather his wheat into the barn, but the chaff he will burn with unquenchable *fire*." (Matt. 3:11–12)

Christ's fire of judgment burns up the chaff, but also purifies believers, as we see when the coming of the Holy Spirit at Pentecost is symbolized by fire (Acts 2:3). Christ is the fulfillment of instances in the Old Testament where God's fire destroys evil and purifies his people. Christ is the fulfillment of Old Testament fire theophanies. (See fig. 3.2.)

Fig. 3.2: Fire Fulfilled in Christ

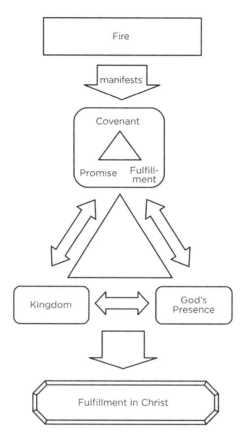

4

Appearing in a Cloud

The pillar of cloud and fire that appears in the exodus leads us to consider the instances where God appears in a *cloud*. The pillar in the exodus is described as appearing as a cloud by day and a fire by night:

> And the Lord went before them by day in a pillar of cloud to lead them along the way, and by night in a pillar of fire to give them light, that they might travel by day and by night. The pillar of cloud by day and the pillar of fire by night did not depart from before the people. (Ex. 13:21–22)

> For the cloud of the Lord was on the tabernacle by day, and fire was in it by night, in the sight of all the house of Israel throughout all their journeys. (Ex. 40:38; cf. Num. 9:15–16; 14:14; Deut. 1:33)

In addition, the cloud on Mount Sinai that Moses entered included fire:

> Then Moses went up on the mountain, and the *cloud* covered the mountain. The glory of the Lord dwelt on Mount Sinai, and the *cloud* covered it six days. And on the seventh day he called to Moses out of the midst of the *cloud*. Now the appearance of the glory of the Lord was like a devouring *fire* on the top of the mountain in the sight of the people of Israel. Moses entered the *cloud* and went up on the mountain. And Moses was on the mountain forty days and forty nights. (Ex. 24:15–18)

In the future day of salvation, God will likewise supply cloud and fire:

Then the LORD will create over the whole site of Mount Zion and over her assemblies a *cloud* by day, and smoke and the shining of a flaming *fire* by night; for over all the glory there will be a canopy. (Isa. 4:5)

Cloud without Explicit Fire

In other instances, God appears in a cloud without the mention of fire:

And as soon as Aaron spoke to the whole congregation of the people of Israel, they looked toward the wilderness, and behold, the glory of the LORD appeared in the *cloud*. (Ex. 16:10)

Since the passage in Exodus 16:10 occurs in the context of the wider exodus experience, we are to understand this cloud as basically similar to the cloud that accompanied the Israelites throughout their wilderness wanderings. Other exodus passages are similar (see, e.g., Ex. 34:5; Lev. 16:2; Num. 11:25; 12:5, 10; 16:42; Deut. 31:15).

A cloud is also mentioned outside the context of the exodus. A cloud fills Solomon's temple after it has been dedicated:

And when the priests came out of the Holy Place, a *cloud* filled the house of the LORD, so that the priests could not stand to minister because of the *cloud*, for the glory of the LORD filled the house of the LORD. (1 Kings 8:10–11; cf. 2 Chron. 5:13–14)

The cloud appears in the temple before God leaves it, in the context of the judgment of exile:

Now the cherubim were standing on the south side of the house, when the man went in, and a *cloud* filled the inner court. And the glory of the LORD went up from the cherub to the threshold of the house, and the house was filled with the *cloud*, and the court was filled with the brightness of the glory of the LORD. (Ezek. 10:3–4)

And we have more general contexts:

"You have wrapped yourself with a *cloud* so that no prayer can pass through." (Lam. 3:44)

He was still speaking when, behold, a bright *cloud* overshadowed them, and a voice from the *cloud* said, "This is my beloved Son, with whom I am well pleased; listen to him." (Matt. 17:5; cf. Mark 9:7; Luke 9:34–35)

The Son of Man Coming with Clouds

Jesus ascends in a cloud, and the Son of Man comes with clouds:

> And when he had said these things, as they were looking on, he was lifted up, and a *cloud* took him out of their sight. (Acts 1:9)

> "I saw in the night visions,
>
>> and behold, with the *clouds* of heaven
>>> there came one like a son of man,
>> and he came to the Ancient of Days
>>> and was presented before him." (Dan. 7:13)

See also Matthew 24:30 (parallel to Mark 13:26; Luke 21:27); Matthew 26:64 (parallel to Mark 14:62; Luke 22:69); Revelation 1:7; 14:14.

The Significance of the Cloud

Sometimes a cloud has the primary function of *concealing* God. But he also *appears* in the cloud. Both functions match the character of God. Human beings never master God or know him exhaustively. So the cloud is a reminder of human limits. At the same time, God does draw near and establish communion with mankind. So the cloud represents his drawing near. Because ordinary clouds are in the sky, the use of cloud symbolism also reminds us that God's dwelling is especially in heaven. A cloud symbolizes his coming near to us from heaven.

When God comes near, he can come to give blessing, but he can also come to give negative judgments. This dual aspect of God's coming belongs to the cloud as well. The pillar of cloud is with Israel to guide them through the wilderness (Ex. 13:21; Num. 9:17–23; Deut. 1:33). The cloud settles on the completed tabernacle structure, symbolizing the blessing of God's presence among the people of Israel (Ex. 40:34). The Lord also appears in a cloud at times when he pronounces judgments against Israel (Num. 12:10; 16:42). A dark cloud can symbolize God's presence in wrath (Pss. 18:11; 97:2–3; Matt. 27:45).

While Israel is in the wilderness, the cloud sometimes appears when God speaks to the people of Israel or when he appears in order to exercise judgments. God's speech from the cloud takes the form of promises and covenantal speech. His judgments from the cloud manifest his kingship. The cloud represents God's presence, and so underlines the character of God's promises, his covenants, and his kingship. The cloud has the function of revealing God and at the same time leaving some things concealed. So it is with God's promises. They reveal God and his purposes, but they do not reveal every detail of how God will bring about later fulfillment. The same is true for God's covenants. God commits himself to his people, but more of the depth of his commitments will be revealed when Christ comes. And the same is true for God's kingly rule. In his powerful acts, God reveals himself. But we do not know every detail of his rule. In all these ways, God reveals himself and at the same time never allows us to master him. (See fig. 4.1.) By reminding us of heaven, the cloud also underlines God's transcendent authority: he is the king of the universe.

Fig. 4.1: The Cloud Manifesting God's Character

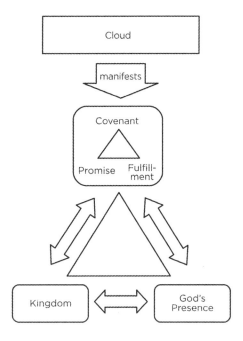

We should note that a cloud is associated with Mount Sinai and with thunderstorm manifestations of God. So there is some overlap between cloud manifestations and thunderstorm manifestations.

Fig. 4.2: Cloud Fulfilled in Christ

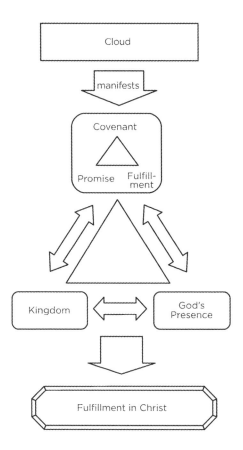

Fulfillment in Christ

How do the appearances in cloud point forward to Christ? The pillar of cloud and fire in the wilderness guided and protected the people, as well as providing a source of God's pronouncements of judgment when the people rebelled. Christ now serves as guide, protector, and judge of his people. The revealing and concealing functions of the cloud point forward to the mystery of Christ. He is revealed to us in his earthly life. He himself reveals the Father (Matt. 11:27) and provides us the way of salvation (John 14:6). At the same time, in his deity and his union with the Father he remains unfathomable. Just as the cloud symbolizes God's heavenly presence, Christ is the one who is God and comes from heaven: "For I have *come down from heaven*, not to do my own will but the will of him who sent me" (John 6:38). In Christ we truly see God. But because Christ is God and is incomprehensible, we still do not have exhaustive knowledge of God.

5

Appearing in Glory

The passages about God appearing in a cloud often mention God's "glory." His glory is represented by the brightness of a cloud. Though the themes of cloud and glory overlap, it is worthwhile mentioning glory as a separate theme of theophany, because some passages describe the appearance of God's glory without any explicit mention of a cloud.[1]

Cloud and Glory

First, note some passages where God's glory is closely linked to the cloud:

> [B]ehold, the *glory* of the LORD appeared in the *cloud*. (Ex. 16:10)

> The *glory* of the LORD dwelt on Mount Sinai, and the *cloud* covered it six days. And on the seventh day he called to Moses out of the midst of the *cloud*. (Ex. 24:16)

> Then the *cloud* covered the tent of meeting, and the *glory* of the LORD filled the tabernacle. And Moses was not able to enter the tent of meeting because the *cloud* settled on it, and the *glory* of the LORD filled the tabernacle. (Ex. 40:34–35)

See also Numbers 16:42; 1 Kings 8:11 (parallel to 2 Chron. 5:14); Isaiah 4:5; Ezekiel 10:4; Matthew 24:30 (parallel to Mark 13:26; Luke 21:27).

---

1. The theme of glory also has a close connection in a number of biblical contexts with the theme of images and reflections, to be discussed in later chapters.

Fig. 5.1: Glory Manifesting God's Character

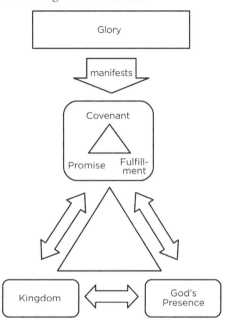

In other passages, the glory of the Lord is mentioned without explicit mention of a cloud:

> "There [at the tabernacle] I will meet with the people of Israel, and it shall be sanctified by my *glory*." (Ex. 29:43)

> And the Lord said, "Behold, there is a place by me where you shall stand on the rock, and while my *glory* passes by I will put you in a cleft of the rock, and I will cover you with my hand until I have passed by. Then I will take away my hand, and you shall see my back, but my face shall not be seen." (Ex. 33:21–23)

> And Moses said, "This is the thing that the Lord commanded you to do, that the *glory* of the Lord may appear to you." (Lev. 9:6)

See also Leviticus 9:23; Numbers 14:10; 16:19; 20:6; Isaiah 6:3; 60:1–3.

Other passages can describe the brightness of God's appearing without using the specific word for glory:

> You who are enthroned upon the cherubim, *shine* forth. (Ps. 80:1)

Restore us, O God; let your face *shine*, that we may be saved! (Ps. 80:3, 7; cf. v. 19; see also Ps. 94:1)

"But for you who fear my name, the *sun* of righteousness shall rise with healing in its wings." (Mal. 4:2)

The Significance of Glory

The term *glory* (Hebrew *kabod*) has associations not only with brightness but with splendor, majesty, and honor. The visible appearing of God manifests his splendor and majesty. It manifests the character of God, which is supremely glorious and worthy of honor. These associations are such that the term *glory* can also be used where it is not clear whether there is any *extraordinary* visible display. In the exodus, God gets "glory" over Pharaoh (Ex. 14:4, 17–18). And in Isaiah 6:3 the whole earth, not merely the vicinity of God's throne, is "full of his *glory*." "The heavens declare the *glory* of God, and the sky above proclaims his handiwork" (Ps. 19:1). The splendor of the character of God is displayed not merely in what is extraordinary, but every day in the things that he has made: "For his invisible attributes, namely, his eternal power and divine nature, have been clearly *perceived*, ever since the creation of the world, in the things that have been made" (Rom. 1:20).

The glory of God, as one form of theophany, has ties with the themes of promise, covenant, and kingdom. Let us briefly consider how.

First, the glory of God is made manifest in God's *promises*. They are glorious promises, exceeding human expectation. Centrally, God promises to make his glory known in all the world, and this display of glory is the culmination of his purposes in history. Next, the glory of God is displayed in his *covenants*. The contents of the covenants express God's majesty. Finally, glory has a connection with *kingship*. When God appears in glory, the glory has associations with the splendor of a great king. God is the great king, and his glory testifies to the exalted nature of his kingship.

Specific instances when God appears in glory also reinforce the claims in his promises, his covenants, and his kingship. For example, the appearances in glory during the exodus confirm God's promise to be with his people. When God appears, he addresses issues that have arisen or will arise concerning covenant faithfulness. In sum, God's glory manifests the nature of God's promises, his covenants, and his kingship (see fig. 5.1).

Fulfillment in Christ

How does the theme of glory come to fulfillment in Christ? Christ is supremely glorious, and reveals the glory of God:

> And the Word became flesh and dwelt among us, and we have seen his *glory*, *glory* as of the only Son from the Father, full of grace and truth. (John 1:14)

> This, the first of his signs, Jesus did at Cana in Galilee, and manifested his *glory*. And his disciples believed in him. (John 2:11)

> "The *glory* that you have given me I have given to them, that they may be one even as we are one." (John 17:22)

> In their case the god of this world has blinded the minds of the unbelievers, to keep them from seeing the light of the gospel of the *glory* of Christ, who is the image of God. For what we proclaim is not ourselves, but Jesus Christ as Lord, with ourselves as your servants for Jesus' sake. For God, who said, "Let light shine out of darkness," has *shone* in our hearts to give the *light* of the knowledge of the *glory* of God in the face of Jesus Christ. (2 Cor. 4:4–6)

The glory of Christ will be revealed in final form in the new heaven and the new earth (Rev. 21:23).

Several instances within the New Testament remind us in special ways about the glory of Christ, because they recount times when his glory was manifested in a visible way. We may include the scene of the transfiguration of Christ (where both Christ and the cloud are bright: Matt. 17:2, 5; Mark 9:2–3; Luke 9:29), Christ's appearance to Saul on the road to Damascus (Acts 9:3; 22:6; 26:13), and Christ's appearance to John in Revelation (Rev. 1:16).

Glory in the Temple

In concluding our focus on cloud and glory, we should observe their relation to the temple theme in the Bible. Cloud and glory function together in close relation to the Mosaic tabernacle and the temple later built by Solomon. When the tabernacle is set up and dedicated, the cloud of glory descends on it, signifying that God is taking up his residence in the tabernacle (Ex. 40:34–38). The same happens

Fig. 5.2: The Temple Theme and the Glory of God

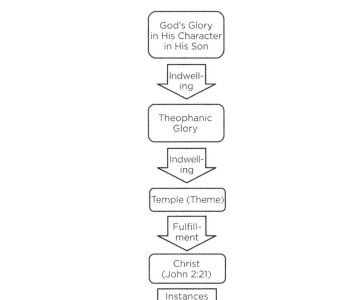

when Solomon's temple is dedicated (1 Kings 8:10–11), and when God comes to the ideal temple envisioned in Ezekiel 43 (especially vv. 4–5). In the New Testament, the church is the temple of God (1 Cor. 3:16; Eph. 2:21; 1 Pet. 2:5). So the same principle holds for the church as was true for the temple: at Pentecost, God descends on the church in the person of the Holy Spirit, represented by a fire theophany (Acts 2:3–4).

The theophany in glory represents an intensive expression of the presence of God with his people. The tabernacle and the temple express the same truth about God's presence. As more permanent structures, they symbolize the continuing character of God's presence with his people, and his covenantal commitment to be with them. Tabernacle and temple and dwelling place of God constitute a single unified theme in Scripture. It is a magnificent, major theme, deserving study on its own account. Because G. K. Beale has already produced such a study,[2] we will be content here to refer readers to his work.

We may summarize by saying that the theme of the temple serves to express the presence of God. It is therefore natural that specific theophanies in cloud and glory take place to inaugurate the tabernacle and the temple. God is present in a special way to bless his people when he meets them in the temple environment. The tabernacle and the temple in the Old Testament both point forward to the climactic dwelling of God with man, in the person of Christ, who is "God with us" (Matt. 1:23; cf. John 2:21). Christ's physical body is the final temple: "he was speaking about the temple of his body" (John 2:21). Through Christ, the church as a whole and each individual Christian is a temple (1 Cor. 3:16; 6:19). The New Jerusalem in the new heaven and new earth constitutes the final dwelling place of God (Rev. 21:3, 22). (See fig. 5.2.)

---

2. See G. K. Beale, *The Temple and the Church's Mission: A Biblical Theology of the Dwelling Place of God* (Leicester, UK: Apollos; Downers Grove, IL: InterVarsity, 2004).

6

Appearances of God's Court

The display of the splendor of God can take the form of showing God as king in the midst of his angelic hosts. The angels are like a heavenly court. They honor him and do his bidding. Let us consider the instances when God appears amid his heavenly court.

Visions of God's Court

In Isaiah 6:1–4 we find a description of God's court as well as God in the midst of the court:

> In the year that King Uzziah died I saw the Lord *sitting upon a throne*, high and lifted up; and the train of his robe filled the temple. Above him stood the *seraphim*. Each had six wings: with two he covered his face, and with two he covered his feet, and with two he flew. And one called to another and said:
>
> > "Holy, holy, holy is the LORD of hosts;
> > the whole earth is full of his glory!"
>
> And the foundations of the thresholds shook at the voice of him who called, and the house was filled with smoke.

The seraphim are angelic creatures who serve God and praise him.

Another passage, in 1 Kings 22, makes a key comparison between God's court and the court of the earthly kings Ahab (king of Israel) and Jehoshaphat (king of Judah). First there is a scene of a court serving the two earthly kings:

> Now the king of Israel and Jehoshaphat the king of Judah were *sitting on their thrones*, arrayed in their robes, at the threshing floor at the entrance of the gate of Samaria, and all the prophets were prophesying before them. And Zedekiah the son of Chenaanah made for himself horns of iron and said, "Thus says the Lord, 'With these you shall push the Syrians until they are destroyed.'" And all the prophets prophesied so and said, "Go up to Ramoth-gilead and triumph; the Lord will give it into the hand of the king." (1 Kings 22:10–12)

The situation involves a council for war, where the two kings receive advice from a company of some four hundred prophets (v. 6) about whether to go to war and try to retake Ramoth-Gilead.

The prophet Micaiah is summoned before this earthly council of kings, and he describes another council in heaven:

> And Micaiah said, "Therefore hear the word of the Lord: I saw the Lord *sitting on his throne*, and all the host of heaven *standing beside him* on his right hand and on his left; and the Lord said, 'Who will entice Ahab, that he may go up and fall at Ramoth-gilead?' And one said one thing, and another said another. Then a spirit came forward and stood before the Lord, saying, 'I will entice him.' And the Lord said to him, 'By what means?' And he said, 'I will go out, and will be a lying spirit in the mouth of all his prophets.' And he said, 'You are to entice him, and you shall succeed; go out and do so.'" (1 Kings 22:19–22)

Ironically, the council in heaven has already determined a kind of "war" against the earthly council, which has led to the corruption in the earthly council. Lying speech goes out from the mouths of the prophets in the earthly council. The scene gains its irony from the contrast between the two kingly councils, the one on earth and the other in heaven. It presupposes that we understand that the Lord's council in heaven is like the council of a king on earth, and yet supremely great and capable of overruling and overthrowing earthly councils. This scene thus presents a clear case of God appearing amid his heavenly court of angelic beings.

Job 1:6–12 involves another case where the narrative gives us access to a heavenly consultation, involving God and angelic beings. This time Satan comes in among the council:

Now there was a day when the sons of God [angelic servants] came to present themselves *before the* LORD, and Satan also came among them. The LORD said to Satan, "From where have you come?" Satan answered the LORD and said, "From going to and fro on the earth, and from walking up and down on it." And the LORD said to Satan, "Have you considered my servant Job, that there is none like him on the earth, a blameless and upright man, who fears God and turns away from evil?" Then Satan answered the LORD and said, "Does Job fear God for no reason? Have you not put a hedge around him and his house and all that he has, on every side? You have blessed the work of his hands, and his possessions have increased in the land. But stretch out your hand and touch all that he has, and he will curse you to your face." And the LORD said to Satan, "Behold, all that he has is in your hand. Only against him do not stretch out your hand." So Satan went out from the presence of the LORD.

A second round of consultation occurs in Job 2:1–6.

Daniel 7:9–10 shows a judgment scene where "a thousand thousands" of angels minister to God:

> "As I looked,
>
>> thrones were placed,
>>> and the Ancient of Days *took his seat*;
>> his clothing was white as snow,
>>> and the hair of his head like pure wool;
>> his throne was fiery flames;
>>> its wheels were burning fire.
>> A stream of fire issued
>>> and came out from before him;
>> a thousand thousands *served him*,
>>> and ten thousand times ten thousand
>> stood before him;
>> the *court* sat in judgment,
>>> and the books were opened."

The Psalms also make reference to God's heavenly court:

> God has taken his place in the *divine council*;
>> *in the midst of the gods* he holds judgment. (Ps. 82:1)

> . . . a God greatly to be feared in the *council* of the holy ones,
>> and awesome above all who are *around him*? (Ps. 89:7)

In Ezekiel 1 we see an aspect of the angelic court in the form of the living creatures or cherubim (Ezek. 10:15) around God's throne:

> Over the heads of the *living creatures* there was the likeness of an expanse, shining like awe-inspiring crystal, spread out above their heads. (Ezek. 1:22)

> And above the expanse over their heads there was the likeness of a *throne*, in appearance like sapphire; and seated above the likeness of a throne was a likeness with a human appearance. (v. 26)

The vision of God in Revelation 4:2–6 picks up on these Old Testament visions of God's court. It gives us a central throne, four living creatures, twenty-four elders, and myriads of angels (Rev. 5:11).

We can clearly see some overlap between the more elaborate court appearances and other kinds of theophany. In court theophanies, sometimes there is thunder or lightning or fire. Sometimes there is smoke or cloud. Whether or not the word *glory* appears in the description, the vision makes manifest the awesome majesty of God—it displays his glory.

Significance of Court Appearances

The court appearances show that God is the majestic king of the universe. They may also show him issuing kingly commands. He renders judgment on the affairs of mankind (Dan. 7:10). The number and power and glory of his attending angels underlines the greatness of his power. The picture of consultation occurs in 1 Kings 22:19–22, Job 1:6–12, and Job 2:1–6. God does not *need* to consult anyone, since he has his own wisdom in the Spirit (Isa. 40:13–14). The visions nevertheless show a consultation with angelic beings in order to underline the overflowing abundance of his wisdom, which is reflected in the angelic beings.

These court theophanies have close ties with the themes of promise, covenant, and kingdom. The most prominent tie is with the kingdom. A court theophany reveals God as king on his throne. So it is a powerful manifestation of God's kingly rule. At the same time, the scenes with God's court imply that, since God is king, he issues orders—decrees. The decrees are like promises of action that will follow. Promises in a literal sense that come from God presuppose that God is the ruler, and so the promises themselves proceed ultimately from the presence of God as the majestic king in his court.

What about the theme of covenant? When God makes a covenant, the covenant is between God as king and the people as his servants. So covenant in turn implies kingship, such as is manifested in a court theophany. A court theophany shows us who God is, so it also shows us the meaning of God's covenants with us.

Conversely, when God appears as the king in his court, this appearance comes in a covenantal context. When God appears, he does so in order to establish or maintain or confirm a covenantal relation to the human beings to whom he appears. For example, Isaiah 6:1–4 comes in a context where Isaiah is being commissioned to go to the people of Israel, who have been disobedient to the covenant that God has established with them. God comes to Isaiah in fulfillment of his promises to remain faithful to the covenant. Similarly, 1 Kings 22:19–22 declares disaster to Ahab in a context in which Ahab has been unfaithful to God's covenant with the people of the northern kingdom of Israel. The council in Job 1:6–12 comes in a context where the main issue is Job's faithfulness or unfaithfulness to God within a covenantal relation. Daniel 7:9–10 brings a vision of universal judgment, which is based on the universal covenantal relation that God has with the kingdoms of the world. The judgment will be conducted in accordance with the standards of the covenantal God.

Fulfillment in Christ

How are court theophanies fulfilled in Christ? In Revelation Christ shares the throne of the Father and the honor of the Father, amid the angelic beings who praise him (Rev. 3:21; 5:9–14). The vision of Christ in Revelation 1:12–16 takes up features of "the Ancient of Days" in the court appearance in Daniel 7:9. He, together with the Father and the Spirit, represents the fulfillment of the court visions in the Old Testament.

Christ is the fulfillment, and as such he is the fulfillment of the promissory aspects implicit in the Old Testament court theophanies. If God appears from time to time to bring preliminary judgments, those preliminary appearances and preliminary judgments imply a future climactic manifestation. Christ is the fulfillment both of the promissory aspect and the covenantal aspect and of the kingly aspect of court theophanies, because in him are manifest the fulfillments of promises, covenants, and kingship.

Only through Christ do God's promises come to fulfillment (2 Cor. 1:20). Only through Christ and his blood can there be a covenantal meeting between God and man, without man being destroyed because of his sin. Only through Christ does God's kingly rule come to us with peace.

7

Appearances of a Man

Next, there are manifestations of God in which the central element is a human form or human-like appearance.

The Relation to God's Court

This appearance of a human form is closely connected to the instances involving God's court. The whole idea of a court surrounding God implies that in the middle of the court there is a central divine figure, who often is described as sitting on a throne. What else would be seen sitting on the throne but a human-like figure? Moreover, in Ezekiel 1 the human-like figure is explicitly described:

> And above the expanse over their heads there was the likeness of a throne, in appearance like sapphire; and seated above the likeness of a throne was *a likeness with a human appearance*. And upward from what had the appearance of his *waist* I saw as it were gleaming metal, like the appearance of fire enclosed all around. And downward from what had the appearance of his *waist* I saw as it were the appearance of fire, and there was brightness around him. (Ezek. 1:26–27)

Other manifestations of God's court have briefer descriptions of the central figure, or mention of the throne with no description of the figure seated on it:

> "As I looked,
>
> > thrones were placed,
> > > and the Ancient of Days took his seat;

his clothing was white as snow,
>   and the hair of his head like pure wool;
his throne was fiery flames;
>   its wheels were burning fire." (Dan. 7:9)

In the year that King Uzziah died I saw the Lord sitting upon a *throne*, high and lifted up; and the train of his robe filled the temple. (Isa. 6:1)

See also Exodus 24:10 and 1 Kings 22:19.

Appearances with Angels but Not a Court

We also have instances where God appears in the company of angels, but without the full context of a kingly court.

And he [Jacob] dreamed, and behold, there was a ladder set up on the earth, and the top of it reached to heaven. And behold, the *angels of God* were ascending and descending on it! And behold, the Lord *stood* above it and said, "I am the Lord, the God of Abraham your father and the God of Isaac." (Gen. 28:12–13)

And the Lord appeared to him by the oaks of Mamre, as he sat at the door of his tent in the heat of the day. He lifted up his eyes and looked, and behold, *three men* were *standing* in front of him. When he saw them, he ran from the tent door to meet them and bowed himself to the earth. (Gen. 18:1–2)

The episode in Genesis 18 invites further reflection. It is introduced with the description, "The Lord appeared to him," but with no immediate explanation for the presence of "*three* men," not just one. As the narrative in Genesis 18 goes on, we find that two of the "men" go off in the direction of Sodom (v. 22) and are later identified as "angels" (Gen. 19:1). They are obviously angels who appear in human form. From 18:22 onward, the third "man" remains with Abraham: "Abraham still stood before the Lord" (v. 22). So the third human appearance is identified as "the Lord." The Lord is accompanied by two angels, but the context is not the full context of the divine court.

An Individual Man

Finally, we have instances where the Lord appears in human form, with no mention of any accompanying figures.

Consider first the figure who appears to Joshua near Jericho:

When Joshua was by Jericho, he lifted up his eyes and looked, and behold, a *man* was standing before him with his drawn sword in his hand. And Joshua went to him and said to him, "Are you for us, or for our adversaries?" And he said, "No; but I am the commander of the army of the LORD. Now I have come." And Joshua fell on his face to the earth and worshiped and said to him, "What does my lord say to his servant?" And the commander of the LORD's army said to Joshua, "Take off your sandals from your feet, for the place where you are standing is holy." And Joshua did so. (Josh. 5:13–15)

The figure in this passage is first identified as "a man," according to his appearance. The subsequent interchange includes several elements: (a) the man identifies himself as "the commander of the army of the LORD"; (b) Joshua falls on his face and offers worship; and (c) the man pronounces that the place is holy. It is reasonable to infer that the human-like figure is not a created angel but the Lord himself. This temporary appearance foreshadows the incarnation and Christ's role as divine warrior fighting against the kingdom of Satan.

God appears to Joshua. Shall we say also that Christ appears? This question touches on the mystery of the Trinity. How do we deal with the fact that Christ is fully God, with the fact that he is distinct from God the Father, and also with the fact that the Old Testament often speaks of God in general terms, without fully articulating the distinction between persons in the Trinity? The Old Testament does not become as explicit as does the New Testament about the Trinitarian character of God. The Old Testament saints would have been able to understand that God appeared. They would also have been able to infer that an appearance of God manifested the God who was the same God behind all appearances. Thus, there is a kind of subtle distinction between any one appearance of God and God who is the same God all the time, even apart from any appearance. That means that Old Testament saints could have seen in a theophany some form of distinction about God. Yet they would not have had all the insight possible on the basis of the fuller teaching in the New Testament.

The full truth about God in his Trinitarian character is revealed only progressively. Fuller teaching appears in the New Testament. This fuller teaching assures us that God, the true Trinitarian God, was present in the Old Testament manifestations. His appearance long ago is consistent with the constancy of his character as God. So the appearances would have involved intrinsically the work of the Father, the Son, and the Holy Spirit—all three. The appearances in the Old Testament anticipate the way in which God the Father shows himself in the New Testament in Christ, through the power of the Holy Spirit. This connection is reinforced by cases in the New Testament where Christ appears with features corresponding to Old Testament theophanies. For example, in Revelation 1:12–16 the appearance of Christ has affinities to Ezekiel 1:27, Daniel 7:9, 13, and Daniel 10:5–6.

We may therefore infer that the human form in an Old Testament appearance points forward to the permanent appearance of God in the human nature of Christ. So God the Son appears in the Old Testament. At the same time, when the Son appears, the Father also appears in the Son, by the power of the Holy Spirit. All three persons are present, because all three persons indwell one another. The appearances in the Old Testament remain mysterious, however, because the incarnation has not yet taken place.

Another instance occurs in Daniel 3:25. Nebuchadnezzar in his fury ordered the three men Shadrach, Meshach, and Abednego to be thrown into the fiery furnace. But then he sees a fourth. The fourth has a human form, like the other three ("I see four *men*") but this fourth man also has a divine quality "like a son of the gods."

Consider another instance. We find that an individual figure appears to Manoah's wife and then to Manoah:

> And the *angel* of the LORD *appeared* to the woman and said to her, "Behold, you are barren and have not borne children, but you shall conceive and bear a son." (Judg. 13:3)

> Then the woman came and told her husband, "A *man of God* came to me, and his appearance was like the appearance of the angel of God, very awesome. I did not ask him where he was from, and he did not tell me his name." (v. 6)

Several things need to be noted about this passage. Underlying the English word *angel* (v. 3) is the Hebrew word for "messenger" (*mal'ak*). It describes the function of the personage: his function is to convey a message, in this case a message from God.[1] The word in itself does

---

1. See the further discussion in appendix A concerning "the angel of the Lord."

not determine what sort of personage is designated, whether divine or human or angelic, in our modern sense of the word *angel*. For example, Malachi uses the same word "messenger" (*mal'ak*), to describe prophetically the coming of John the Baptist as a "messenger" (Mal. 3:1; cf. Matt. 11:10). Also in Malachi, the priest is "the messenger [*mal'ak*] of the LORD of hosts" (Mal. 2:7). The same word is also used for human messengers in ordinary affairs, such as the communications between David, Abner, Ishbosheth, and Joab (2 Sam. 3:12, 14, 26). So, in spite of the fact that in Judges 13:3 many English translations use the word *angel*, we should not assume without further reflection that we have an "angel" in the modern sense, a created spiritual being who serves God.

Manoah's wife describes the appearance as "a man of God." She saw a human-like appearance. She suspected from his awesome appearance that he was "the angel of God," that is, the messenger of God.

According to verse 8, Manoah then prayed to the Lord that he would send "the man of God" again. According to verse 9, the personage came again, and is described once again as "the angel of God." In verse 10 the woman describes him as "the *man* who came to me the other day." Then, Manoah "came to the *man*" (v. 11). After several more interactions, Manoah concluded in the end that "we have seen God" (v. 22). God had appeared in human form. This scene again looks like a case where the figure who appeared is divine, not angelic. The preincarnate Christ appeared to Manoah and his wife, in anticipation of his incarnation. But the Father and the Holy Spirit were also present, as we will confirm later in discussing the Trinitarian background for theophany (chapters 16–17).

Now consider the case with Gideon. In the light of the episode with Manoah, we can tentatively infer that Gideon saw a man-like appearance:

> And the angel of the LORD *appeared* to him and said to him, "The LORD is with you, O mighty man of valor." . . . And the LORD *turned* to him and said, "Go in this might of yours and save Israel from the hand of Midian; do not I send you?" (Judg. 6:12–14)

Daniel 10:5–6 involves another instance of an awesome appearance of a man-like figure:

> I lifted up my eyes and looked, and behold, a *man* clothed in linen, with a belt of fine gold from Uphaz around his waist. His body was

like beryl, his face like the appearance of lightning, his eyes like flaming torches, his arms and legs like the gleam of burnished bronze, and the sound of his words like the sound of a multitude.

It is not clear whether this description refers to a created angel or to an appearance of God in the preincarnate Christ. Features from this passage are taken up in Revelation 1:12–16, which explicitly describes Christ. Moreover, the reaction of the men around Daniel (Dan. 10:7) is similar to the later reaction of the men around Saul on the Damascus road (Acts 9:3–7), when Saul sees the risen Christ.

In a narrow sense, a "theophany" is an appearance of *God*. So the classification of the event in Daniel 10:5–6 depends on whether the key figure is divine or angelic. But on the created level angels reflect the original, uncreated glory of God. Their awesome majesty reflects the majesty of God. So, when a description is fairly sparse, it may not be possible to determine with certainty whether we are dealing with a divine or an angelic figure.

In the end, it does not matter much at a practical level. Angels who function as messengers prefigure Christ as the final messenger. And whenever Christ appears directly in the Old Testament, as he did to Joshua and to Manoah and his wife, these appearances also point forward to the incarnation. Angels who are created beings bear a message that is divine. The divine character of the message implies the presence of God, even if the angel is only an angel. So at a broader level, an appearance of an angelic messenger still has associations with the nature of theophany in the narrow sense. It is nevertheless important to see that there is a clear and firm distinction between the Creator and his creatures. We must worship the Creator alone, not creatures (Rom. 1:25; Rev. 22:8–9). But sometimes, in particular historical events, God does not give us enough detail to enable us to decide for certain the exact status of a messenger of God.

Finally, we should mention the key passage prophesying the coming of one like a son of man:

"I saw in the night visions,

and behold, with the clouds of heaven
    there came one like a *son of man*,
and he came to the Ancient of Days
    and was presented before him." (Dan. 7:13)

We have a human-like figure here, and he is associated with "the clouds of heaven" that typify a cloud theophany. But he is distinguished from "the Ancient of Days," who sits in court according to Daniel 7:9–10.

There is mystery about this passage within its original context in Daniel. The mystery is unveiled when Christ identifies himself as the Danielic son of man (Matt. 26:64; Mark 14:62; Luke 22:69). Christ is himself divine and also distinct from God the Father, who is identified with "the Ancient of Days." Once we have the full revelation of Christ from the New Testament, we can return and confidently identify the Danielic "son of man" as an appearance of God in human likeness. As usual, it points forward to Christ.

Significance of Appearances in Human Form

The appearances in human form have part of their basis in the fact that God created man "in the image of God" (Gen. 1:27). On the level of the Creator, God acts in a way analogous to human action, and his nature is fittingly represented in human form, rather than the form of an animal or a plant. He speaks, he thinks, he knows, he hears, and he acts in power. Human beings through their bodily actions imitate his actions. Their imitation is fitting, because God's action is the archetype or original pattern for human action.

In addition, human appearances of God have a special weight. Even though in the Old Testament such appearances are temporary, they anticipate the permanent coming of God in permanent human form, in the incarnation of Christ.

As usual, these appearances offer perspectives on God's promises, his covenants, and his kingship. For example, in context of the theophany in Genesis 18:1–2, God issues his promise that Sarah will have a son the next year (v. 10). This promise is a key element in the entire spectrum of God's promises, because it concerns the maintenance of the line of promised offspring, the line of the offspring of the woman (Gen. 3:15), leading to Christ. The appearance to Abraham manifests the promise. The appearance to Abraham in Genesis 18:1–2 also involves a continuation of God's covenant with Abraham, and a confirmation and further specification of God's covenantal commitments. The promise of a son to Sarah in her old age also presupposes God's kingship, including his power to overcome her situation of barrenness. The episode in Genesis 18 also leads to the judgment of

God on Sodom and Gomorrah in Genesis 19. God shows his kingship by executing judgment on unrighteousness. Abraham acknowledges God's kingship in saying, "Shall not the Judge of all the earth do what is just?" (Gen. 18:25).

Similarly, when God appears to Joshua in Joshua 5:13–15, the appearance comes in a context where God is fulfilling his promises to Abraham, that his offspring will possess the land of Canaan. He appears in the context of his covenant with Joshua and the people of Israel. He appears as kingly commander over the heavenly army of angels.

Similar observations can be made about the appearances to Gideon and to Manoah. By manifesting the presence of God, the appearances of God also manifest his promises, his covenant, and his kingship.

8

Appearing as a Warrior

Next we consider descriptions of God appearing as a warrior. These descriptions are closely related to appearances of God in human form. When we hear a description of a warrior, it is natural to make a comparison with human warriors, and to think of a human-like figure. But the descriptions of God as a warrior vary in their details. Some descriptions may include the mention of armor or weapons but may not include a direct reference to the physical form of a warrior. They may or may not imply that there is some special physical appearance, either of a human figure or of light or glory or cloud. So, even though we have some overlap between appearances of a human figure and appearances of a warrior, it is appropriate to devote attention specifically to descriptions of God as a warrior or as engaging in warrior-like activity.

A Human-Like Figure as a Warrior

We can begin by recalling the passage in Joshua 5 where a "man" appeared to Joshua and identified himself as "the commander of the army of the Lord" (5:14). The man has a drawn sword in his hand (v. 13). This passage involves God appearing as a man and as a warrior. The two descriptions are two sides of the same thing.

We also have an episode where "the angel of the Lord" appeared to Balaam's donkey and then to Balaam, "with a drawn sword in his hand" (Num. 22:23). We have the usual difficulty in determining whether this "angel" is a divine or an angelic messenger. The mention of "his hand" suggests that the donkey and then Balaam saw a human-like figure. But the text does not give us further details about the form of his appearance. The presence of the sword gives the "angel" a warrior-like appearance.

Figures with a Sword

We can compare the episode with Balaam with other cases of angels with swords. God sends a pestilence after David's foolish census. The key description includes an angelic sword:

> And David lifted his eyes and saw the *angel* of the Lord standing between earth and heaven, and in his hand a drawn *sword* stretched out over Jerusalem. (1 Chron. 21:16)

The angel was "standing between earth and heaven," which magnifies the supernatural character of the angel and his work. We do not know the details of his appearance.

The cherubim that God appointed to "guard the way to the tree of life" in Genesis 3 are accompanied by "a flaming sword that turned every way" (3:24). If we take our cue from the descriptions of the cherubim in Ezekiel 10 and 1:5–22 (cf. 10:20), these angelic beings have "human hands" (1:8; cf. 10:8) and human faces (1:10; 10:14), but each has three additional faces—of a lion, an ox, and an eagle (1:10). Ezekiel 10:14 re-describes the four faces, and there we find that the face of the ox is re-described as "the face of the cherub," suggesting that the ox face is more properly associated with the cherubim. Furthermore, the text says that "the soles of their [the cherubim's] feet were like the sole of a calf's foot" (Ezek. 1:7), and that "each of them had four wings" (v. 6). The cherubim have certain special features similar to a human shape, but overall they are not in human shape.

However that may be, the flaming sword in Genesis 3:24 represents God's power to war against transgressors. The cherubim are creatures, so their appearance is not a theophany in the narrow sense. But, in a broad sense, their appearance is still somewhat like a warrior theophany: God shows a visible phenomenon in a manner demonstrating his power to wage war against sin and evil.

General Imagery of a Warrior or of Fighting

We also have more general pictures concerning God's war against sin and evil.

An "angel" of the Lord "struck down 185,000 in the camp of the Assyrians" (2 Kings 19:35).

God puts on armor to fight on behalf of his people:

> He put on righteousness as a breastplate,
>   and a helmet of salvation on his head;
> he put on garments of vengeance for clothing,
>   and wrapped himself in zeal as a cloak. (Isa. 59:17)

The Lord fights against Pharaoh in the exodus and at the Red Sea:

> "The LORD is a man of war;
>   the LORD is his name. . . .
>
> "Your right hand, O LORD, glorious in power,
>   your right hand, O LORD, shatters the enemy.
> In the greatness of your majesty you overthrow your adversaries;
>   you send out your fury; it consumes them like stubble.
> At the blast of your nostrils the waters piled up;
>   the floods stood up in a heap;
>   the deeps congealed in the heart of the sea.
> The enemy said, 'I will pursue, I will overtake,
>   I will divide the spoil, my desire shall have its fill of them.
>   I will draw my sword; my hand shall destroy them.'
> You blew with your wind; the sea covered them;
>   they sank like lead in the mighty waters.
>
> "Who is like you, O LORD, among the gods?
>   Who is like you, majestic in holiness,
>   awesome in glorious deeds, doing wonders?
> You stretched out your right hand;
>   the earth swallowed them." (Ex. 15:3, 6–12)

We find other descriptions of the Lord fighting for his people: Isaiah 63:1–6; Habakkuk 3:8–15; Zephaniah 3:17; Zechariah 9:14–15; 14:3–5.

We also find instances where God's people or a representative of God's people fight on God's behalf, and God gives them the victory. We think of the offspring of the woman in Genesis 3:15:

> "I will put *enmity* between you and the woman,
>   and between your offspring and her offspring;

> he shall *bruise* your head,
>   and you shall bruise his heel."

And then there is David's victory over Goliath:

> "This day the LORD will *deliver you* into my hand, and I will strike
> you down and cut off your head. And I will give the dead bodies of
> the host of the Philistines this day to the birds of the air and to the
> wild beasts of the earth, that all the earth may know that there is a
> God in Israel." (1 Sam. 17:46)

Instances involving the people of God in battle are too numerous to
mention. Among these are the instances with Joshua, beginning with
the battle of Jericho (Joshua 5).

The Significance of Appearances as a Warrior

The significance of warrior appearances is evident. They show that
God is mighty and powerful to save his people and crush the enemies
of righteousness.

As usual, warrior appearances interlock with the themes of promise, covenant, and kingdom. When God wars against evil, he is faithful
to his promises, including the original promise that the offspring of the
woman would bruise the head of the serpent (Gen. 3:15). God is faithful to his covenant commitments to his people when he protects them
from enemies (Deut. 28:7). And God manifests his kingship in spiritual
warfare. One of the expected functions for kings in the ancient Near
Eastern context was to wage war against enemies (cf. 1 Sam. 8:20).
God as the great king over Israel wages war to defend Israel against
enemies.

Fulfillment in Christ

Christ fulfills the Old Testament depictions of God by fighting against
sin and evil, in both his first coming and his second coming. The first
coming concentrates on warfare against Satan and evil spirits:

> Then a demon-oppressed man who was blind and mute was brought
> to him, and he healed him, so that the man spoke and saw. And all
> the people were amazed, and said, "Can this be the Son of David?"
> But when the Pharisees heard it, they said, "It is only by Beelzebul,
> the prince of demons, that this man casts out demons." Knowing

their thoughts, he said to them, "Every kingdom divided against itself is laid waste, and no city or house divided against itself will stand. And if Satan casts out Satan, he is divided against himself. How then will his kingdom stand? And if I cast out demons by Beelzebul, by whom do your sons cast them out? Therefore they will be your judges. But if it is by the Spirit of God that I cast out demons, then the kingdom of God has come upon you. Or how can someone enter a strong man's house and plunder his goods, unless he first binds the strong man? Then indeed he may plunder his house. Whoever is not with me is against me, and whoever does not gather with me scatters." (Matt. 12:22–30; cf. Mark 3:22–27; Luke 11:14–23).

The climactic triumph over evil comes at the cross:

"Now is the *judgment* of this world; now will the *ruler* of this world *be cast out*." (John 12:31)

The New Testament letters also indicate that Jesus triumphed over the world of evil spirits in his death and resurrection:

He disarmed *the rulers and authorities* and put them to open shame, by triumphing over them in him. (Col. 2:15)

Since therefore the children share in flesh and blood, he himself likewise partook of the same things, that through death he might *destroy* the one who has the power of death, that is, *the devil*, and deliver all those who through fear of death were subject to lifelong slavery. (Heb. 2:14–15)

The second coming of Christ is the time for his final triumph over evil. He is accordingly depicted as a warrior in Revelation 19:11–16:

Then I saw heaven opened, and behold, a white horse! The one sitting on it is called Faithful and True, and in righteousness he judges and makes war. His eyes are like a flame of fire, and on his head are many diadems, and he has a name written that no one knows but himself. He is clothed in a robe dipped in blood, and the name by which he is called is The Word of God. And the armies of heaven, arrayed in fine linen, white and pure, were following him on white horses. From his mouth comes a sharp sword with which to strike down the nations, and he will rule them with a rod of iron. He will tread the winepress of the fury of the wrath of God the Almighty.

On his robe and on his thigh he has a name written, King of kings and Lord of lords.

Since believers in Christ are united to him, they also participate in spiritual war against the demonic forces:

> Finally, be strong in the Lord and in the strength of his might. Put on the whole armor of God, that you may be able to stand against the schemes of the devil. For we do not wrestle against flesh and blood, but against the rulers, against the authorities, against the cosmic powers over this present darkness, against the spiritual forces of evil in the heavenly places. Therefore take up the whole armor of God, that you may be able to withstand in the evil day, and having done all, to stand firm. Stand therefore, having fastened on the belt of truth, and having put on the breastplate of righteousness, and, as shoes for your feet, having put on the readiness given by the gospel of peace. In all circumstances take up the shield of faith, with which you can extinguish all the flaming darts of the evil one; and take the helmet of salvation, and the sword of the Spirit, which is the word of God. (Eph. 6:10–17)

In this passage, the description of the armor is reminiscent of Isaiah 59:17, where God wears the armor himself in order to fight against evil. In Christ we receive the armor that Christ has worn. We fight not with our own power, but on the basis of Christ's victory and with the power of the Holy Spirit, which is the Spirit of Christ. In a broad sense, our own spiritual warfare is a manifestation of God the warrior, fighting with and in us by the power of the Holy Spirit.

9

Appearing with a Chariot

Now we consider instances where God appears with a chariot or with chariots.

Examples with Chariots

A clear instance of God appearing with chariots is found in Isaiah 66:15–16:

> "For behold, the LORD will come in fire,
>   and his *chariots* like the whirlwind,
> to render his anger in fury,
>   and his rebuke with flames of fire.
> For by fire will the LORD enter into judgment,
>   and by his sword, with all flesh;
>   and those slain by the LORD shall be many."

The mention of "fire" and "sword" show that this passage could also be classified with fire theophanies or warrior theophanies. We nevertheless place it in the category of appearances with chariots because of the explicit mention of chariots.

In the ancient Near East, chariots were not commonly owned by ordinary people. They were expensive. They could, of course, be used for mere show. But their main practical use was in war. They provided a mobile platform. So when chariots occur in connection with God appearing, we should think first of all of God waging war against evil. And that is in fact what we find in Isaiah 66:15–16 and other passages.

Here are more instances involving a warlike context:

> Was your wrath against the rivers, O LORD?
> > Was your anger against the rivers,
> > or your indignation against the sea,
> when you rode on your horses,
> > on your *chariot* of salvation?
> You stripped the sheath from your bow,
> > calling for many arrows. *Selah*
> > You split the earth with rivers. (Hab. 3:8–9)

> Then Elisha prayed and said, "O LORD, please open his eyes that he may see." So the LORD opened the eyes of the young man, and he saw, and behold, the mountain was full of horses and *chariots* of fire all around Elisha. (2 Kings 6:17)

See also Psalm 68:17–18.

We also have the well-known instance where chariots of fire come to take Elijah up to heaven:

> And as they still went on and talked, behold, *chariots* of fire and horses of fire separated the two of them. And Elijah went up by a whirlwind into heaven. And Elisha saw it and he cried, "My father, my father! The *chariots* of Israel and its horsemen!" And he saw him no more. (2 Kings 2:11–12)

The main point here seems to be the power and mobility of the chariots, not that they are actually engaged in war.

Cases with Allusion to Chariots

We also have cases that describe God as "riding," but where there is no explicit description of chariots. In the light of clear cases where God uses chariots, these instances also should be understood as involving an allusion to chariots:

> There is none like God, O Jeshurun,
> > who *rides* through the heavens to your help,
> > through the skies in his majesty. (Deut. 33:26)

> Sing to God, sing praises to his name;
> > lift up a song to him who *rides* through the deserts;

his name is the Lord;
  exult before him! (Ps. 68:4)

See also Psalm 68:33; Isaiah 19:1.

Ezekiel 1:15–17 and Daniel 7:9 mention wheels. How do the wheels function, and what is the point of the symbolism? The wheels in Daniel 7:9 are chariot wheels. Daniel 7:9–10 has combined a description of a scene of God's court with a feature from chariots. Ezekiel 1 makes this plain by including more detail. God's throne is at the center (v. 26), and the living creatures are part of the surrounding "court." The wheels come with the living creatures.

In Ezekiel 1, we may infer that the four wheels, with the four living creatures, were spaced around the central throne. There are four wheels, rather than the two wheels that are attached to a normal human chariot. And each wheel is "as it were a wheel within a wheel" (v. 16). These wheels probably symbolize the power of the chariot to move in any direction—unlike an ordinary chariot, built to move in only its "forward" direction. Later on in Ezekiel the whole structure does move: the presence of God, as represented in the structure with the living creatures, departs from the temple and moves toward the east (Ezek. 10:18–19; 11:22–23).

The passage in Ezekiel 1 also makes it clear that there is a close correlation between the wheels and the four living creatures. The two move together (vv. 19–20). This connection is explained: "for the spirit of the living creatures was in the wheels" (1:20; cf. 10:17).

It appears that with the mention of the living creatures and the wheels we have two different symbolic representations of the "vehicle" that carries the throne and the presence of God. The vehicle consists in the four living creatures *and* the wheels, which are closely identified with the living creatures. Together, the four wheels form a chariot to carry the presence of God.

We can add to this picture a key verse in 1 Chronicles 28:18: " . . . also his plan [David's plan given to Solomon; v. 11] for the golden *chariot of the cherubim* that spread their wings and covered the ark of the covenant of the Lord." The overall "plan" in 1 Chronicles 28 specifies designs for various items that will furnish the temple that Solomon is instructed to build. Included in the master plan is a plan for "the golden chariot of the cherubim." What cherubim are in view? From an earlier point in history, the ark of the covenant already had images of two cherubim attached to its cover (Ex. 25:17–21). The plan from David's time also includes two larger cherubim that Solomon made and that were placed in the Most Holy Place of the temple (1 Kings 6:23–28; 2 Chron. 3:10–13). The fact that the cherubim "spread their wings and covered the ark" (1 Chron. 28:18) seems to indicate that the immediate reference is to the two cherubim attached to the cover of the ark (Ex. 25:20).

The point to notice is that the cherubim are identified with "the golden chariot." The cherubim *are* God's chariot. Rather than having some physical structure made of wood or iron, God's chariot is made of living creatures, who are cherubim (Ezek. 10:20).

Once we have this information, other verses fall into place, which describe God as riding on a cherub: "He *rode on a cherub* and flew; he was seen on the wings of the wind" (2 Sam. 22:11; cf. Ps. 18:10). Here the "cherub" functions as the vehicle on which God rides: it is his chariot. The expression "wings of the wind" enjoys a connection with the wings of the cherubim, mentioned in 1 Kings 6:27; 8:6–7; 1 Chronicles 28:18; 2 Chronicles 3:11, 13; 5:8; Ezekiel 1:6, 8, 9, 11, 23, 24, 25.

Significance of Chariots

As we already observed, chariots typically function as equipment in war. God's chariot or chariots symbolize his ability to execute judgment as a warrior whenever and wherever he wishes. He does not have the limitations in space and time of a human warrior.

Like the warrior theophanies, the chariot theophanies manifest God's faithfulness to his promises and to his covenant. They also affirm his kingly power.

Fulfillment in Christ

In the New Testament, Christ comes as the divine warrior warring against sin, evil, and death. In the Old Testament, the two cherubim above the ark of the covenant were attached to the mercy seat (Ex. 25:18–19). In the New Testament, we see that Christ through his sacrifice is the source of all mercy and atonement for us (Rom. 3:25).[1] In addition, Christ's execution of war is depicted especially with reference to his second coming in Revelation 19:11. He rides on a horse, not on a chariot. But the point is similar. It is through Christ that God executes war against evil. In this way, Christ is the fulfillment of the chariot symbolism in the Old Testament.

---

1. I owe to my wife, Diane, this observation about the connection to the cherubim on the ark.

10

Other Appearances

We also find in the Bible descriptions of God appearing where we have little or no detail about *how* he appeared.

> Then the Lord *appeared* to Abram and said, "To your offspring I will give this land." So he built there an altar to the Lord, who had *appeared* to him. (Gen. 12:7)

> When Abram was ninety-nine years old the Lord *appeared* to Abram and said to him, "I am God Almighty; walk before me, and be blameless, that I may make my covenant between me and you, and may multiply you greatly." (Gen. 17:1–2)

> When he had finished talking with him, God *went up* from Abraham. (v. 22)

> But God *came* to Abimelech in a *dream* by night and said to him, "Behold, you are a dead man because of the woman whom you have taken, for she is a man's wife." (Gen. 20:3)

See also Genesis 26:2, 24; 35:9, 13; Exodus 6:3; 1 Samuel 3:21; 1 Kings 3:5 (parallel to 2 Chron. 1:7); 1 Kings 9:2 (parallel to 2 Chron. 7:12); Matthew 1:20; 2:13, 19.

Significance of Appearances without Detail

The lack of detail in some appearances increases the mystery. We do not know exactly what the human recipients saw. Some of the appearances specifically mention "an angel of the Lord," which may suggest a man-like figure. But others mention an appearance without any further detail. Some of the appearances occur in *dreams*. The appearances in dreams may be less startling than appearances in broad daylight or appearances at night in a waking vision. And appearances of an "angel of the Lord" may or may not involve a created angel that would make the vision something less than a direct appearance of *God*. Yet we can classify all these appearances as *theophanies* in the broadest sense of the term. All such appearances build upon the climactic, permanent appearance of God in the person of the incarnate Christ.

11

Appearing in the Created World

God appears in the things that he has made. Romans 1:19–20 speaks about this kind of manifestation of God:

> For what can be known about God is plain to them, because God has *shown* it to them. For his invisible attributes, namely, his eternal power and divine nature, have been clearly *perceived*, ever since the creation of the world, in the things that have been made.

This kind of appearance is subdued in comparison with the special, spectacular appearances that come to individuals here and there in the history of redemption. Because the "appearances" in creation are not momentary, they are not clear examples of "theophanies." But God does show himself through created things. They are "theophany-like." They are not "theophany" in a narrow sense, but may be considered theophany in the broadest sense.

In all these appearances, God is distinct from the world. God is the Creator, and is radically distinct from everything that he created. Romans 1:25—along with many other passages—makes it clear that we must worship God alone and not any creature: "they [idolaters] exchanged the truth about God for a lie and worshiped and served *the creature rather than the Creator*, who is blessed forever! Amen." The distinction between God and created things is underlined in the very same passage (Rom. 1:18–25) that a few verses earlier has indicated how God reveals himself *in* created things. Created things reflect the God who made them. And through created things God shows who he is. He shows how he is distinct from the creatures, in that he alone is eternal and he alone created them. So in all our reflections on how created things reveal God, we must also affirm his distinctness from the things that he has created.

Language Evoking Theophany

Now let us consider some particular passages that explain how God reveals himself. We may begin with Psalm 104:1–4:

> ¹ Bless the LORD, O my soul!
>   O LORD my God, you are very great!
> You are clothed with *splendor* and majesty,
>   ²covering yourself with *light* as with a garment,
>   stretching out the heavens like a tent.
> ³ He lays the beams of his chambers on the waters;
>   he makes the *clouds* his *chariot*;
>   he rides on the *wings* of the *wind*;
> ⁴ he makes his messengers *winds*,
>   his ministers a flaming *fire*.

In this passage, God's work of creation is being compared to a theophany. No one detail in the description proves conclusively that there is an allusion to theophany, but we can see an accumulation of features that also occur in descriptions of God's appearances in theophany. The mention of "splendor" and "light" (vv. 1–2) is similar to a glory theophany. The mention of being clothed and "covered . . . with a garment" (vv. 1–2) suggests a picture of a human-like figure, and so is linked to man-like appearances of God. The cloud and fire (vv. 3–4) are reminiscent of cloud and fire appearances. The chariot (v. 3) is linked to God's appearances with chariots. The winds (vv. 3–4) are one feature sometimes accompanying a thunderstorm appearance:

> He rode on a cherub and flew;
>   he came swiftly on *the wings of the wind*. (Ps. 18:10)

The parallel between Psalm 104:3 and Psalm 18:10 is striking, because there is more than one verbal link. The expression *wings of the wind* occurs in both Psalms 18:10 and 104:3. In both cases it is associated with God *riding*: "he *rides* on the wings of the wind" (104:3), and "he *rode* on a cherub and flew" (Ps. 18:10). Note that Psalm 18:10

says that God "flew." It is an unusual expression, equivalent to God's riding "on a cherub." The descriptions of riding and flying are both poetic, but how would we combine the idea of riding and flying? It would make sense if the cherub itself is flying, using its *wings*. And of course cherubim *do* have wings, according to the descriptions in Exodus 25:20, 1 Kings 6:24//2 Chronicles 3:11, and Ezekiel 1:6. (Note also that a seraph flies to Isaiah in Isa. 6:6, and an angel flies in Rev. 14:6.)

As we saw from 1 Chronicles 28:18, the cherubim serve as God's *chariot*. So the mention of a chariot in Psalm 104:3 has links with the cherub in Psalm 18:10. The clouds that serve as a chariot according to Psalm 104:3 have a link to the clouds that accompany the thunderstorm appearance in Psalm 18:11: "thick *clouds* dark with water." Now Psalm 18:8–15 clearly involves language associated with a thunderstorm theophany. The parallels between Psalm 18:10 and Psalm 104:3 therefore show that Psalm 104:1–4 also has allusions to theophanic themes.

We find a further confirmation about Psalm 104:1–4 by comparing it with Ezekiel 1. The fire in Psalm 104:4 has a link with the cherubim in Ezekiel 1, who have an appearance like fire:

> As for the likeness of the living creatures, their appearance was like burning coals of *fire*, like the appearance of torches moving to and fro among the living creatures. And the *fire* was bright, and out of the *fire* went forth lightning. And the living creatures darted to and fro, like the appearance of a flash of lightning. (Ezek. 1:13–14)

There are still further linkages between the language of Psalm 104:1–4 and theophanies. The poetic lines in Psalm 104:2–3 compare the creation to a tent and a house:

> . . . stretching out the heavens like a *tent*.
> He lays the *beams* of his *chambers* on the waters;

This comparison with a tent or a house occurs in other contexts as well (e.g., Job 38:4–11; Ps. 19:4; Isa. 40:22; Amos 9:6). We might not think much of it, if it were merely a passing comparison. But the tabernacle and the temple are earthly reflections of God's dwelling in heaven. And the cloud of glory comes and dwells on them. So we have an indirect association between the idea of the world as a house or tent and the appearance of God in a cloud of glory. In addition, within the tabernacle and the temple are images of cherubim (Ex. 25:18; 26:31; 1 Kings 6:23,

29//2 Chron. 3:10–14). These parallels show that the analogy with a tent and with chambers in Psalm 104:4 has connections with the temple and the appearances of God in the temple.

What do we conclude about Psalm 104:1–4? There is much in these verses that invites us to see analogies between the way in which God showed his character in creating the world and the ways in which he shows his character in theophanies of a more spectacular kind.

Consider now another psalm that extols God's presence in creation:

The heavens declare the *glory* of God,
   and the sky above proclaims his handiwork.
Day to day pours out speech,
   and night to night reveals knowledge. (Ps. 19:1–2)

The heavens declare "the *glory* of God." Should we think of theophany? In this passage, the associations with theophany are less strong than they were with Psalm 104:1–4. Yet mention of God's glory could make us think of an appearance of the glory of God. And we have seen that such appearances have associations with the phenomena of creation.

In the light of the use of "clothing" and "garment" imagery in Psalm 104:1–2, we may add to our list of creation imagery other passages that speak of God with clothing:

The Lord reigns; he is *robed* in majesty;
   the Lord is *robed*; he has *put on* strength as his *belt*.
Yes, the world is established; it shall never be moved.
Your throne is established from of old;
   you are from everlasting. (Ps. 93:1–2)

On the basis of Psalm 104:1–2, it does not seem accidental that God's being "robed" is mentioned in immediate juxtaposition with the establishment of creation and his rule over it. Creation is like a "robe" displaying his majesty and strength and the firmness of his throne.

Psalm 102:25–27 also suggests a correlation between God's "garment" and creation:

Of old you laid the foundation of the earth,
   and the heavens are the work of your hands.
They will perish, but you will remain;
   they will all wear out like a garment.

You will change them like a robe, and they will pass away,
> but you are the same, and your years have no end.

The "wearing out" of the created world is like the wearing out of a garment, which God changes "like a robe" for another garment (the new heaven and the new earth?).

The Holy Spirit in Genesis 1:2

We should also consider the mention of the Holy Spirit in Genesis 1:2: "And the Spirit of God was *hovering over* the face of the waters." The text does not say explicitly that this presence of the Spirit came in the form of the visible appearance. But the language does suggest a specific location, when it uses the expression "hovering over." It is natural for us mentally to *picture* this presence as similar to the visible presence of God in full-blown theophanies. So did the Holy Spirit appear with some specific physical manifestation in Genesis 1:2? Maybe.

This instance is one of a number that we should integrate into our thinking about theophany, while recognizing that it is less than explicit. Biblical texts that involve an explicit claim about God appearing in a special way are at one end of a spectrum of texts that become less explicit, but that still involve some sense of a special presence of God. Genesis 1:2 is one of these less explicit texts. Granted its mysterious character, it still enjoys a relation to many other texts that express a special presence of God.[1]

We confront a special issue in translating Genesis 1:2. The word translated "Spirit" in the ESV of Genesis 1:2 can also mean *wind*. Accordingly, some interpreters have suggested that in Genesis 1:2 it means *wind* rather than *Spirit*. Genesis 1:2b would be saying, "And a *wind* of God was fluttering over the face of the waters." This interpretation has some attraction, because it makes the half verse 2b a physical description of a physical phenomenon, parallel to the other physically oriented descriptions in Genesis 1. Moreover, the translation as "wind" fits reasonably well with the verb for "hovering," which might possibly mean "fluttering."

But the traditional interpretation "Spirit of God" has at least two

---

1. In fact, Meredith G. Kline sees in Genesis 1:2 an instance of theophany. According to Kline, the Holy Spirit appeared in the form of the cloud of glory that we see later in the exodus (Ex. 13:21–22) (Kline, *Images of the Spirit* [Grand Rapids, MI: Baker, 1980], 13–15). See the further discussion in appendix B of the present work.

main advantages. First, the expression "Spirit of God" is a regular expression in the Old Testament (Gen. 41:38; Ex. 31:3; 35:31; Num. 24:2; 1 Sam. 10:10; etc.). It is natural to interpret this expression in Genesis 1:2 in the same way as in the other occurrences. A writer intending to express the meaning "wind of God" instead of "Spirit of God" would naturally realize that the normal wording would mean "Spirit of God." He therefore would have chosen some alternate wording, such as "a wind *from* God" or "a wind sent from God" to indicate that he intended a different meaning. In fact, Numbers 11:31 contains an example of just such an alternative expression: "Then a *wind from the Lord* sprang up."

Second, there seems to be little point in mentioning "a wind of God" fluttering over the waters. It has no discernible relation to the rest of Genesis 1. By contrast with this lack of relationship, the rest of the elements mentioned in Genesis 1:2 all make a direct contribution to the complete narrative of creation. Let us consider how. The earth is said to be "without form and void," in contrast to the state of the earth by the end of Genesis 1, when it is formed and filled. The darkness in Genesis 1:2 contrasts with the light that God introduces in 1:3. The "deep" in 1:2 is a water-like surface, which underlines the formlessness of the starting situation. It also prepares us for verses 6 and 9, where God separates the waters that are already present in verse 2. And finally, if it is "the Spirit of God" rather than "a wind of God" that is hovering, the resulting picture expresses the presence of God, which is part of the background for the whole series of creative acts in Genesis 1:3–31. If it is said that the point of "a wind of God" is to indicate God's use of an active, moving element in the later formations in creation, this point is more effectively made if the active element is not merely "wind" but God's own Spirit.

All in all, the interpretation "Spirit of God" fits the context better than "a wind of God." But if, for the sake of argument, we postulate that the meaning is "a wind of God," it is best understood as a representation of God's active presence. Later Scripture associates God's active presence with his Spirit. So we would still end up inferring in our theological reasoning that behind the physical manifestation of "wind" stands the activity of the Spirit of God. The wind has a natural correlation with a thunderstorm theophany, and with the later appearance of the Holy Spirit at Pentecost with wind and fire (Acts 2:2–3).

We need to consider one more point of interpretation. Some Old Testament interpreters stress that, within the immediate context of Genesis

1:2, the expression "the Spirit of God" does not communicate explicitly to listeners the doctrine of the Trinity. The doctrine that the Holy Spirit is a person distinct from the Father and the Son becomes explicit in the New Testament. Revelation is progressive. According to his own wise purposes, God reveals more as time passes and he adds to earlier revelation. But that means that the earlier revelation was never intended by God to be neatly "closed off" to the added depth that would come through later revelation. Consequently, in the light of the whole canon, we may confidently say that God intended from the beginning to teach about the distinct role of the Holy Spirit in creation, even though the explicit doctrine of the Holy Spirit was made fully available to human beings only later.

Significance of Appearance in Creation

What is the significance of considering creation as like a theophany or an appearance of God, in a broad sense? We must continue to remember that God is the Creator and is distinct from every creature. It is also true that the God of the Bible is not a God who is aloof and uninvolved in creation. Rather, he is the one who created it. And through "the Spirit of God" he was present in the acts of creation. Through the same Spirit he continues to be present in his acts of providence (cf. Job 32:8; Ps. 104:30). The world around us shows the regularities of God's rule. These regularities are due to God's faithfulness in governing the world. In addition to all these things, man is made in the image of God, and so is an especially intense reflection of God. He is a creature, but in his creatureliness he reminds us of God who made him.

This teaching is important. Modern believers may be tempted to forget that God displays his character in what is regular as well as in what is spectacular (miracle). He displays his character especially in the creation of human beings. Creation psalms (Ps. 19:1–6; Psalm 104; Ps. 147:4–20; Psalm 148) help to reset our thinking by praising God for his majesty in creation. Psalm 136 is striking in that it lays out side by side God's works of creation (vv. 5–9), of providence (v. 25), and of redemption (vv. 10–24); it sees all three as "great wonders" (v. 4).

Spectacular theophanies like Mount Sinai and the descent of fire at Mount Carmel stand out above "routine" providence and "routine" history. But theologically speaking, providence and history are never merely "routine" but serve in a less spectacular way to display the same great truths about the power and greatness and kindness of God. Spectacular theophanies, therefore, can be seen as windows onto the realities about God that are always on display in providence.

The principle of analogy between theophany and providence extends to details. Ordinary thunderstorms are not equivalent to Mount Sinai, but they do display God's power and majesty. They make manifest the character of God. God is present in them, since he is present in the whole world. Thus, theophany in a narrow sense can serve as a perspective on the whole world, and the whole world is analogous to theophanies in the broadest sense.

Ordinary clouds are not equivalent to the cloudy pillar that led the people of Israel through the wilderness. But they do testify to God's exaltedness and to the mystery of his being. God reveals himself to us, but he also remains mysterious. We know him; but since he is infinite, we know him without *comprehending* him fully.

Ordinary fire is not equivalent to the fire of the burning bush or the fiery pillar at night in the wilderness or the tongues of fire at Pentecost. But ordinary fire still reflects the burning and purifying power of God in his justice and his anger against evil.

Ordinary light is not equivalent to the surpassing brightness of God's glory in his special appearances. But ordinary light testifies to God's moral brightness and the purity of his knowledge.

An ordinary human being is not equivalent to the man-like appearance in special theophanies of God. But man is made in the image of God, and constantly testifies to God who made him. Even unbelievers by their human abilities testify in spite of themselves to the glory of God who made them.[2]

An ordinary chariot is not equivalent to the "chariot of the cherubim" (1 Chron. 28:18) on which God rides in executing judgment. But the ordinary chariot testifies to the ingenuity of man, who makes weapons of war. The ingenuity of man is a gift of God, reflecting God's original creativity. And human ability to wage war in order to execute either justice or injustice reflects the original ability of God, who is the original warrior against evil (Ex. 15:3).

In all these instances, such as thunderstorms, fire, light, human beings, and chariots, we should acknowledge a distinction between the

---

2. See Cornelius Van Til, *Introduction to Systematic Theology: Prolegomena and the Doctrines of Revelation, Scripture, and God*, ed. William Edgar (Phillipsburg, NJ: P&R, 2007), 117–189, especially the aspects concerning mankind.

special theophanies and general providence. At the same time, we also acknowledge a relationship between the two. There is an analogy. This analogy is confirmed by the way in which Scripture offers *reports* of theophanies. A report of a theophany, as distinguished from the theophany itself, comes to many people like us who do not directly experience the theophany. For example, the report concerning Moses's encounter with the burning bush comes to those who never saw the burning bush. So how can they understand something that they never saw? Scripture describes what happened using language about burning and about bushes. This language instructs the people by relying on an analogy between ordinary fire and burning on the one hand and the theophanic fire and burning on the other hand. Theophanic fire is *like* ordinary fire, or there would be no point to the description. Similarly, the bush has to be *like* ordinary bushes. Thus, the meaning of the reports depends on a real analogy between special theophanies and general providence.[3] The report in Scripture invites us to start with our experience of ordinary fire and then by analogy use it to understand theophanic fire. But the presence of analogy also allows us to travel in the reverse direction: theophanic fire gives insight into the meaning of ordinary fire. At the same time, we should also affirm that instances of theophanic fire are special in character. The burning bush stood out from other cases of fire because the bush was burning but was not consumed. Moses understood that he was seeing something extraordinary.

When we take seriously the meaning of God's special appearances in theophanies, it has implications for the way in which we view God's creation and his providence. We are dealing with the same God! Creation and providence actually reveal this God.

The modern world is deeply influenced by materialism and deism and atheism, which together say that God—if he exists at all—is absent from the world. In these modern views, the world is the world analyzed by science. And all too often science itself has been transformed into something that forbids us to marvel at the greatness of God as we observe his creation. We make ourselves blind and deaf to the wonder of the created world, which reflects the wonder of God himself. Theophany can aid us in finding a way out of this trap. And if we find a way out, by seeing the reality of who God is and how much he is present and reveals

---

3. I am grateful to Scott Doherty for a personal conversation in which he pointed out the significance of biblical *reports* of theophanies.

himself in his creation, our view of the world itself will be transformed. When I first realized that theophanies had analogies with providence, it transformed my view of the world. I woke up to God's presence in the world and the reflections of his character in the things that he has made.

In short, God is present everywhere and at all times in the created world that he has made. Since we are made in the image of God, our own constitution testifies to the presence of God, and it was originally created to be in tune with God and his majesty.

In addition, God may impress his presence more intensively on our hearts and minds and bodies in particular kinds of events like thunderstorms and fire. In fact, he may draw near whenever and wherever he wishes (e.g., Pss. 21:8–9; 32:4; 38:2; 39:10; the general principle is expressed in Ps. 115:3). Even in a fallen state, people all over the world testify to special experiences in which they have had an intensive encounter of some kind with a transcendent reality.[4] (Remember the dreams of Pharaoh's cupbearer and baker; Genesis 40.) For example, people may experience a special moment, a kind of epiphany that seems transcendently significant, when they see a sunset or a majestic mountain or an ant or a fallen leaf or a flower or a painting or a movie. Or they may have an intense religious experience. But because of sin these encounters may be beset by confusion. We will further evaluate these events at a later point, when we focus on how people *respond* to divine revelation (chapter 24).

---

4. I disagree with some aspects of the approach and the theological conclusions in Robert K. Johnston's book, *God's Wider Presence: Reconsidering General Revelation* (Grand Rapids, MI: Baker, 2014), but I wish to credit the book for drawing my attention to special incidents in which people have an experience with transcendence (19–66).

The expression *general revelation* is not an apt label for this kind of experience. The experiences are *particular*, not general in the sense of being common to the whole human race. They vary from individual to individual, and from one event to another even within the lifetime of a single individual. Because of the particularity of the events, it seems impossible for human analysis to separate the meaning of the presence of God from fallible, sinful human responses.

Difficulties increase, because personal experience has inevitably been digested and interpreted by the individual before and when he reports it to others. His report may acknowledge how little he understood at the time of his initial experience. Yet his report is also inevitably colored by his view or lack of view about the nature of "transcendence," by his faith or unbelief, and by whether he uses Scripture to guide his interpretation.

Given the variety of reports, a vague word like "transcendence" is in some ways appropriate. But it may conceal from view the issue of demonic presence in contrast to divine presence. As in the book of Job, God can use even the presence of the demonic to testify to himself. My wife tells of one American couple with little sense of transcendence who went on a Peace Corps mission to a Third World country. Their encounter with clear demonic activity awakened them to the possibility of the existence of God, and from there they traveled by various routes and finally embraced faith in Christ. God controls all events for his own glory.

Major Themes in Creation

We have seen that theophanies have close connections with the themes of promise, covenant, and kingdom. The same is true of the created world, because it reflects God and is therefore theophany-like. It too reveals the themes of promise, covenant, and kingdom. For example, the themes of both promise and covenant appear in the covenant with Noah. The created world in its regularities conforms to the faithfulness of God, who has promised in his covenant with Noah to preserve regularities: "While the earth remains, seedtime and harvest, cold and heat, summer and winter, day and night, shall not cease" (Gen. 8:22). The theme of kingdom is also manifest in the created world. The world is constantly governed by God, who in his providence rules over it as the everlasting king: "The LORD has established his throne in the heavens, and his kingdom rules over *all*" (Ps. 103:19). In addition, creation reveals the *presence* of God, which is our major theme.

Fulfillment in Christ

Do creation and providence have a relation to Christ and his coming? Christ comes as the redeemer. But before he was redeemer, he was creator. More precisely, he was the *mediator* of creation, in fellowship with God the Father as Creator and the Spirit who hovered over the face of the waters. Colossians 1:15–20 points out the parallels and organic unity between creation and redemption by placing the two side by side, with Christ as mediator of both. He is mediator of creation (v. 15–17) and of redemption (v. 18–20). Through him "all things were created" (v. 16) and through him "all things" are reconciled (v. 20).

Accordingly, the Gospel of John and the Revelation of John point out correlations between Christ and the imagery of the created world. "In him was life, and the life was the *light* of men" (John 1:4). "I am the *light* of the world" (John 8:12). He comes with a *cloud* (Rev. 14:14). "His eyes were like a flame of *fire*" (Rev. 1:14). "His voice was like the *roar* of many waters" (v. 15). "His face was like the *sun shining* in full strength" (v. 16).

To see creation and providence in the right way involves seeing Christ the mediator of creation in them. The glory of creation reflects the glory of Christ the Creator. Understanding creation as we should leads to stirring up praise to God the Father, the Son, and the Spirit. As the psalmist says, "How majestic is your name in all the earth!" (Ps. 8:1, 9). The same is true for unusual, intense experiences of God's presence that people encounter in nature or in culture. God is present in these experiences, in a manner similar to his presence in his daily provisions, "giving you rains from heaven and fruitful seasons, satisfying your hearts with food and gladness" (Acts 14:17). In such ways, people glimpse the reality of God. But they need to move from these experiences to repentance. They need to abandon their idolatrous commitments and find saving knowledge of God through Christ, in order to praise God—the Father, the Son, and the Spirit—for his goodness in creation and salvation.

PART II

THE MYSTERY OF GOD APPEARING

12

Knowing God

We now come to consider more deeply the meaning of God's appearances. Before moving to details, we should reflect briefly on what it means to know God.

The Reality of Knowing God

As we have indicated, God makes himself known in the world. He makes himself known in his word; he makes himself known through his visible appearances in theophany. He also makes himself known through the world that he made and his providential actions in the world. The Bible provides his written speech, which gives us the key guidance in interpreting the rest of his words and actions.

In all these revelations from God, he actually does make himself known. In fact, through the revelation of his character in the created world, every human being knows him:

> For what can be known about God is *plain to them*, because God has *shown it* to them. For his invisible attributes, namely, his eternal power and divine nature, have been *clearly perceived*, ever since the creation of the world, in the things that have been made. So they are without excuse. For although they *knew God*, they did not honor him as God or give thanks to him, but they became futile in their thinking, and their foolish hearts were darkened. (Rom. 1:19–21)

This revelation of God through the created world is called *general revelation*, because it comes to all human beings. Through it, human beings know God and "are without excuse." The passage in Romans 1 indicates not simply that the created world provides ample evidence by which people *could* possibly know God. It does not say merely that people have the inborn *capacity* to know God. It does not say merely that they can infer the existence of God. It says that they *know* him (v. 21). But by itself this knowledge does not result in salvation. God also gives *special revelation* at particular times and places, as recorded in the Old Testament. The special revelation includes theophanies, miraculous works, and verbal revelation. According to God's plan, some of the verbal revelation was written down and has become Scripture. Through the power of the Holy Spirit illumining our minds, we can understand the Bible and know Jesus Christ. Through him, we can know God in a saving way. We can know him more deeply than through general revelation alone.

Nonexhaustive Human Knowledge

In order better to understand theophanies, let us consider what it means to know God. We know God, and we know him truly. But we are creatures; we are not God. We do not know him exhaustively. We do not know him as he knows himself.

Theologians describe God as "incomprehensible." That term means that we do not know him comprehensively. He is God and is unique:

[H]is understanding is unsearchable. (Isa. 40:28)

"For my thoughts are not your thoughts,
    neither are your ways my ways, declares the Lord.
For as the heavens are higher than the earth,
    so are my ways higher than your ways
    and my thoughts than your thoughts." (Isa. 55:8–9)

Affirming Genuine Knowledge and Limitations

In all cases of revelation, we must affirm two complementary truths: (1) God makes himself known, and it really is God that can be known; and (2) through revelation we who are human know God truly but not comprehensively (not exhaustively). The same is true when it comes to cases when God appears: (1) God's appearances make him known. They do show, really and truly, who God is and what he is like; (2) God's appearances never result in our having exhaustive knowledge of him.

God's knowledge of himself always surpasses what he gives to human beings through his appearances.

These two complementary truths can be conveniently summed up in a diagram invented by John Frame.[1] The diagram has come to be known as "Frame's square." The diagram is intended to summarize the nature of God's transcendence and immanence. (See fig. 12.1.)

Fig. 12.1: Frame's Square of Transcendence and Immanence

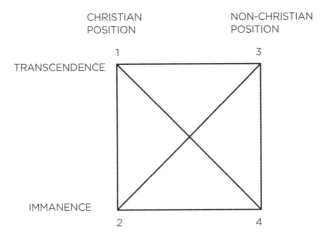

As will become clear in what follows, the left-hand side of the square represents the Christian understanding of God's transcendence and immanence—an understanding derived from the Bible, while the right-hand side of the square represents the non-Christian understanding.

According to the Christian understanding, God's transcendence means that he has supremacy over all that he has made. He exercises authority and power over all the created world. God's immanence means that he is present in the world. He is present to human beings in particular, and also present as ruler in all that he has made. Precisely through his presence he exercises authority and power. Thus God's transcendence and immanence go together.

According to the non-Christian understanding, God's transcendence means that he is far away and uninvolved, while God's immanence means that he is identical with the world. These two poles are in tension with each other.

1. John M. Frame, *The Doctrine of the Knowledge of God* (Phillipsburg, NJ: P&R, 1987), 14.

The diagonal lines in Frame's square represent direct contradictions. The non-Christian view of transcendence, represented by the upper-right corner 3 of the square, contradicts the Christian view of immanence, represented by the lower-left corner 2 of the square. The non-Christian view of transcendence says that God is uninvolved, while the Christian view of immanence says that he is constantly involved. Similarly, the non-Christian view of immanence (corner 4) says that God is identical with the world, and so is trapped in the world. It contradicts the Christian view of transcendence (corner 1), which says that God is supreme and governs the world.

Fig. 12.2: Summary of Transcendence and Immanence

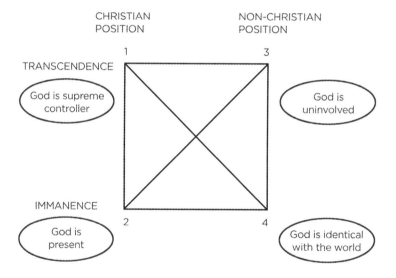

The horizontal lines in Frame's square represent instances of "formal" similarity between the Christian and non-Christian views. The non-Christian view of transcendence (corner 3) can *sound like* the Christian view of transcendence (corner 1). Both sides can use the same word *transcendence* or say that God is "exalted." But they mean different things. Likewise, the Christian view of immanence (corner 2) may sound like the non-Christian view of immanence (corner 4), but they mean different things. To be plausible, the non-Christian view has to seem close to the truth. It does this by imitating the true view, on the left-hand side, but twisting it so that, on the level of actual meaning, the non-Christian view contradicts the Christian view. (See the summary in fig. 12.2.)

Transcendence and Immanence in Knowledge

This square of transcendence and immanence can be applied to summarize how we think about the *knowledge* of God. According to the Christian view of transcendence (corner 1), God knows everything and is the standard for all knowledge. According to the Christian view of immanence (corner 2), God actually makes himself known to human beings, through the world that he has made and through special revelation, so that human beings know the true God. They may and do suppress that knowledge, as Romans 1:18 indicates, but the knowledge is still there, in suppressed form.

According to the non-Christian view of transcendence (corner 3), God is unknowable. He is far away and inaccessible to our knowledge. According to the non-Christian view of immanence (corner 4), our human knowledge of what a god would be is the only thing that we have, and our human knowledge serves as the standard for knowledge. God must conform to our thinking.

Once again, the diagonal lines in Frame's square represent contradictions. The Christian view of transcendence (corner 1) says that God is the standard for knowledge, while the non-Christian view of immanence (corner 4) says that man is the standard. The Christian view of immanence (corner 2) says that we can and do know God, while the non-Christian view of transcendence (corner 3) says that God is unknowable. (See the summary in fig. 12.3.)

From one end to the other, the Bible consistently puts forth what we have called the *Christian* view of transcendence and immanence, and the Christian view of *knowledge*. But it is easy to become confused about these things, because the non-Christian view of transcendence and the non-Christian view of knowledge tend to imitate the Christian view in a "formal" way. The non-Christian view may use similar terms—for example, transcendence and immanence.

We should also note the term *incomprehensible*. According to a Christian view, God's incomprehensibility means that God is the standard for knowledge, while our knowledge of him is true but limited. According to a non-Christian view, "incomprehensibility" might mean *unknowability* (denying corner 2, Christian immanence).

Fig. 12.3: Transcendence and Immanence in Knowledge of God

Fig. 12.3: Transcendence and Immanence in Knowledge of God

CHRISTIAN POSITION — NON-CHRISTIAN POSITION

1 — TRANSCENDENCE — God knows everything and is the standard for knowledge

3 — God is unknowable

2 — IMMANENCE — God is present and gives knowledge of himself and the world to human beings

4 — Our knowledge can serve as our standard; God must conform to it

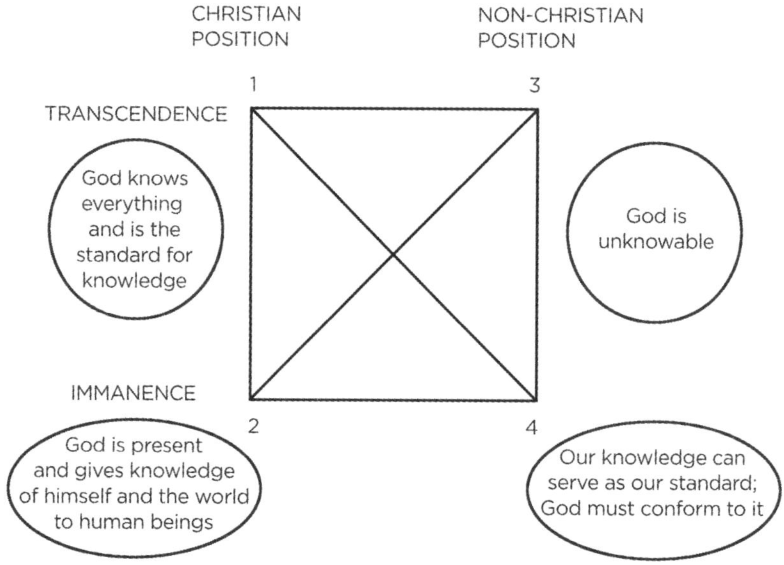

Application to God's Appearances

These principles for knowledge need to be applied when we consider theophany. An appearance of God makes God known. But what does it mean for God to be known? We must interpret theophanies using a Christian view of knowledge.

When God reveals himself in theophany, his revelation never gives us exhaustive knowledge. That is the principle of Christian transcendence. God himself knows himself completely, and remains the standard for knowledge in theophany. At the same time, the revelation of God in theophany is real and effective. We can actually know God and know about him through his appearances. That expresses the Christian principle of immanence in knowledge (corner 2).

God does not have a body and does not have a material composition. Consequently, he is not innately visible or subject to human analysis or human domination. He is the Lord of the universe and cannot be captured within the universe. In this sense God is invisible (1 Tim. 1:17). That expresses the Christian principle of transcendence (corner 1). But we must not use this truth to undercut the reality of his revelation, including his revelation of himself in appearances. God shows his character in profound ways when he appears (the Christian principle of immanence, corner 2).

Suppose that we turn away from treating God's appearances as serious, and we say to ourselves that it is "merely" appearance, and is a kind of illusion. Then we have subtly and unwittingly moved into a non-Christian view of transcendence (corner 3), according to which God is unknowable, a complete blank "behind" his revelation in the appearances.

.

13

Relation of Kinds of Appearances

The appearances of God take quite a few forms. In previous chapters we have looked at thunderstorms, fire, cloud, glory (brightness), king's court, man, warrior, and chariot. Why so many forms? And what is the relation between the different forms?

Distinct Forms

The multiplicity of forms suggests to begin with that God himself in his character and in his actions is richer than what could be captured by any one form by itself. In fact, he is richer than all of them put together. As we mentioned in the previous chapter, theologians describe God as "incomprehensible." The multitude of forms underline his incomprehensibility. At the same time, each form does reveal him and does communicate things about who he is and what he does. Any one form puts to the foreground some aspects of his character more than others. For example, the appearances in a court emphasize his kingship and his authority to judge. The appearances in a cloud emphasize his incomprehensibility—that we do not know him exhaustively. The appearances with a chariot emphasize his power and zeal to make war against evil. They also allude to his omnipresence. The mobility of a chariot poetically suggests his ability to appear anywhere.

The appearances in human form remind us that human beings are created in the image of God. These appearances also foreshadow the coming of Christ, who is "God with us" permanently (Matt. 1:23).

Christ as the permanent "theophany" surpasses any one appearance of God in the Old Testament, and he also surpasses them even when they are all taken together. Hebrews underlines the climactic character of God's appearance in Christ:

> Long ago, at many times and in many ways, God spoke to our fa-
> thers by the prophets, but *in these last days* he has spoken to us *by*
> *his Son*, whom he appointed the heir of all things, through whom
> also he created the world. He is the radiance of the glory of God and
> the exact imprint of his nature, and he upholds the universe by the
> word of his power. After making purification for sins, he sat down
> at the right hand of the Majesty on high. (Heb. 1:1–3)

Given this emphatic claim in Hebrews, we might naively think that we can virtually "throw away" all the earlier instances of theophany, because in Christ we now have the reality to which they pointed. According to this reasoning, we could dispense with not only Old Testament appearances of God but the entire contents of the Old Testament—it has all been superseded. But the rest of the book of Hebrews shows that the opposite is true. Hebrews repeatedly appeals to the Old Testament in expounding the significance of Christ and his work.

Likewise theophanies, as a particular piece of the Old Testament, help us to grow in appreciating the significance of the surpassing revelation of Christ. Consider the expression in Hebrews 1:3, "He is the radiance of the glory of God." Hebrews alludes to the glory and brightness associated with Old Testament theophanies in order to underline the significance of Christ's coming.

The book of Revelation also gives us visions that show similarities to Old Testament appearances of God—we read about a heavenly court, fire, lightning, thunder, and cloud. A variety of imagery continues to function—as it did in the Old Testament—to expound the richness of God.

Overlapping Themes in God's Appearances

Different forms of divine appearance are distinguishable up to a point. But only up to a point. Each appearance is an appearance of the *same* God. Appropriately, we find in some divine appearances combinations and coalescences of multiple imagistic representations.

For example, the appearances of God with chariots have a close connection to God's appearances as a warrior. And since the chariot is identified with the cherubim (1 Chron. 28:18), who are participants in God's court, the chariot imagery passes over into and reinforces the imagery of God's court. The living creatures in Ezekiel 1 are *both* God's court and God's chariot. We have chosen to treat God's appearances with chariots as a distinct kind of theophany, and we have devoted a separate chapter to discussing them (chapter 9). But if we wished, we could also have made the discussion a subdivision of appearances as a warrior or appearances of God in the midst of his court.

We also see instances where biblical passages contain imagery but do not fully develop it. They merely hint at a further development. Daniel 7:9 speaks of the throne of "the Ancient of Days," and says,

> "his throne was *fiery flames*;
> its *wheels* were *burning fire*."

This imagery has links with God's appearances in fire, and the "wheels" designate the wheels of his chariot, the cherubim. But neither of these images is fully developed. Similarly, Deuteronomy 33:26, Psalm 68:33, and Isaiah 19:1 speak of God riding in the heavens, but do not fully develop the picture of riding specifically on a chariot.

We might also consider the way in which a human-like figure is mentioned or at least suggested in several forms of divine appearance: God with his court, God as a warrior, and God as an individual human appearance.

The overlapping themes imply that no one form of divine appearances is isolated from the rest. Any strict and neat classification is artificial.

The overlapping of themes reinforces two points. First, there is only one God. One God is manifesting himself in all the appearances, and this one God is consistent with himself. He is always just, merciful, powerful, and pure, so all his appearances show him as such. Second, God is not masterable. There is always more to his character than what is obvious on the surface from the main features of one of his appearances.

Together, these two points encourage us to worship God and stand in awe of him. His character as revealed in theophany is altogether worthy of our worship and our service. And we should be in awe because he exceeds what we can understand.

14

Reflecting God

We now consider the ways in which a process of reflecting God occurs in God's appearances.[1] In this context, the word *image* needs careful attention. Theologians are accustomed to discuss the fact that man was created "in the image of God" (Gen. 1:26–27). In the discourse of systematic theology, the word *image* and more especially the phrase *image of God* customarily build on the word *image* in Genesis 1:26–27, and often are used to designate whatever is uniquely characteristic of humanity, either in itself or in relation to God.

Genesis 1:26–27 does emphasize the uniqueness of mankind in comparison with other earthly creatures. And there is nothing wrong with developing a technical vocabulary in which the expression *image of God* summarizes the discussion of what is unique about mankind. But the word *image* could also be used in other ways in other contexts. This word and other, related words sometimes occur in contexts where we see broader ways in which God reflects aspects of his character. We could use the English word *image* to express these reflections of God. To avoid confusion, we will primarily use the words *reflect* and *reflection*.

Instances of Reflections in the Bible

Let us consider some instances of reflection. The New Testament describes Christ as the image of God:

---

1. See Meredith G. Kline, *Images of the Spirit* (Grand Rapids, MI: Baker, 1980), for attention to this theme.

In their case the god of this world [Satan] has blinded the minds of the unbelievers, to keep them from seeing the light of the gospel of the glory of Christ, who is the *image* of God. (2 Cor. 4:4)

He is the *image* of the invisible God, the firstborn of all creation. For by him all things were created, in heaven and on earth, visible and invisible, whether thrones or dominions or rulers or authorities—all things were created through him and for him. (Col. 1:15–16)

Colossians 1:15–16 describes the Son of God in the context of creating the world, not merely in the context of redemption. The language of "image" is applied to the role of the Son of God as mediator of creation, a role that he had before his incarnation. So the language of reflection is applied to the Son of God as *God*, not merely to his human nature, which he acquired in the incarnation.

Accordingly, we must adjust our understanding of the word *image*. In some contexts, the word *image* could suggest a *mere* image, an inferior representation. But that is not the meaning here. The Son of God, the second person of the Trinity, is *fully* God. As John 1:1 says, "The Word was God." Being God is not a matter of degree. The Son is God, just as much as the Father is God. Hebrews 1:3 makes a similar point: "He [the Son] is the radiance of the glory of God and the exact imprint of his nature." The Son is "the exact imprint," the exact representation of everything that God is. He exactly represents God because he is God! We are here dealing with an eternal relation between God the Father and God the Son. The Son is eternally the exact reflection of the Father, and is God equally with the Father. Philippians 2:6 makes a similar point: "he was in the *form* of God." This means that the Son is God. He is equal with the Father, not inferior to him.

Now let us consider further the implications of Colossians 1:15, where Christ is "the image of the invisible God." How does this truth fit into the larger context of Colossians 1:15–20? The subsequent verses in Colossians 1 indicate that Christ is mediator of redemption, in a way parallel to his mediation of creation (vv. 18–20). Thus, the role of the Son of God in creation (vv. 15–17) forms the background for understanding how appropriate it is that he should become the mediator of redemption (vv. 18–20). The Son's eternal status as the image of God forms the background for his acquiring human nature, which is made in the image of God in the sense of Genesis 1:26–27. But we can still distinguish creation from redemption.

We conclude, then, that the word *image* or similar words can be appropriately used not only in describing mankind but also in describing the relation of the eternal Son to God the Father. We must simply recognize that we have a different but related use. In this context, we must make distinctions between God and man. We must remember that the Son of God is fully God. He is *always* the image of God. Adam, by contrast, is a creature, *created* in the image of God. We have two levels of existence, not one. There is the Creator, God, and the creature, man.

Now consider the angels. Job describes the angels as "sons of God":

> Now there was a day when *the sons of God* came to present themselves before the Lord, and Satan also came among them. (Job 1:6)

> Again there was a day when *the sons of God* came to present themselves before the Lord, and Satan also came among them to present himself before the Lord. (Job 2:1)

> " . . . when the morning stars sang together
>   and all *the sons of God* shouted for joy?" (Job 38:7)

These verses are also related to the theme of reflecting God. According to Genesis 5:3, Adam "fathered a son in his own likeness, after his image, and named him Seth." It is easy to infer that one implication of being a son is being "in his own likeness, after his image." In a broad sense, angels reflect God, to whom they are "sons." Though they are creatures, they certainly do reflect his majesty, power, glory, and purity, and their voice reflects his voice when they serve as messengers for his announcements.

Once we see that reflecting God takes place in a broader way, we can see instances of reflection in the context of theophany. Ezekiel 1 describes the central throne and the man-like figure as a "likeness":

> And above the expanse over their heads there was the *likeness* of a throne, in appearance like sapphire; and seated above the *likeness* of a throne was a *likeness* with a human appearance. . . . Like the appearance of the bow that is in the cloud on the day of rain, so was the appearance of the brightness all around.
>   Such was the appearance of the *likeness* of the glory of the Lord. (Ezek. 1:26–28)

What does the word *likeness* imply? The word *likeness* (Hebrew *dᵊmût*) is paired with the word *image* (Hebrew *ṣelem*) in the key passages in Genesis 1:26 and 5:3. By using the two words in parallel, the passages focus on their overlapping meaning. That is to say, in the verses in question, the two words function as virtual synonyms, helping to define each other. Ezekiel 1:26–28 uses the word *likeness* but not *image*. But the meaning is similar. Thus, in Ezekiel 1 we can infer that we have a case of reflection in the broad sense. The human figure and the throne *reflect* the nature of God and his ruling power. The manifestation of God in human form is a *reflection* of God.

Reflections in Theophany

Once we have seen the more striking cases of reflections of God, a larger pattern becomes noticeable. There are many instances of reflecting God in a broad sense. Angels reflect God, according to Job. And the cherubim or living creatures of Ezekiel 1 are a subclass of angels. So the cherubim reflect God, at least in some respects. The twenty-four elders in Revelation 4 are seated on twenty-four thrones, imitating the central throne of God (Rev. 4:2). They reflect God by reflecting his power, represented by his throne. Daniel 7:9 mentions not only a central throne on which the Ancient of Days sits, but "thrones," in the plural, so we should think of angelic assistants in God's court, who have thrones that reflect the central throne of God.

Ezekiel 1 is worth our attention, because it is in some ways the most elaborate theophany in the Old Testament. It has three "layers," as it were. The outermost layer is what Ezekiel sees first: "a stormy wind came out of the north, and a great *cloud*" (v. 4). Inside the cloud is a second layer, consisting in the living creatures and the wheels associated with them (vv. 5–25). In the middle and above the living creatures is the throne with the human figure sitting on it (vv. 26–28). The human figure is the most intense and intimate aspect of the entire display. It constitutes a third, innermost layer.

Now consider how this structure of three layers is connected with the process of reflection. The central human figure is itself an image or "likeness," reflecting "the glory of the Lord" (v. 28). It has "the appearance of *fire*" (v. 27). In the second layer the living creatures are full of fire (v. 13). In the outermost layer, the cloud has fire in it: "fire flashing forth continually" (v. 4). Fire appears in all three layers. Since the outer layers are less intense, we can say that the fire in them reflects the inner fire in the innermost layer, the fire of the human figure. The fire in all three layers depicts in visual form the same truth about God that is associated with a fire theophany. God is pure and consumes evil, by both destruction and purification. Or, as Hebrews says, "our God is a consuming fire" (Heb. 12:29).

We may notice also that all three layers have gleaming metal. In the inner layer, Ezekiel describes it as follows: "I saw as it were gleaming metal" (Ezek. 1:27). In the middle layer the living creatures "sparkled like burnished bronze" (v. 7), and their wheels were "like the gleaming of beryl" (v. 16). The cloud also has "as it were gleaming metal" (v. 4). The gleaming metal speaks of the brightness of God's glory. It reflects his splendor. This aspect in theophany is picked up in Revelation 1, where Christ appears: "his feet were like burnished bronze, refined in a furnace" (Rev. 1:15). The primary connotation is probably one of brightness and glory. But it may also have an association with bright metal armor. The contexts in Ezekiel 1 and Revelation 1 include a note of judgment against sin and evil. So we may think of both the splendor of God's nature and his zeal for judgment against evil.

A third feature also occurs in at least two layers of the theophany in Ezekiel 1: a loud voice. In the inner layer, a voice comes "from above the expanse over their [the living creatures'] heads," that is, from the central throne (v. 25). This voice continues in Ezekiel 2:1–2, as is indicated in the expressions "And he said to me," and "And as he spoke to me." In the middle layer, the living creatures make sound: "And when they went, I heard the sound of their wings like the sound of many waters, like the sound of the Almighty, a sound of tumult like the sound of an army" (v. 24). The sound is explicitly compared to "the sound of the Almighty," linking it to the voice from the throne (cf. 10:5).

Ezekiel 1 does not explicitly say whether there is a sound from the cloud (v. 4). But the cloud includes "a stormy wind," suggesting that a sound may have come from the wind. Whether or not a sound is explicitly included in the third, outer layer, the sound from the two inner layers moves outward to the cloud. So all three layers end up having sound coming from them or through them. The sound reflects or expresses God's ability to speak, and to do so with power and efficacy.

The presence of instances of reflection underlines the way theophany expresses and makes known the character of God. God produces reflections of his character in his appearance. Sometimes this reflection is more intense, as with the human likeness sitting on the throne. Sometimes it is less intense, as with the fiery cloud. But all the appearances truly manifest who God is. In all these instances, we continue to have a distinction between God the Creator and the creatures that he made. The metal, the fire, the cloud, and the air waves that carry sound remain creatures. Through creatures who are distinct from God, God manifests his own character as the one who created and maintains them.

Fulfillment in Christ

Revelation 1 shows us that Christ is the fulfillment of Old Testament theophanies. The fire, the gleaming bronze, and the loud voice of Ezekiel 1 are all there in Revelation 1:12–16, as is the representation by means of a human-like figure. But Christ is not merely "human-like"; he *is* human—God and man in one person. He proclaims his humanity in Revelation 1:18: "I died." At the same time he proclaims his deity, by applying to himself the divine name: "I am the first and the last" (v. 17; cf. Rev. 1:8; 21:6; 22:13). So the theophany in Revelation 1:12–16 takes up the features of Ezekiel 1 and at the same time surpasses the Old Testament. When we compare Revelation 1:12–16 with the Old Testament, we see that the Old Testament offers us a shadow or anticipation or reflection of the reality that was to come in Christ.

15

Reflecting God in
Human Appearance

The inner layer in the theophany in Ezekiel 1 consists in the human figure on the throne. The human figure foreshadows the incarnation of Christ. And, as we have seen, specific features about the human figure are taken up in the vision of Christ in Revelation 1. But we can also consider what the human figure suggested in Ezekiel's time. The fire in Ezekiel 1 connotes God's ability and zeal to destroy evil and purify what is contaminated. The voice points to God's ability to speak. Can we similarly see a display of some features of God's character in the human shape?

Divine Attributes Reflected in Eyes

We may conveniently start with eyes as one feature of the human form. Ezekiel 1 does not specifically mention that the central human form has eyes, but of course we can infer that they belong there. The vision of Christ in Revelation 1, which partly builds on Ezekiel 1:27, mentions that "His eyes were like a flame of fire" (Rev. 1:14). This feature is repeated in Revelation 2:18: "The words of the Son of God, who *has eyes like a flame of fire*, and whose feet are like burnished bronze." The message to the church in Thyatira includes the line, "And all the churches will know that I am he who *searches mind and heart*, and I will give to each of you according to your works" (2:23). The reference to searching mind and heart alludes back to 2:18 and 1:14, with their symbolism of "eyes like a flame of fire." Christ's eyes symbolize his ability to penetrate to the inner reality of who a person is. He knows the heart.

More broadly, the Old Testament already speaks of "the eyes of the Lord," in order to describe his knowledge of all things:

> "For the *eyes of the* Lord run to and fro throughout the whole earth, to give strong support to those whose heart is blameless toward him." (2 Chron. 16:9)

> The *eyes of the* Lord are toward the righteous and his ears toward their cry. (Ps. 34:15; cf. 1 Pet. 3:12)

> The *eyes of the* Lord are in every place, keeping watch on the evil and the good. (Prov. 15:3)

See also Psalm 11:4–5; Proverbs 5:21; 22:12; Jeremiah 32:18–19.

God in his divine nature does not have a body and does not have physical eyes. Theologians therefore say that this language is *anthropomorphic*. It is metaphorical. It describes God *by comparison* with a human figure, with human eyes. But it does describe something real about God, namely his knowledge.

Though Ezekiel 1 does not mention explicitly the eyes of the central human figure, it does describe eyes in connection with the wheels (v. 18; cf. 10:12). In Revelation 4–5 eyes belong both to the living creatures (4:6, 8) and to the Lamb (5:6).

Divine Attributes Reflected in Hand and Arm

Consider next the feature of hands. Ezekiel 1 does not explicitly mention the hands of the human figure, but it is supplemented by 2:9–10, which does: "And when I looked, behold, a *hand* was stretched out to me, and behold, a scroll of a book was in it. And *he spread it* before me. And it had writing on the front and on the back, and there were written on it words of lamentation and mourning and woe." We may infer that the spreading out of the scroll in verse 10 was done with the hand or hands. The pronoun *he* in "he spread it" refers most naturally to the "he" who has been speaking to Ezekiel since verse 1. It is the Lord. So the "hand" is the hand of the central human figure. This idea is confirmed by Revelation 5:1. This verse mentions "a scroll written within and on the back," which is "in the right hand of him who was seated on the throne." Revelation 5:1 obviously builds on Ezekiel 2:9–10, and in Revelation 5 the hand belongs to God, who is seated on the throne. The living creatures also have hands, according to Ezekiel 10:7–8.

These visions of hands, with functions given to the hands, show the ability of the Lord to manipulate created objects and thereby to act with power and precision in the world that he has made. The same is true here as with the *eyes* of the Lord. God does not have a body and does not have physical hands. But he does have power to act on and within the world. His limitless power is reflected in the living creatures, who have hands. The living creatures imitate God's power, though they are creatures and therefore have only finite power.

The Old Testament contains other passages referring to "the hand of the Lord":

> "behold, *the hand of the Lord* will fall with a very severe plague upon your livestock that are in the field, the horses, the donkeys, the camels, the herds, and the flocks." (Ex. 9:3)

> and the people of Israel said to them, "Would that we had died by the *hand of the Lord* in the land of Egypt, when we sat by the meat pots and ate bread to the full, for you have brought us out into this wilderness to kill this whole assembly with hunger." (Ex. 16:3)

See also Deuteronomy 2:15 and Joshua 4:24.

The feature of the "hand" is closely related to "arm." The expression "the arm of the Lord" is used to express his power, sometimes in parallel with "hand":

> "You shall remember that you were a slave in the land of Egypt, and the Lord your God brought you out from there with a mighty *hand* and an outstretched *arm*." (Deut. 5:15)

> "And the Lord brought us out of Egypt with a mighty *hand* and an outstretched *arm*, with great deeds of terror, with signs and wonders." (Deut. 26:8)

See also 1 Kings 8:42; Psalms 44:3; 98:1.

Both God's "hand" and his "arm" symbolize his power to save and to destroy. His hand and his arm work both to save his people and to destroy his enemies, as we see clearly in the narrative of the exodus from Egypt:

"Or has any god ever attempted to go and take a nation for himself from the midst of another nation, by trials, by signs, by wonders, and by war, by a mighty *hand* and an outstretched *arm*, and by great deeds of terror, all of which the LORD your God did for you in Egypt before your eyes?" (Deut. 4:34)

Divine Attributes Reflected in Other Human Features

We can extend our list to include other features of the human body. The Lord's *ears* are open to hear prayers:

And when Samuel had heard all the words of the people, he repeated them in the *ears* of the LORD. (1 Sam. 8:21)

"In my distress I called upon the LORD;
    to my God I called.
From his temple he heard my voice,
    and my cry came to his *ears*." (2 Sam. 22:7; cf. Ps. 18:6)

See also 2 Chronicles 6:40; Psalms 34:15; 130:2. God's ears indicate his ability to hear prayers.

The Lord's *feet* symbolize his dominion:

The glory of Lebanon shall come to you,
    the cypress, the plane, and the pine,
to beautify the place of my sanctuary,
    and I will make the place of my *feet* glorious. (Isa. 60:13)

See also 2 Samuel 22:10; Psalm 18:9; Nahum 1:3; Zechariah 14:4. Or, the language of *treading* is used without specific reference to feet:

"I have *trodden* the winepress alone,
    and from the peoples no one was with me;
I *trod* them in my anger
    and *trampled* them in my wrath;
their lifeblood spattered on my garments,
    and stained all my apparel." (Isa. 63:3)

The Lord's *mouth* is associated with his articulate speech:

"And the glory of the LORD shall be revealed,
    and all flesh shall see it together,
    for the *mouth* of the LORD has *spoken*." (Isa. 40:5)

The Lord's *face* symbolizes his presence:

> Thus the LORD used to speak to Moses *face* to face, as a man speaks to his friend. (Ex. 33:11)

> the upright shall behold his *face*. (Ps. 11:7)

See also Exodus 33:20; Psalms 13:1; 17:15; 27:8–9.

Significance of Human Features

As we observed, God is a spirit and does not have a body. But Scripture uses language referring to his eyes, ears, hand, and so on, when it represents his knowledge, power, and presence. This use of language is *anthropomorphic*, using human characteristics by way of analogy in order to describe God. Why does it work? As Genesis 1:26–27 indicates, man is made in the image of God. He is *like* God in certain ways. And we can be so bold as to say that the similarities extend to include the bodily powers of mankind.

A human being has eyes, enabling him to see. He has ears, enabling him to hear. He has hands and arms, enabling him to act and manipulate things in the world. Human beings are able to do these things in imitation of God, who has perfect knowledge and power. Human beings imitate God with their finite knowledge and power. God's knowledge is the original knowledge. Human knowledge, obtained through the eyes, is derivative and finite knowledge. But it is imitative of God. Human knowledge *reflects* divine knowledge. So it is fitting that God gave human beings eyes to see and ears to hear. The original for these eyes and ears is not man but God—not that God has a body, but that he has knowledge. God's knowledge is the original eyes and ears. Human eyes and ears are imitative of the original.

Similarly, the language of God's "hand" symbolizes his power, which is the original power. God's "hand" *is* his power. God made human hands and arms in imitation of his power.

We have said that the language about eyes and ears and hands used to describe God is *anthropomorphic* language. It depicts God *as if* he were "anthropomorphic," that is, in the form of a human being. It works because, first of all, as the foundation for meaning, God made man in the image of God. Man is *theomorphic* (in the "morph" or "form" of God).[1] In a sense the word *anthropomorphic* has the order

---

1. This insight came from a remark made years ago by J. I. Packer.

exactly backwards. God is the original, and human beings are derivative. The relation of reflection in which human beings stand to God includes many aspects. Among them are aspects of the human body—not because God has a physical body, but because the body represents the outward side of human abilities that imitate and reflect the original divine abilities.

So the human-like figure at the center of the theophany in Ezekiel 1 makes sense. The human shape symbolizes personal capabilities of God, and these capabilities in God have a reflection in man. This relationship is true because of *creation*. It is not merely a product of later *redemptive* work, which looks forward to the incarnation of Christ. Christ did take on human nature, and his identifying with our humanity is crucial for the efficacy and sufficiency of the redemption that he accomplished. But even apart from redemption and its needs, it would still have been true that man is made in the image of God, and that the full relationship in which man reflects God extends to the human body. The human body reflects original divine capabilities in knowledge, power, and presence.

16

Reflections and the Spirit

Attributes of God are reflected in the fact that God manifests himself in human form. In the previous chapter we saw that the eyes and ears of God symbolize his knowledge; the hand of God and the arm of God signify his power; and so on. The human-like features of face, eyes, hand, and arm also have close links to the presence of the Holy Spirit. This correlation should not be surprising, because the Holy Spirit is himself God. The Bible teaches that God is Trinitarian: God is three persons—the Father, the Son, and the Holy Spirit. Let us now explore the relation of the Holy Spirit to the language of face, eyes, hand, and arm.

The Face of God

The *face* of God is closely linked with the Holy Spirit, who manifests the presence of God.

> Cast me not away from your presence [*face* in Hebrew],
>   and take not your Holy Spirit from me. (Ps. 51:11)

> Where shall I go from your Spirit?
>   Or where shall I flee from your presence [*face* in Hebrew]?
>   (Ps. 139:7)

See also Ezekiel 39:29.

The Eyes of God

The eyes of the Lord are also linked with the Holy Spirit:

> I saw a Lamb standing, as though it had been slain, with seven horns and with seven *eyes*, which are the *seven spirits* of God sent out into all the earth. (Rev. 5:6)

The "seven spirits of God" are a symbolic representation of the sevenfold fullness of the Holy Spirit. This representation is confirmed by Revelation 1:4–5, where grace and peace come both from "the seven spirits of God" and from the Father and the Son:

> John to the seven churches that are in Asia:
>   Grace to you and peace from him who is and who was and who is to come, and from the *seven spirits* who are before his throne, and from Jesus Christ the faithful witness, the firstborn of the dead, and the ruler of kings on earth.

Only God can be the source of grace, so it is evident that "the seven spirits" stand for the Holy Spirit (see Rev. 4:5). Revelation 5:6 then equates the seven spirits with "seven eyes" of the Lamb.

The Hand of God

The hand of God represents his power. In Ezekiel, the "hand" of the Lord "fell upon" Ezekiel to give him a vision (Ezek. 8:1–2). Later "the Spirit of the Lord fell upon" him to give him the word of God (11:5). The parallel shows that the Lord's hand expresses the presence of his Spirit. In Luke 1:35 the Holy Spirit is set in parallel with the power of God:

> And the angel answered her, "The *Holy Spirit* will come upon you, and the *power* of the Most High will overshadow you; therefore the child to be born will be called holy—the Son of God."

The "hand" of God and the "Spirit" work closely together in other verses in Ezekiel:

> The *Spirit* lifted me up and took me away, and I went in bitterness in the heat of my spirit, the *hand* of the Lord being strong upon me. (Ezek. 3:14)

He put out the form of a *hand* and took me by a lock of my head, and the *Spirit* lifted me up between earth and heaven. (Ezek. 8:3)

See also Ezekiel 37:1.

The Finger of God

Next, consider the expressions that talk about the "finger" of God. The finger of God, like the hand of God, signifies his ability to act on the world. But it seems that the focus may be more on the power of God not merely to act but to signify meaning. The finger of God functions in a way similar to the Spirit of God in parallel passages in the Gospels:

"But if it is by the *Spirit* of God that I cast out demons, then the kingdom of God has come upon you." (Matt. 12:28)

"But if it is by the *finger* of God that I cast out demons, then the kingdom of God has come upon you." (Luke 11:20)

The law of Moses is written "with the finger of God," while the corresponding new covenant is written "with the Spirit of the living God":

And he gave to Moses, when he had finished speaking with him on Mount Sinai, the two tablets of the testimony, tablets of stone, written with the *finger* of God. (Ex. 31:18; cf. Deut. 9:10)

And you show that you are a letter from Christ delivered by us, written not with ink but with the *Spirit* of the living God, not on tablets of stone but on tablets of human hearts. (2 Cor. 3:3)

The Breath of God

The breath of God has a close correlation with the Holy Spirit. This correlation is reinforced by the fact that some Old Testament passages play on two meanings of the same Hebrew word: *ruach* (רוּחַ) in Hebrew means *spirit*, *breath*, or *wind*. We can also find passages that make the correlation direct:

"Thus says the Lord God: Come from the four winds, O *breath*, and *breathe* on these slain, that they may live." (Ezek. 37:9)

"And I will put my *Spirit* within you, and you shall live." (v. 14)

"as long as my *breath* is in me,
    and the *spirit* of God is in my nostrils, . . . " (Job 27:3)

"The *Spirit* of God has made me,
    and the *breath* of the Almighty gives me life." (33:4)

See also Job 34:14.

Multiple Features during the Exodus

The time of the exodus involves multiple actions through the Holy Spirit:

> [10] But they rebelled
>   and grieved *his Holy Spirit*;
> therefore he turned to be their enemy,
>   and himself fought against them.
> [11] Then he remembered the days of old,
>   of Moses and his people.
> Where is he who brought them up out of the sea
>   with the shepherds of his flock?
> Where is he who put in the midst of them
>   *his Holy Spirit*,
> [12] who caused his glorious arm
>   to go at the right hand of Moses,
> who divided the waters before them
>   to make for himself an everlasting name,
>   [13] who led them through the depths?
> Like a horse in the desert,
>   they did not stumble.
> [14] Like livestock that go down into the valley,
>   *the Spirit* of the LORD gave them rest.
> So you led your people,
>   to make for yourself a glorious name. (Isa. 63:10–14)

This passage mentions "his glorious arm" (v. 12). It refers back to the crossing of the Red Sea and the pillar of cloud and fire. In this passage the Holy Spirit is closely associated with the appearance of God in the pillar of cloud and fire.

If we go back to the earlier description of the events in Exodus 14–15, we see several instances of features involving human-like action:

And in the morning watch the Lord in the pillar of fire and of cloud *looked* down on the Egyptian forces and threw the Egyptian forces into a panic. (Ex. 14:24)

"Your right *hand*, O Lord, glorious in power,
your right *hand*, O Lord, shatters the enemy. . . .
At the blast of your *nostrils* the waters piled up;
　　the floods stood up in a heap;
　　the deeps congealed in the heart of the sea." (15:6, 8)

"You stretched out your right *hand*;
　　the earth swallowed them." (v. 12)

The Significance of the Holy Spirit

We conclude, then, that quite a few passages make an association between the Holy Spirit (who is God) and one or more attributes of the Trinitarian God that are signified by a human-like feature, such as face, eyes, hand, finger, or breath. It should not be too surprising to see this association with the Holy Spirit, because the Holy Spirit especially expresses the *presence* of God. For example, he shows the presence of God in the world in a passage like Genesis 1:2:

> The earth was without form and void, and darkness was over the face of the deep. And the *Spirit* of God was hovering over the face of the waters.

He expresses the presence of God among believers in many New Testament passages:

> Do you not know that you are God's temple and that God's *Spirit dwells in* you? (1 Cor. 3:16)

> Or do you not know that your body is a temple of the *Holy Spirit within* you, whom you have from God? (1 Cor. 6:19)

In expressing the presence of God most specifically and immediately, the Holy Spirit also expresses the knowledge, power, and speech of God. In a manner similar to the way in which a person's body expresses his actions in the world and his body makes immediate contact with the world, part of the work of the Holy Spirit is to express God's actions in the world and make immediate contact with the world (and with us!).

17

Reflections and the Trinity

Now let us consider the relation of theophanies to the *Trinitarian* character of God. What can we say?

Progressive Revelation

The books of the Old Testament make contributions to a history of revelation that is *progressive*. God in his wisdom undertakes to reveal truths about himself and his salvation progressively in time. Among those truths are the truths about the Trinity. God always is the Trinitarian God. But the teaching about the Trinity comes into view in its fullest and clearest form in the New Testament.

Old Testament theophanies anticipate the Trinity but do not include by themselves the fullness of the New Testament teaching. For example, theophanies in human form anticipate the incarnation of Christ. They foreshadow not only the incarnation but the New Testament teaching about the distinction between God the Father and God the Son. The human form in an Old Testament theophany represents God, but in its specific form as an appearance it is in some sense distinguishable from God as well. Similarly, the figure of the "angel of the Lord" in the Old Testament is sometimes said to have a divine name (Ex. 23:21), or is revealed with divine prerogatives. He is divine, and in addition is sent by God as a messenger of God, thus distinguishing him from the person who sent him. Yet to a reader without the fuller knowledge given in the New Testament, these things are mysterious.

Theophany in the Light of the Whole of the Bible

We receive fullest illumination in our understanding of the Bible if we take into account progressive revelation and use the whole canon of the Bible for fuller understanding. In the light of fuller understanding of the Trinity in the New Testament, we can more confidently see how Old Testament theophanies already involve a revelation of the Trinity, but in less than the fullest clarity.

The appearances of God in human form have a link to Christ in his incarnation. The temporary appearances in human form anticipate the permanent appearance of Christ, who takes to himself a human nature and remains God and man ever since his incarnation.

What about the Holy Spirit? As we saw in the previous chapter, the Holy Spirit is associated in various texts with individual human features, such as face, eyes, and hand. The Holy Spirit expresses the presence of God and brings about powerful contact between God and the world, between God and humanity. This role of the Holy Spirit also means that the Holy Spirit expresses particular attributes of God that are represented by the imagery of face, eyes, ears, and hand. For a human being, his face, eyes, ears, and hands are means by which he makes immediate contact with the world. In a similar way, God is present in the world through the immediacy of the presence of the Holy Spirit. Christ, as one person with divine nature and human nature, draws together in one person the attributes shown by the Holy Spirit in particular manifestations of face, eyes, and hand.

We can also see a connection between the Holy Spirit and the cloud of glory in the Old Testament. Meredith G. Kline sees a reference to the cloud of glory when Genesis 1:2 mentions the Spirit "hovering over the face of the waters."[1] To arrive at this conclusion, Kline relies on a *select* set of associations, rather than all the possible associations with later instances of theophany. Yet the fundamental point about an association between the Holy Spirit and the cloud of glory is sound, as we can see from other passages:

> If you are insulted for the name of Christ, you are blessed, because the *Spirit of glory* and of God rests upon you. (1 Pet. 4:14)

First Peter identifies the Spirit (of God) with "glory." Moreover, the

---

1. Meredith G. Kline, *Images of the Spirit* (Grand Rapids, MI: Baker, 1980), 13–19. See discussion in appendix B of the present work.

verse goes on to describe the Spirit as one who "rests upon you," which is reminiscent of the cloud "resting" on the tabernacle:

> And Moses was not able to enter the tent of meeting because the cloud *settled on* it, and the glory of the LORD filled the tabernacle. (Ex. 40:35)

> As long as the cloud *rested over* the tabernacle, they remained in camp. (Num. 9:18)

Isaiah, in reflecting on the exodus from Egypt, indicates that the Holy Spirit was in the midst of Israel:

> Then he remembered the days of old,
>   of Moses and his people.
> Where is he who brought them up out of the sea
>   with the shepherds of his flock?
> Where is he who put *in the midst of them*
>   *his Holy Spirit*,
> who caused his glorious arm
>   to go at the right hand of Moses,
> who divided the waters before them
>   to make for himself an everlasting name . . . ? (Isa. 63:11–12)

The reference may well be specifically to the cloud of glory.[2]

All three persons of the Trinity indwell each other; each is present with the others. Therefore, the Father and the Son as well as the Holy Spirit are present in the cloud of glory. But it is also true that in the activities of God we can see some mysterious differentiation in the *roles* of the three persons. The Holy Spirit is most directly associated with the presence of God in the world. During the exodus and the wilderness wanderings, the cloud manifests most directly the presence of God among his people. So, we can infer that it represents the presence of the Holy Spirit, even if we did not have the specific passages that confirm the association of the cloud with the Spirit.

In the New Testament, Jesus promises to send the Spirit as "another Helper" (John 14:16), who will express the presence of Jesus to the disciples. The Spirit dwells in believers, and through him Christ dwells in believers (Rom. 8:9–10). The Old Testament cloud of glory

---

2. See discussion of the Holy Spirit, glory, and the cloud in Meredith M. Kline, "The Holy Spirit as Covenant Witness" (ThM thesis, Westminster Theological Seminary, 1972).

anticipates this later role of the Spirit. Through the cloud, which represents the Spirit, God dwells with Israel. The cloud represents the presence of God the Father and the presence of the "angel of the Lord."

Similarly, it is the Holy Spirit who makes present and reflects the attributes of God, such as are represented by the language of eyes, ears, hand, arm, and face.

Theophany in Revelation 4–5

We can also see specific representations of all three persons of the Trinity in the theophanic vision of Revelation 4–5. The "one seated on the throne" (4:2; cf. 5:1) represents God the Father. The Lamb, also identified as "the Lion of the tribe of Judah," represents God the Son (5:5–6). The Holy Spirit is symbolized by "the seven spirits of God sent out into all the earth" (5:6; cf. 4:5).

Taken together, the vision in Revelation 4–5 is most easily classified as an appearance of God in his court. The court is constituted by the four living creatures and the twenty-four elders (4:4, 6; 5:6, 8), which are two distinct groups of angelic beings. These are created beings. But, according to the general pattern of reflections, they reflect at the created level features of God the Creator. We also see in the extended description of Revelation 4–5 other features that are reminiscent of the Old Testament appearances of God in a thunderstorm and in fire (4:5).

The entire scene, then, is a theophany. The larger scene eventually encompasses "many angels" (5:11) and "every creature in heaven and on earth and under the earth and in the sea" (v. 13). Within this scene, the four living creatures and the twenty-four elders represent an intermediate circle. At the center is the one on the throne and the Lamb. Once we see the entire scene, we can see that a principle of reflection is at work in several "layers."

The ultimate origin of the scene lies in the Trinity. The one God is three persons—the Father, the Son (the Lamb), and the Holy Spirit. Within the Trinity, the Son is the "exact imprint" of the nature of the Father (Heb. 1:3). He is the image of God (Col. 1:15). The full pattern of reflections has its foundation and its origin in God, and especially in the relation of the Father to the Son.

Second, the Trinity is reflected in the specific vision in Revelation 4–5, which has the three persons in three imagistic representations, namely, the one on the throne, the Lamb, and the seven eyes of the Lamb, which represent the Holy Spirit (cf. 1:4).

Third, these visionary representations also reflect the attributes of God—the attributes are reflected in the specific imagery of the vision.

Fourth, the specific imagistic representation of the Trinity in the center of the vision is reflected in the features of the court and its accompaniments in fire, lightning, and thunder (4:5).

Fifth, the glory of God is reflected in the larger circle of angels and "every creature" mentioned in 5:11, 13, who proclaim the glory of God in their praise.

This succession of reflections not only magnifies the glory of God in an immediate way but also anticipates the consummation of all things. The consummation comes when the praise of God and the vision of the glory of God that are described in Revelation 4–5 become a universal reality, filling the new heaven and the new earth (Rev. 21:1, 23; 22:3–4). The whole universe comes to reflect the glory of God intensively.

Significance of Trinitarian Theophany

When we put all the information together, we can see that the Trinity is at the heart of theophany. The Trinity is incomprehensible and incomprehensibly deep. The imagery for the Trinity, by referring itself to the ultimate reality of the Trinity and by having its meaning rooted in the Trinity, is also incomprehensibly deep. It is inexhaustible. Nevertheless it is understandable by finite human beings, because we can see that it genuinely reveals the God who is, and it reveals him in harmony with who he is. Theophany in Revelation 4–5, like theophany everywhere else, is in harmony with the nature of Christian transcendence and Christian immanence in knowledge (as summarized in Frame's square of transcendence and immanence, discussed in chapter 12).

The very concept of reflections also has its ultimate roots in the Trinity. The Son is the eternal image of the Father. This archetypal instance of reflection is itself reflected at a created level in the living creatures and the lightning, thunder, and fire around the throne. Because of the association of the Holy Spirit with the presence of Christ and the presence of the cloud, and because the Spirit executes the will of Christ who is the image of the Father, the Holy Spirit also reflects the Father. We may infer that, in a broad sense, the Spirit reflects the presence of the Father and the Son.

The vision of Revelation 4–5 calls on us to stand in awe of God. We stand in awe of the Lamb along with the Father; they are worshiped and praised together:

> "To him who sits on the throne and to the Lamb
> be blessing and honor and glory and might forever and ever!"

And the four living creatures said, "Amen!" and the elders fell down and worshiped. (Rev. 5:13–14)

Themes from the Trinity: Covenant, Kingdom, and Presence

We may also consider how the interlocking themes of covenant, kingdom, and divine presence participate in the structure of reflections of God. In covenants, God expresses his *speech*. In kingdom, he expresses his *rule*. In presence, he expresses his *communion* with mankind. But, as we have already seen, these three expressions are not three utterly *separate* expressions. They are three ways of considering all of God's relations to the world. They are perspectives on the whole.

The three perspectives have ties with the three main Old Testament offices of prophet, king, and priest. The prophet represents the fact that God undertakes to speak to his people. The king represents the fact that God undertakes to rule over his people. Faithful earthly kings who rule according to God's law express God's own rule in justice. Priests raised up by God offer the people mediated communion with the presence of God. The three offices of prophet, king, and priest function as expressions and reflections of three themes in God's work, the themes of covenant, kingdom, and presence. And the three themes in turn offer reflections of three attributes of God. God's speaking ability has an expression and a reflection in covenant and prophetic work; God's power has an expression and a reflection in kingdom and kingly work; God's omnipresence has an expression and a reflection in communion and priestly work. (See table 17.1.)

Table 17.1: God's Attributes and Human Offices

	Speaking	Ruling	Dwelling
Attributes	Speaking Ability	Omnipotence	Omnipresence
Offices	Prophet	King	Priest

These three attributes of God in turn have correlations with the three distinct persons of the Trinity. The attributes are manifestations of the Trinity. God's speaking ability is shown especially by God the Father, who is speaker in relation to God the Son, who is the Word. God's power is shown especially by God the Son, who in time carries out in power the purposes specified by the Father. God's omnipresence is shown especially by God the Holy Spirit, who expresses in himself the presence of God.

All the persons of the Trinity are present in all of God's works in the world. Even though each person has a distinct role, they are present in one another. So the distinctions in role are subtle and mysterious. But we can see the presence of the three themes of speech, power, and presence, operating together. God the Trinity reflects himself in speech, power, and presence. So it is understandable that his manifestations in theophany express speech, power, and presence. Therefore theophany is reflected in covenant, kingdom, and presence, as these three themes are expressed throughout the Bible. Theophany especially expresses the theme of *presence. Presence* becomes in this way a window or perspective through which God reveals himself, his character, and his purposes. (See table 17.2.)

Table 17.2: The Triune God Manifesting Himself

God:	Father	Son	Holy Spirit
attributes:	speech	power	communion/presence
			theophany
particular instance:			
perspective:	theophany manifesting speech	theophany manifesting power	theophany manifesting presence
themes:	covenant	kingdom	presence
offices:	prophet	king	priest

The same truths can be represented diagrammatically (fig. 17.1).

Fig. 17.1: Triunal Manifestations

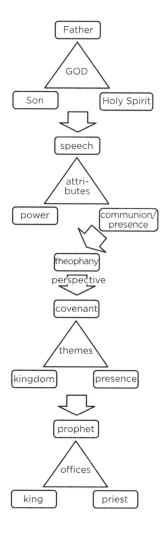

18

Reflections of God in the Book of Revelation

When we touched on the vision of Revelation 4–5, in the previous chapter, we were focusing on a central hub within the book of Revelation. Theophany is a central theme within Revelation, so we should consider how it functions within Revelation. We will see that in fact the theme of theophany is pervasive.

The Appearance of Christ in Revelation 1

We meet with an appearance of God already in Revelation 1:12–16. It is Christ who appears. Several features in his appearance repeat themes from Old Testament appearances, especially from Ezekiel 1:26–28; Daniel 7:9–10, 13; and 10:5–6.

It is noteworthy that the vision of Christ in Revelation 1:12–16 has allusions to two distinct figures in Daniel 7. The first allusion is to the Ancient of Days in Daniel 7:9. Christ in Revelation 1:14 is described with respect to his hair: "The hairs of his head were white, like white wool, like snow." This description is similar to the Ancient of Days in Daniel 7:9: "his clothing was white as snow, and the hair of his head like pure wool." In addition, the fire in God's throne in Daniel 7:9 is linked to the fiery eyes of Christ in Revelation 1:14.

The second allusion is to the "one like a son of man" in Daniel 7:13. Revelation 1:13 has the same expression, "one like a son of man."

In Daniel 7:13 we see a clear distinction between the "one like a son of man" and "the Ancient of Days":

> "and behold, with the clouds of heaven
>   there came *one like a son of ma*n,
> and he came to the *Ancient of Days*
>   and was presented before him."

On the other hand, in Revelation 1:13–16 the vision *combines* features from Daniel's "son of man" and his "Ancient of Days." Revelation 1 does not directly take up the topic of the doctrine of the Trinity, but the presence of both a distinction of persons and common Godhead is presented imagistically.

The direct description of the vision of Christ is found in Revelation 1:12–16. But the experience of the vision by John continues through the rest of chapter 1 and through all of chapters 2–3. Christ continues to interact with John. He addresses John directly in 1:17–20. Then he gives John messages to the seven churches in chapters 2–3. Moreover, five of the messages to the seven churches have near their beginning a description of Christ that takes up some feature of the vision in 1:12–20:

> "'The words of him who holds the seven stars in his right hand, who walks among the seven golden lampstands.'" (Rev. 2:1)

> "'The words of the first and the last, who died and came to life.'" (2:8, alluding to 1:17–18)

> "The words of him who has the sharp two-edged sword." (2:12)

> "'The words of the Son of God, who has eyes like a flame of fire, and whose feet are like burnished bronze.'" (2:18)

> "'The words of him who has the seven spirits of God and the seven stars.'" (3:1)

So in a larger sense the vision of Christ continues through the whole of Revelation 2–3.

Links between the Vision of Christ and the Throne Vision of Revelation 4–5

At the end of Revelation 3 we are not finished with the theme of the appearing of God. Revelation 4:1 mentions "the first voice, which I had heard speaking to me like a trumpet." This voice must be the one described in 1:10–11: "I was in the Spirit on the Lord's day, and I heard behind me a loud *voice like a trumpet* saying, 'Write what you see.'" In the next verses John turns around "to see the voice that was speaking to me," and then he sees the vision of Christ. The voice must be the voice of Christ. The identity is confirmed by the fact that, in the messages to the seven churches, Christ repeats the command to "write," given in 1:11.

The vision of Christ in 1:12–16 is thus linked to the vision given in Revelation 4–5. While the vision of Christ is best classified as a man theophany, the vision of Revelation 4–5 is a court theophany. The vision has expanded to encompass a larger circle of activity.

Some features in the appearance of Christ in 1:12–16 reappear in Revelation 4–5 (see Table 18.1).

Table 18.1: Features in Revelation 1:12–16 and Revelation 4–5

Features in 1:12–16	Features in 4:1–5:14
in the Spirit (1:10)	in the Spirit (4:2)
flame of fire (1:14)	torches of fire (4:5)
powerful eyes (1:14)	powerful eyes (5:6)
loud noise (1:10, 15)	loud noise (4:5; 5:2, 12)
centrality of Christ (1:13)	centrality of Christ (5:5–6)

At the same time, there are many differences, because of the shift from a man theophany to the wider court theophany. The general theme of theophany continues through the end of Revelation 5.

The First Cycle of Judgment

The theme of theophany continues beyond chapter 5. Revelation 6:1 is a continuation of the same scene, with a focus on the actions of the Lamb in opening the seven seals on the scroll. The entire series of actions in Revelation 6 issue from the Lamb and the seven seals, both of which have been introduced in Revelation 5. The Lamb and the seals mentioned in Revelation 6 continue to belong within the larger scene of Revelation 5.

Thus, the theophany introduced in Revelation 4:1 continues through Revelation 6:17. What happens after Revelation 6:17? As many interpreters recognize, Revelation 7:1–17 introduces an interlude with two distinct visions: the vision of the four angels and the 144,000 in 7:1–8; and the vision of the great multitude in 7:9–17. Both still belong within the larger context of theophany. The four angels in 7:1 and the sealing angel of 7:2 are servants of God, who is "seated on the throne" (4:2). The commands of God the king are implicitly in the background of the angelic responsibilities. The angels could easily be among the myriads of angels mentioned in 5:11.

The second vision, the vision of the great multitude in 7:9–17, explicitly refers to features of the court theophany in Revelation 5: the throne (7:9), the Lamb (v. 9), white robes (v. 9), a loud voice (v. 10), praise for salvation (v. 10), the angels around the throne (v. 11), the elders (v. 11), the four living creatures (v. 11).

After the interlude in Revelation 7, the Lamb opens the seventh seal (8:1). This action completes the process in 6:1–8:1 of opening all seven seals. It completes the first cycle out of several cycles of judgment. The seventh seal remains within the framework of the sealed scroll introduced in 5:1. The entire sequence of judgments in 6:1–8:1 resides within the framework of theophany, and the actions all issue from theophany. Moreover, the specific judgments with the first four seals take place in response to orders coming from the living creatures (6:1, 3, 5, 7). The living creatures, as we have seen, reflect the character of God. The passages describe judgments from *God*, not merely random instances of unaccountable suffering. They reflect the anger and justice of God. In a broad sense, the visions are instances of judgment *reflecting* the justice of God. This justice is executed through the Lamb and the "seven spirits" (the Holy Spirit).

The actual judgments take place with the opening of the seven seals in 6:1–8:1. But from one point of view we may include within the cycle of judgment not only the actual opening of the seals but also the earlier description in Revelation 5:1, where the sealed scroll is first introduced, and 5:5–6, where the Lamb is introduced. Revelation 5:1–17 is significant in many respects. One aspect of its significance is that it functions as the opening scene that indicates the origin for the judgments that take place in 6:1–8:1. The opening scene begins at 5:1 with the sealed scroll, or even at 4:1, with the introduction of a vantage point for the entire vision of the throne and its environment.

Other Cycles of Judgment in Revelation

What happens in the book of Revelation after 8:1? Quite a few interpreters of Revelation recognize that the cycle of judgments with the seven seals (6:1–8:1 or 5:1–8:1) is only the first of several cycles of judgment.[1] Interpreters differ on the details but usually recognize one cycle of seven trumpets (8:2–11:19), one of symbolic histories (12:1–14:20), and one of seven bowls (15:1–16:21). Beyond 17:1 there is no longer any explicit numbering of a group of seven, so disagreements about a structural outline become more pronounced.

By focusing on the climax of the second coming of Christ, we can detect three more cycles, each of which ends with the second coming: (1) seven pronouncements of judgment on Babylon, plus the vision of the Bride as the holy counterpart to the unholiness of Babylon (17:1–19:10); (2) the vision of Christ as holy warrior executing judgment on the beast and the false prophet (19:11–21); and (3) the visions of judgment on Satan and his followers (20:1–15). These three cycles address the final destiny of the main opponents of God: Babylon (17:1–19:10); the beast and the false prophet (19:11–21); and Satan himself (20:1–15). The vision of the new heaven and new earth, together with the New Jerusalem, offers an eighth and climactic picture, on the other side of the second coming (21:1–22:5).[2]

Since these cycles all point forward to the second coming of Christ, they are all oriented to a theophany, namely, the appearing of Christ in glory. The second coming is the goal of the cycles of judgment.

Theophany in the Later Cycles

Can we also see a relation between theophany and the *origin* of the cycles of judgment? The second cycle consists in the judgments of the seven trumpets (8:2–11:19). The cycle has its origin described in Revelation 8:2:

> Then I saw the seven angels who stand before God, and seven trumpets were given to them.

The judgments then take place in 8:6–11:19 as one angel after another blows his trumpet.

These specific seven angels do not receive direct mention in

---

1. E.g., G. K. Beale, *The Book of Revelation: A Commentary on the Greek Text* (Grand Rapids, MI: Eerdmans, 1999), 108–151; William Hendriksen, *More Than Conquerors: An Interpretation of the Book of Revelation* (Grand Rapids, MI: Baker, 1939), 30; Dennis E. Johnson, *Triumph of the Lamb: A Commentary on Revelation* (Phillipsburg, NJ: P&R, 2001), 25–48; Vern S. Poythress, *The Returning King: A Guide to the Book of Revelation* (Phillipsburg, NJ: P&R, 2000), 60–64.

2. Revelation 21:1–8 can be seen as a transition piece. It has a relation to 20:11–15, because it expresses the positive counterpart to the primarily negative judgment in 20:11–15. At the same time, it provides an overview that is a fitting introduction to the detailed vision of the New Jerusalem in 21:9–22:5.

Revelation 4–5. But in the context of theophany they are part of the divine court that serves God's bidding. Moreover, the seven angels "stand before God." They start out from his presence. Later, the seven judgments will issue in response to each of the angels blowing a trumpet. From where do the trumpets come? "Seven trumpets *were given* to them." The immediate agent for giving the trumpets could be the one on the throne, or the Lamb, or the Spirit, or some angelic agent. The text does not provide specific detail. But since the giving takes place while the angels are standing "before God," the ultimate agent is God.

The angels and their trumpets appear amid a theophanic context. In a broad sense, the trumpets also reflect the trumpet-like voice of Christ (1:10; 4:1). From God, and more immediately from the angels in his court, spring forth the seven trumpet judgments described in detail in the subsequent text (8:6–11:19). The judgments manifest God's anger and his justice. The fire mentioned in 8:7, 8, and 10 at least loosely reflects the fire of God's anger and purity, represented in 4:5 and 1:14. The judgments reflect who God is, and so belong in a broad sense to theophany.

Revelation 10:1–11:14 represents an interlude between the sixth and seventh trumpets. Its role is similar to the role of the interlude in Revelation 7:1–17.

The next cycle of visions begins in 12:1. This cycle has two counterposed personages, namely the woman clothed with the sun and the dragon. Both are depicted in what might be called "cosmic" imagery. The imagery in this section shows us more about the depth and the scope of the conflict between God and his servants on the one side and the dragon and his servants on the other.

The depiction of the woman has at least faint echoes of theophanic language. She is clothed with the sun (12:1), reminding us of the angel in Revelation 10:1–2, of whom it is said, "his face was like the sun." My own opinion is that the angel in 10:1–2 is a created angel, who reflects the glory of God and of Christ. But some interpreters think that the description refers to Christ directly—that the angel *is* Christ. And indeed Christ in 1:12–16 is described as having a face "like the sun shining in full strength," and "his feet were like burnished bronze," corresponding to the angel's "legs like pillars of fire" (10:1; cf. Ezek. 1:27; Dan. 10:6). The woman of Revelation 12 reflects the brightness of theophanic glory.

The dragon, of course, is not so glorious. In the end, he is hideous. But he has cosmic power, in that "his tail swept down a third of the stars of heaven and cast them to the earth" (Rev. 12:4). A number of interpreters have recognized that the dragon is one of three demonic figures that together form a trio that functions as a counterfeit of the Trinity.[3] The most obvious counterfeit figure is the beast, as described in Revelation 13:1–8. He is a counterfeit Christ (that is why Bible students often call him "the Antichrist"). He is in the image of the dragon, and functions to execute the will of the dragon. The dragon "stood on the sand of the sea," and out of the sea comes a kind of counterfeit creation, imitating the way that God brought the created world out of a formless "deep" (Gen. 1:2; "out of water," 2 Pet. 3:5). The beast is the image of the dragon, which counterfeits the fact that Christ the Son is the image of God the Father. The false prophet depicted in Revelation 13:11–18 promotes worship of the beast, in a manner that functions as a counterfeit to the role of the Holy Spirit in Acts. The Holy Spirit promotes the worship of Christ.

Thus even the principal evil figures in the book of Revelation function in relation to theophany. They are a counterfeit to theophany. They reflect in a counterfeit way the appearance of God, employing an evil and hideous twist.

We can pass on to consider the later cycles of judgment in Revelation. After the cycle of symbolic histories in Revelation 12:1–14:20 comes the cycle of seven bowls in 15:1–16:21. The cycle of bowls also begins with angels: "seven angels with seven plagues, which are the last" (15:1). The angels, as usual, function as participants in the court of God. We are still within the larger context of theophany.

What about the bowls themselves? The bowls are given to the seven angels in the context of the temple (15:5–6). The temple is a location for theophanic appearances, as we are reminded by the appearance of smoke and glory:

and the sanctuary was filled with *smoke* from the *glory* of God and from his power. (15:8)

The next cycle is the cycle of judgments on Babylon (17:1–18:24). It includes an antithetical passage about the reward for the Bride (19:1–10). Babylon is the satanic counterfeit of the Bride. As with the earlier instances of counterfeiting, this counterfeiting is a twisted kind of reflection of the original. Babylon is a counterfeit reflection of the Bride. The Bride reflects the glory of God in her adornment of "fine linen, bright and pure" (19:8).

---

3. G. R. Beasley-Murray, *The Book of Revelation* (Greenwood, SC: Attic; London: Marshall, Morgan, & Scott, 1974), 207; Poythress, *Returning King*, 16–22.

The next cycle is the cycle of judgment by the warrior Christ on "a white horse" (19:11–21). This cycle clearly begins with a warrior theophany: Christ is the divine warrior, who will war against the beast and the false prophet and all God's enemies.

The final cycle begins with "an angel coming down from heaven," who binds Satan (20:1–2). It continues with a scene of "thrones, and seated on them were those to whom the authority to judge was committed" (20:4). The scene is reminiscent of the multiplicity of thrones in Daniel 7:9. We are still in the realm of theophany. It is not immediately clear who is seated on the thrones. Is it angelic beings, as it presumably was in Daniel 7:9–10? Or is it "the souls of those who had been beheaded for the testimony of Jesus and for the word of God" (Rev. 20:4)? The latter group "came to life and reigned with Christ for a thousand years" (v. 4). They "reigned," which suggests that they occupy the thrones, either alongside angels or instead of angels. One way or another, we are still in the realm of theophany.

At the end of the thousand years, we find the judgment of the great white throne in 20:11, which provides another instance of theophanic imagery.

After the seven cycles comes a final vision of the New Jerusalem (21:1–22:5). This vision too contains the imagery of theophany. At its center is "the throne of God and of the Lamb (22:1). "His servants will worship him. They will see *his face*, and his name will be on their foreheads" (22:3–4). The city is filled with the theophanic light of God's glory (21:23; 22:5).

Theophany as Pervasive

Thus the theme of theophany runs through the entire visionary center of the book of Revelation, from 1:12 to 22:5. At some points the focus rests on central aspects of theophany, as with the vision of Christ in 1:12–16 and the vision of God's throne in 4:2–3. At other times the visionary description travels outward to the court of God and to larger vistas, where we see the effects of God's judgments. These judgments never lose their connection with God, who is their origin. They reflect his justice. And so, in a broad sense, the entire central vision of Revelation, from 1:12 to 22:5, is a gigantic theophany—a gigantic appearance of God. Such a thing is fitting for a book that is designed to stir up our longing for the consummate manifestation of God, in the New Jerusalem. It is fitting also for a book whose endpoint lies in the final, consummate theophany, seeing God face to face (Rev. 22:4).

19

Reflections of God in Structures in Revelation

We may be able to discern a further pattern in the use of reflections in the book of Revelation. Near the beginning, each of the cycles of judgment in Revelation has a vision that shows some aspect of the origin of the entire cycle. For example, the cycle of seven seals (Rev. 6:1–8:1) has its origin determined by the sealed book that appears in 5:1, and the Lamb who appears in 5:6. The cycle of seven trumpets has its origin in the seven angels with seven trumpets, who appear in 8:2.

All seven cycles have an origin in a visionary description related to theophany. At the same time, each cycle has different details in its origin. Is there a pattern in these differences?

The Beginning of a Pattern

The first cycle, as we observed, begins with the sealed book and the Lamb. And the sealed book is "in the right hand of him who was seated on the throne" (Rev. 5:1). The vision of origin gives us God himself, including two distinct persons of the Trinity. (The third person, the Holy Spirit, is also represented in 5:6 with "seven eyes, which are the seven spirits of God.")

The second cycle begins with seven angels, who serve as members of God's court. We have moved out from God, who is at the center of theophany, to the angels, who are in the court.

The third cycle, consisting of symbolic histories (Rev. 12:1–14:20), begins with the woman and the dragon depicted in cosmic imagery. The cosmic imagery is a key element. We have moved out from the court of God to the surrounding cosmos, which was represented within 4:1–5:14 by "every creature in heaven and on earth and under the earth and in the sea" (5:13).

These three starting points represent respectively the king of the universe, his court, and the realm over which he rules.

Using Kingship

Let us then consider the meaning of God's kingship. In the midst of his court, God rules over the universe. The first three cycles of judgment all have their background in God's kingship. The first cycle (seven seals) starts from God the king. The second starts from God's court, represented by the seven angels in Revelation 8:2. The third cycle starts from cosmic imagery. The three starting points enjoy relations involving reflections. The angels in God's court reflect his power and glory. And the cosmos reflects God's glory—with a lower level of intensity, we might say. (See fig. 19.1.)

Fig. 19.1: God's Dominion

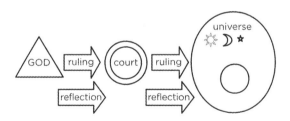

Now consider the reflection of God's kingship on earth. God has made man in his image (Gen. 1:26–27). Man has a key role. Man is a subordinate king, imitating God's kingship. God has assigned to him the task of dominion:

> "And let them have *dominion* over the fish of the sea and over the birds of the heavens and over the livestock and over all the earth and over every creeping thing that creeps on the earth." (Gen. 1:26; see also v. 28)

If man is imitating God, the imitation may extend to the pattern of the court. Earthly kings have their earthly courts. Even apart from the fall, we can infer that Adam would be a kind of king, with other human beings as his assistants in the task of dominion. So mankind is imitative of God in the structure of dominion. (See fig. 19.2.)

Fig. 19.2: God's Dominion Reflected in Human Dominion

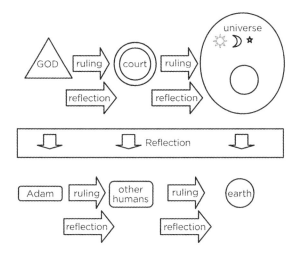

Using Spaces

Kingship is only one way of looking at God's relation to creation. We can also use the theme of dwelling, which is related to spatial areas. God dwells first of all in himself, through the indwelling of the persons of the Trinity in one another (John 17:21, 23). The book of Revelation represents this mystery of indwelling pictorially by the vision of Christ in Revelation 1:12–16, where Christ combines features from the Ancient of Days and the "one like a son of man" (Dan. 7:9, 13). This imagery hints at the fact that the Father ("the Ancient of Days") dwells in the Son. This indwelling between the persons of the Trinity is unique, because God is unique. That is to say, the Creator is distinct from all creatures. But, like other characteristics of God, the pattern of indwelling has reflections on the creaturely level. God dwells in the midst of his angelic court. And God dwells in the entire universe by filling all things with his presence: "Do I not *fill* heaven and earth? declares the LORD" (Jer. 23:24).

God's redemptive purpose also includes his presence among human beings. Each believer has his body as a temple of the Holy Spirit (1 Cor. 6:19). And the church as a whole is the temple of the Holy Spirit (1 Cor. 3:16). In the Old Testament the tabernacle of Moses and the temple of Solomon were special spatial areas where God dwelt in a special way in order to be among his people and meet with them.

We can reformulate the diagram of God's rule and man's rule in order to represent this spatial pattern of indwelling (see fig. 19.3).

Fig. 19.3: God's Dwelling

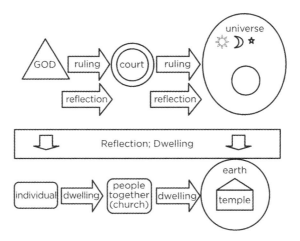

The structure of the temple belongs in the diagram, because the tabernacle and the temple in the Old Testament were earthly reflections of God's dwelling place in the cosmos as a whole, and especially in heaven (1 Kings 8:30, 32; Heb. 8:5). In the New Testament, of course, we learn that the Old Testament symbolism of the temple is fulfilled in Christ, whose body is the final temple of God (John 2:21). Because of being united to Christ and being indwelt by the Holy Spirit, the church is a temple (1 Cor. 3:16). And the body of an individual Christian is a temple (1 Cor. 6:19). So in the New Testament the idea of "temple" gets closely aligned with Christ himself, with the individual saint, and with the Christian community. We can nevertheless still distinguish the *symbolism* of the temple as a distinct kind of imagery. The symbolism uses a distinct space that is marked out as holy.

Spatial Origin of the Cycles of Judgment

The first three cycles of judgment in Revelation originate from three successive spatial regions. The first, the cycle of the seven seals, originates from the indwelling of God in himself, in his Trinitarian nature: it starts from the Lamb, in whom dwells God the Father and God the Holy Spirit. The second cycle starts from the angels, who compose God's court, which is a wider arena in its spatial visualization. The third cycle starts from the cosmos as a whole, viewed as the arena reflecting the glory of God and the arena in which the cosmic conflict takes place.

Now what about the remaining cycles of judgment in Revelation? We begin with the fourth cycle. The fourth cycle is the cycle of the seven bowls of God's wrath. It starts from the temple of God (Rev. 15:5–6). This spatial point of origin is also found in our diagram of distinct spaces (fig. 19.3). Why start with the temple instead of with the individual human being as a dwelling place for God? From the standpoint of Old Testament imagery, the temple as an external structure represents the way that the individual and the community come to have access to God. It has more intensive holiness and a more intensive presence of God than does the individual and the community. It is a reflection of the "cosmic" dwelling place of God, the universe as a whole.[1]

Now what about the fifth cycle of judgments in Revelation? The fifth cycle consists in the judgments on Babylon and the reward for the virgin church (Rev. 17:1–19:10). The two main symbols, Babylon and the Bride, are both symbols of *communities*. They represent the false church and the true church, respectively. Thus, they correspond well to the fifth spatial arena in our diagram of the various spaces for God's indwelling.

The sixth cycle of judgment consists in the war waged by the rider on the white horse, who is Christ (19:11–21). Its origin is in the rider. He is a single person. He is the divine warrior, with the divine name, "The Word of God" (19:13). At the same time, we can see that he

---

1. See Vern S. Poythress, *The Shadow of Christ in the Law of Moses* (reprint; Phillipsburg, NJ: P&R, 1995), chapter 2.

is the representative of humanity. He wages war against two beasts, and achieves complete victory and *dominion* over them. In so doing, he fulfills the task at which Adam failed. Christ functions here not only as the divine warrior but also as the last Adam (1 Cor. 15:45; cf. 15:25).

Thus Christ functions in a way that combines features from two points in our diagram of spatial arenas. He combines the roles of the human individual in whom God dwells, and the divine presence of the Trinity. (See fig. 19.4.)

Fig. 19.4: Dual Functions of Christ's Triumph

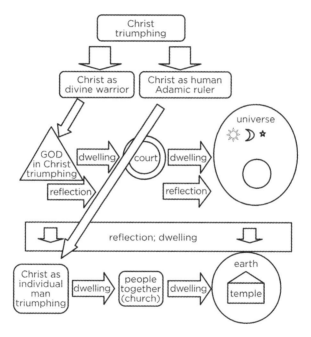

The seventh cycle of judgments has its origin in the power of the thrones mentioned in Revelation 20:4. As we observed, these are reminiscent of the thrones of God's court angels, mentioned in Daniel 7:9. But the passage indicates that the saints rule, either with the angels or instead of them (Rev. 20:4; cf. 1 Cor. 6:3). So the vision in Revelation 20:4 combines features from the court of angels and the "court" consisting in human worshipers of God, belonging to the church. (See fig. 19.5.)

Fig. 19.5: The Function of Human Rulers

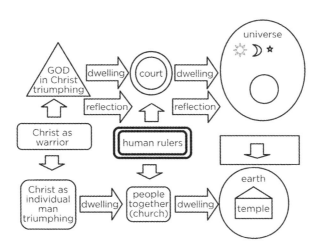

The Consummate Vision of God's Dwelling

The final vision in Revelation is the vision of the New Jerusalem, found in 21:1–22:5 and especially in 21:9–22:5. It is a vision of the final, consummate dwelling place of God. It combines features from all the spatial arenas that we have seen earlier.

(1) It has one throne, described as "the throne of God and of the Lamb" (Rev. 22:1). This description reminds us in visionary imagery of the indwelling of the persons of the Trinity.

(2) It has angels at the twelve gates, representing the court of God (21:12).

(3) It has cosmic imagery, both in the fact that it descends from heaven (21:2) and in the fact that it has the glory of God shining in it instead of sun and moon (21:23). In addition, as some interpreters think, the twelve jewels of the twelve foundations correspond to the twelve constellations of stars through which the planets travel (21:19–20).[2] This function would be in addition to the twelve jewels functioning as a match for the twelve stones on Aaron's breastpiece (Ex. 28:17–20).[3]

(4) It has no temple, that is, no smaller structure inside it that serves as a temple in a special way. There is no need for a temple, since God and the Lamb dwell in immediate presence in the whole city (Rev. 21:22).

---

2. G. R. Beasley-Murray, *The Book of Revelation* (Greenwood, SC: Attic; London: Marshall, Morgan, & Scott, 1974), 324–325.

3. G. K. Beale, *The Book of Revelation: A Commentary on the Greek Text* (Grand Rapids, MI: Eerdmans, 1999), 1080–1081.

The city as a whole is in the shape of a perfect cube, which is also the shape of the Most Holy Place in the tabernacle and the temple of Solomon. So the whole city is not only like a temple, but a Most Holy Place.

(5) The city is the Bride, which represents the church, the entire *community* of God's people.

(6) Each individual has immediate access to God:

> No longer will there be anything accursed, but the throne of God and of the Lamb will be in it, and his servants will worship him. They will see his face, and his name will be on their foreheads. (Rev. 22:3–4)

The fact that God's "name will be on their foreheads" corresponds to the clothing of the high priest in Israel. God instructed Israel to make special holy garments for the high priests. Among these is a plate for the turban, with the engraving "Holy to the LORD" (Ex. 28:36). The word "LORD," the tetragrammaton, the most holy name of God, is on it. The high priest is supposed to wear it on his forehead (v. 37). The name signifies the presence of God, and this presence is symbolically resting on him. The vision of the name of God in Revelation 22:4 indicates that God's presence is on the saints. And, as we know from other parts of the New Testament, his presence is also *in* each one of them. Each individual believer is indwelt by God in a consummate way.

Thus the New Jerusalem in Revelation 21:1–22:5 sums up all the symbolism for earlier dwellings of God. (See fig. 19.6.)

Fig. 19.6: The Consummate Dwelling of God

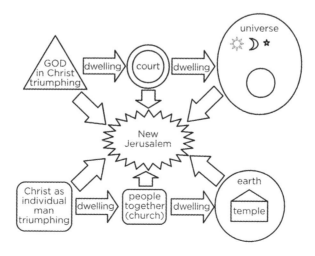

They all come together in the consummate dwelling of God, as is fitting for the nature of the consummation of all things:

> And I heard a loud voice from the throne saying, "Behold, the dwelling place of God is with man. He will dwell with them, and they will be his people, and God himself will be with them as their God." (Rev. 21:3)

This description is the fulfillment of God's purpose for history, to sum up all things in Christ:

> . . . making known to us the mystery of his will, according to his purpose, which he set forth in Christ as a plan for the fullness of time, to *unite all things in him*, things in heaven and things on earth. (Eph. 1:9–10)

It is a magnificent vision, which not only should evoke our praise and awe but should stir us up to loyalty to God and to his Christ, and to longing for the complete manifestation of his triumph and his presence.

20

Patterns of Multiple Reflections

We can use the structure of spatial indwelling from the previous chapter to understand patterns of multiple reflections.

Reflections of Light

Consider first the theme of light. The Bible in more than one place indicates that God himself is the original light—light in an uncreated sense. First John 1:5 sets it out boldly by saying that "God is *light*, and in him is no darkness at all." We are also familiar with Jesus's statement, "I am the *light* of the world" (John 8:12; cf. 9:5). Jesus makes the claim to be the light of the world in the context of bringing redemption. He is redemptive light, guiding and illumining people so that they find redemption in him. But the Gospel of John also indicates that this redemptive role of Jesus has a background in Jesus's role in creation:

> All things were made through him, and without him was not any thing made that was made. In him was life, and the life was the *light* of men. The *light* shines in the darkness, and the darkness has not overcome it. (John 1:3–5)

John 1:3–5 is already moving toward the proclamation by John the Baptist, who bears "witness about the light" (v. 7). But the earlier verses have connections with the account in Genesis 1:3–5, where God creates the light and separates the light from the darkness. Created light is a reflection of the Word, God the Son, who is uncreated light.

We still need to bear in mind that the Creator is distinct from all the creatures that he has made. There is a fundamental distinction between God and created light. God is not created. He is not to be confused with created light. When we say that God is light, we mean light at the level of the Creator. Created light *reflects* who God is, but it does so at the level of the creature.

If God the Father is light (1 John 1:5), and God the Son is light (John 1:4–5; 8:12; 9:5), what about God the Holy Spirit? In their description of Daniel, Belshazzar and his wife link spirit and light:

> "There is a man in your kingdom in whom is the *spirit* of the holy gods. In the days of your father, *light* and understanding and wisdom like the wisdom of the gods were found in him." (Dan. 5:11)

> "I have heard of you that the *spirit* of the gods is in you, and that *light* and understanding and excellent wisdom are found in you." (v. 14)

But Belshazzar and his wife are polytheists, so they might be considered as questionable witnesses. We can find scriptural verses that link the Holy Spirit with light indirectly. The Holy Spirit has the role of *illumining* Christians in knowledge of the truth (John 16:13; Eph. 1:17). We saw earlier that the Spirit is closely linked with the cloud of glory in the exodus (chapter 17). And this cloud can have light in it (Ex. 13:21; Neh. 9:12, 19; Matt. 17:5).

Thus all three persons of the Trinity are associated with light. The uncreated light in the Trinity corresponds to the first of the kinds of indwelling that we have cataloged in fig. 19.2. God dwells in himself, and this dwelling is filled with light.

We can now go through the pattern of indwelling given in fig. 19.3, and ask whether light occurs in other cases of spatial regions indwelt by God. The six "regions" are (1) God himself; (2) God's court; (3) the created universe; (4) the temple; (5) God's people as a community (the church); and (6) an individual human being. We have already dealt with the first: (1) God himself has light in himself; he is light.

(2) What about God's court? Does it have links with light? In Revelation 1:20 "the seven *stars* are the *angels* of the seven churches." Some interpreters of Revelation believe that the "angels" in this verse are the pastors of the churches or human messengers sent to the churches. But Revelation as a whole is visionary and filled with apocalyptic imagery. In such a context, we expect that these mes-

sengers are angels (like the angels that appear frequently throughout the book of Revelation). So I believe that the reference is to angels as spiritual beings. These angels are representative of the churches, and perhaps representative of the pastors of the churches. But they are still angels. They are symbolized as "stars," indicating that they are light bearing in a symbolical sense.

In addition, angels frequently appear in bright clothing (e.g., Ezek. 1:13; Acts 10:30; Rev. 15:6). The angel in Revelation 18:1 is "bright" with glory. The brightness of angels reflects the brightness of God.

(3) The universe is made bright with light from sun, moon, and stars. The stars as physical sources of light reflect the angels, who bear spiritual light.

(4) What about the temple? The temple of Solomon had within it ten lampstands that provided light (1 Kings 7:49). These ten lampstands were an enhancement of the single lampstand that stood in the tabernacle (Ex. 25:31–40). "And the lamps shall be set up so as to *give light* on the space in front of it" (v. 37). The tabernacle and the temple as a whole were copies of God's dwelling in heaven (v. 40; Heb. 8:5; 9:23). The lights of the lampstands reflect and imitate the lights of heaven— sun, moon, and stars. As we have seen, the stars imitate the light of the angels. And the angels reflect the light of God.

(5) What about the community of God's people? Is it a light? Revelation 1:20 says that "the seven lampstands are the seven churches." The churches give light. In so doing, they reflect and imitate the light coming from Christ the Son: "his face was like the sun shining in full strength" (Rev. 1:16).

(6) Do individual believers reflect God's light? Yes. Jesus speaks concerning the plurality of disciples: "Let your *light shine* before others, so that they may see your good works and give glory to your Father who is in heaven" (Matt. 5:16).

The apostle Paul speaks similarly:

for at one time you were darkness, but now you are *light* in the Lord. Walk as children of *light* (for the fruit of *light* is found in all that is good and right and true), and try to discern what is pleasing to the Lord. Take no part in the unfruitful works of *darkness*, but instead expose them. For it is shameful even to speak of the things that they do in secret. But when anything is exposed by the *light*, it becomes visible, for anything that becomes visible is *light*. Therefore it says,

> "Awake, O sleeper,
>   and arise from the dead,
>   and Christ will *shine* on you." (Eph. 5:8–14)

The final verse, which says that "Christ will shine on you," indicates that the light that Christians have imitates and reflects the light of Christ himself.

In sum, all six points in the diagram of spatial regions show the manifestation of light (see fig. 20.1).

Fig. 20.1: Reflections of Light

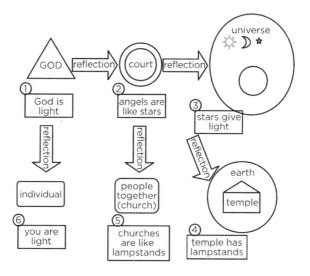

The pattern shows that God is light and that he chooses to reflect the glory of his character in several ways and in several "layers" in the things and persons that he has created. Praise the Lord for these signs of his magnificence!

Reflections of Glory

Let us now consider the theme of *glory*. Glory is closely related to the theme of light and brightness. So we should not be surprised to see God's glory reflected in the six spatial regions of God's dwelling.

(1) God is glorious in himself. Jesus speaks of "the glory that I had with you [the Father] before the world existed" (John 17:5), indicating

that there is an uncreated, divine glory with the Father and the Son. As we saw earlier, the Holy Spirit is also associated with glory (chapter 17).

(2) Do the angels reflect the glory of God? They do:

> And an angel of the Lord appeared to them, and the *glory* of the Lord shone around them, and they were filled with great fear. (Luke 2:9)

> "For whoever is ashamed of me and of my words, of him will the Son of Man be ashamed when he comes in his glory and the *glory* of the Father and of *the holy angels*." (Luke 9:26)

(3) Heaven and earth are filled with God's glory:

> And one called to another and said:
>
>> "Holy, holy, holy is the LORD of hosts;
>> the whole earth is full of his *glory*!" (Isa. 6:3)

> The heavens declare the *glory* of God,
>> and the sky above proclaims his handiwork. (Ps. 19:1)

The new heaven and new earth will be filled consummately with God's glory:

> "But truly, as I live, and as all the earth shall be filled with the *glory* of the LORD, . . . " (Num. 14:21)

> Blessed be his glorious name forever;
>> may the whole earth be filled with his *glory*!
>>> Amen and Amen! (Ps. 72:19)

See also Habakkuk 2:14 and Revelation 21:23.

(4) Does the glory of the Lord appear in the temple? The Old Testament explicitly describes the appearing of the glory of the Lord during the consecration of the tabernacle and the consecration of the temple:

> Then the cloud covered the tent of meeting, and the *glory* of the LORD filled the tabernacle. And Moses was not able to enter the tent of meeting because the cloud settled on it, and the *glory* of the LORD filled the tabernacle. (Ex. 40:34–35)

> And when the priests came out of the Holy Place, a cloud filled the house of the LORD, so that the priests could not stand to minister

because of the cloud, for the *glory* of the LORD filled the house of the LORD. (1 Kings 8:10–11; cf. 2 Chron. 5:14)

(5) Glory is given to the church as God's people:

" . . . it was granted her to clothe herself
with fine linen, *bright and pure*"—

for the fine linen is the righteous deeds of the saints. (Rev. 19:8)

. . . so that he [Christ] might present the church to himself in *splendor*. (Eph. 5:27)

We may also reflect on Isaiah 62:2: "The nations shall see your righteousness, and all the kings your *glory*." The context of this verse is talking about "Zion" and "Jerusalem," which are Old Testament types pointing forward to the church.

(6) Finally, each believer as an individual is to be filled with glory:

"All mine are yours, and yours are mine, and I am *glorified* in them." (John 17:10)

. . . and if children, then heirs—heirs of God and fellow heirs with Christ, provided we suffer with him in order that we may also be *glorified* with him. (Rom. 8:17)

those whom he justified he also *glorified*. (v. 30)

If the goal of history is that the earth will be filled with the *glory* of the Lord (Num. 14:21), it is fitting that his glory be reflected comprehensively—in angels, in the universe as a whole, in the corporate community of God's people, and in each individual among his people. (See fig. 20.2.)

Reflections of Fire

We can also see the imagery of fire reflected at the different levels that we have enumerated.

(1) Fire symbolizes God himself, as illustrated by the appearances of God in fire:

And the angel of the LORD appeared to him in a flame of *fire* out of the midst of a bush. (Ex. 3:2)

Fig. 20.2: Reflections of Glory

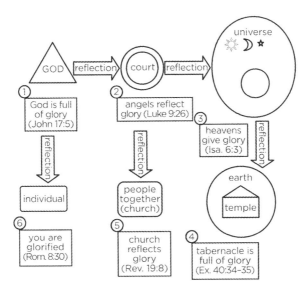

When the sun had gone down and it was dark, behold, a smoking *fire* pot and a flaming torch passed between these pieces. On that day the LORD made a covenant with Abram, . . . (Gen. 15:17–18)

for our God is a consuming *fire*. (Heb. 12:29)

Fire is especially used in symbolizing the Holy Spirit:

And divided tongues as of *fire* appeared to them and rested on each one of them. And they were all filled with the *Holy Spirit* and began to speak in other tongues as the Spirit gave them utterance. (Acts 2:3–4)

From the throne came flashes of lightning, and rumblings and peals of thunder, and before the throne were burning seven torches of *fire*, which are *the seven spirits of God*. (Rev. 4:5)

(2) Fire occurs among the living creatures in Ezekiel 1, who are angelic beings:

As for the likeness of the living creatures, their appearance was like burning coals of *fire*, like the appearance of torches moving to and fro among the living creatures. And the *fire* was bright, and out of the *fire* went forth lightning. (Ezek. 1:13)

(3) Fire occurs in the world as a whole, as God has created it to be.

(4) Fire burns in the tabernacle and the temple, in connection with the bronze altar:

"The *fire* on the altar shall be kept burning on it; it shall not go out. The priest shall burn wood on it every morning, and he shall arrange the burnt offering on it and shall burn on it the fat of the peace offerings. *Fire* shall be kept burning on the altar continually; it shall not go out." (Lev. 6:12–13)

(5) and (6) The church and the individuals in it have fire rest upon them at Pentecost:

And divided tongues as of *fire* appeared to them and rested on each one of them. And they were all filled with the *Holy Spirit* and began to speak in other tongues as the Spirit gave them utterance. (Acts 2:3–4)

Thus fire appears as a symbol of God's presence within all the layers of spatial regions that we have distinguished. (See fig. 20.3.)

Fig. 20.3: Reflections of Fire

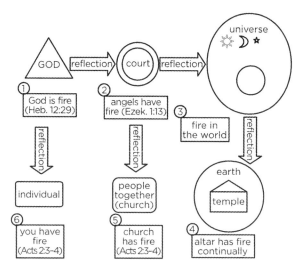

Reflections of Jewel-Like Beauty

We may also consider the way in which the beauty of God is displayed. (1) In Revelation 4 God is represented through the beauty and splendor of precious jewels and a rainbow:

> And he who sat there had the appearance of *jasper* and *carnelian*, and around the throne was a *rainbow* that had the appearance of an *emerald*. (Rev. 4:3)

Does jewel-like splendor occur in the other spatial regions that reflect him?

(2) Angelic beings have gleaming beryl associated with them:

> As for the appearance of the wheels and their construction: their appearance was like the *gleaming of beryl*. (Ezek. 1:16)

(3) The created world has jewels that are present in it according to God's design:

> And the gold of that land is good; bdellium and *onyx stone* are there. (Gen. 2:12)

(4) The New Jerusalem, which is shaped like the Most Holy Place of the temple, has jewels as its foundations:

> The foundations of the wall of the city were adorned with every kind of jewel. The first was jasper, the second sapphire, the third agate, the fourth emerald, the fifth onyx, the sixth carnelian, the seventh chrysolite, the eighth beryl, the ninth topaz, the tenth chrysoprase, the eleventh jacinth, the twelfth amethyst. (Rev. 21:19–20)

(5) The church is the Bride, which is identified with the New Jerusalem in Revelation 21:2, 9. So the church also is adorned in jewel-like splendor:

> I will greatly rejoice in the LORD;
>   my soul shall exult in my God,
> for he has clothed me with the garments of salvation;
>   he has covered me with the robe of righteousness,
> as a bridegroom decks himself like a priest with a beautiful
>   headdress,
>   and as a bride adorns herself with her *jewels*. (Isa. 61:10)

Fig. 20.4: Reflections of Beauty

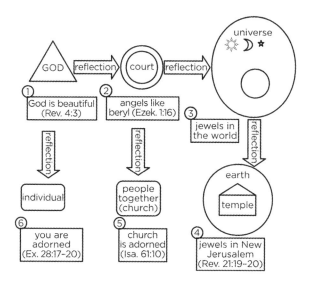

(6) Individual believers, through Christ, now have access to the Most Holy Place in heaven (Heb. 10:19–20). We may infer that they are suitably clothed for their approach. In fact, they are "clothed" with Christ, who is their high priest: "For as many of you as were baptized into Christ have put on Christ" (Gal. 3:27). So they have jewel-like splendor: "For like the jewels of a crown they shall shine on his land" (Zech. 9:16).

Because of Christ, Christians have now all become priests (1 Pet. 2:5). They therefore have adornment that is the fulfillment of the adornment foreshadowed in the high priestly clothing in Exodus 28. Among the clothing is the breastpiece, which has precious jewels (Ex. 28:17–20). The clothing as a whole is meant "for glory and for beauty" (v. 2).

Women are counseled to adorn themselves as Christians:

Do not let your adorning be external—the braiding of hair and the putting on of gold jewelry, or the clothing you wear—but let your adorning be the hidden person of the heart with the imperishable beauty of a gentle and quiet spirit, which in God's sight is very precious. For this is how the holy women who hoped in God used to adorn themselves, by submitting to their own husbands. (1 Pet. 3:3–5)

In sum, the beauty of God, which is represented symbolically by the precious jewels with which he appears in Revelation 4:3, is reflected in his creatures. (See fig. 20.4.)

This pattern of reflections encourages us to appreciate the beauty of God, for who he is, and the beauties in the created world as reflecting his original beauty.

21

Reflections of God in Creation

The world that God created testifies to him and reflects his glory, as a number of biblical passages declare:

> The heavens *declare the glory of God*,
>   and the sky above *proclaims* his handiwork.
> Day to day *pours out speech*,
>   and night to night *reveals knowledge*. (Ps. 19:1–2)

> For what can be known about God is plain to them, because God has *shown it* to them. For his invisible attributes, namely, his eternal power and divine nature, have been *clearly perceived*, ever since the creation of the world, in the things that have been made. So they are without excuse. (Rom. 1:19–20)

See also Psalm 104:31–34.

As we discussed in an earlier chapter (chapter 11), Psalm 104:1–4 describes God's work of creation in language reminiscent of theophany. So is creation a theophany? Psalm 104:1–4 suggests that creation is in some sense "theophany-like." And Genesis 1:2 indicates that God through his Holy Spirit was present in a special way. But we should continue to acknowledge the fundamental distinction between God the Creator and the creation that he has made. God shows himself and reflects his character through created things. But he is never *identical* to those created things.

If we emphasize that creation as a whole is theophany-like, we may also fail to notice or communicate the specially intense character of appearances of God that take place at special times: the appearance at Mount Sinai, the pillar of cloud and fire in the wilderness, and the appearances to Isaiah (Isaiah 6), to Ezekiel (Ezekiel 1), and to Daniel (Dan. 7:9–10). On the other hand, if we say that creation is *not* theophany-like, we may overlook the way in which Psalm 104:1–4 invites us to see it as at least a reflection *analogous* to the intense theophanies at Mount Sinai and elsewhere.

Analogies with Theophany

So what should we say? It is wisest to acknowledge a number of biblical truths. We acknowledge the Creator-creature distinction. We acknowledge the special character of special theophanies. At the same time, we acknowledge that one of the benefits of special theophanies is to reveal who God is in ways that enable us more effectively to notice who he is *all the time.* The special theophanies do not actually *compete* with God's works of creation. Neither are they on the same level as God's works of creation. Rather, they give us understanding of God that opens our eyes to who God is, and therefore also opens our eyes to who he is in revealing himself in creation. Theophanies in the special sense offer us a *perspective* on God, and therefore also a perspective on God's work of creation.

The same principle can be extended from God's works in creating the world (Genesis 1) to God's works of providence. God continually governs the world that he made. His continual governance, up to this day, is what we call *providence.* God's providential government shows us the *same* God who powerfully created the world in his original six days of work (Genesis 1).

We might say that providence shows analogies with God's works of creation, and God's works of creation show analogies—at a lower level—with theophanies in intense form. We could use the word *theophany* in either a narrow way or a broad way. If we use it in a narrow way, only the most intense appearances of God count as "theophany." If we use the word in a broad way, we could expand it so broadly that every providential act of God is "theophany-like," a created reflection of the Creator. God is *present* all the time in all his works, governing the universe and human affairs. He makes himself known all the time through his presence in his works.

We can also use the language of reflections. God has the "exact" image of himself in his Son (Heb. 1:3). Subordinately, in imitation of this exact image, God reflects his character in theophanies of an intense kind, such as at Mount Sinai. A further subordinate, less intense reflection is found in his works of creation. And providence offers us reflections of creation.

Reflections in Particular Works of Creation and Providence

The preceding chapter has shown how a pattern of reflections occurs with several themes, such as brightness, fire, and jewel-like beauty. According to the pattern of fig. 19.3, God has reflections (1) in himself, (2) in his angelic court, (3) in the created universe, (4) in the temple, (5) in the corporate people of God, and (6) in individual saints. The third of these, the reflection of God in the created universe, is particularly pertinent. God's glory is reflected in particular ways in some of the things that he has made.

For example, within the created universe, the brightness of the sun, as a created thing, reflects the uncreated, original "brightness" or splendor of God's character. It is fitting that the nature of Christ is expressed at one point in the transfiguration when Christ appears in brightness:

> And he was transfigured before them, and his face *shone like the sun*, and his clothes became *white as light*. (Matt. 17:2)

Christ appears in a similar way in Revelation 1: "and his face was *like the sun shining* in full strength" (v. 16).

God the Son, as the eternal image of the Father, is the original image of the glory of God. The special theophanic appearances of Christ in his incarnation reflect this original glory. Christ describes this glory as "the glory that I had with you before the world existed" (John 17:5).

Idolaters substitute false images for the true God (Rom. 1:23, 25). They may worship the sun. This worship is a perversion. But it is a perversion of something true, namely that the sun does reflect the glory of its Creator. The sun ought to stir us up to worship the Creator with greater fervor.

Once we have noticed a pattern of reflected glory in one created thing, such as the sun, it becomes more natural to notice it in other created things. What about fire? Fire theophanies involve special appearances of God. But do they also provide an analogy or a perspective on fire as one element within the created world? Fire as an ordinary phenomenon within the created world reflects in the sphere of the "ordinary" the extraordinary appearances of God in fire, and these extraordinary appearances express and reflect God's purity and his power to destroy sin and evil.

In chapter 11 we noted some particular phenomena in providence that reflect the character of God:

- thunderstorms reveal the power of God
- clouds reveal the mystery of God
- fire reveals the purity of God and his destructive power against evil
- light reflects the light of God's character, his moral purity
- human beings made in the image of God reflect the personal character of God
- chariots and other implements of war reflect God's zeal in war against evil

We can add more elements to this list.

Jewels on earth reflect the beauty of God.

The tree of life in the garden of Eden (Gen. 2:9) was a special tree, specially set apart as a kind of "sacramental" expression of the communion in life that Adam and Eve were designed to enjoy with God. It reflects the life of God and his life-giving power. Subordinately, ordinary trees show us created life, which reflects the uncreated life of God.

Bread reflects Jesus, who is the bread of life (John 6:35).

Water reflects Jesus, who is the water of life through the Spirit (John 7:37–39; 4:14).

The imagery of the bread of life, the water of life, and "the light of the world" are used in the Gospel of John to link creational imagery directly with Jesus as the incarnate Son. But in fact God in his Trinitarian character is the original behind all created manifestations of his glory. So each particular manifestation in creation and providence has a link with God the Son, who is the mediator of creation:

> Yet for us there is one God, the Father, from whom are all things and for whom we exist, and one Lord, Jesus Christ, *through whom are all things* and through whom we exist. (1 Cor. 8:6)

He is the image of the invisible God, the firstborn of all creation. For *by him all things were created*, in heaven and on earth, visible and invisible, whether thrones or dominions or rulers or authorities—all things were created through him and for him. And he is before all things, and in him all things hold together. (Col. 1:15–17)

Earthly prophets, kings, and priests reflect God. God is the original prophet, by speaking. God is the original king, by ruling. God is the original priest, by being in communion with himself and then with the world that he created. Man made in the image of God is the created reflection of God.

22

A Pattern of Reflections
in Clothing

Some of the appearances of God in the Bible pay attention to clothing.

Clothing in God's Appearances

Appearances of God as a warrior may describe the armor that he wears (Isa. 59:17). In other instances, God may appear in a long robe, or in linen, or in bright clothing:

"As I looked,

> thrones were placed,
>> and the Ancient of Days took his seat;
> *his clothing was white as snow*,
>> and the hair of his head like pure wool;
> his throne was fiery flames;
>> its wheels were burning fire." (Dan. 7:9)

And he was transfigured before them, and his *clothes became radiant, intensely white*, as no one on earth could bleach them. (Mark 9:2–3; cf. Matt. 17:2; Luke 9:29)

See also Revelation 1:13; 15:6; 19:13–14.

We find additional cases that may not involve any literal man-like figure with clothing, but where in a poetic context God is described in terms of clothing. Especially noteworthy is the passage in Psalm 104:1–2, which we discussed earlier (chapter 11):

> Bless the LORD, O my soul!
>   O LORD my God, you are very great!
> You are *clothed with splendor and majesty*,
>   *covering yourself with light as with a garment*,
>   stretching out the heavens like a tent.

This passage has themes common with theophanies. It is likening God's work of creation to what happens in theophanies. It therefore invites us to pay more attention to other passages that speak in terms of God being clothed:

> "Out of the north comes golden splendor;
>   God is *clothed with awesome majesty*." (Job 37:22)

> "Adorn yourself with majesty and dignity;
>   *clothe* yourself with glory and splendor." (Job 40:10)

(In context, God is issuing a challenge to Job, but it implies that God does what man cannot do.)

> He put on righteousness as a breastplate,
>   and a helmet of salvation on his head;
> he put on garments of vengeance for *clothing*,
>   and wrapped himself in zeal as a cloak. (Isa. 59:17)

The Larger Pattern for Clothing

The use of clothing imagery in connection with God fits into a larger pattern in the Bible. For human beings, appropriate clothing expresses the character or status of those who are clothed. For example, the special clothing for the high priest expresses his special status, with respect to the people and with respect to God. Sackcloth as clothing expresses the grief and humility of the person who chooses this clothing. We can say that, in this respect, clothing reflects the person who is clothed. Likewise, clothing in the context of God reflects the character of God or the character of the work that he is performing.

As usual, the imagery does not ultimately originate with human beings but with God. The *original* clothing is the "clothing" of divine majesty: "You are clothed with splendor and majesty" (Ps. 104:1). God's character *is* his "clothing" In imitation of God as the original, it is appropriate that human beings use clothing as an expression or reflection of the particular person who is wearing the clothing.

Clothing with Christ

Since Christ is the climactic revelation of God and the final "theophany," it is fitting that the imagery of clothing is used with him, as in the transfiguration: "And he was transfigured before them, and his *clothes* became radiant, intensely white, as no one on earth could bleach them" (Mark 9:2–3). Those who become followers of Christ are called to become Christlike, and this reality can be expressed in the language of reflections: we reflect Christ: "And we all, with unveiled face, beholding the glory of the Lord, are being transformed into *the same image* from one degree of glory to another. For this comes from the Lord who is the Spirit" (2 Cor. 3:18). This transformation into the likeness of Christ can also be expressed in the language of clothing:

> But *put on* the Lord Jesus Christ, and make no provision for the flesh, to gratify its desires. (Rom. 13:14)
>
> For as many of you as were baptized into Christ have *put on* Christ. (Gal. 3:27)
>
> . . . and to *put on* the new self, created after the *likeness* of God in true righteousness and holiness. (Eph. 4:24)
>
> . . . and have *put on* the new self, which is being renewed in knowledge after the *image* of its creator. (Col. 3:10)

As we have noted repeatedly, Christ is "the exact imprint" (Heb. 1:3) or image of the divine nature. The calling to "put on Christ" means reflecting Christ, who is the image of God. Clothing is an expression of who a person is, and of whether he is reflecting Christ.

23

The Dynamics in
Reflections of God

What should we appreciate about the *dynamics* of God's appearances? The dynamics of action goes together with the stability of the actors who act and of the environment in which their actions take place. In theophany, dynamic action takes place in harmony with the stability of God's character. Let us see how this works.

We have repeatedly seen ways in which appearances of God show who God is. They show God as the God of power, holiness, omniscience, and justice. Though a particular appearance in theophany does not last forever, the God who appears does remain forever. And he is forever the same God.

Theophany often has as one of its functions the establishing of a permanent representation of God's presence. For example, in theophany God announces to Abraham and Sarah the promise of a son (Gen. 18:10). After the end of the theophany, what remains is the continuing promise, and then, a year later, the son himself. After the theophany at Mount Sinai, Israel has the covenant words of the Ten Commandments as a permanent representation of God's presence. And in connection with Mount Sinai, Moses also receives the instructions to build the tabernacle, which offers a more enduring representation of the presence of God that accompanies the people through the wilderness.

In these cases, the theophany and the permanent representations of God's presence function in harmony. The God who appeared temporarily in theophany shows who he always is; he is the same God who is also more permanently present.

Stability and Dynamics Together

When we start thinking about God's character—his attributes— we might pay attention *only* to what is the same. But this would be a mistake. The God who is the same God throughout history is also the God who *acts* in history. The God who has planned the whole history of the world from eternity is also the God who *carries out* his plans in the dynamics of historical processes, leading from one event to another. The features of God's character that remain the same are significant. But these features also get expressed and manifested in God's actions. So God's actions are also significant. The same is true of theophanies. In theophany, the God who is the *same* appears. So we can emphasize the stability of God's character. But we can also choose to emphasize the dynamics involved in his appearing. God *appears*, and by appearing he changes the world.

Some people might reason that, since God is always the same, sta- bility has a kind of metaphysical ultimacy; process and activity belong only to this created world, which is subordinate to God. Or they could observe that God's plan, which is the same for all time, has a priority over the actual events and processes in history, which work out in time successively.

It is indeed true that God is always the same. So we need to empha- size his stability. It is a source of practical comfort, because we can rely on him always to act in a manner consistent with his eternal character. He is always faithful, kind, loving, all-powerful, and all-knowing (Ex. 34:6–7). But it is also true that God is always *active*. The Father loves the Son, in the fellowship of the Holy Spirit. The Father *begets* the Son, in an eternal act of begetting. The Father speaks the eternal Word, in an eternal act of speaking. In God's own nature, his activity is just as fundamental as his stable character. We need to emphasize this activity, because it too is a source of practical comfort. The same God who eter- nally loves his Son has come to us in his Son and extended his love to *us*.

Similar principles hold when we consider the dynamics of history. Both stability and change are involved. First, consider the importance of stability. The dynamics of history have meaning only because the events take place within a relatively stable environment, created by

God's original acts of creation. We ourselves can act meaningfully in history only because we have relatively stable personalities, and stable bodies, created by God. At the same time, events and developments in time—the changes—are significant. God's actions are significant, because they express who he is. God is always *acting* in history, sustaining and governing the events and directing all of history toward the goal of the consummation in Christ (Rev. 21:1–22:5). We ourselves, as creatures of God, have significant actions, which express who we are.

Let us go behind history to God's plan for history. God's plan is always the same, as we have said, because he has planned the end from the beginning (Isa. 46:9–10). At the same time, this plan encompasses all the dynamicity of history! God has not only planned the end; he has also planned all the events along the whole course of history leading to the end. The events, the activities, and the turmoil of history—they all make sense only because they belong to a whole that has significance in relation to God's governance and his plan. The processes and activities matter!

Dynamics in Theophany

What we have observed in a broad way concerning God we can also apply to theophany. Theophany, we have observed, reveals God. If so, it reveals God *in action*. The accounts of theophany in the Bible mostly occur in narratives, reports about certain processes and series of events. The first instance of a theophany-like appearance, with the Spirit of God in Genesis 1:2, contains action: "And the Spirit of God was *hovering* over the face of the waters." This initial action anticipates in seed form the later actions and processes that God undertakes to accomplish during the ensuing six days of creation activity. God dynamically created the world. He acted. He brought about changes. And the world, having been created, dynamically manifests the character and activity of the God who created it and who sustains it.

Or consider the theophany at Mount Sinai (Ex. 19:1–20:26). There is plenty of activity. God instructs Moses on how the people are to prepare. They prepare for three days (19:15). They have also experienced a kind of earlier preparation, when God brought Israel out of Egypt (19:3–4). After these preparations, God manifests his might in the thunder of Mount Sinai. And he speaks to Israel in an audible voice. The people respond with fear (Ex. 20:18). This kind of sequence, going from preparation to appearance to divine speech to human response, can be found in some other instances of theophany.

The theophany at Mount Sinai has a further purpose. The awesome appearance of God and the speech of God have the purpose of forming Israel into a people who are "my treasured possession," "a kingdom of priests and a holy nation" (Ex. 19:5–6). The theophany transforms the people. And the temporary theophany at Mount Sinai has a close relation to a more permanent manifestation of God, in the form of the cloud of fire and the tabernacle. It also has a close relation to the law. Out of the theophany on Mount Sinai, God delivers the Ten Commandments to the people. He does it first with an audible voice, then with the two tablets of the covenant, written in stone by the finger of God (Ex. 24:12; 31:18; Deut. 9:10). The law is like a constitution, to define and form and guide the people of Israel.

Theophany is always purposeful. God appears in a way that changes things. Moreover, he appears in a context where he gives a verbal explanation to indicate the significance of what people see. Verbal explanation and visible appearance go together. The one interprets the other. On this basis, we might also say that every word that God speaks is a theophany-word, in the broadest sense of theophany. It manifests who God is. Conversely, the visual manifestation in theophany harmonizes with what God says. Theophany has as one purpose the provision of a permanent word of God, which abides with God's people and continues to guide and shape them long after the theophany is completed. The theophany has meaning; it is a kind of word-theophany.

God Manifesting Himself in History

The large plan for history is that God would dwell with man. God's fellowship with Adam and Eve was ruined by the fall, but through the work of redemption the endpoint is still attained: "Behold, the dwelling place of God is with man" (Rev. 21:3). "They [his servants] will see his face, and his name will be on their foreheads" (22:4). In Revelation, the consummate dwelling of God with man is a scene of activity. The throne of God in Revelation 22:1 represents his activity in ruling. The saints "will worship him" (v. 3) and "will reign forever and ever" (v. 5).

All the earlier theophanies through the course of creational history and redemptive history build toward this goal. In fact, the goal is intrinsic to the nature of theophany. Theophany reveals God. And this

God is a God who has unbreakable plans. The plans are in harmony with his character and express his character. His plan is to fill the world with his presence—with theophany. The theophanic scene in Revelation 21:22–22:5 is the final expansion of the same presence that God manifested in his throne vision in Revelation 4:1–5:14. Note how the throne vision in Revelation 4–5 already anticipates that God's presence will dominate. It describes a scene where all creation gives him praise: "And I heard every creature in heaven and on earth and under the earth and in the sea, and all that is in them, . . . " (5:13).

We may also express the same truth in terms of the pattern of reflections. The Father loves the Son, who is "the exact imprint of his nature" (Heb. 1:3). It is therefore the Father's purpose that the glory of his Son should be imprinted and displayed with all intensity in the entire universe. The original process of imaging in the begetting of the Son finds its fitting reflection in the manifestation of the glory of the Son in the new heaven and the new earth, which are filled with the glory of God (Rev. 21:23). This glory is simultaneously the glory of the Holy Spirit (1 Pet. 4:14), so that the glory manifests the full Trinitarian character of God. The archetypal pattern is found in the eternal begetting of the Son. Then God reflects this pattern in all of history. The reflections have their beginning in time with God's acts of creation, such as the creation of light (Gen. 1:3). The reflections find their consummation in the final appearing of God (Rev. 22:4). In between these two endpoints lies the reality of God producing reflections of himself by appearing theophanically from time to time in history. The climactic appearance of God is his permanent appearance, in the incarnation of Christ.

The early theophany at Mount Sinai takes place in a context where God reveals his glory. Once we have the fuller New Testament revelation concerning the Trinity, we can see how God the Father, God the Son, and God the Holy Spirit are involved in the revelation at Mount Sinai. God the Father reveals himself in the glory of his Son, who is his Word, and whose glory is reflected in the law given to Israel. The glory is a representation of the Holy Spirit, who is the Spirit of glory (1 Pet. 4:14). Moses's face shone with a reflection of this glory (Ex. 34:29–30). This glory was to form and shape Israel as a people. Unfortunately, the people of Israel were often objects of God's fiery wrath, because their hearts were hard. The glory of the old covenant anticipates the greater glory of the new covenant, which results in positive conformity to the glory of Christ (2 Cor. 3:18). So the Sinai theophany has within it the same fundamental dynamic of reflections that is realized in the glory of Christ. We who are united to Christ reflect his glory in an inaugurated way. The reflection of glory will be realized consummately, on a cosmic scale, in the new heaven and the new earth.

The dynamics of theophany involves God revealing his glory. The compressed revelation of God's glory in theophany is analogous to the more extended revelation of God in the course of history. Thus theophanies show us, in God himself, a pattern representing the dynamics of all of history.

History as Reflections of the Trinity

We can see more than one way in which God's Trinitarian nature is manifested or reflected in history.

First, the relation between stability and dynamics in history is a reflection of the Trinity. We may see this truth by using several steps of reasoning. First, let us remind ourselves that the persons of the Trinity are equal in deity and equal in glory. But there is also a mystery of order among the persons: typically we speak of the Father, the Son, and the Spirit in that order. God the Father, as the first person in that order, preeminently represents the stability of God being the same. The Son, who executes the purposes of God in time, represents the dynamicity of God's activity. He executes the stable purposes of God the Father. And the Holy Spirit brings communion with God—in him we have fellowship with God. He establishes our *relation* to God. Stability, dynamics, and relations reflect respectively the Father, the Son, and the Holy Spirit. All of history holds together. Stability, dynamicity, and relations all form the necessary framework for there to be history at all. (See table 23.1.)

Table 23.1: Stability, Dynamicity, and Relationality

Persons:	Father	Son	Holy Spirit
Features of history:	stability	dynamicity	relations

Second, the purposes of God are manifested in the movement of history from plan to execution to the attainment of the goal. The Father is more closely associated with the plan. The Son executes the plan. The Holy Spirit through his presence brings the execution into full effect. In the consummation, he fills the earth with his glory. The dynamicity of history, in its movement from plan to execution to attainment, reflects the Trinitarian differentiation of action within God. (See table 23.2.)

Table 23.2: Unfolding of Purpose in History

Persons:	Father	Son	Holy Spirit
Roles in events:	planning	executing	achieving, consummating

Third, the common structure of theophanic manifestation expresses the dynamicity of God's purposes. Earlier in this chapter, we mentioned that often theophanies involve a movement in four stages: (1) preparation; (2) appearance; (3) divine speech; and (4) human response. Sometimes there may also be (5) an aftermath, which may include discussion of further consequences. The preparation and the aftermath represent natural boundaries to the intense center of a theophanic event. But they are not indispensable. Some accounts of theophanies do not mention a preparation or an aftermath. So at the heart of theophany we have a series of three events: (1) appearance; (2) divine speech; and (3) human response.[1]

These three can be viewed as a way of spreading out in time the natural character of divine communication. There is a source in the divine speaker, who is represented by the appearance of a theophany; there are the contents of communication, represented by the speech itself; and there is the reception of the communication, involving human response. These three in turn offer us a mirror of divine Trinitarian life. With the Trinity, it is the Father who is preeminently the speaker, the source of communication. It is the Son who, as the Word of God, is present in the speech. And it is the Holy Spirit who is present to work human transformation through the reception of the speech. The inner source of theophany is God. And God reflects himself in the very way in which the theophany unfolds in time. Its unfolding is itself a manifestation that reflects the Trinitarian character of God. (See table 23.3.)

Table 23.3: Unfolding Purposes in Theophany

Persons:	Father	Son	Holy Spirit
Roles in events:	planning	executing	achieving, consummating
Reflections:	↓	↓	↓
Roles in theophany:	appearance	speech	response

---

1. George W. Savran, though not sharing the presupposition of divine authorship of Scripture, has noted some of this pattern (Savran, *Encountering the Divine: Theophany in Biblical Narrative* [London/New York: T&T Clark, 2005]).

Fear in Responding to Theophany

The human response to theophany often shows awe. For a human being to meet God in his appearance is a stupendous privilege. In many cases, God establishes a relation with *one* selected human being. This relation is more intimate, more specific, and more revealing than what we ordinarily see in the surrounding environment of the world. This intimacy expresses God's character. God shows his character in love and in establishing knowledge. At the same time, in the context of sin, a human meeting with God is potentially deadly. The holiness of God is a threat to sin. So, even with Moses, God limits the intensity of intimacy (Ex. 33:20). In other cases, people express fear that they will die, or astonishment and gratitude that they have not died, or fear or wonder over the fact that they have had the encounter. We may think of Hagar (Gen. 16:13), Jacob at Bethel (Gen. 28:17), Jacob at Peniel (Gen. 32:30), Moses at the burning bush (Ex. 3:6), Israel after hearing the voice of God (Ex. 20:18–19), the elders of Israel (Ex. 24:11), Manoah (Judg. 13:20, 22), and Isaiah (Isa. 6:5).

The expressions of fear show the need for mediation. They show that God has a purpose to draw near, but also that some way must be provided to overcome the barrier created by sin. Moreover, the meeting with God usually focuses on an individual. The focus on the individual indicates the way in which one individual can function to mediate the presence of God to a larger group. The exceptional case occurs with Mount Sinai, because in that case God appears before all the people of Israel. But this exception underlines the principle of mediation, because Moses is active as a mediator throughout the encounter. And at the end of the encounter the people beg for God to use Moses as the continuing mediator, in order not to subject them to such a frightening experience again (Ex. 20:18–19). So God appoints Moses as an individual who functions as mediator for the whole nation. Consequently, this aspect of theophany offers an anticipation of the coming of Christ and his atoning work as the final mediator between God and man (1 Tim. 2:5).

We see similar principles with Solomon's temple. The Aaronic priests serve as mediatorial figures, who stand between the presence of God in the temple and the people who are outside the inner part of the temple. When God appeared in a cloud at the time of the dedication of the temple, even the priests could not enter his immediate presence (1 Kings 8:10–11).

The Narrative Environment of Theophany

The necessity of mediation also provides a theological understanding for the events that often surround the occurrence of a theophany. Sometimes, but not always, the description of a theophanic experience may be preceded by preparation, and may be followed by an aftermath.

The preparation for theophany often singles out the human recipient, and thereby prepares him for his unique mediatorial role in bringing the presence of God to bear on the larger group that he represents or to whom God commissions him to go. So, for example, Jacob has left his family and is alone when he lies down at Bethel and receives his revelatory dream (Gen. 28:10–12). God does not immediately commission Jacob to tell anyone, but the dream is significant not only for the subsequent life of Jacob but also for his family and his descendants, who will eventually have the story told to them. Moses travels with his flock to an isolated place before seeing the burning bush (Ex. 3:1). This placement of Moses surely shows God's providential control over history. But, more pointedly, it shapes Moses and the situation in preparation for his unique role in mediating the revelation of God and the presence of God to the people of Israel. Moses as mediator experiences an intimate relation to God that Israel herself could not bear. Similarly, Samuel before his call is lying alone in the temple, near the ark (1 Sam. 3:3). Only afterward does he convey God's message to Eli. Ezekiel says that he "was among the exiles by the Chebar canal" (Ezek. 1:1), which integrates him with the group to which he is primarily sent. But the subsequent experience of theophany also isolates him. He, and not the people, receives the vision in Ezekiel 1:4–3:14.

Now consider what happens in the aftermath of an appearance of God. An account of the aftermath of a theophanic experience does not always occur in biblical texts. But when it does, it often includes information that shows the reintegration of the human recipient into a larger social group or a larger historical context. For example, when Jacob wakes up after the dream, he marks the place and names it Bethel, which clearly indicates his awareness of the importance of his experience for a larger social environment (Gen. 28:18–19). Jacob also makes a vow, which touches on his subsequent life in ordinary environments (vv. 20–22). After the meeting at the burning bush, Moses goes back to talk to Jethro and Aaron, and then to all of Israel (Ex. 4:18–31). After going up to Mount Sinai and receiving the law, Moses comes down again to the people (32:15). Samuel, after privately receiving the word of God, opens the doors of the house of the Lord, delivers the word of God to Eli, and then comes to be publicly recognized as a prophet (1 Sam. 3:15–21). Ezekiel sits overwhelmed after his vision, and then begins to function as prophetic mouthpiece to the people (Ezek. 3:15, 26–27).

In these cases, the aftermath shows how the function of mediation establishes a relation between the mediatorial figure and the people—or, in Jacob's case, at least a relation to a larger life environment. Mediation, founded in the nature of the holiness of God and his purposes in Christ the mediator, is reflected in the narratives describing a divine encounter with a prophetic figure.

24

Responding to God's Presence

Let us consider more closely the human responses to theophanies. The responses have significant meaning. For one thing, a response by a mediator like Moses often has a key role in the major events in redemptive history. The human response functions as one part of God's purposes at the time. But a single response can also offer significant insights into the larger patterns involving God's presence with human beings. As we have already seen, theophany offers us a window or perspective onto the meaning of God's presence everywhere. Therefore, a *response* to a theophany may offer insight into the broader pattern of responses that take place in many manifestations of the presence of God.

Degrees of Responsibility

When people receive revelation and when they respond to God's presence, the general principle holds that they are responsible for what God has given them, not for what he has not. "Everyone to whom much was given, of him much will be required" (Luke 12:48). The principle of general revelation, as articulated in Romans 1:18–23, implies that everyone has received *something*. In fact, they have received quite a notable amount: everyone knows God (Rom. 1:21). But some people have been given more than others. The Israelites, to whom God gave the Ten Commandments and the law, became more deeply guilty than the pagan nations around them when they fell into disobedience. Christian believers who now have access to the whole canon of Scripture and the completed record concerning Christ's redemption are more deeply responsible still. So we must always come to God for mercy, rather than priding ourselves that we are better off than others (Luke 18:11–12; Rom. 3:9).

In addition, some people may at some times have an intensified awareness of God, due to the work of the Holy Spirit. Such experiences may come to non-Christians as well as Christians, because in common grace the Holy Spirit can be at work in situations even when people are not saved. Often, these experiences may be difficult for us to evaluate from a merely human point of view. But since God governs all of history, he knows all about them. He has made them what they are. In such special experiences, God may give to one person what he has not given to others. People are responsible in all such cases for what they receive.

Mediators

With the principle of responsibility in mind, let us now think about the responses to theophanies. As we have seen, in many cases God appears to a single individual. That individual may later serve as a mediator, bringing the gist of the theophany to a larger group. Jacob's dream at Bethel mediates a message that has pertinence for his descendants (Gen. 28:13–15). Moses in his encounter at the burning bush mediates for Israel (Ex. 3:7–22). Likewise, Joshua in his encounter with the commander of the army of the Lord mediates for Israel (Josh. 5:13–15). Isaiah mediates for the people of Israel of his time (Isa. 6:8–10). In these cases God requires a response from the mediator, and then later a response from the people who receive his mediation.

Old Testament mediators foreshadow Christ. So one part of the response is that people would recognize their need for a mediator. They should then repent and ask God for his mercy. They should also thank God and praise him for his grace. When they have a temporary mediator like Moses, they should understand that the pattern of mediation looks forward to a climax. Ultimately, they should have faith in God and his promises. His promises point to the final mediator whom Moses and other figures anticipate. Since the Old Testament mediators are imperfect, they themselves still need the final mediation of Christ, and they are called to have faith in the coming mediator, to thank God, and to praise his name for his grace.

This principle of mediation, which often expresses itself in theophanies, has implications for any response to the presence of God. We need mediation when we receive God's manifestation in creation and providence. People also need mediation on the special occasions when they have an especially intense experience of God's presence. We may start with Scripture, which gives clear teaching about mediation. God the Father speaks to us in Scripture. And he speaks through the mediation of God the Son and God the Spirit, so that we will not die when we receive his word (Rev. 1:1, 10; 2:7).

In analogy with theophanies and with special revelation, we can infer that the Son and the Spirit always work with the Father in manifesting the presence of God. The Son and the Spirit were agents with the Father in creation (John 1:3; Gen. 1:2) and in providence (Heb. 1:3; Ps. 104:30). That is to say, the Son and the Spirit mediate the objective revelation in nature. They also mediate the subjective appropriation of revelation in human knowledge. The Son is the source of wisdom for human beings (Col. 2:3), and the Spirit teaches mankind (Job 32:8). The Bible, as the written word of God, comes through the Son and the Spirit to enable us to interpret properly this revelation of God in nature. Gratitude is the proper response.

Faith and Obedience

The reflections on mediation also show the need for faith in the God who reveals himself, and then obedient response to explicit and implicit commands that accompany his appearance. In the record of Scripture, not everyone responds in an ideal way. Moses and Jeremiah know that they are meeting God, but both initially express reluctance (Ex. 3:11; Jer. 1:6). Moses continues to be reluctant until God becomes angry over his responses (Ex. 4:14–15). God's grace appears when he continues to supply support in the face of Moses's reluctance. The presence of reluctance shows something about the insufficiency of merely human mediators. In the end, God sends Christ, who is the divine and human mediator, and who is without sin.

We may infer that the same principles concerning faith and obedience hold in human responses to all manifestations of God's presence. For example, with respect to the revelation of God in the created world, the key passage in Romans 1:21 mentions that people fail to give thanks. Acts 14:17 and 17:25 implicitly ask for thanksgiving and therefore convict pagans for not having been thankful to God, who is the true source of creational and providential benefits. The sermon in Acts 17 leads up to a call to faith in Christ the mediator (vv. 30–31). The truths that are manifest in general revelation, when properly interpreted by the apostles and by the Bible as whole, lead to the truths of special revelation, climaxing in Christ.

(Acts 14:17–18 does not include a proclamation of Christ's resurrection as its endpoint, probably because of the disrupted situation. The discussion did not come to completion. But at a later, calmer point in time, we see that a church is growing up in Lystra; Acts 14:21–23.)

Doing Something with What God Gives

In all this, it is important to see that human response to theophany has a significant, even vital role. The responses can be of several kinds. They sometimes include an event in which God purifies the human respondent, and the respondent shows faith and obedience. There are also imperfect responses, or temporary responses that fall short, or even complacent responses that achieve nothing, or resistant, hostile responses (such as those of Jesus's religious opponents). The people involved can show strong faith in God, or wavering faith, or pretended faith, or confusion, or raw unbelief, or even defiance.

Moses, though initially reluctant, in the end functions as a wonderful mediatorial deliverer.

Isaiah sees his unworthiness, but then he is cleansed:

> And I said: "Woe is me! For I am lost; for I am a man of *unclean* lips, and I dwell in the midst of a people of unclean lips; for my eyes have seen the King, the Lord of hosts!"
>   Then one of the seraphim flew to me, having in his hand a burning coal that he had taken with tongs from the altar. And he touched my mouth and said: "Behold, this has touched your lips; your *guilt* is taken away, and your sin *atoned* for." (Isa. 6:5–7)

We can also see temporary responses that fall short in the long run. The people of Israel seem receptive and humble when they receive the Ten Commandments (Ex. 20:19). But not long afterwards they fall into the terrible sin of the golden calf (32:9), and they repeatedly rebel in the wilderness (Heb. 4:2).

We can also see responses that amount to nothing. Balaam, for example, seems not to have changed or repented in a fundamental way during the events of Numbers 22–24, even though he received spectacular revelations confirming God's special purposes for Israel (cf. Josh. 13:22; 2 Pet. 2:15), and even though he was confronted visibly by an angel of the Lord who threatened death (Num. 22:32–33). Balaam's case is reminiscent of Jesus's parable about the rich man and Lazarus, where he makes a point about lack of repentance even in response to a spectacular revelation: "He said to him, 'If they do not hear Moses and the Prophets, neither will they be convinced if someone should rise from the dead'" (Luke 16:31).

Likewise, Belshazzar seems not to have repented even after seeing the hand writing on the wall and hearing Daniel's interpretation (Dan. 5:30).

Or we may consider a more quiet case, namely the dreams that came to Pharaoh's cupbearer and baker in Genesis 40. The two of them received revelatory dreams and a revelatory interpretation from Joseph. Possibly one or both of them repented and asked Joseph about the true God that he served. But we have no record of it. And the cupbearer forgot (Gen. 40:23).

Here the cupbearer had a golden opportunity, a once-in-a-lifetime opportunity to ask Joseph freely about the God of power and providence who gave the cupbearer his dream. Apparently he did nothing. His religious experiences, his reception of divine revelation, did not fundamentally alter him. Or at least so it appears—the text does not record any fundamental change. It is true that later on he made a confession of "offenses" (Gen. 41:9), but that response may have been minimal. The fact that he forgot Joseph is telling. He almost certainly also forgot the God who had given him the dream, who had given him a new lease on life, and who had restored him to his position under Pharaoh. Even if he did respond robustly to God, we know enough about human nature to know that other people often do not. In this respect, not the mere reception of revelation but the response is key.

Jesus's words about prophesying in his name show the same pattern:

On that day many will say to me, "Lord, Lord, did we not *prophesy* in your name, and cast out demons in your name, and do many mighty works in your name?" And then will I declare to them, "I never knew you; depart from me, you workers of lawlessness." (Matt. 7:22–23)

Jesus does not say that these people were *false* prophets. It looks as though they spoke words of true prophecy. But they themselves never exercised true faith in Christ for salvation. Their reception of prophetic revelation did not help them. Indeed, it only made them more guilty in the end.

We also see openly hostile responses in the case of the Pharisees of Jesus's time. After seeing spectacular miracles where Jesus cast out demons, they grew in hostility instead of repenting (Matt. 12:24). The presence of revelation, whether spectacular or quiet, does not by itself imply a faithful reception of the revelation. For faithful reception, evil hearts must be changed (Matt. 12:34–35). This lesson pertains not only to outsiders but to insiders as well. The Pharisees themselves were in a sense insiders. They were not only inside Israel, that is, sons of Abraham according to the flesh, but insiders socially and religiously speaking. They were admired for their piety and learning.

The Danger of Remaking God in Our Image

The response by the Pharisees also illustrates that the problem of idols, substitutes for God, and counterfeits for God is a wide and subtle one. The pagans around Israel worshiped idols and many gods. It was easy for a Jew who was instructed by Scripture to see their obvious errors. But it was not so easy to realize that similar errors of a more subtle kind could infiltrate "nice"-looking worship. The Pharisees thought they knew quite a bit about the God of Israel and the way in which he would bring a Messiah. They read the Scriptures, but they were unaware of ways in which they subtly remade their view of God to conform to their desires and expectations (cf. Matt. 22:29). If it could happen to them, it can happen to anyone.

The pattern of replacing truth with falsehood about God illustrates Frame's square of transcendence and immanence (chapter 12). The Christian view (the left-hand side of the square) and the non-Christian view (the right-hand side of the square) superficially look similar. It is all too easy for sinful desires to move us partway toward the right-hand side, or somehow to mix the left-hand and right-hand sides of the square.

In short, people manufacture substitutes for God. They make physical idols as symbols for transcendence, or they make within their minds counterfeit conceptions of God. The counterfeit conceptions may be *close* to the truth. That is the way a counterfeit works. A counterfeit must be close to the truth in order to seem plausible. It expresses fragments of the truth about God. In spite of itself, it testifies to God—but in a distorted way.

Counterfeits may arise when people react in a distorted way to general revelation. Romans 1:21–25 describes just such a distorted reaction. People do not react by merely suppressing all religious impulses or merely ignoring what they know. Precisely because people know God, they react by producing a distortion, a substitute—an idol. Similarly, people may remain satisfied with vague experiences of "transcendence" rather than earnestly seeking to respond to God, whose worthiness and holiness are all-surpassing. They may treat their vague religious experiences as if they needed no further reflection. And that is in itself already a distortion of their real meaning. Or, through the grace of God and the working of the Holy Spirit in special grace, some *do* respond to God and begin to travel along a path leading to fuller understanding of salvation in Christ.

Applying to Us

The problem also affects Christians, who have access to the Bible and who should know better. We too can be complacent. We too can make substitutes. If we do not obviously worship money or pleasure, we may still subtly conform our picture of God to what we want him to be. So for us as well, it is important to continue to assess the nature of creation and providence using biblical instruction. We need to continue to respond in faith and obedience to the God who has shown us such love (Rom. 8:32) and continues to lavish his love on us (Rom. 5:8). We need to submit to God and his ways, rather than substituting for him a picture of what we want God to be like.

The record of theophanies in the Bible provides resources to sustain us. God reveals himself powerfully in theophanies. His power also functions as purifying power. He is able in Christ through the Spirit to purify not only our motives and our actions but our minds. He reforms us so that we can know him better: "Do not be conformed to this world, but be transformed by the renewal of your mind, that by testing you may discern what is the will of God, what is good and acceptable and perfect" (Rom. 12:2).

It is significant that theophanies express the Trinitarian character of

God (as in chapter 17). The grace of God, the purity of Christ, and the sanctifying work of the Holy Spirit need to work in us as we respond to theophanies, in order that we may respond in a manner worthy of the God we serve (cf. Eph. 4:1). The work of the Trinity *in* us, as God comes to indwell us through the Holy Spirit, imitates the pattern of the work of the Trinity in theophany itself.

Reflecting God in Our Lives

Because we are made in the image of God, God's design is that we should reflect his glory in our own nature. Second Corinthians 3:18 speaks about a transformation: "And we all, with unveiled face, beholding the glory of the Lord, are being transformed into the same image from one degree of glory to another." The expression "beholding the glory of the Lord" is the language of theophany. And the preceding verses have referred to the theophany in Exodus 34 in which Moses saw the glory of the Lord. By analogy with Moses, we behold the glory of Christ. By beholding his glory, we are transformed into his image. This transformation implies that we ourselves display the glory of God, by reflecting the glory of Christ in our own persons and our words and deeds. "Let your light shine before others, so that they may see your good works and give glory to your Father who is in heaven" (Matt. 5:16). We ourselves become sources of light, reflecting the light of theophany.

Much could be said about the multitude of ways in which human beings imitate God. One form of imitation is found in the offices of prophet, king, and priest.

First, consider the office of prophet. Prophets speak the word of God. Jesus is the final prophet (Heb. 1:1–2). In union with Christ, we become prophets in a subordinate sense, by speaking the word of God (Col. 3:16).

Second, consider the office of king. Kings rule in the name of God, and bring God's justice to bear on others. Jesus is the supreme, messianic king (Eph. 1:20–22). In union with Christ, we become kings in a subordinate sense (Eph. 2:6). In situations where God has given us authority, we should reflect the wisdom, kindness, and justice of God's rule over us.

Third, consider the office of priest. Priests represent mankind before God, intercede on their behalf, and bring God's blessings to others. Jesus is the supreme and final high priest (Heb. 7:26–8:1). In union with Christ, we become priests (1 Pet. 2:5). Christ's atoning sacrifice happened once and for all, and is not repeatable. But we may intercede before God for others, and bring God's blessings to others.

In all three ways, as prophets, kings, and priests, we are reflecting the offices of Christ himself.[1] We are reflecting the glory of God, in a manner analogous to theophanies.

---

1. *The Heidelberg Catechism* summarizes Christ's offices:
Q. 31. Why is he called "Christ," that is anointed?
A. Because he is ordained of God the Father, and anointed with the Holy Ghost, to be our chief *Prophet* and Teacher, who has fully revealed to us the secret counsel and will of God concerning our redemption; and to be our only *High Priest*, who by the one sacrifice of his body, has redeemed us, and makes continual intercession with the Father for us; and also to be our eternal *King*, who governs us by his word and Spirit, and who defends and preserves us in that salvation, he has purchased for us. (*The Heidelberg Catechism*, http://reformed.org/documents/index.html ?mainframe=http://reformed.org/documents/heidelberg.html, accessed June 24, 2016; italics are mine; notes providing scriptural texts have been omitted).

PART III

A HISTORY OF
GOD APPEARING:
THE OLD TESTAMENT

25

Universal Presence of God in History

In discussing the theme of God's appearances, we have so far focused mostly on *special* appearances of God and *special* times and for special purposes. The key word *theophany* is used mostly to designate these special appearances. Can we move beyond these special cases, and identify themes associated with theophany in broader contexts?

Theophany as a Perspective

Already in chapters 11 and 21 we have seen that creation and providence enjoy thematic relationships with theophany. This breadth in relationships is part of a larger pattern. The most spectacular appearances of God can be compared with *less* spectacular cases. In some of these cases, it may not be clear whether there are special visual phenomena. For example, Genesis 12:7 says that "the LORD appeared to Abram," without describing any particular details. Genesis 12:1 mentions that "the LORD said to Abram," without indicating whether a visual appearance accompanied the speech. In addition, poetic passages use the language of theophany to describe God's care, and some of these cases may not involve literal visual phenomena—we may consider David's praise to God for his powerful acts in 2 Samuel 22:8–16, or the description of God's acts in warrior-like imagery in Isaiah 59:16–17 and Habakkuk 3:11–13.

Such passages invite us to see the special appearances of God as offering perspectives on the character of God, and therefore also perspectives on the acts of God in less spectacular cases. In other words, *theophany* offers us a perspective on God's acts in general.

The Presence of God

We can also look at the special appearances of God as intense instances of a broader principle, namely the principle of God's *presence* (see fig. 1.5 in chapter 1). According to biblical teaching, God is present as ruler and Lord in all places and at all times (Jer. 23:24; Rev. 1:8). This universal presence of God goes together with his *special* presence with the people that are his. He is present to have personal fellowship with his people, to act in power in order to bless them, to discipline them (Heb. 12:3–11), and to punish those who are unfaithful and disobedient. This special presence is promised, for example, when Jacob is leaving Canaan to go to Paddan-aram:

> "Behold, I am *with you* and will keep you wherever you go, and will bring you back to this land. For I will *not leave you* until I have done what I have promised you." (Gen. 28:15)

During the exodus from Egypt, God is specially present with the people of Israel. His special presence is symbolized by the pillar of cloud and fire (Ex. 14:19–20; Num. 9:16–23). God's presence becomes a specific topic for discussion after the difficulties raised by the incident of the golden calf:

> And he [God] said, "*My presence* will go *with you*, and I will give you rest." And he [Moses] said to him, "If *your presence* will not go *with me*, do not bring us up from here. For how shall it be known that I have found favor in your sight, I and your people? Is it not in your going *with us*, so that we are distinct, I and your people, from every other people on the face of the earth?" And the LORD said to Moses, "This very thing that you have spoken I will do, for you have found favor in my sight, and I know you by name." (Ex. 33:14–17)

The tabernacle of Moses is a symbolic expression of God's presence with the Israelites: "And let them make me a sanctuary, that I may *dwell in their midst*" (Ex. 25:8).

Thus the special appearances of God, whether as "the angel of the Lord" or at Mount Sinai or in the pillar of cloud and fire, are all expressions of the broader theme of God's *presence with* his people. The spectacular events at Mount Sinai inaugurate a permanent covenantal relationship between God and his people, and one feature of this relationship is God's special presence as redeemer and shepherd. Theophany is an intense expression of the broader theme of God's *presence*.

We can follow the theme of God's presence all the way through the Bible. It is there continually, as an expression of his covenantal relation to his people, a relation that comes to climactic fulfillment in Christ. One of the names given to Christ is *Immanuel*, meaning "God with us": "'Behold, the virgin shall conceive and bear a son, and they shall call his name Immanuel' (which means, *God with us*)" (Matt. 1:23; cf. Isa. 7:14).

Accordingly, a number of modern books show how the theme of God's presence and the theme of his *dwelling-place* (tabernacle and temple) go through the whole of the Bible.[1] We need not go over again the same ground that they have covered. But we should note that the presence of God at unique places, such as the tabernacle and the temple of Solomon, is an intense expression of a still broader theme, the theme of God's *universal* presence with his people. And his presence with his people in blessing and salvation goes together with his broader presence as ruler of the entire universe. Special instances of theophany cohere with this universal presence.[2]

The special instances of theophany in the Old Testament point forward to the incarnation of Christ. He is the climactic and permanent theophany. But he is also mediator of creation, and accordingly he plays an essential role in God's universal providential presence, as well as God's presence in bringing redemption to his people.

The Presence of God in Relation to Promises, Covenants, and Kingdom

As usual, the theme of God's presence interlocks with other major themes: the themes of God's promises, God's covenant, and God's

---

1. G. K. Beale, *The Temple and the Church's Mission: A Biblical Theology of the Dwelling Place of God* (Leicester, UK: Apollos; Downers Grove, IL: InterVarsity, 2004); G. K. Beale and Mitchell Kim, *God Dwells among Us: Expanding Eden to the Ends of the Earth* (Downers Grove, IL: InterVarsity, 2014); J. Ryan Lister, *The Presence of God: Its Place in the Storyline of Scripture and the Story of Our Lives* (Wheaton, IL: Crossway, 2014); although Samuel L. Terrien does not share the presupposition of divine authorship of Scripture, he has extensively addressed the theme of God's presence in his book *The Elusive Presence: Toward a New Biblical Theology* (San Francisco: Harper & Row, 1978).

2. John Frame has the theme of "presence" as one of three main perspectives on God's lordship (John M. Frame, *The Doctrine of the Knowledge of God* [Phillipsburg, NJ: P&R, 1987], 15–18; John M. Frame, *The Doctrine of God* [Phillipsburg, NJ: P&R, 2002], 94–102). Since God is Lord over all, this perspective implies that God's presence is pervasive, in time and space.

kingdom (see chapter 1). The entire history of God's presence involves his being present in covenant and in kingly rule. So in following the theme of God's presence, we should recognize the simultaneous presence of the other themes. In subsequent chapters, we will make these connections explicit in a few cases. But many more instances of the connections could be added.

26

God's Presence in Creating
the World (Day One)

If God is present in all of history, it remains for us to trace instances of his presence through the course of history as recorded in the Bible.[1] How shall we go about it?

Principles for Interpretation

We cannot here introduce a long discussion of how to interpret Scripture.[2] But we should clarify a few fundamental principles that we use.

The most fundamental issue affecting interpretation is the issue of whether God exists, and what *kind* of God he is. Is he the kind of God who rules and governs all of history for his own wise purposes? Is he a God who works miracles? Is he the kind of God who, when he wishes, appears amid startling, spectacular visual phenomena? Did he, for example, appear at Mount Sinai in thunder and fire, and speak with an audible voice to the people of Israel gathered at the foot of the mountain (Ex. 19:16–20; 20:19–22)? Are the words that he speaks perfectly true and reliable?

---

1. See also Jeffrey J. Niehaus, *God at Sinai: Covenant and Theophany in the Bible and the Ancient Near East* (Grand Rapids, MI: Zondervan, 1995), who discusses theophanies in biblical history, and also points out parallels with polytheistic descriptions of the appearing of gods in ancient Near Eastern literature.
2. For my own views, see Vern S. Poythress, *God-Centered Biblical Interpretation* (Phillipsburg, NJ: P&R, 1999); Vern S. Poythress, *Reading the Word of God in the Presence of God: A Handbook for Biblical Interpretation* (Wheaton, IL: Crossway, 2016).

Many modern biblical scholars in the "critical" tradition do *not* believe that God (if he exists) is that kind of God. If he were, it would disrupt their whole understanding of history—indeed, of the world itself. So we cannot assume that everyone is coming to the Bible with the same assumptions about the nature of history. But in fact the God who rules the universe *is* the God described in the Bible, the God who does these things. So in interpreting the Bible and interpreting history, we should reckon with who he is.

The second major issue is what kind of book the Bible is. Is it the very word of God, as Jesus taught and demonstrated by his own life? Or is it a merely human product, a human *record* of various religious thoughts and possible "encounters" with some mysterious divine presence?

I believe that it is the very word of God, as the Bible itself testifies.[3] So the canonical documents as we have them should be our principal focus, rather than some speculatively constructed, hypothetical story of how they were composed out of diverse sources and previous layers of thinking. Moreover, the history they record gives us descriptions of events that actually happened. These events have theological significance and exercise weighty influence in the religious community of Israel and in the church. They have hortatory value. But these effects of the documents belong together with their affirmation of the reality of events. So, for example, when we consider the description of the events at Mount Sinai in Exodus 19–20, we can have confidence that God did appear in thunder and fire and smoke. It is a vain denial of divine authority when, instead, scholars replace *this God* of the Bible, a God who has *this manner of appearing and speaking*, with a god of their imagination. They then claim, for example, that Israelites gradually embellished a story for theological reasons and produced a made-up account of the events at Sinai.

The various books of the Bible were written under the inspiration of the Holy Spirit at various times (Heb. 1:1). God had the purpose of addressing his people who lived at the time of writing. At the same time, he purposed that a body of canonical documents should grow that would *also* form a permanent record to speak to coming generations (cf. Deut. 31:9–13, 24–29). We can therefore deepen our understanding of the full import of God's word by reading the earlier portions in the light of later

---

3. See John Murray, "The Attestation of Scripture," in *The Infallible Word: A Symposium by Members of the Faculty of Westminster Theological Seminary*, ed. N. B. Stonehouse and Paul Woolley, 3rd rev. ed. (Philadelphia: P&R, 1967), 1–54.

revelation, as well as in the historical and social context in which God originally produced them.

God's Work of Creation as a Whole

We begin with creation, as narrated in Genesis 1–2. How is God's presence manifested in the creation of the world? We cannot give a thorough discussion to all the issues that arise in the interpretation of Genesis 1–2. We must leave that to the commentaries and to discussions of the relation of Genesis 1–2 to modern science.[4] Here we focus on the theme of God's presence.

We have discussed at earlier points the fact that God's works of creation manifest his presence (chapters 11 and 21). In particular, God's presence is proclaimed in the hovering of the Spirit over the face of the waters (Gen. 1:2), and in the poetic celebration of creation in Psalm 104:1–4. Let us now look at some details.

The Initial Creation of the World (Genesis 1:1)

First, God is present in the initial act of creating the world out of nothing (Gen. 1:1; Col. 1:16). Interpreters of Genesis disagree over the function of Genesis 1:1. I think that Genesis 1:1 is describing God's initial act of creation, with nothing preceding it. But there are alternative interpretations. One interpretation is that Genesis 1:1 functions as a *title* introducing Genesis 1:2–31. According to this view, Genesis 1:1 summarizes Genesis 1:2–31 rather than referring to an initial event of original creation.

We cannot enter into a full discussion of the details. Both the grammar and the structure are consistent with the interpretation in which Genesis 1:1 refers to the initial act of creation.[5] But even if we were to allow another interpretation of this one verse, the message of the absolute sovereignty of God in creation *implies* his sovereignty over the very beginning. And later scriptural passages unambiguously assert God's creation of all the aspects of the world, including any initial stage of unformed matter (John 1:1–3; Col. 1:16–17; Rev. 4:11).

---

4. The literature is voluminous. Readers who want to know my own views should look at Vern S. Poythress, *Redeeming Science: A God-Centered Approach* (Wheaton, IL: Crossway, 2006); see also C. John Collins, *Genesis 1–4: A Linguistic, Literary, and Theological Commentary* (Phillipsburg, NJ: P&R, 2006). Among many excellent commentaries by evangelical scholars, Collins's commentary is perhaps the closest to my own preferred interpretation.

5. See, e.g., Collins, *Genesis 1–4*, 50–55.

Was God present in a special way in the initial act of creating the world? Since the initial creation of the world was uniquely special and spectacular, God was especially present. Does Genesis 1 explicitly speak about his presence? Genesis 1:1 by itself does not explicitly mention his presence, but it does say that God did it! The special presence of the Holy Spirit is mentioned beginning with Genesis 1:2, and Genesis 1:2 describes a situation some time *after* the initial beginning. We can nevertheless infer the presence of God in the initial work of creation, for at least two reasons.

1. John Frame, through his theology of lordship, shows how the presence of God is involved in *all* his works and at every point in his lordship. Since the initial creation of the world involves God's lordship over creation, we can infer that God is specially present in the work of initial creation.

2. The presence of the Holy Spirit at Genesis 1:2, and the presence of the Holy Spirit in the work of creating generations of animals in Psalm 104:30, point to a general principle, according to which the Holy Spirit expresses the presence of God in all his works. Creation is the work of God the Father, God the Son (1 Cor. 8:6), and God the Holy Spirit (by analogy with Ps. 104:30).

The Hovering of the Holy Spirit (Genesis 1:2)

The next verse, Genesis 1:2, directly expresses the presence of God in creation: "And the Spirit of God was hovering over the face of the waters." The narrative in Genesis 1 does not mention the Holy Spirit again, but his presence at this early point implies his presence throughout the work of creation over the space of six days. As Meredith Kline has endeavored to show, the presence of the Spirit in a spatially specific way is reminiscent of theophany, and *may* be an instance of theophany.[6]

Like other instances of God's acts, the movement of the Spirit has an inherently dynamic quality. It reveals a God who acts in power, a God who acts to accomplish his purposes. His purposes travel all the way from creation to consummation. The movement of God the Spirit is the source not only for the acts of creation in the next verses of Genesis 1 but also for the acts of providence, redemption, judgment, and consum-

---

6. Meredith G. Kline, *Images of the Spirit* (Grand Rapids, MI: Baker, 1980), 14–26. See discussion in appendix B.

mation through the entirety of history. Genesis 1:2 gives us the whole of history in a nutshell, because it gives us God with his comprehensive purposes expressed in his acts.

God Speaking

Genesis 1:3 describes the first of ten instances in Genesis 1 when God speaks: "And God said, 'Let there be light,' and there was light." The language of speaking makes us think of oral communication, not a visible manifestation. But there are still links with the theme of God's appearing. When God appears, his speech is often a central component of meeting with him. And in a broad sense, God is present in his speech. Since God manifests himself when he speaks, his speech is a form of divine manifestation, and therefore can be seen as "theophany" in the broadest sense of the term.

John Frame makes the same general point through his theology of lordship. God's speech is an expression of his lordship, and consequently it manifests the attributes of lordship, including presence. The recipient experiences God's presence because he hears *God*, not simply words. To hear God is one mode of experiencing his presence. God's speech is a kind of auditory analogue to visible manifestations, such as we see in the major theophanies in the Old Testament.

We conclude that all ten speeches of God in Genesis 1 are manifestations of the presence of God, reflective of God. He is the same God who appears in theophanies. If God's speeches manifest the presence of God, so do the *effects* of the speeches, which we see in the rest of the narrative in Genesis 1.

The archetypal image of God is God the Son, who is the image of the Father and who is the Word of God (John 1:1). God's particular speeches reflect this original speech. The power to speak and to name derives from God the Son. Speaking reflects God the Son, who is the Word.

Light as Theophanic

Does the light that God created reflect God? Yes. "God is light," according to 1 John 1:5. We saw earlier how various elements within creation reflect the character of God (chapter 21). Light is one of them. As we saw in chapter 11, Psalm 104 makes a connection between the creation of light and theophany:

> You are clothed with splendor and majesty,
>> covering yourself with *light* as with a garment,
>> stretching out the heavens like a tent. (Ps. 104:1–2)

In the creation of light, God manifests his speaking capability and his power. He also manifests himself in the light as the thing created. Light as a created thing foreshadows the coming of Christ, who is "the light of life" and "the light of the world" (John 1:4; 8:12). God is present in light, as one created manifestation of his presence in all of the world.

God Evaluates

The text of Genesis 1:4 says, "And God saw that the light was good." He evaluated it as good. The process of evaluation has affinities with theophanies, because God often comes to judge by appearing in theophany. Daniel 7:9–10 is an obvious, dramatic case where God appears in order to judge. Less obviously, Ezekiel 1:1–28 prefaces the commission of Ezekiel to prophesy, and the prophetic messages in the first half of the book are predominantly messages of judgment and condemnation. In addition, the last judgment of Revelation 20:11–15 is a theophany of God on his throne.

All preliminary judgments foreshadow the last judgment. Even the evaluation in Genesis 1:4 reveals God's ability and competence to judge with righteousness and discrimination. By revealing God as one who cares for what is good, it already anticipates that the same God will at last judge the world in righteousness:

> and he *judges* the world with *righteousness*;
>> he *judges* the peoples with *uprightness*. (Ps. 9:8)

> for he comes,
>> for he comes to *judge* the earth.
> He will *judge* the world in *righteousness*,
>> and the peoples in his *faithfulness*. (Ps. 96:13)

See also Psalm 98:9; Acts 17:31.

Separations Reflecting God's Character

The narrative in Genesis 1 next describes the first of several *separations*: "And God separated the light from the darkness" (1:4). The separation goes together with supplying a distinct name for each of the two elements that are separated: "God called the light Day, and the darkness he called Night" (v. 5).

The description of separation indicates God's power to *make* separations. As usual, according to Frame's discussion of lordship, God's lordship includes control and presence. God's control is manifested in making the separations. God's presence is manifested in his intimate involvement in the world, as he brings form to the world through separations. So God is *present* through making the separation between light and darkness.

Though God's act of separating is not a theophany in the narrow sense, it has thematic associations with some of the acts of God in theophany. Light and darkness often symbolize good and evil (cf. 1 John 1:5–7). God's separation of physical light and darkness calls to mind his acts in which he brings judgments to distinguish between good and evil. God is the righteous judge who "separates" the righteous from the wicked. Indeed, John 3:19–21 uses the language of light in darkness to discuss God's judgment:

> "And this is the *judgment*: the *light* has come into the world, and people loved the *darkness* rather than the *light* because their works were evil. For everyone who does wicked things hates the *light* and does not come to the *light*, lest his works should be *exposed*. But whoever does what is true comes to the *light*, so that it may be clearly seen that his works have been carried out in God."

An earthly king imitates God by making discriminate judgments or rulings in the cases that come before him: "A king who sits on the throne of judgment *winnows* all evil with his eyes" (Prov. 20:8; cf. Deut. 16:18–20). God illustrates his ability to make moral distinctions when he brings the ninth plague on Egypt, the plague of darkness. The Egyptians lived in darkness, but "all the people of Israel had light where they lived" (Ex. 10:23). The separation between darkness and light symbolizes that the Egyptians were in the wrong and the Israelites in the right. It was a form of evaluative judgment.

In sum, the physical distinctions that God pronounces and puts in place in creation foreshadow the moral distinctions that belong to his judgments in history. And his judgments in history foreshadow the last judgment, which takes place as a climactic theophany. God distinguishes the righteous from the wicked (cf. Matt. 25:33, 46).

God Gives Names

In Genesis 1:5 God also shows his ability to *name* things: "God called the light Day, and the darkness he called Night." His ability to name reflects the archetypal Word of God, who is the Son of God. Naming is a manifestation or reflection of God. It conforms to God's character, and it thus manifests the God who speaks and who names.

After the completion of the sixth day of creative activity, the cycle of day and night that all human beings experience continues to manifest the faithfulness of God:

> "While the earth remains, seedtime and harvest, cold and heat, summer and winter, day and night, shall not cease." (Gen. 8:22)

> Day to day pours out speech,
>   and night to night reveals knowledge. (Ps. 19:2)

In Genesis 8:22, God's promise to continue the cycle of day and night comes in the context of covenant making. God responds to Noah's sacrificial offering (8:20–21) with promises that are elaborated in an official covenant (9:9): "Behold, I establish my *covenant* with you and your offspring after you." A covenant is an expression of God's presence, in which he officially binds himself to people and thereby expresses his presence.

God Makes a Pattern of Time

The creation of light on day one establishes a pattern for time. On the basis of God's acts of creation, night and day now follow one another. God is Lord of time and Lord of history. The alternation between night and day offers one testimony to God in his control, and therefore also God in his presence in history. He brings the night and the day:

> You *make darkness*, and it is night,
>   when all the beasts of the forest creep about. (Ps. 104:20)

> "For he makes his *sun rise* on the evil and on the good, and sends rain on the just and on the unjust." (Matt. 5:45)

The Themes of Promise, Covenant, and Kingdom

By proclaiming the presence of God, the first few verses in Genesis 1 also include implicitly the themes of promise, covenant, and kingdom.

Let us focus on God's speech. Genesis 1:3 contains the first record of a specific command: "Let there be light." In giving a command, God acts as the great king of the universe. So this command is expressive of the theme of kingdom.

Since God speaks, his speech also has ties with covenant and with promise. The later parts of the Bible focus predominantly on God's covenants with human beings. But here his words shape the environment in which human beings will later live. We can also see an implicit promise, that the light will continue to be available for human beings, and that God will preserve the separation between light and darkness that he has ordained. God's rule over the created world is later compared to a covenant (Jer. 31:35–36; 33:25–26). God's faithfulness and care for human beings, expressed explicitly in biblical covenants, is also expressed more broadly in his wise governance of the environment in which human beings live. So even in Genesis 1:1–5 God is showing *covenantal* actions and covenantal commitments with respect to the created world.

27

God's Presence in Creating the World (Days Two–Six)

Now that we have seen the pattern of God's manifestations in the works of day one of creation, we can note more briefly the continuation of similar patterns through the remaining days. All the works of all the days manifest God's character and his presence in various ways.

God's Presence Manifested in Creating the Expanse (Genesis 1:6–8)

On the second day, God creates an "expanse" that separates the waters above from the waters below. In this narrative of the second day, several features run parallel to what we saw with the first day.

To begin with, God acts by *speaking*. Speaking manifests his presence and is climactically expressed in instances of theophany where God speaks.

The work of God on the second day also involves the creation of a *separation*. So we may draw the same connection with God's ability to make judicial separations and evaluations.

God also engages in another act of *naming*, by calling "the expanse Heaven" (1:8). This act of naming manifests God's ability to speak and name, as in the earlier naming in 1:5. It also displays God's authority over the thing that is named.

In the context of 1:8, the name "Heaven" is given to the visible sky. The same name is used, of course, in other contexts to describe God's invisible dwelling place among the angels (1 Kings 22:19; Ps. 89:5–7; Rev. 4:2). The exaltedness of the visible sky imitates and reflects the exaltedness of God and his invisible heavenly dwelling place. The visible "heaven" is a kind of reflection of the invisible heaven, which in turn is a reflection of God's exaltedness, his transcendence.

We may also have a case of reflections in the specific structure of the expanse. Sometimes the visions of God include an expanse:

> and they saw the God of Israel. There was under his feet as it were a *pavement* of sapphire stone, like the very heaven for clearness. (Ex. 24:10)

> And above the *expanse* over their heads there was the likeness of a throne, in appearance like sapphire; and seated above the likeness of a throne was a likeness with a human appearance. (Ezek. 1:26; see also v. 22)

> And before the throne there was as it were a *sea* of glass, like crystal. (Rev. 4:6; see also 15:2)

> And I saw what appeared to be a *sea* of glass mingled with fire—and also those who had conquered the beast and its image and the number of its name, standing beside the *sea* of glass with harps of God in their hands. (Rev. 15:2)

Given the presence of reflections of God's heavenly presence, the presence of an expanse in heaven suggests that the expanse within the visible world in Genesis 1:6 imitates the expanse in the court of angelic beings. The different verses do not use identical wording. But there seems to be a relationship. The "pavement" in Exodus 24:10 is more specifically described as "sapphire stone." The expanse in Ezekiel 1 is "in appearance like sapphire (v. 26) and "shining like awe-inspiring crystal" (v. 22). The "sea of glass" in Revelation 4:6 is "like crystal." The "sea of glass" in Revelation 15:2 seems to be basically the same sea as in Revelation 4:6. But this time it appears in the context of the conquerors who sing:

> And they sing the song of Moses, the servant of God, and the song of the Lamb, saying,

"Great and amazing are your deeds,
    O Lord God the Almighty!
Just and true are your ways,
    O King of the nations!" (Rev. 15:3)

The reference in Revelation 15:3 to the song of Moses leads us naturally back to Exodus 15, where the people of God sing in celebration of God's deliverance from the Red Sea. God triumphs over Pharaoh and his army, and over the waters that threaten death. So, through a number of connections, the Red Sea on earth gets an association with the sea or expanse in heaven. The sea in heaven is not tumultuous, but crystalline. One point of the visions seems to be that God is fully master of created things, including the seas on earth. The sea in heaven is, as it were, a reflection of God's mastery and control. And God's separation of the waters on earth in Genesis 1:6 is then a demonstration of his mastery. It reveals God and expresses the presence of God.

Separation of Earthly Waters to Make Dry Land (Genesis 1:9–11)

On the third day God speaks again to produce a separation between seas and dry land. His speech and the act of separating both manifest his presence, in a manner parallel to what we have seen with day one and the second day.

This initial separation of sea and dry land shows God's mastery over the waters. It has a natural association with the later redemptive act at the Red Sea. God there separates the sea and the dry land for the sake of redeeming his people:

> Then Moses stretched out his hand over the sea, and the LORD drove the sea back by a strong east wind all night and *made the sea dry land*, and *the waters were divided*. And the people of Israel went into the midst of the sea on *dry ground*, the waters being a wall to them on their right hand and on their left. (Ex. 14:21–22; see also v. 29)

During the exodus, at the crossing of the Red Sea, God is present theophanically through the pillar of cloud and fire (cf. Ex. 14:19–20, 24). The intense presence of God at the Red Sea crossing provides an association between Genesis 1:9–11 and a later theophany. In Genesis 1:9–11, God is present to master the sea, for the sake of creating a space where human beings can later live (Gen. 1:26–30). The process showing his mastery over the sea is emblematic for all the other cases in history where God comes to exert his mastery over anything that threatens the life of his chosen people. In the new heaven and new earth, "the sea was no more" (Rev. 21:1), which signifies the final disappearance of all threats to human life.

God's Presence in Creating Vegetation

Next, let us consider God's creation of vegetation on the third day (Gen. 1:12–13). God creates by *speaking*, as before (1:11; cf. 1:3, 6, 9). He creates distinct *kinds* of plants and vegetation, and the distinction of kinds shows us an instance of *separation*. When the plants have come forth, God *evaluates* the situation and pronounces it "good," giving us another instance of the theme of evaluation.

God also shows himself in a particular way in what he has created, namely vegetation. In an earlier chapter (chapter 21) we considered how the tree of life reflects the archetypal life in God himself. The tree of life in Genesis 2:9 has a special role, but it has thematic connections with trees in general. God reflects his life at the created level in the life of the plant kingdom. He is present through this symbolic reflection of his character.

One of the distinctive things about living creatures is that they *reproduce*. Plants produce more plants, "each according to its kind" (1:11). So do land animals, sea animals, and birds (1:24, 21). This pattern of reproduction dimly reflects a kind of process of reflections, as we can see by several stages of reasoning.

First, man is made "in the image of God" (Gen. 1:26–27). Second, in human reproduction, Adam fathers Seth as a son "in his own likeness, after his image" (5:3). So human reproduction reflects the character of man made in the image of God. Adam is imitating God, who created man. Third, animal reproduction and human reproduction have obvious likenesses. We might even be bold and say that in this respect animals—especially mammals and other higher animals—are made in the image of man. Fourth, plants in their reproduction imitate animals, and then also human reproduction.

Man, of course, is distinguished from animals by being made in the image of God. But the distinction does not undermine subtle likenesses between the two. And then there are more distant likenesses with plants as well. Finally, man being the image of God is an imitation of Christ, who as the eternal Son is eternally the image of God (Heb. 1:3; Col. 1:15).

The presence of God is in Christ, who is God. Subordinately, and in a different way, the presence of God is with man, who is made in the image of God and can represent God in ruling and in executing judgment (Gen. 1:28; 9:6). Plants, in imitating man, reflect the glory and life of God, and God shows his character when the pattern of creation is reflected in the capacity of plants to reproduce after their kinds.

God's Presence in Creating the Heavenly Lights (Genesis 1:14–19)

Next, consider the fourth day, when God creates the heavenly lights. He creates them by *speaking*, as usual (1:14). He uses them to maintain a *separation*: "And God said, 'Let there be lights in the expanse of the heavens to *separate* the day from the night'" (v. 14). The heavenly lights, and especially the sun, provide a concentrated area of light, and thereby express in concentrated form the reflection of God's character that we see in the light created on day one. A number of times, theophanic language includes a description of brightness like the sun:

> The *sun* shall be no more
> your light by day,
> nor for brightness shall the moon
> give you light;
> but the LORD will be your everlasting *light*,
> and your God will be your glory.
> Your *sun* shall no more go down,
> nor your moon withdraw itself;
> for the LORD will be your everlasting *light*,
> and your days of mourning shall be ended. (Isa. 60:19–20)

> "But for you who fear my name, the *sun* of righteousness shall rise with healing in its wings. You shall go out leaping like calves from the stall." (Mal. 4:2)

> And he was transfigured before them, and his face shone like the *sun*, and his clothes became white as light. (Matt. 17:2)

See also Acts 26:13; Revelation 1:16; 10:1; 21:23.

In addition, the heavenly lights are said to "rule" over the day and the night (Gen. 1:16, 18). Their rule imitates and reflects the greater *rule* of God over all things. He is present, establishing and maintaining the "rule" of the heavenly lights.

God's Presence in Creating the Sea Creatures and the Birds (Genesis 1:20–23)

Next let us consider the creation of sea animals and birds. God creates by speaking, and produces separations of the *kinds* of animals. As we observed in discussing plants, the sea animals, birds, and land animals reflect God's presence through the way in which they reproduce after their kinds. In addition, God's design is that the sea creatures should "be fruitful and multiply," which is similar to the command for mankind in Genesis 1:28: "Be fruitful and multiply and fill the earth and subdue it, and have dominion over the fish of the sea and over the birds of the heavens and over every living thing that moves on the earth." The command to "subdue" and "have dominion" is unique to mankind. But the command to "be fruitful and multiply" comes to all the kinds of sea animals and birds. In this respect, what the sea animals and birds do is a kind of reflection of what human beings are called to do.

As we look forward through redemptive history, we see that Adam as head of the human race radically failed to carry through his calling from God. But the calling is explicitly renewed in the time of Noah (Gen. 9:1–3). We find that it is fulfilled through Christ, who is the "last Adam" (1 Cor. 15:45). According to Ephesians 1 and 4, Christ has full dominion and fills all things:

> And he put all things *under his feet* and gave him as head over all things to the church, which is his body, the fullness of him who *fills all in all.* (Eph. 1:22–23)

> He who descended is the one who also ascended *far above* all the heavens [implying rule], that he might *fill all things.* (Eph. 4:10)

The Bible also reveals that Christ has a multitude of spiritual offspring, namely those who believe in him. He thereby fulfills the commandment to "be fruitful and multiply" (Isa. 53:10; Heb. 2:13).

The climactic form of being fruitful and multiplying and filling the earth takes place in Christ. From our vantage point in redemptive history, we can see that the commission given to sea animals and birds anticipates in smaller form this later climax. God shows his presence in his design to fill all things with his glory.

God's Presence in Creating the Land Animals

God's creation of the land animals shows patterns parallel to the creation of sea animals and birds. God creates by *speaking*. He separates the land animals into *kinds*. The narrative does not include a specific command for the land animals to be fruitful and multiply, but we can infer it from the parallels with sea animals and birds.

In addition, the land animals and birds enjoy connections with the cherubim around God's throne. The cherubim have the faces of a lion, an ox, a man, and an eagle. The lion is preeminent among wild animals; the ox is preeminent by its strength among domestic animals. The eagle is preeminent among the birds. The lion, the ox, and the eagle may be considered as representative for all the animals in the general category—wild animals, domestic animals, and birds. Each of these animals is a reflection of one aspect of the heavenly cherubim. And the cherubim as angelic creatures reflect the glory of God himself. Man alone is made "in the image of God" in a unique way. But in a broader way the animals reflect the power and glory of the cherubim, who in turn reflect the glory of God. In this way also as created things they reflect the presence of God.

In the original creation, evil has not yet intruded. After it has intruded, God uses the imagery of human dominion over the "beasts" in order to express the conflict between Christ and the beast in Revelation. Human dominion over the animals in Genesis 1:28 anticipates Christ's triumph over the beast in Revelation 19:11–21.

God's Presence in Creating Mankind

The creation of mankind stands at the climax of the narrative in Genesis 1. Mankind is uniquely made "in the image of God" (Gen. 1:27), and uniquely receives dominion over the other creatures of the earth (vv. 28–29). As we have indicated, human dominion reflects the archetypal dominion of God. Humanity reflects God, as we are reminded when we have a theophany with a human form at the center. In a broad sense, humanity as a whole and each human being as an individual reflects God and expresses the presence of God by reflecting his character at the created level.

In sum, all the aspects in God's work in creating the world express God's character and reflect it. God is present in all his work. In all his work God is revealed, as Romans 1:18–23 has indicated.

Promise, Covenant, and Kingdom

As usual, God's presence includes an implicit expression of the themes of promise, covenant, and kingdom. Implicit in God's acts of creation is his commitment to maintain the order that he has established by the end of the sixth day. So there is a promissory aspect in the works of creation. The works of creation also point forward to the day when mankind will have completed the work of dominion and will enter into rest. We have the implicit promise of an eschatological goal.

God's presence in the works of creation also has a *covenantal* character. His works have in mind the benefit of mankind, and so they reflect the covenantal commitments that he makes with mankind. The works of creation point forward to a final realization of covenantal intimacy in the new heaven and the new earth.

Finally, God's works in creation are works of kingship. Every act of creation shows the power of his kingly rule. This kingly rule then continues during later times, as God rules in harmony with the creation he has established.

28

God Appearing on
the Seventh Day

Next, let us consider what Genesis 2:1–3 says about the seventh day:

> And on the seventh day God finished his work that he had done, and
> he rested on the seventh day from all his work that he had done. So
> God blessed the seventh day and made it holy, because on it God
> rested from all his work that he had done in creation. (Gen. 2:2–3)

God's Work and Man's

In the light of later revelation to Israel, we understand that God's work
and rest form the pattern for man's work and rest. Man is made in the
image of God, and this status involves imitation of God, on the level of
man as a creature:

> "Remember the Sabbath day, to keep it holy. Six days you shall
> labor, and do all your work, but the seventh day is a Sabbath to the
> Lord your God. On it you shall not do any work, you, or your son,
> or your daughter, your male servant, or your female servant, or your
> livestock, or the sojourner who is within your gates. For in six days
> the Lord made heaven and earth, the sea, and all that is in them,
> and *rested on the seventh day*. Therefore the Lord blessed the Sab-
> bath day and made it holy." (Ex. 20:8–11)

For human life, the Sabbath day is "blessed" and "made . . . holy."

It is a special day not only for human rest but for celebrating the goodness and holiness of God. We may infer that the seventh day described in Genesis 2:2–3, on which God himself rested, is a special manifestation of the goodness, holiness, and intrinsic blessedness of God. Genesis 2:1–3 does not contain any specific wording that indicates that God manifested his presence in a visible form in a special way on the seventh day. But God showed his holiness and goodness on the seventh day. For God to manifest his character has similarities to a theophany where God manifests himself in a visible way.

If we pay attention to later reflections on the Sabbath, particularly in Hebrews 4:8–10, we understand that the Sabbath for man is a symbol of rest, pointing forward to the final rest in the time of consummation. Let us see how it works by comparing God's work with human work.

God worked for six days to create the world. His seventh day of rest is the time when he has "finished his work that he had done" (Gen. 2:2). God continues working in providentially governing the world. And he continues working in saving people from sin (John 5:17). So his rest is rest from "all his work that he had done *in creation*" (Gen. 2:3). He has finished creating the distinct spaces, heaven and sea and dry land. He has finished creating the kinds of "inhabitants" that will fill these spaces, namely plants and sea animals and birds and land animals, and finally man, who will rule over them all. God has entered into his rest.

Mankind now has a task, the task given in Genesis 1:28: "Be fruitful and multiply and fill the earth and subdue it, and have dominion over the fish of the sea and over the birds of the heavens and over every living thing that moves on the earth." Mankind will accomplish this task over a considerable period of time—which has now extended to thousands of years. Human beings are supposed to celebrate a *temporary* rest every night in sleep, and then a longer rest of a whole day on the Sabbath day. But then they go back to work. The narrative in Genesis 1–2 implies that the time will come when mankind's work is finished, just as God finished his work. Mankind will have been fruitful, and will have filled the earth with image-bearers (other human beings), and will have accomplished dominion. Then comes a consummate rest, when human beings enter into the rest from all their labors in multiplying and subduing the earth. This rest is the new heaven and new earth described in Revelation 21:1.

This program is made more complicated by the fall into sin in Genesis 3:1–7. It is through Christ as the "last Adam" (1 Cor. 15:45) that the plan for mankind is finally fulfilled. Through his resurrection and exaltation, Christ has already "subdued" and "filled" the earth, according to Ephesians 1:22–23. But the full working out of his triumph will take place when he returns.

The Manifestation of God's Glory

The special times of rest are also special times for the manifestation of God's glory. The consummation in the new heaven and new earth represents the time of consummate manifestation of God's glory in theophany:

> And the city has no need of sun or moon to shine on it, for the *glory of God* gives it light, and its lamp is the Lamb. (Rev. 21:23)

> They will *see his face*, and his name will be on their foreheads. And night will be no more. They will need no light of lamp or sun, for the Lord God will be their *light*, and they will reign forever and ever. (Rev. 22:4–5)

Short of this consummation, we also see the glory of God manifested in Christ through his exaltation, when he rests from his finished work on earth (John 19:30; Acts 2:33; Rom. 1:4). God's rest from his work of creation in Genesis 2:3 and man's temporary rest on weekly Sabbath days imitate and foreshadow the consummate rest. God is intensely present in all these special times.

The Theme of Cosmic Temple

The world that God made according to Genesis 1 is like a cosmic temple in which he dwells. Genesis 1 does not make the temple theme explicit, but the later revelations in Exodus and in Solomon's time compare the tabernacle and the temple to God's dwelling in heaven:

> "And see that you make them after the pattern for them, which is being shown you on the mountain." (Ex. 25:40)

> "But will God indeed dwell on the earth? Behold, heaven and the highest heaven cannot contain you; how much less this house that I have built!" (1 Kings 8:27)

> "And listen to the plea of your servant and of your people Israel, when they pray toward this place. And listen in *heaven your dwelling place*, and when you hear, forgive." (1 Kings 8:30)

They [things related to the tabernacle] serve a *copy and shadow of the heavenly things*. For when Moses was about to erect the tent, he was instructed by God, saying, "See that you make everything according to the pattern that was shown you on the mountain." (Heb. 8:5)

We can see that various details in the tabernacle and the Solomonic temple correspond to features of heaven and earth. The lampstand in the tabernacle is a copy of the lights of heaven; the table with the bread of the presence points to the manna that God gave as bread from heaven. The ark of the covenant is a footstool for God's throne in heaven (1 Chron. 28:2; Isa. 66:1). And the images of cherubim correspond to the real cherubim that surround God's throne in heaven. Various authors have seen this correspondence and have discussed the idea of creation as a cosmic temple.[1]

If the creation is a cosmic temple, we expect that, in analogy with the tabernacle and the Solomonic temple, it will be filled with the presence of God, as symbolized by the cloud of glory in Exodus 40:34–38 and 1 Kings 8:10–11. The cloud of God's presence filled the tabernacle after it was complete, and likewise the Solomonic temple. The seventh day of God's rest, in Genesis 2:2–3, is naturally interpreted as the time of "consecration" of the cosmic temple, parallel to the consecration of the tabernacle of Moses and the temple of Solomon. The Old Testament symbolism also has its parallel with the New Testament church. The church is consecrated and made holy by the special presence of God on the day of Pentecost (Acts 2:1–4).

In sum, in several respects the narrative in Genesis 2:1–3 concerning God's seventh day of rest proclaims the special presence of God, and this presence has associations with theophany.

---

1. G. K. Beale, *The Temple and the Church's Mission: A Biblical Theology of the Dwelling Place of God* (Downers Grove, IL: InterVarsity, 2004), 29–80; Meredith G. Kline, *Kingdom Prologue: Genesis Foundations for a Covenantal Worldview* (Overland Park, KS: Two Age, 2000), 49; Meredith G. Kline, *Images of the Spirit* (Grand Rapids, MI: Baker, 1980), 20–21; Vern S. Poythress, *The Shadow of Christ in the Law of Moses* (reprint; Phillipsburg, NJ: P&R, 1995), chapter 2.

29

God Appearing in the Creation of Man (Genesis 2:4–25)

Consider now the narrative of Genesis 2:4–25. This passage focuses on the creation of Adam and Eve and the formation of the garden in which they would live. God was present and manifested his glory in every aspect of his works of creation in Genesis 1:1–2:3. Because of the significant connections between creation and providence, we expect that God is present and manifests his glory in the works of providence as well, throughout the section Genesis 2:4–4:26 and beyond it. Genesis 2:4–25 has some overlap with Genesis 1:1–2:3. The creation of Adam and Eve makes more specific the general statement in Genesis 1:26–27 about the creation of mankind.

Several events in 2:4–25 stand out because they suggest a more intensive presence of God: the creation of Adam in 2:7, the creation of Eve in verses 21–22, the mention of the tree of life in 2:9, and the specific speech given by God in 2:16–17. We will consider them one by one.

The Presence of God in Creating Adam

God shows an intimacy with man in the way in which he creates Adam. He "*formed* the man . . . " and "*breathed* into his nostrils." Classical theologians have often observed that this language is "anthropomorphic." God does not have physical hands to form man; nor does he have a physical body with lungs and physical breath to breathe into his nostrils. So they infer that the language is colorful language, depicting divine action in human-like terms.

The observation about God not having a physical body is of course correct. But we must avoid depreciating the kind of description that God offers us. Certainly the depiction in Genesis 2:7 indicates the intimacy with which God interacts with the dust and with the man whom he is forming. This creation of man is to be something special, as we have already learned from Genesis 1:26–30. Moreover, the concreteness of the depiction is suggestive of theophany. Did God appear in physical form, perhaps even human form, in a manner analogous to later appearances such as in Genesis 18:2? A physical appearance is quite possible. It is suggested by the general theme of specially intimate presence, a presence that in later revelation often takes the form of a theophany. It is also suggested by the physicality of the depiction, as it involves forming and breathing. Language about forming and breathing may be used metaphorically, but the text does not definitely inform us that we have metaphors. The metaphor, if that is what we want to call it, may be the innate "metaphor" or analogy of theophanic revelation rather than a metaphor of nonphysical action analogous to physical formation and physical breathing. It seems that we *are* to infer that there was a physical formation of dust into human shape.

Whether God appeared in human form or in a cloud to bring about the formation is not indicated, but the resulting process of formation is indicated. Similarly, we are not told whether God used some physical means to generate the breath. But we are to think of a process of animation, of bringing to life, and that animation would include the beginning of physical breathing as well as the beginning of other dimensions of activity in the man whom God created.

So should we classify Genesis 2:7 as a theophany? As usual, it depends on how expansively we want to use the term *theophany*. And we have to make the qualification that Genesis 2:7 is a sparse account. It does not state with specificity the details of how God brought about the formation and the breathing. He *could* have done it by a literal theophany with special visual effects. But the text does not guarantee that there were visible effects, outside of the movement of dust and the movement of the man who had been formed. Genesis 2:7 counts as "theophany" only if we use the word expansively, to cover virtually any intensive presence of God.

The Presence of God in Creating Eve

Similar observations hold for the narrative describing the creation of Eve. Several physical effects were involved—a deep sleep coming on Adam, the removal of a rib, the making of the rib into a woman, and finally the bringing of the woman to the man. Any or all of these specific events may or may not have involved a specific visible manifestation in theophany. All of them involved an expression of the special presence of God. He manifested his goodness and his wisdom.

I understand the text to be describing physical events, rather than being merely a kind of parable to tell us about the relationship that men in general should have to women in general, or the relation that husbands should have to their wives. The events here are unique events with Adam and Eve. The descriptions in Genesis 2 are not just statements of general principles. Yet they do have implications for the subsequent conduct of human beings, because they hint at what makes men and women different and yet related.[1] In addition, they have theological connections with Christ, who is the last Adam and becomes the husband to his Bride, the church (1 Cor. 15:45–49; Eph. 5:25–27).

The fact that the events have a physical side suggests that they may have involved theophany. But the text does not give us more information. We do not know whether we have here a specific visible manifestation of God's presence or a more general and diffuse expression of his presence.

The Presence of God in the Tree of Life

The tree of life (Gen. 2:9) reflects the eternal life that God has in himself, and then the created reflection of that life that he grants to his people. We see a picture of eternal life especially in the New Jerusalem in Revelation 21:1–22:5. As many have suggested, the tree of life is like a "sacrament," signifying life, and capable of being the means of giving life, when its fruit is received in the context of communion with God, who is the source of life.

The tree of life is then an especially intensive expression of the presence of the God who is life and who gives life. It is not a "theophany" in the narrow sense, but it is a visible expression of the character of God. So it belongs to the less intensive analogues to theophany.

---

1. For a defense of the physical side of the narrative, see Vern S. Poythress, *Redeeming Science: A God-Centered Approach* (Wheaton, IL: Crossway, 2006), 249–251.

The Presence of God in Speaking to Adam

Genesis 2:16–17 records a specific speech that God gave to the man:

> And the LORD God commanded the man, saying, "You may surely eat of every tree of the garden, but of the tree of the knowledge of good and evil you shall not eat, for in the day that you eat of it you shall surely die."

As we observed with the speeches of God in Genesis 1, divine speech frequently takes place in the context of theophany. This speech may have theophanic accompaniment, but the text does not say. It is an appearance or manifestation of God in a broad sense.

The Garden of Eden as a Sanctuary

A number of interpreters have observed that certain hints in Genesis 2–3 and explicit statements in later revelation indicate that the garden of Eden was a kind of sanctuary, a special, holy space where God dwelt and where he undertook to have communion with mankind.[2] Most decisive is a passage from Ezekiel:

> [13] "You [the king of Tyre; 28:12] were in *Eden*, the *garden* of God;
>   every precious stone was your covering,
> sardius, topaz, and diamond,
>   beryl, onyx, and jasper,
> sapphire, emerald, and carbuncle;
>   and crafted in gold were your settings
>   and your engravings.
> On the day that you were created
>   they were prepared.
> [14] You were an anointed guardian *cherub*.
>   I placed you; you were on the *holy mountain* of God;
>   in the midst of the stones of fire you walked.
> [15] You were blameless in your ways
>   from the day you were created,
>   till unrighteousness was found in you.
> [16] In the abundance of your trade

---

2. E.g., Meredith G. Kline, *Images of the Spirit* (Grand Rapids, MI: Baker, 1980), 35–36; Meredith G. Kline, *Kingdom Prologue: Genesis Foundations for a Covenantal Worldview* (Overland Park, KS: Two Age, 2000); G. K. Beale, *The Temple and the Church's Mission: A Biblical Theology of the Dwelling Place of God* (Leicester, UK: Apollos; Downers Grove, IL: InterVarsity, 2004).

you were filled with violence in your midst, and you sinned;
so I cast you as a *profane* thing from the *mountain* of God,
    and I destroyed you, O guardian cherub,
    from the midst of the stones of fire." (Ezek. 28:13–16)

The passage is introduced as "a lamentation over the king of Tyre" (v. 12). But the king of Tyre is described in language reminiscent of Adam in Eden, and possibly behind Adam the figure of Satan and his fall. Without trying to untangle all the interpretive issues, we can see that the garden of Eden in verse 13 is identified as "the holy mountain of God" in verse 14. From this holy presence the king of Tyre or Adam or Satan is "cast" out as "profane" (v. 16).

The narrative in Genesis 2–3 confirms this picture in its final scene, in 3:24. Guardian cherubim bar the way into the garden and bar the way to the tree of life. These cherubim have an affinity to the cherubim figures in the curtain of the tabernacle and over the ark (Ex. 25:18–22; 26:1). There too the cherubim are guardians along the way to the presence of God.

We can conclude that the garden of Eden is to be understood as a sanctuary or holy place where God is uniquely present. And indeed we find him appearing in a special way in Genesis 3:8. The entire garden of Eden is thus associated with an intense presence of God. God designed it as a place where he could have communion with Adam and Eve. And the communion would have proceeded without a problem, except for the fall into sin.

Creation and Temple

The Bible as a whole also shows us a correlation between the triumph of God and the building and/or consecration of a temple dwelling place in honor of God's triumph.[3] Though not everything is made explicit in the narrative of creation in Genesis 1–2, we can see a pattern when we compare it to later redemptive episodes.

The triumph of God in the exodus from Egypt is followed by lawgiving and the building of the tabernacle at Mount Sinai. Likewise, the triumph of God in giving victory over surrounding nations is followed by the building of the Solomonic temple. The triumph of God in redeeming from exile is followed by the building of the second temple (after the

---

3. See Kline, *Images of the Spirit*, 37–38.

exile). The triumph of God in the crucifixion and resurrection of Christ goes together with the fact of Christ's physical body being a temple and the church being formed as a temple. The triumph of God in the new heaven and the new earth is accompanied by the New Jerusalem, which is also a new holy of holies (a perfect cube in shape).

In the light of this pattern, we can also add the narrative of creation as one more instance. The triumph of God in completing his work in creation is accompanied by the presence of three "sanctuaries." The cosmos itself is a cosmic temple. Second, the garden of Eden is a microcosmic reflection, a sanctuary at a particular place where God's presence is celebrated and adored. Finally, man made in the image of God is a special reflection of God in his holiness. As Ezekiel 28:12 puts it, "you were the signet of perfection." Man himself was to be a holy "dwelling place" for God's presence.

Covenant and the Presence of God

Another theme related to Genesis 2 is that of *covenant*. The word *covenant* does not occur in the book of Genesis until 6:18. But several features characteristic of later covenants occur in the initial situation with Adam. God has a personal relationship to Adam, and then to Eve. And there are binding expectations for both parties in this relationship. God always acts in accord with his own character as the righteous and good and merciful God (Ex. 34:6–7). Adam and Eve must refrain from eating from the tree of the knowledge of good and evil (Gen. 2:16–17). In addition, Adam and Eve and their descendants have a broader task to "fill the earth and subdue it" (1:28). The broader implication of their nature as being made "in the image of God" implies that they should be imitators of God. So, by implication, the entire moral law is relevant to them.

So how do biblical covenants by God relate to the appearances of God? Key events in establishing and confirming covenants often involve a visible appearance of God. But even when they do not, they involve God's voice, which brings to bear his presence and in this way is analogous to a literal visible appearance. Covenants express God's presence, and are therefore closely related to theophany, as we saw in chapters 1 and 17. Covenant commitment establishes a permanent form of God's presence by giving people God's promises, and we can therefore see covenants as enduring forms of divine *appearance* or *theophany*, in a broad sense.

30

God Appearing in the Fall (Genesis 3:1–24)

Now let us consider the theme of God's presence and his appearing in Genesis 3:1–24. The theme functions in several ways.

God's Presence through the Covenantal Commitments in Creation

First, God is present in the events of Genesis 3 by covenantal commitment. As we observed in the previous chapter, when God has established a covenantal relation, he continues to be present with those to whom he is covenantally committed. Adam and Eve continue to experience the presence of God, because they are obligated by his moral law and by his specific commandment concerning the tree of the knowledge of good and evil. His words follow them at all times and in all places, and his word is itself a manifestation of his presence.

Satan Counterfeiting God's Presence

Second, God's presence in this chapter is imitated in *counterfeit* form by Satan. The theme of counterfeiting is especially evident in the book of Revelation, where the triad consisting of the dragon, the beast, and the false prophet (Rev. 16:13) represents a counterfeit opposite to the true Trinity of God the Father, God the Son, and God the Holy Spirit (see chapter 18).[1] Once we have seen the theme in Revelation, it becomes easier to see that Satan uses the strategy of counterfeiting throughout the history of the spiritual warfare between God and Satan.

In Genesis 3:1–5 Satan produces a counterfeit to God in several ways. First, the serpent that appears to Eve represents a counterfeit to theophany. I think that there was a visible serpent that talked to Eve. But animals do not normally talk, and ancient people knew this as well as moderns do. Something highly unusual is going on in Genesis 3:1–5, and the unusual events show that the serpent is not merely an ordinary snake, but has become the mouthpiece of a hideous evil. That hideous evil is further defined and delineated in later revelation—it is Satan, "that ancient serpent" (Rev. 12:9).

The point to notice here, with respect to the theme of counterfeiting, is that Satan is a spirit being, but that he takes on visible appearance in the snake. This taking on of visible appearance is a counterfeit—an evil, twisted imitation—of God's appearing in theophany or in the incarnation.

Satan not only appears, but he *speaks*. His speech is a counterfeit speaking, a perverse imitation of God's covenantal speech to Adam. And indeed, the counterfeit is all the closer, because the contents of Satan's speech quote pieces of God's speech, and yet they pointedly oppose God's speech and attempt to introduce confusion and doubt as to what are God's intentions. "You will not surely die," Satan says (Gen. 3:4). This assertion directly contradicts God's warning, "You shall surely die" (2:17). Satan also offers a more elaborate competing narrative, giving a counterfeit explanation about God's intentions and about the effects of eating from the tree: "For God knows that when you eat of it your eyes will be opened, and you will be like God, knowing good and evil" (Gen. 3:5). Satan offers in effect a counterfeit covenant, with a counterfeit history and counterfeit sanctions. In this case, the sanctions are the alleged advantages that Eve will receive by eating: "your eyes will be opened, and you will be like God, knowing good and evil."

Satan is in the business of trying to replace true worship and true allegiance with a counterfeit worship and counterfeit allegiance. It is as if he had said, "Worship yourself, and worship my voice, and give al-

---

1. Vern S. Poythress, "Counterfeiting in the Book of Revelation as a Perspective on Non-Christian Culture," *Journal of the Evangelical Theological Society* 40/3 (1997): 411–418, http://www.frame-poythress.org/counterfeiting-in-the-book-of-revelation-as-a-perspective-on-non-christian-culture/; Vern S. Poythress, *The Returning King: A Guide to the Book of Revelation* (Phillipsburg, NJ: P&R, 2000), 16–22.

legiance to my promises rather than God's." Satan exerts his presence, including visible presence, in order to displace the presence of God in the mind and life of Eve. The Satanic strategy is all the more horrifying because it is near to the truth. Satan is imitating aspects of God's ways of appearing, and yet he is blasphemous in his rebellion against God and in defaming God's name.

The Appearing of God in Judgment

Next, consider the way the narrative describes God's judgment on Adam and Eve. It begins with a note about an especially intense presence of God in the garden:

> And they heard the sound of the LORD God walking in the garden in the cool of the day, and the man and his wife hid themselves from the presence of the LORD God among the trees of the garden. (Gen. 3:8)

Does the presence of the Lord God constitute a theophany? As usual, we have to deal with a sparse description. The text does not clearly say one way or the other whether there was a special *visible* appearance, nor, if so, what *kind* of appearance. We clearly should think in terms of a localized special presence of God, manifested by sound—"the sound of the LORD God walking." God was intensely present, in order to meet with Adam and Eve. Adam and Eve "hid themselves," probably implying that they had some rough sense as to the location of the presence of the LORD God. They moved away from this presence and away from any location from which they supposed they might be visible to this presence.

Of course the whole attempt was futile. The Lord knew them, where they were, and what they had done. He interrogates, "Where are you?" and "Have you eaten . . . ?" He issues the questions as part of a judicial process to convict the offenders. It is a mistake to see the questions as merely seeking information. The questions are designed to convict the guilty. This judicial process is one aspect of covenantal responsibility. Violators of God's covenant receive condemnatory judgment. And this judgment comes from God personally. He becomes intensely present as part of the process. In later revelation, we see instances of judgment where his presence takes visible form.

By analogy with the later instances of judgment, it is easy to infer that a visible presence was there in the garden. The language of "walking" in 3:8 suggests a man-like appearance.[2] But we must as usual respect the fact that analogies are not the same as identities. We can also see analogies between this case of judgment and later instances of God's judgment, instances that include a special visible manifestation. In the context of the entire canon, the text here invites us to see this one case of judicial process as analogous to cases like Daniel 7:9–10 and Revelation 20:11–15, which involve a solemn weighing of evidence and pronouncement of judgment from God's throne.

The Possibility of Theophany in "the Cool of the Day"

Are we to see some special meaning in the phrase that the ESV translates, "the cool of the day" (so also KJV, ASV, NASB)? The Hebrew word *ruach* (רוּחַ), translated "cool," can mean "spirit," "wind," or "breeze," as marginal notes in some Bible versions indicate.[3] The expression "wind of the day" probably designates the time of day in the afternoon or evening when a wind regularly springs up.[4]

Meredith G. Kline, however, finds in the verse a reference to a Spirit theophany (in accord with his interpretation of Gen. 1:2).[5] He translates the phrase as "the Spirit of the Day." The "Day" in view is the day of God's judgment—the day of the Lord. I agree that the context introduces a scene with a judicial component, and that the reference to the sound of the Lord God walking has affinities with theophany. But, as usual, the presence of analogies and associations does not necessarily lead to a pure identification.

God is especially present on each of the six days of Genesis 1, and then climactically on the seventh day. The seventh day has a correlation with the consummation of history as the final day for rest for mankind. And the final day is also the day for evaluation and for judgment. Every

---

2. In the context of theophany, Ezekiel 1:13 uses the Hebrew verb for walking to describe the movement of fire: "like the appearance of torches *moving to and fro*." By analogy with Ezekiel 1:13, should we picture for ourselves a fire theophany in Genesis 3:8? But in Genesis 3:8 the subject of the verb is a personal being, "the LORD God," rather than fire. "Walking" is the more natural translation for the verb, and suggests a human-like theophany rather than a fire theophany.

3. HCSB and NRSV have in the text, "at the time of the evening breeze."

4. C. John Collins, *Genesis 1–4: A Linguistic, Literary, and Theological Commentary* (Phillipsburg, NJ: P&R, 2006), 151n8; Victor P. Hamilton, *The Book of Genesis Chapters 1–17* (Grand Rapids, MI: Eerdmans, 1990), 192; Gordon J. Wenham, *Genesis 1–15*, Word Biblical Commentary, vol. 1 (Waco, TX: Word, 1987), 76.

5. Meredith G. Kline, "Primal Parousia," *Westminster Theological Journal* 40 (1978): 245–280; Meredith G. Kline, *Images of the Spirit* (Grand Rapids, MI: Baker, 1980), 97–131; also Jeffrey Jay Niehaus, *God at Sinai: Covenant and Theophany in the Bible and the Ancient Near East.* (Grand Rapids, MI: Zondervan, 1995), 155–159. For further discussion of Kline's view, see appendix C of the present work. On Genesis 1:2, see appendix B.

day in history anticipates this final day either more closely or more remotely. Thus, the day in Genesis 3:8 turns out to be a day of God's judgment. So, yes, it also anticipates final judgment. But we need not overread Genesis 3:8. It does not say "the day of the Lord," but rather merely "the day," that is, the same day on which Adam and Eve sinned by eating the fruit.

Likewise, wind or breeze has an association with the Spirit of God[6] and with thunderstorm theophanies. But that does not mean that the starting meaning in Genesis 3:8 is "Spirit of the Day." Rather, as commentaries have recognized, the phrase indicates the time of day, "in the cool of the day." The associations with theophany spring primarily from the judicial context and the description of the "sound of the LORD God walking."

God's Presence in Covenantal Promise (Genesis 3:15)

God's judgments pronounced in Genesis 3:14–19 are not wholly negative in character. They also include a promise: "I will put enmity between you and the woman, and between your offspring and her offspring; he shall bruise your head, and you shall bruise his heel" (Gen. 3:15). This promise has a key role, because, in the light of later revelation, we know that the "offspring" who "shall bruise your head" is ultimately a reference to Christ. The rest of Genesis begins to trace the line of this offspring, through Seth, Noah, and Abram. God is with his people through his promises until the time when the promise is fulfilled in Christ (Gal. 4:4–5). He is present to preserve the line of offspring from the time of Eve all the way down to the time of Christ's coming in the flesh. In Christ, God manifests his presence and the reality of his promises climactically: "For all the promises of God find their Yes in him [Christ]" (2 Cor. 1:20).

The promises of God fit into the context of covenant. As we observed, the specific word *covenant* does not occur in the Bible until Genesis 6:18, but the concept of a binding personal relation between God and his people is expressed throughout, especially in the form of the promise of Genesis 3:15. In this promise God commits himself to his people, to save them and to bring a remedy for sin, and to heal, undo, and reverse the various effects of the fall. God is present with his people

---

6. Bruce K. Waltke with Cathi J. Fredricks, *Genesis: A Commentary* (Grand Rapids, MI: Zondervan, 2001), 92.

through his promise. The promise is like a continuing deposit, left after the temporary time in which God appears with special intensity to confront Adam and Eve and the serpent.

Guarding the Way to the Tree of Life

Genesis 3:21–24 contains some final notes about the presence of God. It is through the authority, control, and *presence* of God as Lord that he executes the judicial sentence:

> [21] And the LORD God made for Adam and for his wife garments of skins and clothed them.
> [22] Then the LORD God said, "Behold, the man has become like one of us in knowing good and evil. Now, lest he reach out his hand and take also of the tree of life and eat, and live forever—"
> [23] therefore the LORD God sent him out from the garden of Eden to work the ground from which he was taken. [24] He drove out the man, and at the east of the garden of Eden he placed the cherubim and a flaming sword that turned every way to guard the way to the tree of life. (Gen. 3:21–24)

God's special presence appears first of all when he makes garments (v. 21). Then the Lord God sends Adam away: "the LORD God sent him out from the garden of Eden" (v. 23). This language again suggests a special presence, though as usual it does not tell us whether there was a literal visible presence in theophany. The same action is expressed yet more vigorously in the next verse: "He drove out the man" (v. 24).

Genesis 3:24 has connections with theophany. It mentions the cherubim and the tree of life. The cherubim, as we have observed, are heavenly creatures that appear in the context of theophany (such as Ezekiel 1 and Revelation 4). They are guardians of the presence of God, which is represented by the tree of life. Adam and Eve by their sin have profaned themselves and disqualified themselves from communion with God. They are barred from God's presence. God's presence is represented in Genesis 3:24 in a visible way through the "sanctuary" of Eden, in which is the tree of life. It is as if we are invited with Adam and Eve to cast a final longing glance backward, with regret for what has been lost.

And yet, in view of the promise in Genesis 3:15, not all is lost forever. The tree of life reappears in Revelation 22:2. Communion with God, and therefore also communion with the life of God, is restored through the work of Christ. In this respect, Genesis 3:24 gives us a glance at not only what we have lost but also what will be regained, and in far more glorious form. Revelation 22:1–5 does not literally return us to Eden and the original test for Adam; rather, it moves us forward in the purpose of God, to enter the consummation. The glance back to Eden is indirectly a glance forward to the consummation. And since the consummation is the consummation of the presence of God in theophany, the barred way to Eden also resonates with the theme of God's appearing.

31

God Appearing in Two Lines of Offspring

Now let us consider Genesis 4–5. Chapters 4–5 develop the story of two lines of offspring, the godly line of Abel and Seth, and the ungodly line of Cain. God is providentially present in the whole of history, including this history.

God's Presence with the Godly Line

In the light of later revelation, we can also infer that God gives a special presence in blessing to the people who are his. He providentially cares for the line of offspring through whom the Messiah, the offspring of the woman, will come.

But we must respect the limits of the information that Genesis 4–5 provides. Genesis 5 provides the names of intermediate generations, leading to Noah. This list follows the line of the offspring of promise, leading to Christ. Included are commendations of a few of the people in the list, but we cannot be sure that all of the people in the list were godly in character.

Who is commended? Noah especially:

But Noah found *favor* in the eyes of the LORD.
These are the generations of Noah. Noah was a *righteous* man, *blameless* in his generation. Noah *walked with* God. (Gen. 6:8–9)

We also find a commendation of Enoch (Gen. 5:22–24), an expression of faith and hope by Lamech (vv. 28–29), and a note concerning the time of Seth and Enosh: "At that time people began to call upon the name of the LORD" (4:26). In the light of later revelation, we may infer that God was especially present with these individuals not only to bless them but also to produce the faith and righteousness that led to blessings. Yet only a few details are provided by the passage itself.

God's Presence with the Line of Cain

God is also present among those who rebel against his ways. He is present to curse and to bring consequences for sin. He is also present in common grace, mitigating the consequences of sin. We can see a few instances of both.

God speaks to warn Cain in Genesis 4:6. The warning represents a special presence in common grace. Many later cases of God's speech come in the context of a theophanic appearance, as we have noted. Did God appear to Cain in a theophany? We are not told. God's speech to Cain is one of many instances where we do not know the details. But we may say that we have an expression of God's presence, his "appearing" in a broad sense.

Then God confronts Cain after he has killed his brother (Gen. 4:9–15). The confrontation is judicial in character, and therefore has a thematic connection with biblical theophanies for judgment. God speaks, but once again we do not know whether his appearing to Cain involved a special visual element. God also "put a mark on Cain, lest any who found him should attack him" (Gen. 4:15). God is specially present to produce the mark. God expresses his presence in common grace, by mitigating the judgment.

The subsequent narrative mentions a number of generations of descendants from Cain (4:17–24). Cain receives protection from the Lord (v. 15), and his life is preserved. He also has descendants. These events show God's undeserved mercy on him. God is present to mitigate the curse of death.

Cultural Developments

We also see in the narrative the mention of a number of cultural activities—building a city (Gen. 4:17), dwelling in tents (v. 20), husbanding livestock (v. 20), making and playing musical instruments (v. 21), and practicing metallurgy (v. 22). Even though these developments come in the context of the line of Cain, cultural activities should be seen as positive in themselves, an expression of one aspect of the rich capabilities that God gave mankind in creation. Sinful human beings twist the meaning and direction of development of human projects, but the power and structure for the projects are still due to the God of creation.

The human projects express two sides. Since they are founded in the resources of creation and the creation of man in the image of God, they express and reflect the character of God and manifest his presence. Since they are twisted by sin, they express rebellion against God. But even rebellion has its meaning in relation to God against whom the rebellion takes place; rebellion has meaning only in opposition to standards for righteousness and truth that derive from God.

Marriage and Children

We see the same duality when we look at the record of marriage and children in Genesis 4. Marriage and family are intrinsically good, as ordained by God. But sin perverts both.

Marriage, the begetting of children, and their rearing all have a foundation in the creational order established by God (Gen. 2:24–25; 5:1–3). God carefully and specifically designs marriage in the narrative of Genesis 2:18–25, in accordance with what is "good" for man (v. 18). The begetting and rearing of children is implicit in the mandate in Genesis 1:28 to "be fruitful and multiply." It takes specific form in the description in 5:1–3:

> [1] When God created man, he made him in the likeness of God. [2] Male and female he created them, and he blessed them and named them Man when they were created. [3] When Adam had lived 130 years, he fathered a son in his own likeness, after his image, and named him Seth.

In verse 3, Adam "fathered a son" in harmony with the original, archetypal act of God, who "made him in the likeness of God" (v. 1). Thus every case where a man fathers a son reflects and expresses the character of God, who created Adam with the status of son (see Luke 3:38).

In Genesis 4 we can also see the corruption of marriage and family by sin. Cain murders his own brother. He has corrupted the family, which should be characterized by love. In 4:17 Cain has a wife who bears a son, Enoch. Wife and child are intrinsically good gifts from the Lord (Prov. 18:22; Ps. 127:3–5). But it looks like there is a hint of sinful aggrandizement of self and family in the fact that Cain named the city after his son, Enoch (Gen. 4:17).

True power and fame come from God. We should seek God's approval and give glory to his power. But sinful human beings desire to become small-scale gods themselves. This desire is a perversion of the original pattern of man made in the image of God. Cain wants power and fame for *himself*. He begins on a smaller scale the same project that Babel undertook on a larger scale, to make himself a name:

> Then they said, "Come, let us build ourselves a city and a tower with its top in the heavens, and let us make a *name* for ourselves, lest we be dispersed over the face of the whole earth." (Gen. 11:4)

God judges the project of Babel. In contrast to his negative judgment on Babel, he makes a positive promise to Abram; he promises to give Abram a name: "And I will make of you a great nation, and I will bless you and make your name great, so that you will be a blessing" (Gen. 12:2).

Abram's name will be great, not because by his own might he has overseen and accomplished the building of a city or a high tower, but because of the gift of the grace of God. The subsequent narrative shows that Abram's name becomes great because of the presence of the greatness of the name of God. God places his own name on Abram, when he says, "I am the God of Abraham" (Gen. 26:24; 28:13; etc.).

The name of God reveals the character of God, and so manifests God and his presence. In longing for fame in the wrong way, Cain twisted the original purpose of God for naming and becoming famous. Even in the twisting, Cain shows that he cannot escape being an imitator of God. But he is doing it in the wrong way.

We also see continuations of the blessings of marriage and family in the subsequent generations of Cain, in Genesis 4:18–22. But there are corruptions. "Lamech took two wives" (v. 19). He deviates from the pattern of Adam and Eve. Marriage as designed by God expresses on a human level intimate personal communion, and the original personal communion is with God, among the persons of the Trinity, and then communion between God and man. God is present in the world in common grace through the blessing of marriage. But his presence is in tension with sinful corruption.

Vengeance

Finally, the discussion of the line of Cain ends with Lamech boasting of vengeance. Proverbs 20:22 and Romans 12:19 indicate that vengeance belongs to the Lord. He is a God of justice, and he is the judge of all the world. He delegates authority for retribution to human authorities in government, according to Romans 12:19–13:4, but private individuals should not take vengeance into their own hands. Lamech rightly sees a parallel between himself and Cain (Gen. 4:24). But he misconstrues the parallel by putting himself in the role of God, who himself promised vengeance in the case of Cain by giving him the mark (v. 15).

Thus Lamech's boast about vengeance has the duality that we have already seen. The very idea of vengeance depends on God's justice. According to the principle of the creation order, Lamech's interest in vengeance derives from the God of vengeance, in whose image Lamech has been made. But Lamech perverts God's standard of justice by seizing a God-like prerogative for himself. He is in effect expressing the desire to *be* God—a counterfeit form of reflecting God. Even in this counterfeit he indirectly reflects God and the inescapability of the presence of God's justice.

The Birth of Seth

At the birth of Seth, God is specially present in several respects. First, as we have observed, "children are a heritage from the LORD" (Ps. 127:3). Any child that is conceived comes from the Lord, as a gift of his power, presence, and lordship.

Second, Eve explicitly recognizes that she has received a gift from God:

> . . . she said, "*God has appointed* for me another offspring instead of Abel, for Cain killed him." (Gen. 4:25)

Third, we see in the entrance of Seth a faint instance of the principle of substitution. Until the consummation, it is not yet time for God to bring about the general resurrection of the dead. But God has appointed that there would be small-scale imitations of the reversal of sin. If Abel is not yet resurrected, the next best thing is for him to have a replacement—a substitute. And this substitute is Seth. Eve sees it: "another offspring *instead of* Abel." The general principle of substitution will have its ultimate fulfillment when Christ comes as the last Adam.

He is then the substitute for Adam, who rebelled, because he is perfectly obedient and refuses rebellion. He is the substitute for sinners when he dies as sin-bearer:

> He himself *bore our sins* in his body on the tree, that we might die to sin and live to righteousness. By his wounds you have been healed. (1 Pet. 2:24)

> For our sake he *made him to be sin* who knew no sin, so that in him we might become the righteousness of God. (2 Cor. 5:21)

We conclude that when God gave Seth to Eve, he expressed beforehand by foreshadowing what he would do with the coming of Christ. Christ would be the substitute for us. So Seth is a shadow of the theophanic work of God in Christ. He manifests the grace of God that comes to full flower and fruition when Christ comes.

Now consider again what Genesis 5:3 says about the fathering of Seth. We already gave attention to the way in which Adam fathering Seth in Genesis 5:3 reflects the work of God in fathering Adam. And the work of God in fathering Adam has its archetype in the role of God the Father in fathering ("begetting") God the Son as an eternal act (not in time). God the Son is the ultimate manifestation or "appearing" of God. Adam is an "appearance" or manifestation of the presence of God through man as a creature. And so is Seth, who is an image of his father, Adam.

The Genealogy of Genesis 5

The general pattern of the genealogy in Genesis 5 also manifests the character of God and his presence. On the one hand, death is pervasive. On the other hand, so is the continuation of life.

First, there is death. "And he *died*" is one of the refrains. God is present to maintain faithfulness to his covenantal words, which said that death would follow sin (Gen. 2:17; 3:19). The repeated occurrence of death underlines the seriousness of God's words, the seriousness of his justice, and the black-and-white contrast between life in the garden and life under the curse.

Next, there is life. The generations continue to succeed one another: "When Seth had *lived* . . . " (Gen. 5:6); and "Seth *lived* after he fathered Enosh . . . " (v. 7). People continue to have children, fulfilling the plan of

God for them to "be fruitful and multiply" (1:28). The genealogy also supplies numbers of years, indicating that the men in question lived long lives in comparison with the decreasing numbers of years after the flood of Noah. It is as if some blessings of life still trailed tenuously out of Adam's previous access to the tree of life. God was present with the blessing of life. The patriarchs are manifestations of God's life-giving power.

Enoch

Now consider Enoch (Gen. 5:21–24). Enoch stands out, because he did not die: "Enoch walked with God, and he was not, for God took him" (v. 24). The language of this verse reflects associations with theophany. God met Enoch during his life: "Enoch walked with God" (v. 22). Did God appear visibly to Enoch? The text does not say explicitly. But God gave personal intimacy to Enoch, and the experience of "walking with" was reminiscent of theophany. At the end of his time on earth, "God took him" (v. 24). In the context of the whole canon, we naturally think of Elijah, whom God took up to heaven in a whirlwind (2 Kings 2:11). The parallel is real. We do not know the details of what happened in the case of Enoch, but there are certainly associations with the case of Elijah, where there are definite visible phenomena.

32

God Appearing in the Flood

Next let us consider the narrative of the flood in Genesis 6–9. God acts in judgment against evil. This judgment foreshadows the final day of judgment, as 2 Peter 3 confirms by comparing the two:

> For they deliberately overlook this fact, that the heavens existed long ago, and the earth was formed out of water and through water by the word of God, and that by means of these the world that then existed was deluged with water and *perished*. But by the same word the heavens and earth that now exist are stored up for fire, being kept until *the day of judgment* and destruction of the ungodly. (2 Pet. 3:5–7)

There are several ways in which we see, in the flood, an especially intense manifestation of the presence of God.

The Multiplication of Evil

First, God's character is reflected in a counterfeit way by the multiplication of evil in Genesis 6:1–5. God gave to mankind the task of being fruitful and multiplying (Gen. 1:28). Now that human nature is twisted by sin, that multiplication can consist in a multiplication of evil. As we saw earlier, the ability of human beings to reproduce and have children reflects an archetype in God, namely that God created man in his image. Multiplication among human beings reflects in a positive way the original creativity of God. Being fruitful and multiplying in evil still manifests mankind's character as created in the image of God; but now that nature is twisted toward evil and sin.

Evaluation and Pronouncement of Judgment

Second, God shows his lordship by evaluating human conduct and condemning it. These acts manifest God's presence in judgment. They may include an actual theophany, but the text does not give us details. It says that "the LORD *saw* that the wickedness of man was great in the earth" (Gen. 6:5). The picture here is analogous to later evaluations, when the Lord "came down to see" Babel (Gen. 11:5) and when the two angels went to evaluate the conduct of Sodom and Gomorrah: "I will go down to see . . . " (Gen. 18:21). This latter case involves specific visible phenomena, in the human-like appearance of the Lord and the two angels. Genesis 6:5 involves a presence and an activity of the Lord that is analogous to a visible appearance, but where we do not know the details.

The Lord also speaks in judgment:

> Then the LORD said, "My Spirit shall not abide in man forever, for he is flesh: his days shall be 120 years." (Gen. 6:3)

> So the LORD said, "I will blot out man whom I have created from the face of the land, man and animals and creeping things and birds of the heavens, for I am sorry that I have made them." (v. 7)

Like the other cases of God's speech, these acts of speaking manifest a special presence of the Lord. They are theophany-like, but we do not know whether a special visible phenomenon accompanied them. These manifestations of God show God as a God of justice, who executes justice throughout history, and climactically brings justice through the cross of Christ and then through the consummate judgment of the last day (Rev. 20:11–15).

The Instructions to Noah

God also comes to Noah and instructs him to build the ark. Here we find another case of divine speech, which may or may not have been accompanied by visible phenomena. The key word *covenant* occurs for the first time in Genesis 6:18: "I will establish *my covenant* with you." The covenantal relation includes the speech, the power, and the presence of God. Through Noah the benefits of the covenant extend also to his wife, his sons, his sons' wives, and the animals in the ark (vv. 18–20).

The Flood Itself

The flood itself foreshadows the final judgment. The final judgment takes place through theophany (Rev. 20:11–15). This preliminary judgment in the flood also manifests the presence of God, but not quite with the same intensity. It shows not only the power of God but also his holiness in reaction to sin. The use of water for judgment has associations with the waters of the Red Sea, where God will later act through a visible appearance. Wind also occurs (Gen. 8:1), with a loose association with the wind occurring in some later theophanies.

The flood means not only destruction of wickedness but also salvation for Noah and his family and his animals. As many Bible interpreters have observed, the flood returns the world to a state of watery chaos, similar to the waters that covered the earth in Genesis 1:2. After the waters have covered everything, God brings about a return of order: the dry land is separated from the waters again (Gen. 8:3); the plants grow (v. 11); the animals are released from the ark and begin to multiply (v. 19). Mankind is given dominion (9:2–4). God manifests his grace in bringing re-creation. God is present in these events, as we may infer by analogy with his presence in the original acts of creation in Genesis 1. God underlines his comprehensive control over the world of nature by giving the promise that there will not be another comprehensive flood, and he confirms this promise with the sign of the rainbow (9:13–17).

The Post-Flood Covenant with Noah

God also makes a covenant with Noah, the effects of which extend to all of Noah's descendants (Gen. 9:1–17). The covenant expresses the presence of God in blessing. This blessing extends even to unbelievers in later generations. It expresses common grace.

The covenant also includes a visible sign, the rainbow (Gen. 9:12–17):

> And God said, "This is the sign of the covenant that I make between me and you and every living creature that is with you, for all future generations: I have set my *bow* in the cloud, and it shall be a sign of the covenant between me and the earth. . . . " God said to Noah,

"This is the *sign of the covenant* that I have established between me and all flesh that is on the earth."

Interpreters discuss whether at this point the rainbow is an utterly new phenomenon, or whether God appoints a previously existing visible phenomenon to have a special covenantal meaning, like the bread in the Lord's Supper. Whichever is the case, the rainbow manifests the presence of God and his commitment to his promise.

33

God Appearing at Babel

Now we turn to the portion of Genesis describing the events after the flood, up through the genealogy of Abram in Genesis 11:10–32. Prominent among them is the episode of the tower of Babel (Gen. 11:1–9). But, in addition to Babel, God manifests his special presence at a number of points.

Noah's Life after the Flood

We begin with the description in Genesis 9:18–28 of the life of Noah and his sons after the flood.

At an early point, Noah tends the soil and plants a vineyard (9:20). We can say concerning his work what we earlier observed about cultural endeavors in the line of Cain. Cultural endeavors are part of the human task, reflecting the plan of God and the capabilities and calling of man made in the image of God. God reflects his character in human endeavor.

The narrative continues with Noah getting drunk. Many cultures embellish the stories of their "founding fathers" out of admiration. The Bible does not hide from us the failings of the patriarchs who were the founding fathers leading to Israel. God manifests his grace by continuing to deal in faithfulness with the patriarchs.

On learning of the actions of his sons in response to his drunkenness, Noah makes a speech, recorded in Genesis 9:25–27. Despite the background in Noah's drunkenness, this speech is prophetic, as later events show. God speaks through Noah in prophecy. God's speaking is a form of his presence. This instance is particularly noteworthy because it is the first recorded instance where God uses a human being as an instrument for prophecy. The use of a human intermediary foreshadows Christ, who is the final prophet and who is human as well as divine (Heb. 1:1–3). It also manifests the grace of God, in that God is willing to use a sinful human being as his spokesman.

The Genealogy of the Nations (Genesis 10:1–32)

Next we encounter the genealogy of the nations in Genesis 10:1–32. This genealogy repeats the points made in the genealogies of Genesis 4–5. God is active in maintaining human life, manifesting his life-giving power and his grace. The principle of multiplication imitates and reflects God's original creation of man in his image. Death also continues in the world, in fulfillment of the curse from Genesis 2:17 and 3:17, but here it is implied rather than emphasized.

This genealogy sets the stage for the life of Abraham. In the initial call of Abram in Genesis 12:1–3, God already makes it explicit that Abram will be a source of blessing to the nations: "and in you *all the families* of the earth shall be blessed" (v. 3). God's covenant with Abraham is a manifestation of his presence to Abraham. But subordinately it also manifests his presence toward the nations, whom he includes in the implications of the covenant. In the light of this inclusion, we can infer a covenantal care for the nations during the previous generations, as delineated in Genesis 10. Genesis 10 is not just a record but by implication a reminder that God is at work among the nations. It is he who orchestrated the multiplication of nations and their dispersion (Gen. 10:5, 25, 32). This dispersion of the nations links itself to the account of Babel in 11:1–9. The events at Babel are one of the chief causes of the dispersion. The details given concerning Babel underline the role of the hand of God in creating the nations with "their clans, their *languages*, their lands, and their nations" (10:31).

The Tower of Babel

The tower of Babel (11:1–9) involves the special presence of God in a notable way. The plans of the people (vv. 3–4) illustrate the capabilities of man made in the image of God. Man still imitates God in planning and constructing, even though the plans and their execution are twisted by sin. But at the center of the story is the judicial activity of God:

> And the Lord *came down* to see the city and the tower, which the children of man had built. And the Lord said, "Behold, they are one people, and they have all one language, and this is only the beginning of what they will do. And nothing that they propose to do will now be impossible for them. Come, let us *go down* and there confuse their language, so that they may not understand one another's speech." So the Lord dispersed them from there over the face of all the earth, and they left off building the city. (Gen. 11:5–8)

Twice the narrative speaks about the Lord "coming down" or "going down." The language implies a special presence in specific locations, and therefore suggests theophany. God's inspection of the situation is reminiscent of Genesis 1, where God pronounces things "good." It also calls to mind God's inspection of the situation before the flood (Gen. 6:5), and his inspection of Sodom and Gomorrah in Genesis 18:21. But as usual, the description is sparse. We do not know whether there were visible phenomena accompanying God's special inspection of the tower building.

God executes judgment on Babel. This judgment prefigures the final judgment, which occurs in the context of theophany. The judgment on Babel anticipates the judgment executed on Babylon in Revelation 17:1–19:3.

The Genealogy of Shem

The next piece in the Genesis narrative is the genealogy of Shem (Gen. 11:10–26) and the genealogy of Terah (vv. 27–32) introducing the life of Abraham. This genealogy follows the line of promise, which will lead to the offspring of the woman, the Messiah (cf. 3:15). God is providentially present with this line, in order to establish his purpose of redemption, year by year, generation by generation, until its climactic fulfillment in Christ.

No outstanding special events are recorded in these verses, but the genealogy of Shem, like the earlier genealogy of Adam (chapter 5), contains the themes of life, of death, and of human reproduction. All of these manifest the character of God. Human life reflects the archetypal life of God. Human death reflects the holiness and righteousness of God, who has pronounced the curse of death as punishment for sin. It also reflects the faithfulness of God to his earlier pronouncement of curse. Human reproduction is reproduction in the image of God, reflecting the original creation of man in the image of God.

34

God Appearing to Abraham

Next let us consider the appearances of God and the presence of God in the life of Abraham (Gen. 11:27–25:11). The genealogical section focusing on Abraham begins in Genesis 11:27 with the genealogy of Terah (vv. 27–32). God is providentially present with the line of promise leading from Noah to Abram, and from Abram to the people of Israel and to David.

The Call of Abram

The first special encounter between God and Abram is recorded in Genesis 12:1–3. God calls him from the land of his origin to the Land of Promise. God speaks to Abram. This speech has associations with theophanies, which are often the occasion for the most significant speeches of God. This first speech to Abram may or may not have been accompanied by visible phenomena of theophany.

God's Covenant with Abraham

The first speech is *covenantal* in character. The text in Genesis 12 does not use the specific word for covenant, but the commitment that God makes goes together with later expansions of his commitment that are specifically called a covenant:

> On that day the Lord made a *covenant* with Abram, saying, "To your offspring I give this land, from the river of Egypt to the great river, the river Euphrates." (Gen. 15:18)

"Behold, my *covenant* is with you, and you shall be the father of a multitude of nations." (Gen. 17:4)

God's covenant with Abraham involves a commitment to be with him continually, and it extends to his offspring as well:

"And I will establish *my covenant* between me and you and *your offspring* after you throughout their generations for an everlasting covenant, to be *God to you* and to your offspring after you." (Gen. 17:7)

God said, "No, but Sarah your wife shall bear you a son, and you shall call his name Isaac. I will establish *my covenant* with him as an everlasting covenant for his offspring after him. (v. 19)

God's Presence

God's speech in the form of promise accompanies Abram and his offspring. So God himself accompanies Abram through this speech. It is fitting that the founding events for God's covenant should involve an intensive presence of God.

In some cases these events involve specific visible manifestations of God's presence. The visible manifestations underline the solemnity of the occasion, the reality of God's presence, the character of his faithfulness, and the permanence of his commitment. So the significance of theophany extends beyond the specific occasions and covers the whole life of Abraham after his initial call.

Specific Appearances of God

We find several central episodes where God appears to Abraham in specific visible form. The first is found in Genesis 12:7:

Then the LORD *appeared* to Abram and said, "To your offspring I will give this land." So he built there an altar to the LORD, who had *appeared* to him.

This appearance comes shortly after Abram has obeyed the call to go out to the Land of Promise. The Lord makes the promise more specific by positively identifying the land that he is giving to Abram and his descendants: "To your offspring I will give *this land*." A specific appearance underlines the significance and the reliability of the covenant and God's promises in it.

Next we have Genesis 15,[1] where God speaks in promise and also appears in the form of "a smoking fire pot and a flaming torch" (v. 17). The fire passes between the animal pieces. Interpreters have long recognized that the action of passing between the parts of a divided carcass constitutes an oath ceremony:

> The covenant ritual resembles that of Jeremiah 34:18. In its full form, probably both parties would pass between the dismembered animal to invoke a like fate on themselves should they break their pledge.[2]

God emphasizes the firmness of his commitment to his word and the overcoming of opposition (Gen. 15:13–14).

In Genesis 17 and 18, two separate occasions for God's appearance concentrate on the promise of the birth of Isaac. The birth of Isaac is a significant stage in the working out of God's promise concerning the offspring of the woman (Gen. 3:15), so the appearances of God on those occasions underline the importance of his birth.

The first appearance is described in Genesis 17:1, without further detail:

> When Abram was ninety-nine years old the Lord *appeared* to Abram and said to him, "I am God Almighty; walk before me, and be blameless."

The second involves the appearance of three men:

> And the Lord appeared to him by the oaks of Mamre, as he sat at the door of his tent in the heat of the day. He lifted up his eyes and looked, and behold, *three men* were standing in front of him. When he saw them, he ran from the tent door to meet them and bowed himself to the earth. (Gen. 18:1–2)

During the development of the doctrine of the Trinity in the patristic church, this text was seen as an early adumbration of the Trinity. But the narrative later indicates that two of the men separate from the third

---

1. Some interpreters have thought that Melchizedek in Genesis 14:18–20 is a preincarnate appearance of Christ, mostly on the basis of what Hebrews 7:1–3 says. But Hebrews 7:1–3 is better interpreted as teaching that Melchizedek is a *type* of Christ. He is both king and priest; the lack of *mention* of genealogy shows that his priesthood does not depend on tribal descent; the lack of *mention* of his beginning or end indicates a similarity to the coming greater priesthood of Christ.

2. Derek Kidner, *Genesis: An Introduction and Commentary* (London/Downers Grove, IL: InterVarsity, 1967), 124.

and go off toward Sodom (18:22; 19:1). The two that come to Sodom are identified as "the two angels," which makes it seem more likely that they are angelic beings. The third, who remains standing with Abraham, is definitely identified as "the LORD" (18:22).

Yet there is a grain of truth in what the patristic church did with this passage. At a deep level, the plurality among created beings reflected the original plurality among the persons of the Trinity. So there *is* a reflection of the Trinity in the plurality of the angels—but not quite what the fathers of the church thought when they simply identified the three men as appearances of the three persons of the Trinity.

The kind of appearance suits the circumstances. Genesis 15 involves a solemn oath that God will overcome opposition (15:13–14). Given the somber nature of the prediction of affliction for Abraham's descendants, the overall mood is somber, and the visible representation of God in fire emphasizes his divine holiness and power. By contrast, the appearances of God that promise the birth of Isaac are more positive in tone, even including laughter (18:12–15; cf. 21:6). God appears in *human* form, thereby underlining his intimacy with Abraham and Sarah and the human offspring in Isaac. The kind of appearance of God emphasizes God's intimacy with his people, as is suitable to the occasion.

Other Expressions of the Presence of God

It remains to note other instances where God is with Abraham in a special way, but mostly without the note of a direct visible appearance.

When Abram went down to Egypt, God acted with favor to Abram, both in multiplying his flocks and in preserving Sarah (Gen. 12:16, 17).

The Lord spoke to Abram after he separated from Lot (13:14–17).

The Lord gave victory to Abram and his men in the battle with the kings who had taken Lot captive (14:13–16).

The Lord met Abram through Melchizedek, the priest-king representative of the presence of "God Most High" (v. 19).

Abram confessed that he depended on God and God's presence to give him prosperity (vv. 22–24).

The "angel of the LORD" appeared to Hagar after she separated from Sarai (Gen. 16:7). With this episode we have the usual difficulty in determining whether the appearance was a created angel or a visible form of God himself—that is, an appearance of the preincarnate Son of God. After the encounter, Hagar concludes that she has seen God: "So she called the name of the LORD who spoke to her, 'You are a God of seeing,' for she said, 'Truly here I have seen him who looks after me'" (v. 13). The narratival voice speaks of "the name of the LORD who spoke to her," confirming that she was right in thinking that she had seen a visible appearance of God.

In Genesis 17, God gives Abraham the covenantal sign of circumcision. Circumcision is a permanent visible expression of the abiding character of the covenant, and therefore also the abiding character of the presence of God with Abraham and his descendants.

We may move on to Genesis 19. We earlier decided that the two angels that come to Sodom are created angels rather than a direct appearance of God. But it is still true that they are participants in the "court" of God, and that they come to Sodom reflecting the glory of God. Here we see the presence of God in a broad sense, through the presence of angelic representatives who bear his word and his authority. The rescue of Lot and the destruction of Sodom and Gomorrah both reflect the glory of God and his power. The destruction of Sodom and Gomorrah becomes a permanent example of God's just judgment and a permanent picture foreshadowing the last judgment:

> "but on the day when Lot went out from Sodom, fire and sulfur rained from heaven and destroyed them all—*so* will it be on the day when the Son of Man is revealed." (Luke 17:29–30)

And as Isaiah predicted,

> "If the Lord of hosts had not left us offspring,
>   we would have been *like Sodom*
>   and become *like Gomorrah*." (Rom. 9:29)

See also 2 Peter 2:6–7; Jude 7. The presence of God in the destruction of Sodom and Gomorrah is a foretaste of the theophany of God's presence at the last judgment.

In Genesis 20:3, God comes to Abimelech in a dream, warning him about Sarah. The dream-like encounter with God is more indirect, as is suitable with relation to someone like Abimelech, who shows respect for the God of Israel but is outside the Abrahamic covenant. There is some irony, because Abimelech behaves more honorably than Abraham, and has more of a sense of the fear of God than does Abraham.

In Genesis 21:1, God visits Sarah and Abraham by giving them Isaac.

He also speaks to Abraham as to what to do when strife breaks out between Sarah and Hagar's families (v. 12). The "angel of God" meets Hagar again after she has separated from Abraham and Sarah (v. 17).

In Genesis 22, God speaks to Abraham again, commanding him to sacrifice his son Isaac (Gen. 22:1–2). At the last minute "the angel of the Lord called to him from heaven and said, 'Abraham, Abraham!' And he said, 'Here I am'" (v. 11). The angel of the Lord also speaks to Abraham after his faithful obedience, confirming the promise (vv. 15–18).

The angel of the Lord also goes before Abraham's servant, as he travels to the city of Nahor to find a wife for Isaac (Gen. 24:7, 40). The Lord prospers the servant's commission, and Rebekah returns with him to become Isaac's wife. The hand of God is evident in the events. But we probably should not think of a visible appearance of God to the servant or to the household of Laban. Laban and his family become convinced that God is at work because of the narrative of the servant meeting Rebekah at the well (vv. 34–49):

> Then Laban and Bethuel answered and said, "The thing has come from the Lord; we cannot speak to you bad or good. Behold, Rebekah is before you; take her and go, and let her be the wife of your master's son, as the Lord has spoken." (vv. 50–51)

The providential work of God always displays his character. But in this case his providential work is particularly striking, and Laban and Bethuel recognize it as a manifestation of his presence and his glory.

The Significance of Abraham

All in all, a considerable number of encounters are recorded in Genesis 12–25, some with Abraham himself and some with those interacting with Abraham. God chose Abraham to be the beginning of the chosen people of Israel, and to make his name great. It is understandable that an unusual cluster of divine encounters would underline the presence of God in Abraham's life and in key events that take place.

35

God Appearing to the Patriarchs

Next let us consider how God shows himself in the life of the patriarchs after the time of Abraham.

The Genealogy of Ishmael

God shows faithfulness to his promise to Abraham by caring for the line of Ishmael, about which he spoke in Genesis 17:20: "As for Ishmael, I have heard you; behold, I have blessed him and will make him fruitful and multiply him greatly. He shall father twelve princes, and I will make him into a great nation." Though Ishmael does not belong to the line of promise (v. 21), God is present in a broad sense with him and his descendants, for the sake of Abraham and the promise to Abraham.

The Birth of Esau and Jacob

If God is present with the line of Ishmael, how much more with Isaac and his descendants, who represent the line of promise. The text of Genesis first records an obstacle: Rebekah was barren (Gen. 25:21). God manifests his presence and his grace to Isaac and Rebekah by answering Isaac's prayer: "And Isaac prayed to the LORD for his wife, because she was barren. And the LORD granted his prayer, and Rebekah his wife conceived" (v. 21). Small miracles like this one foreshadow even greater miracles to come. God gives conception to the Virgin Mary. And, as he brought life to wombs that were in a state of figurative death, so climactically, out of physical death he brings life to Christ in his resurrection.

The Lord also gives a specific prophecy to Rebekah while the children are still in her womb: "And the LORD said to her, 'Two nations are in your womb, and two peoples from within you shall be divided; the one shall be stronger than the other, the older shall serve the younger'" (Gen. 25:23). As is often the case, we are not told whether specific visual phenomena accompanied God's communication to Rebekah. Any divine speech represents the presence of God. A visual accompaniment would intensify this presence. But any divine speech is akin to theophany.

In this case, the speech to Rebekah also indicates something about the future days. God controls and is present in the providential developments concerning Esau and Jacob. God's providential involvement includes the birth itself. We understand that it is significant that Esau comes out first and is the firstborn, concerning whom God's prophecy spoke. The characteristics of the two sons at their births already anticipate something of the subsequent history.

The History of Jacob and Esau

The narrative concerning Jacob and Esau is of special interest to the later generations of Israelites. It serves to indicate the providence of God that has located them genealogically in relation to the blessing of God through Abraham, and in relation to the neighboring nation of Edom. Readers are invited to see God's presence and his care for the later generations, even though there are no visual theophanic phenomena.

In the ancient Near East the right of primogeniture belonged ordinarily to the firstborn. So the narrative also undertakes to describe the reversals that took place later on: the sale of the birthright (Gen. 25:29–34), Jacob's deception of Isaac (27:1–29), and the checkered nature of Jacob's subsequent relation to Esau (27:41; 33:1–17). The Lord works out the prophecy that he made in Genesis 25:23.

Amid these events we should note that Isaac's blessings to Jacob (27:27–29) and to Esau (vv. 39–40) contain prophecy. God speaks through these words, and so a distinct presence of God is manifested in them.

Confirmation of the Promise to Isaac

Several specific theophanic events occur in the lives of Isaac and Jacob. The first noteworthy event is God's appearance to Isaac, telling him not to go down to Egypt: "And the LORD *appeared to him* and said,

'Do not go down to Egypt; dwell in the land of which I shall tell you'" (Gen. 26:2). The text provides no details about how and in what form the Lord "appeared." This appearance has special significance because the Lord specifically confirms to Isaac the promises made to Abraham:

> "Sojourn in this land, and I will be with you and will bless you, for to you and to your offspring I will give all these lands, and I will establish the oath that I swore to *Abraham* your father. I will multiply your offspring as the stars of heaven and will give to your offspring all these lands. And in your offspring all the nations of the earth shall be blessed, because Abraham obeyed my voice and kept my charge, my commandments, my statutes, and my laws." (Gen. 26:3–5)

The visible appearance of God confirms and solemnizes the promise. God is present both in the special appearance and in the promise.

As a result, Isaac remains in the land of Canaan, and settles in Gerar (Gen. 26:6). He then comes into contact with Abimelech and his people. Isaac tries a trick similar to what we saw with Abraham in Egypt (12:10–20) and in Gerar (20:1–18). God providentially preserves Isaac and protects the genealogy of the line of promise.

After the episode is over, Isaac goes to Beersheba. The Lord appears to him again and confirms the Abrahamic promise: "And the LORD *appeared* to him the same night and said, 'I am the God of Abraham your father. Fear not, for I am with you and will bless you and multiply your offspring for my servant Abraham's sake'" (Gen. 26:24). This appearance again underlines the importance of the promise.

Jacob's Dream

Two special theophanic events occur in Jacob's life. The first is Jacob's dream, recorded in Genesis 28:

> [12] And he dreamed, and behold, there was a ladder set up on the earth, and the top of it reached to heaven. And behold, the angels of God were ascending and descending on it! [13] And behold, the LORD stood above it and said, "I am the LORD, the God of Abraham your father and the God of Isaac. The land on which you lie I will give to you and to your offspring. [14] Your offspring shall be like the dust of the earth, and you shall spread abroad to the west and to the east and to the north and to the south, and in you and your offspring shall all the families of the earth be blessed. [15] Behold, I am with you

and will keep you wherever you go, and will bring you back to this land. For I will not leave you until I have done what I have promised you." (Gen. 28:12–15)

This episode is significant for Jacob because it is his first real experience with God. God speaks to Jacob himself, rather than simply to his ancestors Abraham and Isaac. In this theophany the contents of the speech concern the promises to Abraham and his descendants. What is new is primarily that God applies these promises specifically to Jacob.

God also promises to be present with Jacob throughout the time of his sojourning: "Behold, I am with you and will keep you wherever you go, and will bring you back to this land. For I will not leave you" (Gen. 28:15). The theophany represents an intensive, special presence. But the significance of this presence spreads through the whole life of Jacob. This whole episode is a good illustration and confirmation of the principle that theophany forms the foundation for covenantal words, and that the principle of the presence of God in theophany applies to the times of providential action subsequent to the time of the theophany itself.

We should also note the character of the theophany. It involves (1) a ladder[1] reaching to heaven; (2) angels ascending and descending; and (3) the Lord standing "above it" (v. 13). The description of the Lord as standing suggests a man-like figure. The angels belong to God's court. So even though the scene is not a courtroom scene, the appearance of God here has the greatest affinity to court theophanies.

There is a difficulty in translation. In verse 13 the ESV has the wording, "the LORD stood above it." But in the margin it offers, as an alternative, "the LORD stood beside him." So is the Lord at the top of the ladder or near the bottom? The Hebrew text has "upon him/it," where the preposition for "upon" (Hebrew *'al* [עַל]) can mean either "above" or "beside," depending on the context. "Above" seems more likely in this

---

1. The Hebrew word (סֻלָּם), translated *ladder*, occurs only here in the Old Testament. So there is some uncertainty about its meaning. The Brown-Driver-Briggs lexicon offers the meaning *ladder* (Francis Brown, S. R. Driver, and Charles A. Briggs, *A Hebrew and English Lexicon of the Old Testament with an Appendix Containing the Biblical Aramaic* [Oxford: Oxford University Press, 1953], 700); later Hebrew attests the same meaning (Marcus Jastrow, *A Dictionary of the Targumim, the Talmud Babli and Yerushalmi, and the Midrashic Literature*, 2 vols. [New York: Pardes, 1950], 2:964); Koehler-Baumgartner prefers a "**stepped ramp, flight of steps**" (Ludwig Koehler and Walter Baumgartner, *The Hebrew and Aramaic Lexicon of the Old Testament*, 5 vols. [Leiden/New York/Köln: Brill, 1995], 2:758; boldface emphasis is original). One way or another, it offers an entrance to heaven and the presence of God.

context, but both interpretations are possible. We cannot be certain. The ladder symbolizes access to heaven, and therefore access to the presence of God. This presence could be depicted either with the Lord appearing from heaven at the top of the ladder or with the Lord appearing in human form on earth at the bottom of the ladder. Either way, the vision as a whole emphasizes the importance of God's promise and his commitment to be with Jacob. God has given Jacob access to God himself, even though in human terms he is alone, leaving his family and being in danger from the murderous plans of Esau.

It is noteworthy that Jesus makes reference to this vision of Jacob in John 1:51: "And he said to him, 'Truly, truly, I say to you, you will see heaven opened, and the angels of God ascending and descending on the Son of Man.'" It could be that Jesus is inviting the disciples to identify him with the figure of the Lord who appeared in Jacob's vision. But the specific language that Jesus uses connects the *ladder* and *the Son of Man*. In Jacob's vision, the angels ascend and descend "on it," that is, on the ladder (Gen. 28:12). In Jesus's statement, the angels ascend and descend "on the Son of Man." If Jesus is proclaiming himself as the true ladder, it fits with his statement later in John that he is "the way" (John 14:6). He is the way to heaven, the way to God, the ladder to God. As Jesus says elsewhere, he is "the door" (John 10:7). He is also a descendant of Jacob, and this line of descent reinforces the connection between Jacob and Jesus.

Jacob's response to the vision shows that he at least partly understands its awesome character and its significance:

> [16] Then Jacob awoke from his sleep and said, "Surely the LORD is *in* this place, and I did not know it." [17] And he was afraid and said, "How awesome is this place! This is none other than the *house of God*, and this is the *gate of heaven*." [18] So early in the morning Jacob took the stone that he had put under his head and set it up for a pillar and poured oil on the top of it. [19] He called the name of that place Bethel, but the name of the city was Luz at the first. [20] Then Jacob made a vow, saying, "If God will be with me and will keep me in this way that I go, and will give me bread to eat and clothing to wear, [21] so that I come again to my father's house in peace, then the LORD shall be my God, [22] and this stone, which I have set up for a pillar, shall be God's house. And of all that you give me I will give a full tenth to you." (Gen. 28:16–22)

Jacob acknowledges the *presence* of the Lord: "Surely the LORD is in this place" (v. 16). He also calls it "the house of God" and "the gate of heaven." The phrase "gate of heaven" is understandable, given the symbolism of a ladder giving access to heaven and to the presence of God in heaven.

The parallel phrase "the house of God" is worth reflecting on. There is no physical structure in which Jacob is dwelling. He has only the stone, which he will set up as a memorial pillar. The meaning of "the house of God" is bound up with the presence of God, not primarily with a physical structure. The house of God is the place where God dwells, where he is present. Later on in history, the consecration of a house of God can be marked by theophany, as an indication that God has come and is establishing his dwelling on earth. Here in Genesis 28 there is already a theophany, marking not only the place but Jacob himself as a site of God's dwelling on earth. The symbolism anticipates the time when God will dwell on earth climactically in the incarnation of Christ (John 2:19–21), and then the time when God will dwell in the church as his temple (1 Cor. 3:16; cf. Acts 2:2–4).

It is fitting, then, that at the first instance where a house of God is explicitly discussed, the "house" is inaugurated by a theophany. Jacob calls the name of the place "Bethel," which means "house of God" (Gen. 28:19).

Jacob's Encounter with Angels

As Jacob is returning to the land of Canaan, we get a brief description of an appearance of angels:

> Jacob went on his way, and the angels of God met him. And when Jacob saw them he said, "This is God's camp!" So he called the name of that place Mahanaim. (Gen. 32:1–2)

What is its significance? It is not so easy to say. In his speech, Jacob probably is implying that the "camp" of angels is a war camp (the same Hebrew word occurs in Deut. 23:14, Josh. 6:11, and other places involving war). Though the vision is momentary, it offers a long-range reassurance of God's protection for Jacob, in confirmation of the promise made at Bethel in Genesis 28:15. It is a fitting prelude to the confrontation with Esau that Jacob dreads (Gen. 32:6–7, 11).

Jacob's Wrestling Match

One of the more unusual theophanies in the Old Testament is Jacob's wrestling match in Genesis 32:24–32. When Jacob was left alone, "a man wrestled with him until the breaking of the day" (v. 24). We gradually find out that the "man" is a supernatural being. With only a touch he dislocates Jacob's hip (v. 25). The man refuses to give his name (v. 29), but gives Jacob the new name *Israel* with the explanation, "You have striven with *God* and with men, and have prevailed" (v. 28). That declaration seems to imply that the man is in fact an appearance of God. And this implication is confirmed by Jacob giving a name to the place:

> So Jacob called the name of the place Peniel, saying, "For I have *seen God* face to face, and yet my life has been delivered." (Gen. 32:30)

So this episode is one instance of the appearance of God in human form. The human form is suitable. God takes on human form so as to present a figure who can stand opposite Jacob and wrestle with him.

But why should God wrestle with Jacob? If it is indeed God, he has power to bless or curse or destroy Jacob in a moment. Why does he engage in wrestling? And, if it is God, how is it that Jacob "prevails"? The whole thing seems peculiar to modern readers. The text is quite brief and does not answer all our questions. Much mystery remains. And after all, mystery is characteristic of theophanies. We must not expect to have everything explained.

Given the context, it seems best to attempt what explanation we can give by seeing the theophany as a response to Jacob's prayer in Genesis 32:9–12, and then more broadly to the whole life of Jacob up to this point. Jacob's life has been a life of striving and contending and scheming to get blessing. At birth he seized his brother's heel (25:26). He seized a weak moment when Esau was exhausted in order to bargain for the birthright (vv. 32–34). With Rebekah's urging, he schemed to get his father's blessing (27:1–29). He bargained for Rachel, though in this case he met in the person of Laban someone who was his equal in scheming. Jacob's vow in Genesis 28:20–22 ("If God will . . . then . . . ") might just be an expression of gratitude and worship. But in the light of the pattern of scheming, it just may be that Jacob was trying to create a bargaining relationship with God.

God then brings to a climax this pattern of scheming by confronting Jacob in person. Jacob's habit is to strive with circumstances and with other people to obtain blessing. So he will strive even with God. It is right that he should seek blessing from God. But the ways in which he does it reveal complex, mixed motives. By prolonging the match, God tests Jacob's commitment. By touching his hip, he shows Jacob how ridiculous it is to think that a human being could flat-out prevail against God. And yet God *lets* Jacob prevail in a sense at the decisive point by giving him a blessing (Gen. 32:29).

The entire encounter conveys a message of grace and an act of grace, undermining the willful attitude in Jacob's striving. At the same time, by meeting Jacob on his own turf of striving, God graciously recognizes amid the mixed motives Jacob's real desire for God's blessing, and he establishes and affirms a relation of blessing with Jacob. At the same time, by disabling Jacob, he makes it clear that Jacob has not received the blessing by manipulating God. That is what I think we should infer. But much is left unsaid. The actions, and not the mere multiplication of words, must have their effect in giving blessing and working sanctification in Jacob.

The Confirmation of the Covenant with Jacob

The narrative includes one final case of a special encounter between God and Jacob, as Jacob returns to Bethel (Gen. 35:1–15). Bethel had been the site of an earlier spectacular theophany, by which God initiated a more direct, personal relation with Jacob. It is fitting that we should come full circle and God should encounter Jacob again as he returns to Bethel.

The narrative has two main stages. First, in Genesis 35:1, God speaks to Jacob and commands him to go to Bethel: "God said to Jacob, 'Arise, go up to Bethel and dwell there. Make an altar there to the God who *appeared* to you when you fled from your brother Esau.'" God explicitly recalls the earlier appearance. God's direct speech to Jacob is akin to an appearance. But the text does not say that there was any special visual form.

The second main stage takes place when Jacob arrives at Bethel. God gives another speech (35:10–12). This time, the text says that God appears: "God *appeared* to Jacob again, when he came from Paddan-aram, and blessed him" (v. 9). At the conclusion of God's dialogue with Jacob, it says that "God *went up* from him in the place where he had spoken with him" (v. 13). The expression *went up* implies spatial movement, confirming that the encounter included a special visual appearance of God.

The theophanies at the beginning (Bethel in Genesis 28) and the end (Bethel in Genesis 35) round out the crucial period in Jacob's life, when God protected him, made him fruitful with sons, and brought him back to Canaan, in fulfillment of his promise (Gen. 28:15).

Joseph's Dreams and Interpretations

From the life of Jacob we pass in Genesis 37–50 to narratives focusing primarily on the life of Joseph. These narratives contain a prominent emphasis on the providential acts of God that operated in the life of Joseph and that brought him to his position of authority in Egypt. God primarily operates "behind the scenes," so to speak. But the fact that he is controlling events is made more evident especially in prophetic dreams. These dreams are not full-blown theophanies in the narrowest sense. But they are dreams given by God, and they manifest his presence. They are also predictive, and in looking back we see that God demonstrates his control over the future by predicting the crucial events.

There are several such dreams. While still united to his family, Joseph has two dreams about his brothers bowing down to him (Gen. 37:5–11). The subsequent history confirms that these are revelatory dreams and that, however unlikely they seem at the time, they come true in the end.

Later, Joseph interprets two revelatory dreams given to the cupbearer and the baker in prison (Gen. 40:9–19). God gives the dreams to pagans. It is fitting that they can be interpreted only by a faithful servant of God who has a positive covenantal relation to God.

Then Joseph interprets two revelatory dreams given to Pharaoh (Gen. 41:25–36). In a manner similar to his role with the cupbearer and the baker, Joseph serves as a mediatorial figure in explaining the will of God.

The Confirmation of Jacob Going to Egypt

Next, God speaks to Jacob in a dream to confirm that he should go to Egypt and to confirm God's faithfulness to his covenant:

> And God spoke to Israel in visions of the night and said, "Jacob, Jacob." And he said, "Here I am." Then he said, "I am God, the God of your father. Do not be afraid to go down to Egypt, for there

> I will make you into a great nation. I myself will go down with you
> to Egypt, and I will also bring you up again, and Joseph's hand shall
> close your eyes." (Gen. 46:2–4)

The emphasis here is on God speaking. But the text also speaks of "visions of the night," which involve a visual component. We do not know whether there was a theophany of a detailed and spectacular kind. It is not necessary for us to know. God is present in speech, and present in the vision. And by his words God confirms that he will be present during the whole sojourn in Egypt.

Jacob's and Joseph's Prophecies

Finally, we should note that, at the end of their lives, Jacob and Joseph both give prophetic speeches (Gen. 48:19–22; 49:1–27; 50:24–25). The text does not describe any unusual visual appearance of God, but God is present through his speech. And his speech addresses events of future generations. By so doing, God is underlining his covenant with the people of Israel and with each tribe (Gen. 49:3–27). God is present in power through the generations, both in a general way as he oversees their ways, and in specific events, some of which are detailed in Genesis 49:3–27. Jacob's prophetic poem in Genesis 49 is particularly significant, because in its scope it reaches out through countless generations. It also singles out the tribe of Judah as the tribe that will rule, thereby looking forward to the climactic rule that will eventually come to Jesus the Messiah, of the tribe of Judah (Matt. 1:2, 16; 2:6).

36

God Appearing in the Exodus

Next let us consider the presence of God in the events of the exodus.

Fulfilling Prophecies

God shows his presence in providence even in the first lines of the book of Exodus. Exodus 1:1–5 repeats the names of the sons of Israel, thereby recalling God's care for Jacob and his descendants as recorded in Genesis. Exodus 1:7 then notes that the people were fruitful and multiplied in Egypt, in fulfillment of specific prophecies:

> But the people of Israel were *fruitful* and *increased greatly*; they *multiplied* and grew exceedingly strong, so that the land was filled with them. (Ex. 1:7)

> "I will make your offspring *as the dust* of the earth, so that if one can count the dust of the earth, your offspring also can be counted." (Gen. 13:16)

> And he brought him outside and said, "Look toward heaven, and number the stars, if you are able to number them." Then he said to him, "*So* shall your offspring be." (Gen. 15:5)

Similar promises appear in Genesis 17:6; 22:17; 26:24; 28:3; 35:11; and 48:4. The record in Exodus 1:7 implies that God continues to be with his word to fulfill it, and he continues to care for the people of Israel.

The record in Exodus (1:8–22) then describes the oppression of the people of Israel, which also fulfills earlier prophecy: "Then the LORD said to Abram, 'Know for certain that your offspring will be sojourners in a land that is not theirs and will be servants there, and they will be *afflicted* for four hundred years'" (Gen. 15:13). In addition, the entire story of the exodus from Egypt fulfills prophecy:

> "But I will bring judgment on the nation that they [the Israelites] serve, and afterward they shall *come out* with great possessions." (Gen. 15:14)

> Then Israel said to Joseph, "Behold, I am about to die, but God will be with you and will *bring you again* to the land of your fathers." (Gen. 48:21)

Joseph confirms God's plan for the exodus in Genesis 50:24–25.

The Burning Bush

God is present throughout the events of the exodus. But, as usual, theophanies represent events of intensive presence that underline the principle that he is always present with his people and that he is faithful to his word and his covenant.

The first theophanic appearance in the record of Exodus is the burning bush (Ex. 3:1–4:17). In terms of classification, it is a fire theophany (see our discussion in chapter 3). The appearance of fire results in a connection forward to the fire and storm at Mount Sinai (Exodus 19). The Sinai theophany is a large-scale theophany, of central importance for the exodus from Egypt and the formation of the people of Israel into a holy nation (Ex. 19:6).

The same God who will speak to all Israel first speaks to Moses as their spokesman. In harmony with the fact that God addresses only one individual, the theophany is, as it were, scaled down. We do not have a full thunderstorm, or fire from heaven, but fire in a bush. But this appearance of God still communicates his divine power and sovereignty. He can work miracles at will. And the fact that the bush is not consumed (3:2) hints at the eternal nature of God and his independence from the world that he created.

As with many other theophanies, the visual phenomena go together with verbal communication. God has a fairly long dialogue with Moses, revealing the key divine name "I AM," dealing with Moses's apprehensions and objections, and indicating what Moses will say to the people. The visual appearance of God reinforces the authority of God's instructions and the ability of God to make Moses successful, in spite of his apprehensions.

The Plagues in Egypt

The plagues in Egypt constitute unusual visual phenomena. And they manifest the hand of God. They are divinely worked plagues. So they offer an instance of manifestations of God's power, akin to theophany. But they are lesser cases than the focal theophanies at the burning bush and at Mount Sinai.

God Appearing at Mount Sinai

The gigantic, central theophany of the period of the exodus occurs at Mount Sinai. The earlier appearance in the burning bush already looks forward to it: "He said, 'But I will be with you, and this shall be the sign for you, that I have sent you: when you have brought the people out of Egypt, you shall serve God on this mountain'" (Ex. 3:12). The importance of Mount Sinai can be measured partly by the fact that the narrative in Exodus spends a whole chapter describing the preparations and the nature of the theophany on the mountain. It is a thunderstorm theophany (see chapter 2). It includes a whole series of visual and aural effects. It is awesome and terrifying:

> Now when all the people saw the thunder and the flashes of lightning and the sound of the trumpet and the mountain smoking, the people were *afraid* and *trembled*, and they stood far off and said to Moses, "You speak to us, and we will listen; but do not let God speak to us, lest we die." (Ex. 20:18–19)

But the power of the visual effects is not the only thing that gives importance to the events. God speaks the Ten Commandments, which form the heart of his covenant with the people of Israel. He shapes them into a holy nation, and testifies that he will be with them in harmony with what he has already done in bringing them out of Egypt: "And God spoke all these words, saying, 'I am the LORD your God, who brought you out of the land of Egypt, out of the house of slavery'" (Ex. 20:1–2). For the rest of history, the people look back on this event as a founding event, defining them as a nation. The events in which God appeared took up only a limited span of time. But their significance stands forever. The God who appeared at Sinai is the God who claims the people of Israel as his own, and who is *with* the people, in his authority and power and presence, for the rest of the Old Testament.

Seeing God (Exodus 24:9–11)

We should also reflect on the events described in Exodus 24:9–11:

> Then Moses and Aaron, Nadab, and Abihu, and seventy of the elders of Israel went up, and they *saw* the God of Israel. There was under his feet as it were a pavement of sapphire stone, like the very heaven for clearness. And he did not lay his hand on the chief men of the people of Israel; they *beheld* God, and ate and drank.

Here a visible appearance of God comes not only to Moses but to Aaron, Nadab, Abihu, and seventy elders of Israel. It comes in close connection with the making of the covenant in Exodus 24:3–8. The meal with God is a covenantal meal, confirming the commitments of God and the people. The intimacy of the meal also underlines the intimacy of God's presence with his people. This temporary meal foreshadows and anticipates the final feast of intimacy at the consummation of history (Isa. 25:6–9; Rev. 19:9). The preliminary vision of God in Exodus 24:9–11 anticipates the final vision of God's "face" in Revelation 22:4.

Exodus 24:10 says, "they *saw* the God of Israel." God appeared in theophany. What exactly did they see? The text mentions "his feet." We infer that this was a theophany in human-like form. But the text does not go into further detail about the nature of this form, or mention a throne on which he might be seated. It is a sparse description, in keeping with the fact that God's appearance was temporary and anticipatory of greater revelations that were to come only in the future.

The New Testament brings changes. But the changes are not a sidetrack to the Old Testament. They are its fulfillment. Jesus speaks from a mountain when he gives the Sermon on the Mount (Matt. 5:1). His speech is the fulfillment of the earlier speech of God from Mount Sinai (v. 17). We may therefore also infer that his appearance is the fulfillment of the earlier appearance of God on Mount Sinai. Hebrews 1:1–3 is relevant:

> Long ago, at many times and in many ways, God spoke to our fathers by the prophets, but in these last days he has spoken to us by his Son, whom he appointed the heir of all things, through whom

also he created the world. He is the *radiance of the glory* of God and the exact imprint of his nature, and he upholds the universe by the word of his power.

The language of "the radiance of the glory of God" shows that Jesus fulfills the earlier appearances of the glory of God, including the glory of God at Mount Sinai.

The Pillar of Cloud and Fire

The appearance of God at Mount Sinai includes as one central element the appearance of "a thick cloud" (Ex. 19:16). The cloud at Mount Sinai has an obvious link to the pillar of cloud and fire that accompanies the people of Israel during the time in the wilderness.

Even before God's appearance at Mount Sinai, the narrative of Exodus describes the appearance of the pillar of cloud and fire. It is first introduced in Exodus 13:

And the LORD went before them by day in a *pillar of cloud* to lead them along the way, and by night in a *pillar of fire* to give them light, that they might travel by day and by night. The *pillar of cloud* by day and the *pillar of fire* by night did not depart from before the people. (Ex. 13:21–22)

This pillar combines elements from cloud theophany and fire theophany. It is a striking kind of theophany, because it did not disappear after a momentary appearance. As the text indicates, it was constantly with the people during their time in the wilderness.

A number of additional texts mention the pillar. In Exodus 14 the pillar moved between the people of Israel and the army of Pharaoh, to protect them:

Then the angel of God who was going before the host of Israel moved and went behind them, and the *pillar of cloud* moved from before them and *stood behind them*, coming *between* the host of Egypt and the host of Israel. And there was the *cloud* and the darkness. And it lit up the night without one coming near the other all night. (Ex. 14:19–20)

The pillar also appears in order to answer two complaints. God appears in the pillar to answer Miriam and Aaron (Num. 12:5, 10); he appears again when the people complain about the death of Korah and his company (Num. 16:42).

The pillar descends to meet Moses when God speaks to Moses:

> When Moses entered the tent, the pillar of cloud would *descend* and *stand* at the entrance of the tent, and the LORD would speak with Moses. And when all the people saw the pillar of cloud standing at the entrance of the tent, all the people would rise up and worship, each at his tent door. Thus the LORD used to speak to Moses face to face, as a man speaks to his friend. (Ex. 33:9–11)

It is clear that the pillar signifies an intensive presence of God: "Thus the LORD used to speak to Moses face to face, as a man speaks to his friend."

Moses Seeing the "Back" of God

These conversations with Moses are surpassed by a still more intensive meeting between God and Moses. After the incident with the golden calf (Exodus 32), Israel's future appears to be in doubt. Moses requests that God show him his glory (Ex. 33:12–18). In this more intensive meeting, described in Exodus 34:5–28,

> The LORD *descended* in the *cloud* and *stood* with him there, and proclaimed the name of the LORD. The LORD *passed before him* and proclaimed, "The LORD, the LORD, a God merciful and gracious, slow to anger, and abounding in steadfast love and faithfulness, keeping steadfast love for thousands, forgiving iniquity and transgression and sin, but who will by no means clear the guilty, visiting the iniquity of the fathers on the children and the children's children, to the third and the fourth generation." (Ex. 34:5–7)

As is usual with theophany, the visual phenomena reinforce the significance of God's speech. The divine appearance reveals the character of God, and so does the heart of God's speech. God "proclaimed the name of the LORD" (v. 5).

Before the theophany takes place, God also indicates its limitation:

> And he said, "I will make all my goodness pass before you and will proclaim before you my name 'The LORD.' And I will be gracious to whom I will be gracious, and will show mercy on whom I will show mercy. But," he said, "you *cannot see* my face, for man shall not see me and live." And the LORD said, "Behold, there is a place

by me where you shall stand on the rock, and while my glory passes by I will put you in a cleft of the rock, and I will cover you with my hand until I have passed by. Then I will take away my hand, and you shall see my back, but *my face shall not be seen*." (Ex. 33:19–23)

So what exactly did Moses see? Did he see a man-like appearance? Or is the language about "my back" a metaphor to indicate the less-than-full nature of the revelation? Mystery remains. Did Moses see the back of a human figure or a vision like Ezekiel 1 or a bright cloud? Whatever the details, Moses saw a theophany of God, and yet one that was less than the fullest possible exposure to the presence of God. The allusion to human-like features builds on the fact that man was made in the image of God. And of course, along with all theophanies, this one also foreshadows the appearance of God in Christ, who is the permanent and climactic theophany. In him, and through his atonement, we can see God's face and not die (John 14:9; Rev. 22:4).

After this climactic experience with God, Moses's face shone:

When Moses came down from Mount Sinai, with the two tablets of the testimony in his hand as he came down from the mountain, Moses did not know that the skin of his face *shone* because he had been talking with God. Aaron and all the people of Israel saw Moses, and behold, the skin of his face *shone*, and they were afraid to come near him. (Ex. 34:29–30)

An appearance of God may include brightness. The striking thing about Moses is that now the brightness of God's appearance is reflected in Moses himself, who has seen God. This radiance from Moses anticipates the climax in Christ. Christ is "the radiance of the glory of God" (Heb. 1:3). In a manner similar to Moses's reflection of the glory of God, Christians who have communion with Christ are transformed so as to reflect the glory of Christ:

And we all, with unveiled face, beholding the glory of the Lord, are being transformed into the same image from one degree of glory to another. For this comes from the Lord who is the Spirit. (2 Cor. 3:18)

The Cloud Covering the Tabernacle

We should also note that, after the tabernacle is completed, the pillar of cloud descends on it:

> So Moses finished the work. Then the *cloud* covered the tent of meeting, and the glory of the LORD filled the tabernacle. And Moses was not able to enter the tent of meeting because the *cloud* settled on it, and the *glory* of the LORD filled the tabernacle. (Ex. 40:33–35)

The descent of the cloud signifies that God himself now consecrates the tabernacle. It functions as a permanent dwelling place for God, a permanent site for his intensive presence on earth. The cloud is not mentioned after the Israelites enter the Promised Land, until the time when Solomon dedicates the temple (1 Kings 8:10–11). But the tabernacle continues to function as a center where people seek God. Theophany results in the establishment of a permanent way of fellowship with God.

The cloud settling on the tabernacle offers a prelude to the coming of Jesus, whose body is the temple of God: "But he was speaking about the *temple* of his body" (John 2:21).

The Angel of the Lord

The angel of the Lord also appears in connection with the exodus from Egypt. He is present with the burning bush: "And the *angel* of the LORD appeared to him in a flame of fire out of the midst of a bush. He looked, and behold, the bush was burning, yet it was not consumed" (Ex. 3:2). As we indicated in chapter 7, the word translated *angel* means *messenger*.[1] Depending on the context it can refer to a created angel or to a divine appearance. The angel is also closely linked to the pillar of cloud: "Then the *angel* of God who was going before the host of Israel moved and went behind them, and the pillar of cloud moved from before them and stood behind them" (Ex. 14:19). The angel guides and guards them, in a manner parallel to the function of the cloud:

> "Behold, I send an *angel* before you to guard you on the way and to bring you to the place that I have prepared. Pay careful attention to him and obey his voice; do not rebel against him, for he will not pardon your transgression, for my name is in him." (Ex. 23:20–21)

This latter passage is particularly striking. God says that "my *name* is in him." The name is the divine name. For the name to be "in him" implies that the "angel"—the messenger—is himself divine. This messenger is then similar to the instances in Genesis where "the angel of

---

1. See also appendix A.

the Lord" has divine attributes. We are dealing with a preincarnate appearance of Christ, anticipating his incarnation. At the same time, it is God the Father who appears in the Son, and through the presence of the Holy Spirit. The theophany is Trinitarian. Since Christ is closely linked to this messenger, he is also linked to the pillar of cloud and fire. It is Christ who leads Israel through the wilderness.

All in all, the several kinds of theophany in the exodus, with their several functions, all foreshadow the appearing of God in Christ in "the fullness of time" (Gal. 4:4).

God Appearing in Fiery Judgment

God promised Moses that he would go with the people of Israel on their way to the Promised Land (Ex. 33:14–17). But the people were disobedient and hard-hearted, so the presence of God could also take the form of judgment: " . . . lest I consume you on the way, for you are a stiff-necked people" (v. 3). We see several striking instances of judgment.

In Leviticus 10:1, Nadab and Abihu, the sons of Aaron, offer "unauthorized fire." In response, fire comes from the Lord: "And fire came out from *before the* Lord and consumed them" (Lev. 10:2). The expression "from before the Lord" indicates a source in the special presence of God. So the fire is theophanic fire, manifesting the anger of the Lord and his just judgment against unholiness.

We may also list, as a background for the Nadab and Abihu incident, the fire coming from the Lord to consume the offering at the time of Aaron's consecration: "And *fire* came out from *before the* Lord and consumed the burnt offering and the pieces of fat on the altar" (Lev. 9:24). The fire is theophanic fire, confirming in an intense way God's acceptance of the offering and the consecration of Aaron and his sons. At the same time, since the animals are offered as innocent substitutes for the sake of purification of Aaron and the people, the fire also contains an element of judgment. God's judgment falls on the animals instead of on the sins of the people.

Other episodes in Numbers also show the appearance of theophanic fire in judgment. At Taberah, the people complained against God, and "the *fire* of the Lord burned among them and consumed some outlying parts of the camp" (Num. 11:1). In response to Korah's rebellion, "*fire* came out from the Lord and consumed the 250 men offering the incense" (Num. 16:35). As in the case with Nadab and Abihu, the

Lord's fire responded to unholy fire that Korah and his people offered in incense burners (vv. 18, 37).

Appearance to Balaam

We should also note the peculiar combination of features in God's relations to Balaam, narrated in Numbers 22–24. When Balak's request is first presented to Balaam, Balaam undertakes to consult with God (Num. 22:7–8). The text says, "God came to Balaam" (v. 9). There is an oral exchange between God and Balaam, but no indication of whether God's coming had any special visual form.

During Balaam's journey (Num. 22:21–35) we find something else. We read that "the angel of the Lord took his stand in the way as his adversary" (v. 22). The angel appears to the donkey "with a drawn sword in his hand" (v. 23). This appearance has affinities with warrior theophanies. It expresses the power of God and his opposition to evil. But we receive no indication as to whether the angel was a divine appearance or a created angel. The Lord finally "opened the eyes of Balaam" (v. 31). There is much irony in the passage. Balaam has been sought out because he is a famous visionary, and yet he cannot see the angel until God opens his eyes.

When Balaam arrives in Moab, he gives three successive discourses based on three successive encounters with God. In the first, "God met Balaam" (Núm. 23:4) and "the Lord put a word in Balaam's mouth" (v. 5). Balaam experiences intimacy with God, but we hear no mention of a visual experience. The second encounter is similar (v. 16). In the third encounter, "the Spirit of God came upon him" (24:2), but still with no mention of a visual appearance. Yet when Balaam opens his mouth, he describes his experience in visionary terms:

> "The oracle of Balaam the son of Beor,
> the oracle of the man whose *eye* is opened,
> the oracle of him who hears the words of God,
> who *sees* the *vision* of the Almighty,
> falling down with his *eyes* uncovered:" (vv. 3–4)

Balaam did see the angel of the Lord at an earlier point. But at this later point, when Balaam undertakes to pronounce prophecies, the overall impression left is that Balaam did not see anything special at a physical level. He functions to deliver a message, not to deliver a description of a vision. What he "saw," he saw in an ordinary physical way: "And Balaam lifted up his eyes and *saw* Israel camping tribe by tribe" (Num. 24:2). The message from God serves as a kind of functional equivalent to theophany, rather than Balaam having a literal experience of theophany in a narrow sense.

In the narrative of Balaam, Balaam himself is an ambivalent figure. He receives genuine prophetic messages from God and yet is tempted to religious and moral compromise with respect to his own role. In the book of Joshua, he is described as "the one who practiced divination" (Josh. 13:22), a practice forbidden to God's people (Deut. 18:10, 14; see also 2 Pet. 2:15–16; Rev. 2:14). He encounters God's presence in intensive form, in a theophany-like way, and yet he is not morally transformed through the encounter. In its peculiarities, the story of Balaam shows another side to the issue of mediation. Prophetic mediation is necessary because of the sinfulness of human inquirers. Yet if the mediator himself is sinful, the whole process of communication remains problematic and paradoxical. God condescends to communicate with Balaam, but it is on account of his love for Israel, not his love for Balaam (Deut. 23:5).

37

God Appearing in Conquering the Land

Next we consider how God shows his presence in the time of conquest, which is covered by Joshua, Judges, and Ruth.

The Program of Conquest under Joshua

God manifests his presence at the beginning of the book of Joshua by speaking to Joshua, encouraging him to continue in obedience to the law, and promising success:

> [1] After the death of Moses the servant of the LORD, the LORD said to Joshua the son of Nun, Moses' assistant, [2] "Moses my servant is dead. Now therefore arise, go over this Jordan, you and all this people, into the land that I am giving to them, to the people of Israel. [3] Every place that the sole of your foot will tread upon I have given to you, just as I promised to Moses. . . . [5] No man shall be able to stand before you all the days of your life. Just as I was with Moses, so I will be with you. I will not leave you or forsake you. . . . [7] Only be strong and very courageous, being careful to do according to all the law that Moses my servant commanded you. . . . [8] This Book of the Law shall not depart from your mouth, but you shall meditate on it day and night, so that you may be careful to do according to all that is written in it. For then you will make your way prosperous, and then you will have good success. [9] Have I not commanded

you? Be strong and courageous. Do not be frightened, and do not be dismayed, for the LORD your God is with you wherever you go." (Josh. 1:1–9)

As in many cases when God speaks, the narrative gives no indication as to whether there was a visible appearance of God or an angel. God is present in his speech, and his faithfulness guarantees the efficacy of his speech. That is enough.

God's speech addresses the whole period of conquest (vv. 3–5). So it implies that God will be present and will be at work in the battles and struggles through the course of the whole book. And the allotment of land in the second half of the book (Joshua 13–21) also takes place according to God's will. God's presence and his power are pervasive. The opening speech of God offers a more intensive expression of his presence, so that we may understand the rest of the narrative in light of it.

The involvement of God in the conquest confirms what God had said earlier through Moses. In particular, in Exodus 23:23, God indicates that the same "angel" (messenger) who guided and guarded the people in the wilderness will work in the time of conquest to blot out the enemies: "When my *angel* goes before you and brings you to the Amorites and the Hittites and the Perizzites and the Canaanites, the Hivites and the Jebusites, and I blot them out, . . ."

It remains to note a few cases where the presence of God is expressed in a more spectacular way.

The Appearance of the Commander of the Lord's Army

God appears in theophany in Joshua 5:13–15:

When Joshua was by Jericho, he lifted up his eyes and looked, and behold, a man was standing before him with his drawn sword in his hand. And Joshua went to him and said to him, "Are you for us, or for our adversaries?" And he said, "No; but I am the commander of the army of the LORD. Now I have come." And Joshua fell on his face to the earth and worshiped and said to him, "What does my lord say to his servant?" And the commander of the LORD's army said to Joshua, "Take off your sandals from your feet, for the place where you are standing is holy." And Joshua did so.

In the light of Joshua's reaction and the holiness of the figure, we may conclude that this commander is the same as the "angel" mentioned in

Exodus 23:23. He is a divine messenger, foreshadowing the incarnation of Christ and Christ's role as warrior (Rev. 19:11). This theophany is both a man theophany and a warrior theophany. It is suitable that God appears in human form to depict to Joshua, the human commander, what role God will have in the conquest. Joshua as commander imitates and reflects the divine commander. The timing of the divine appearance also makes sense. The earlier speech of God in Joshua 1 governs the whole conquest. Now God comes in a more specific way, just before Joshua and the people are about to engage in the first battle, the battle of Jericho.

Earlier in Joshua 5, the Lord instructs the people to be circumcised (v. 2). Circumcision is a sign of God's covenant (Gen. 17:10–14). It confirms God's presence among his people, and his faithfulness to the promises he made to Abraham.

The Battle of Jericho

The battle of Jericho plays a key role as the opening battle for the entire conquest. It serves as an exemplar, a key case that is a model for the conquest as a whole. It establishes the principles governing the entire conquest. The conquest succeeds by obedience to God, not merely by force of human power or by clever stratagems. Conquest fails if the people compromise their loyalty and allegiance to God, as the incident with Achan shows (Joshua 7). God himself is the central figure in the battle, as the ritual of carrying the ark around the city illustrates. The miraculous acts involving the parting of the Jordan River and the fall of the walls of Jericho manifest God's power and presence in specific, concrete ways.

The Day the Sun Stood Still

We see another spectacular manifestation of the presence of God through the miracles accompanying Joshua's battle against Adonizedek and his allies (Joshua 10). God throws stones from heaven and makes the sun stand still:

> [10] And the LORD threw them into a panic before Israel, who struck them with a great blow at Gibeon and chased them by the way of the ascent of Beth-horon and struck them as far as Azekah and Makke-dah. [11] And as they fled before Israel, while they were going down the

ascent of Beth-horon, the LORD threw down large stones from heaven on them as far as Azekah, and they died. There were more who died because of the hailstones than the sons of Israel killed with the sword.

¹² At that time Joshua spoke to the LORD in the day when the LORD gave the Amorites over to the sons of Israel, and he said in the sight of Israel,

> "Sun, stand still at Gibeon,
>   and moon, in the Valley of Aijalon."
> ¹³ And the sun stood still, and the moon stopped,
>   until the nation took vengeance on their enemies.

Is this not written in the book of Jashar? The sun stopped in the midst of heaven and did not hurry to set for about a whole day.

¹⁴ There has been no day like it before or since, when the LORD heeded the voice of a man, for the LORD fought for Israel. (Josh. 10:10–14)

"The LORD fought for Israel," it says (v. 14). This expression is the language of a warrior theophany. The Lord made his presence known through the heavenly phenomena of "large stones from heaven" (v. 11) and the sun and moon standing still.

Assessing the Conquest

As Joshua reaches the end of his life, he rehearses before Israel the significance of the conquest (Josh. 23:1–24:13). We see again the theme of God's prophetic word, his faithfulness to his word, and the fulfillment of the prophecies of the conquest. Joshua himself gives a word from God in the first person, functioning as a prophet and thereby expressing in his own person the presence of God, who is speaking through his servant (Josh. 24:2).

The Troubles in Judges

We move next to the book of Judges. We are still dealing with the theme of conquest, but now it is articulated in terms of failure as well as temporary successes that take place through the judges that God raises up. The pattern for the book of Judges is articulated in Judges 2 in connection with "the angel of the LORD":

Now the angel of the LORD went up from Gilgal to Bochim. And he said, "I brought you up from Egypt and brought you into the land that I swore to give to your fathers. I said, 'I will never break my covenant with you.'" (Judg. 2:1)

The fact that the angel of the Lord "went up from Gilgal to Bochim" suggests a localized presence, but it does not become explicit as to whether there was a special visual appearance. The angel speaks on behalf of the Lord in the first person, and warns of the troubles to come because of the people's disobedience. This speech, and the later expanded explanation in Judges 2:16–23, are programmatic for the whole book of Judges. As is often the case, the word of God, spoken once, continues to be present and governs the whole period of time that is to follow.

The judges themselves are raised up by God's power and grace. So they are themselves human representatives who express the presence of God with his people. For the most part, the raising up of these judges and God's acts of judgment and deliverance through them offer the principal path by which God expresses his presence with the people.

We may illustrate with the song of Deborah, a poetic reflection on the presence of God in the battle of Barak (Judg. 5:2–31). The poetic language includes resonances with the language of warrior theophany and the theophany of Sinai:

> "Lord, when you went out from Seir,
>   when you *marched* from the region of Edom,
> the earth trembled
>   and the heavens dropped,
>   yes, the *clouds* dropped water.
> The mountains *quaked before* the Lord,
>   even Sinai *before* the Lord, the God of Israel." (Judg. 5:4–5)

But in addition, we find a few cases where God appears in a theophany to prepare for the work of one of the judges.

The Appearance to Gideon

"The angel of the Lord" appears to Gideon:

> Now the *angel* of the Lord came and *sat* under the terebinth at Ophrah, which belonged to Joash the Abiezrite, while his son Gideon was beating out wheat in the winepress to hide it from the Midianites. And the angel of the Lord *appeared* to him and said to him, "The Lord is with you, O mighty man of valor." (Judg. 6:11–12)

Is this instance an appearance of a created angel or of a messenger (angel) who is divine? After the encounter, Gideon is afraid, because he has "seen the angel of the LORD face to face" (v. 22). The intensity of the experience suggests that he has encountered a messenger who is divine.

On this occasion, Gideon encounters a man-like appearance. It is suitable to the occasion. Gideon himself, after extensive interaction with the angel (messenger), becomes a man willing to serve as judge, and in his own person he represents the presence of God with Israel.

The Appearance to Manoah's Wife

The last judge in the book of Judges, Samson, has the most elaborate story. The length of the story shows both Samson's greatness and his weakness. In keeping with this more elaborate story, there is preparation that begins with his parents-to-be:

> And the angel of the LORD appeared to the woman and said to her, "Behold, you are barren and have not borne children, but you shall conceive and bear a son. Therefore be careful and drink no wine or strong drink, and eat nothing unclean." (Judg. 13:3–4)

Samson too, like earlier judges, will represent the power and presence of the Lord to the people. The parents need to receive instructions, since his calling as a Nazirite—and his failure to live up to it—is a key element in the story of his life. The deliverance of this message and this plan for his life is made more solemn and holy by the special appearance of the angel of the Lord to deliver it. Samson himself later becomes a messenger of the Lord by his actions as a judge for Israel. But his failures show in a dramatically concentrated way the failures of Israel during the whole period of the judges.

The Way toward a King

As many commentators have observed, Judges ends on a depressing note:

> In those days there was no king in Israel. Everyone did what was right in his own eyes. (Judg. 21:25)

The failures in Judges indicate the need for a king. A king, even more than a temporary judge, can express the presence of God with Israel, through his role in ruling the people according to the law of God. The king foreshadows Jesus Christ, the great king and Messiah. And thus also, in a subordinate way, the judges foreshadow him too. The presence of God supremely in Christ is foreshadowed by his presence and his mercy expressed through Israelite judges and kings. Their failures, which are manifold, show the need for a perfect king.

The Book of Ruth

The book of Ruth shows how God is present in his providence to take care of Naomi and Ruth. Boaz is a redeemer figure, foreshadowing the coming of Christ. Through him and through his son, God's presence in blessing is experienced by Naomi and Ruth. And of course God is preparing providentially the line of David, which leads forward to Christ (Ruth 4:18–22).

38

God Appearing during
the Monarchy

Now we turn to the period of the monarchy, from the time of Samuel to the beginning of the exile (1–2 Samuel; 1–2 Kings; 1–2 Chronicles). This time period overlaps with some of the prophetic and poetical books. But for convenience we focus first on the prose historical accounts of this period.

God's Presence through Prophets and Kings

The historical books invite us to see the hand of God's providence in all of the events during these times. But we may also ask about ways in which, from time to time, he expresses his presence in an especially intensive or striking way. God works particularly through prophets and kings during these times. The kings are supposed to follow God's ways as expressed in the law (Deut. 17:18–20). When they do, they are a channel for the presence of God and the blessing of God on the people as a whole.

From time to time the kings receive, in addition, special messages from prophets (e.g., 2 Kings 19:20–34; 20:1–11). But at many points the prophets have to redirect or oppose the ways of the kings, because the kings fail to be faithful to God. The prophets express the presence and power of God through delivering the word of God and sometimes through miracles.

Samuel in particular should be mentioned, since he is both a prophet (1 Sam. 3:20; 9:9) and the last of the judges (7:6, 15–17). Through Samuel God brings about the key transition from the time of the judges to the time of the monarchy.

God's Presence with the Ark

During the time of Samuel, God's presence is especially associated with the ark of the covenant. The ark symbolically represents the presence of God, as was established in the time of Moses (Ex. 25:22). First Samuel 4–6 provides the story of the capture of the ark in battle and then its return to Israel.

First Samuel 4:1–10 is deeply ironic. The Israelites propose to bring the ark into the war camp so that God may fight for them. They indeed recognize a special presence of God with the ark, and they hope that he will manifest his presence in battle. God might work providentially, or work in a miracle, or even manifest himself in a warrior theophany as at the exodus (Ex. 15:3). Even the Philistines recognize some of the dangerous significance of the ark:

> And when they learned that the ark of the LORD had come to the camp, the Philistines were afraid, for they said, "A god has come into the camp." And they said, "Woe to us! For nothing like this has happened before. Woe to us! Who can deliver us from the power of these mighty gods? These are the gods who struck the Egyptians with every sort of plague in the wilderness." (1 Sam. 4:6–8)

All of this is painfully close to the truth. God is present, and he may indeed break out in judgment on his enemies. But neither the Philistines nor the Israelites anticipate the actual result: God lets the ark, the symbol of his presence, be captured! He judges the Israelite army and the sons of Eli, not the Philistines.

The sequel shows, however, that God is still powerfully present with the ark. The Philistines suffer plagues. The statue of Dagon falls down before the ark (1 Sam. 5:3–4). Finally, the Philistines send the ark back to the Israelites. The return of the ark includes a miracle, consisting in the fact that the mother cows ("milk cows") go straight toward Israel, overruling their instinct to go back to their calves (6:10–12). Even Israelites who look into the ark are punished by death (6:19). Later Uzzah experiences the same punishment for touching the ark (2 Sam. 6:6–7).

The ark is almost like a miniature theophany. It manifests the holiness of God. God does as he pleases in connection with the presence of the ark—and woe to the person who does not respect his holiness!

The Thunderstorm of Wrath in Samuel

Moving past the providential events that lead to Samuel establishing Saul as the first king, we come to a spectacular event in the form of a thunderstorm:

> So Samuel called upon the LORD, and the LORD sent *thunder and rain* that day, and all the people greatly feared the LORD and Samuel. (1 Sam. 12:18)

The storm itself, together with the people's reaction, make us think about Mount Sinai. But is the storm a *theophany* in the narrow sense of the word? Or is it just a providential thunderstorm, in response to Samuel's prayer? As is often the case, the boundary between a "strict" theophany and a broader providence is not clear-cut. God manifests his power and his wrath in the storm. So in a broader sense, God shows himself as he manifests his presence to the people in the storm. The people are meant to take this storm with uttermost seriousness, even if it is not completely on the level of the theophany at Mount Sinai.

David and Goliath

The battle of David and Goliath in 1 Samuel 17 is one of many battles that David fights for God on behalf of the people of Israel. It stands out not only because it is the first, not only because the narrator devotes more space to it, but also because of the striking way in which David wins the victory. It is so improbable in human terms. A mere boy wins against a giant who is a seasoned warrior.

There is nothing impossible in the narration, when we see it against the background of ordinary providence. David's stone hits Goliath in just the right place. According to regularities of providence, stones violently hitting the forehead can knock people out, give them a concussion, or even kill them.

But within the environment of the ancient Near East, all the observers would understand the theological significance of the event. The ancient Near East thought that victory in battle did not come merely from superior weapons or superior training or superior tactics. The patron gods of the armies could get involved in battle, and their participation could be decisive. In fact, Goliath sets up the situation, not only in terms of himself and a single Israelite soldier as two champions representing the two armies, but in terms of the participation of the sphere of the gods: "The Philistine cursed David *by his gods*" (1 Sam. 17:43). David understands the significance of his encounter with Goliath:

> "For who is this uncircumcised Philistine, that he should defy the armies of the *living God*?" (v. 26)

So now,

> David said to the Philistine, "You come to me with a sword and with a spear and with a javelin, but I come to you in the *name of the Lord of hosts*, the God of the armies of Israel, *whom* you have defied. This day *the Lord* will deliver you into my hand, and I will strike you down and cut off your head. And I will give the dead bodies of the host of the Philistines this day to the birds of the air and to the wild beasts of the earth, that all the earth may know that there is *a God in Israel*, and that all this assembly may know that the Lord *saves* not with sword and spear. For the battle is *the Lord's*, and *he will give* you into our hand." (vv. 45–47)

We are invited to see the battle as a display of the work of God the divine warrior, working through David the human warrior and through his acts of providence. So this battle is akin to a warrior theophany.

The Witch of Endor and the Appearance of Samuel

We may venture to consider also the strange and disturbing narrative of Samuel appearing to Saul in connection with the witch of Endor (1 Sam. 28:12–19). This is a real appearance of Samuel, not a fake one, as we can tell from the fact that the witch herself reacts violently when Samuel appears (v. 12).

This appearance is in some ways antithetical to a theophany. Rather than an appearance of the *living God*, it is an appearance of a *dead person*. It reeks of death and horror. It suits the situation of Saul, because in his own life he has spiraled down toward death, spiritually speaking. His willingness to consult with the dead, in defiance of his own earlier ban on mediums (v. 9), shows a further step in his descent into wickedness.

One of the ironies, then, is that Samuel really does appear. And Samuel has a prophetic message from God. By speaking on behalf of God, Samuel manifests the presence and power of God right in the midst of the atmosphere of death. But Samuel does not really add much to what he has been saying all along to Saul, if only Saul would have listened: "The LORD has done to you as he spoke by me, for the LORD has torn the kingdom out of your hand and given it to your neighbor, David" (1 Sam. 28:17). Saul is headed for death, in accord with the atmosphere of death in which he is currently living: "Moreover, the LORD will give Israel also with you into the hand of the Philistines, and *tomorrow* you and your sons shall be *with me*. The LORD will give the army of Israel also into the hand of the Philistines" (v. 19). We have a kind of antitheophany of grim judgment.

David's Reflections on God's Deliverance

In 2 Samuel 22 David reflects on a lifetime of experiences in which God acted to deliver him (Psalm 18 is largely parallel). Part of the song describes the deliverances using language of a thunderstorm theophany (vv. 8–16). This constitutes poetic use of theophanic language in order to make plain the close theological relation between theophanies and providential acts of God. We have discussed this passage earlier (chapter 2).

The Lord Bringing Pestilence on Israel

In 2 Samuel 24, we have one of the few visual appearances of God, or his angel, in the account of David's foolish census and the subsequent selection of the future temple site:

> And when the *angel* stretched out his hand toward Jerusalem to destroy it, the LORD relented from the calamity and said to the angel who was working destruction among the people, "It is enough; now stay your hand." And the angel of the LORD *was by* the threshing floor of Araunah the Jebusite. Then David spoke to the LORD when he *saw the angel* who was striking the people, and said, "Behold, I have sinned, and I have done wickedly. But these sheep, what have they done? Please let your hand be against me and against my father's house." And Gad came that day to David and said to him, "Go up, raise an altar to the LORD on the threshing floor of Araunah the Jebusite." (2 Sam. 24:16–18)

The special appearance befits the solemnity of judgment against God's own people. It also fits the deep holiness to be associated with what would later become the site of Solomon's temple.

The Lord's Appearance to Solomon

The Lord appears to Solomon in a dream in 1 Kings 3:3–15. The text does not give us any visual details. What it does give is the verbal contents of the communication between God and Solomon. As in many other cases, the main function of theophany is to underline and make firm the verbal covenantal commitments that belong to the divine communication that comes in the context of theophany. This commitment is confirmed in the subsequent narration, which illustrates the operation and demonstration of the wisdom of Solomon (vv. 16–28). The narrative concludes by remarking on Solomon's wisdom: "And all Israel heard of the judgment that the king had rendered, and they stood in awe of the king, because they *perceived* that the *wisdom* of God was in him to do justice" (1 Sam. 3:28). The Israelites "perceived" the wisdom of God that Solomon manifested. He manifested the wisdom and therefore also the presence of God. God's wisdom *appeared* in Solomon.

God Appearing to Consecrate the Temple

In 1 Kings 8:10–11, the ceremonies that complete the setting up of Solomon's temple find their climax in the manifestation of God. God comes and fills the temple with his glory:

> And when the priests came out of the Holy Place, a *cloud filled* the house of the LORD, so that the priests could not stand to minister because of the *cloud*, for the *glory* of the LORD *filled* the house of the LORD.

This appearance of the cloud is an instance of cloud theophany. It has thematic connections with the cloud in the wilderness, which in the days of Moses came down to consecrate the tabernacle (Ex. 40:34–38). In the case of the Solomonic temple, it seems that the appearance of the cloud is temporary. But it makes a permanent statement. It says that God officially (and dramatically!) recognizes the temple as his special covenantal dwelling place. It gives weight to Solomon's subsequent prayer, that the Lord would answer his people and bless them from this center (1 Kings 8:12–53).

In response to Solomon's prayer and the ceremonies of dedication, the Lord appears to Solomon again:

> As soon as Solomon had finished building the house of the LORD and the king's house and all that Solomon desired to build, the LORD *appeared* to Solomon a second time, as he had appeared to him at Gibeon. (1 Kings 9:1–2)

The text provides no information about visual details. The appearing of God introduces a speech in which God confirms his covenant with David, Solomon, and the people (vv. 3–9). The theophany is *covenantal* in its function. It confirms the contents of God's word, which expresses his covenantal commitment.

Solomon's Wisdom before the Queen of Sheba

Solomon's display of wisdom before the queen of Sheba does not involve any unusual visual phenomena. They are not needed. God is manifesting himself, in a broad sense, through the human Solomon, who is blessed with the wisdom of God himself. Solomon foreshadows the wisdom of Christ, who is the source of all wisdom. The Gentile nations seek out Solomon for his wisdom (1 Kings 4:34; 10:1). Likewise, in the time of fulfillment, the Gentiles come to Christ not only for wisdom but for salvation (John 12:20–21; 1 Cor. 1:22–24).

Later Communication to Solomon

Later, Solomon strays from his exclusive loyalty to the Lord. In its comments, the text recalls the two earlier appearances to Solomon but does not suggest that there was a third appearance. Instead, it mentions only that God *spoke* to Solomon:

> And the LORD was angry with Solomon, because his heart had turned away from the LORD, the God of Israel, who had *appeared to him twice* and had commanded him concerning this thing, that he should not go after other gods. But he did not keep what the LORD commanded. Therefore the LORD *said* to Solomon, "Since this has been your practice and you have not kept my covenant and my statutes that I have commanded you, I will surely tear the kingdom from you and will give it to your servant." (1 Kings 11:9–11)

After Solomon's disloyalty, the kingdoms of Judah and Israel mostly spiral downward. There are a few good kings in the southern kingdom. God's hand of providence is still in it all. Particularly, there is a repeated note that God will preserve the line of Solomon for the sake of David:

> "Yet for the sake of *David* your father I will not do it in your days, but I will tear it out of the hand of your son. However, I will not tear away all the kingdom, but I will give one tribe to your son, for the sake of *David my servant* and for the sake of Jerusalem that I have chosen." (1 Kings 11:12–13)

But the dramatic appearances of God come mostly through the prophets, whom God raises up to rebuke the kings and the people and to call them to repentance.

The Confrontation with Jeroboam

In one of the early cases of prophetic confrontation, God sends a prophet to confront Jeroboam concerning his apostate worship. It is a dramatic confrontation, with divine miracles when Jeroboam's arm dries up (1 Kings 13:4), when it is restored by prophetic word (v. 6), and when the altar is torn down and its ashes are poured out (v. 5). God is present, though we do not hear of any special visual appearance of God.

Elijah and Mount Carmel

Further miracles come through Elijah—a whole string of them. All miracles manifest a special presence of God. These miracles confirm the divine authenticity of Elijah's messages. Such confirmation stands in antithesis to the widespread unbelief and devotion to false gods among the people of Israel.

The climactic confrontation comes at Mount Carmel. And the climax of the confrontation comes with the descent of fire from heaven:

> "Answer me, O LORD, answer me, that this people may know that you, O LORD, are God, and that you have turned their hearts back." Then the *fire* of the LORD fell and consumed the burnt offering and the wood and the stones and the dust, and licked up the water that was in the trench. And when all the people saw it, they fell on their faces and said, "The LORD, he is God; the LORD, he is God." (1 Kings 18:37–39)

We see a fire theophany: "the fire of the LORD fell." The power and presence of the Lord comes with such intensity and with such spectacular display that—at least temporarily—the people are overwhelmed and turn toward God: "they fell on their faces and said, 'The LORD, he is God.'"

The theophany is impressive not merely because of an impressive visual display but because it manifests the character of God. He is master over fire and storm. He is the true God who has power over all. He answers the prayers of his servants. This manifestation of God anticipates the climactic revelation of God in the person of Christ. Christ reveals who God is: "Whoever has seen me has seen the Father" (John 14:9). Christ comes with the fire of judgment and purification:

> "I [John the Baptist] baptize you with water for repentance, but he who is coming after me [Christ] is mightier than I, whose sandals I am not worthy to carry. He will baptize you with the Holy Spirit and fire. His winnowing fork is in his hand, and he will clear his threshing floor and gather his wheat into the barn, but the chaff he will burn with unquenchable fire." (Matt. 3:11–12)

But in the time of Elijah, the people's hearts are fickle. Their turn toward God is only temporary. The temporary effect shows the inferiority of the theophany at Mount Carmel to the theophany in Christ. And yet even the appearing of Christ receives a faithful response only if the Holy Spirit works a change in people's hearts. We still await the final act in God's redemption, at the time of the return of Christ, when "every knee should bow" (Phil. 2:10). This final bowing will take place both among those who are saved and among those who are lost. The latter will submit without the change of heart that brings salvation, forgiveness, and spiritual communion with the benefits of Christ's redemption.

Elijah and the Confrontation on Mount Horeb

Immediately after the confrontation on Mount Carmel, Elijah flees. God sends "an angel" and guides Elijah to Horeb, the mount of God (1 Kings 19:6–8). The angel is specifically identified as "the angel of the LORD" (v. 7). We are not given enough information to determine whether this angel is a manifestation of the preincarnate Christ or a created angelic being. He bestows mercy from God, mercy such as, in the end, comes from the person and work of Christ.

When Elijah comes to Horeb, "the word of the LORD" comes to him

(v. 9). As in many other cases, the visual manifestations of God serve to underline the revelation of God through speech.

After some back-and-forth dialogue about Elijah, God tells him to "Go out and stand on the mount before the LORD" (v. 11). This instruction recalls Moses's role in meeting the Lord on Mount Sinai. The location—"Horeb, the mount of God" (v. 8)—is Mount Sinai. We are prepared to expect next an account of God coming in theophany to meet Elijah, in a manner parallel to the earlier theophany at Mount Sinai in the days of Moses.

"And behold, the LORD passed by" (v. 11). This stage in the account already indicates a theophany.

Then we have "a great and strong wind," "an earthquake," and "a fire" (vv. 11–12). But the Lord is "not in" them. It is a curious note, given that we have been set up to expect a theophany like Mount Sinai. This narrative, and the appearance of God to Elijah that it narrates, deliberately breaks human expectations. One can imagine that it also breaks the expectations of Elijah himself. In the light of the introductory words, "And behold, the LORD passed by," we should see the wind and earthquake and fire as the outer edge of the manifestation of the Lord in theophany. But the text denies that they represent the inner side. The Lord is "not in" them.

Well, what is he in? The KJV says, "A still small voice" (v. 12). ESV has "the sound of a low whisper." NASB has "a sound of a gentle blowing."[1] Elijah's response, in going out of the cave, seems to indicate that he senses that in this sound is the heart of the matter. The most intensive revelation of God comes through meanings, not through spectacle. Those meanings, because they are the meanings of God, have God's presence in them, and also God's power. God tells Elijah, without loud volume, what he will do through Hazael and Elisha. The subsequent narration shows that God does just as he said he would.

The point of theophany, then, is not spectacle in itself. The point is to meet and understand God. And also to be blessed by him. That blessing takes place only through communion, and communion with the holy God must overcome sin and its stain. That problem of communion is always in the background in the Old Testament. And sometimes, as at Mount Sinai and with the institutions of sacrifice and priesthood, it is

---

1. The Hebrew phrase is mysterious, and some interpreters go in a different direction, by claiming that it is a thunderous sound.

in the foreground. The animal sacrifices and the priesthood instituted in the time of Moses symbolize the fact that the people are sinful and need mediation in order to endure the presence of God. When an animal is slaughtered in sacrifice, the innocent animal signifies the need for a substitute for sin. It prefigures the fact that Christ will offer himself as a substitute for sin (2 Cor. 5:21; 1 Pet. 2:24).

Micaiah's Vision

Next, consider the narrative in 1 Kings 22. There is no outward theophany visible to all. But Micaiah recounts a theophanic vision given to him alone:

> And Micaiah said, "Therefore hear the word of the LORD: I saw the LORD sitting on his throne, and all the host of heaven standing beside him on his right hand and on his left; and the LORD said, 'Who will entice Ahab, that he may go up and fall at Ramoth-gilead?' And one said one thing, and another said another. Then a spirit came forward and stood before the LORD, saying, 'I will entice him.' And the LORD said to him, 'By what means?' And he said, 'I will go out, and will be a lying spirit in the mouth of all his prophets.' And he said, 'You are to entice him, and you shall succeed; go out and do so.'" (1 Kings 22:19–22)

We have here what we have described earlier as a court theophany (chapter 6). It suits the occasion. The vision comes to Micaiah alone, partly because the others in the company are not worthy recipients. But in addition, it comes to Micaiah in antithetical contrast to the counsel that the lying spirit gives through prophets to Ahab and Jehoshaphat (vv. 6, 24). Only Micaiah sees and hears the heavenly council, so that the two kings remain trapped by the lying voices that they hear on earth. A full theophany is suitable, to answer the cultural weight that would be felt in a solemn council involving two kings and four hundred prophets (v. 6). A court theophany is suitable, because the divine court in heaven is the suitable counterweight to the earthly court composed of the two kings and their counselors.

The irony is striking. The Lord says, in effect, "You think to take solemn counsel for war. But I am holding another council above you, which not only overrules yours but dictates its contents in a manner that undermines completely its humanly intended purpose." Micaiah's vision says a lot about theophany. The Lord rules, and his will is done—even as in heaven, so, in the end, on earth. This lesson may stand as a statement of principle valid for the whole period of the monarchy. In the way in which the people of Israel asked for a king, they repudiated God as their king (1 Sam. 8:7). But God is nevertheless still king! His will supersedes all human plots, and undermines them when appropriate. Indeed, the principle is valid for all of history.

The Consumption of Companies of Fifty

The next theophany-like event in the monarchy comes when Ahaziah sends out companies of fifty to bring Elijah to him. The first two companies perish:

> But Elijah answered the captain of fifty, "If I am a man of God, let *fire* come down from heaven and consume you and your fifty." Then *fire* came down from heaven and consumed him and his fifty. (2 Kings 1:10)

> Then the *fire* of God came down from heaven and consumed him and his fifty. (v. 12)

The descent of fire is reminiscent of the descent of fire at Mount Carmel (1 Kings 18:38). It is "the fire of God" (v. 12). It manifests God's judgment and the power of God's word as spoken through Elijah. The two instances are appearances of God in a broad sense.

Elijah Goes Up to God in a Whirlwind

Second Kings 2 describes the time when Elijah is taken up to heaven alive. The account of Elijah's ascent is bookended by two miracles, in both of which the Jordan River divides (2:8, 14). The two instances of division are reminiscent of the dividing of the Red Sea and the dividing of the Jordan at the time of Joshua. The miracles manifest the special presence of God with Elijah, and then Elisha as Elijah's successor. The latter of the two miracles confirms that Elisha does indeed have the spirit of Elijah on him and is his divinely appointed successor: "Now when the sons of the prophets who were at Jericho saw him opposite them, they said, 'The spirit of Elijah rests on Elisha'" (2:15).

The narrative of the actual ascent of Elijah has theophanic features: "And as they still went on and talked, behold, *chariots* of *fire* and horses of *fire* separated the two of them. And Elijah went up by a *whirlwind* into *heaven*" (v. 11). The chariots have a link with chariot theophanies. The fire has links with fire theophanies. The whirlwind reminds us of the wind sometimes accompanying a thunderstorm theophany (2 Sam. 22:11). Finally, note that Elijah ascends to *heaven*, the special abode of God.

The Vision of the Chariots of God
Given to Elisha and His Servant

Next, theophanic features occur in the vision that God gives to Elisha and then to his servant concerning the provision for Elisha's protection:

> When the servant of the man of God rose early in the morning and went out, behold, an army with horses and chariots was all around the city. And the servant said, "Alas, my master! What shall we do?" He said, "Do not be afraid, for those who are with us are more than those who are with them." Then Elisha prayed and said, "O Lord, please open his eyes that he may see." So the Lord opened the eyes of the young man, and he saw, and behold, the mountain was full of horses and chariots of fire all around Elisha. (2 Kings 6:15–17)

In a manner similar to the narrative in 1 Kings 22, we can see a marked contrast. The "army with horses and chariots" on a human level surrounds the city. The angelic army is then dramatically juxtaposed to it. This manifestation, like many, emphasizes the reality and efficacy of the divine presence. God is in heaven, but his works are also seen on earth. He works for those who fear him, even when we cannot see behind the scenes into heaven or the angelic realm.

The Slaughter of the Assyrian Army

We should note a significant case of the powerful presence of the Lord in answer to Hezekiah and the distress of Jerusalem. At the end of the complex events involving the king of Assyria, the Rabshakeh, King Hezekiah, his assistants, and Isaiah, there comes a resolution: "And that night the angel of the Lord went out and struck down 185,000 in the camp of the Assyrians. And when people arose early in the morning, behold, these were all dead bodies" (2 Kings 19:35).

The mention of "the angel of the Lord" gives us, figuratively speaking, a kind of glimpse into the divine realm and the realm of the angels.

But the text does not suggest that the presence of the angel included a spectacular visual form. It is enough that he acted, and the effects were powerful and devastating. We have an appearance of the power and judgment of God. He is specially present in killing the Assyrians.

The End of the Monarchy

The end of the monarchy comes not with a "bang" of visual display in spectacular theophany, but with the "whimper"[2] of being dragged into exile (2 Kings 25:21). The narration makes it plain that God is not absent:

> Still the Lord did not turn from the burning of his great wrath, by which his anger was kindled against Judah, because of all the provocations with which Manasseh had provoked him. And the Lord said, "*I will remove Judah* also out of my sight, as I have removed Israel, and I will cast off this city that I have chosen, Jerusalem, and the house of which I said, My name shall be there." (2 Kings 23:26–27)

The Lord says, "I will remove Judah"—it is not Nebuchadnezzar, ultimately, but the Lord who does it. The Lord does it, not as an arbitrary act of power but as an act of wrath, of justice, and of holiness: "his anger was kindled against Judah, because of all the provocations with which Manasseh had provoked him" (v. 26).

Second Chronicles makes a similar point:

> The Lord, the God of their fathers, sent persistently to them by his messengers, because he had compassion on his people and on his dwelling place. But they kept mocking the messengers of God, despising his words and scoffing at his prophets, until the wrath of the Lord rose against his people, until *there was no remedy*.
>
> Therefore he brought up against them the king of the Chaldeans. (2 Chron. 36:15–17)

In short, the exile is a manifestation of the presence of God in wrath.

---

2. Alluding to the final lines of T. S. Eliot's poem "The Hollow Men": ". . . This is the way the world ends. Not with a bang but a whimper."

39

God Appearing in the Prophets: Isaiah

Now we consider ways in which God expresses his presence in the books of the prophets (Isaiah to Malachi). These writings belong to the time extending from the monarchy until after the exile. Some prophetic books, like Joel, Obadiah, and Nahum, do not contain specific information about their dating. For convenience, we will consider them in the order in which they normally appear in English Bibles.

Patterns of God's Presence in the Prophets

The prophets are men commissioned by God to deliver the word of God to the people. God expresses his authority, power, and presence in his word. So, in this way, he is present on every page and in every verse in the prophetic writings. That principle is important. But it does not lead us in the direction of singling out any particular passage.

Descriptions of theophanies or expressions akin to theophany most often occur in four contexts.

Appearances for commissioning. First, God may appear in a vision or a dream to commission the prophet for his task. This appearance at the beginning means that God underlines his presence with his word and the solemnity belonging to words that come from God. It reminds the prophet himself as well as all his readers and listeners that it is God who speaks. Theophany introduces the message of God, which continues to abide even after the theophany is completed.

Isaiah testifies to a strong reaction when God appears to him: "And I said: 'Woe is me! For I am lost; for I am a man of unclean lips, and I dwell in the midst of a people of unclean lips; for my eyes have seen the King, the Lord of hosts!'" (Isa. 6:5). He is overwhelmed by the holiness of God in contrast to his own unworthiness.

When God commissions Jeremiah, there is no specific indication that a visual appearance accompanies the commission. But Jeremiah, like Isaiah, sees his own inadequacy: "Then I said, 'Ah, Lord God! Behold, I do not know how to speak, for I am only a youth'" (Jer. 1:6). Ezekiel also has a moving reaction: "And when I saw it, I fell on my face, and I heard the voice of one speaking" (Ezek. 1:28).

The reaction of prophets has a lesson for the readers and listeners. The text calls on us to respond with awe and reverence to God, who speaks from his majesty.

Appearances for judgment. Theophany-like descriptions also come into the prophetic books in contexts threatening or announcing God's judgment. The final judgment will be a time when God *appears* as judge (Rev. 20:11–15). It is fitting that he often proclaims earlier judgments in connection with courtroom scenes. We will consider these scenes individually as they come up in the prophetic writings.

Appearances for salvation. Descriptions of God appearing or of his intensive presence also come up in the context of promises of salvation and deliverance. Salvation includes the aspect of judgment against enemies, whether these enemies are physical or spiritual. But the context may emphasize the positive aspects of salvation rather than the negative aspects of judgment.

Remembering appearances in the past. Some passages, such as Isaiah 51:9–10, call to remembrance God's mighty deeds in the past:

> Awake, awake, put on strength,
>   O arm of the Lord;
> awake, as in days of old,
>   the generations of long ago.
> Was it not you who cut Rahab in pieces,
>   who pierced the dragon?
> Was it not you who dried up the sea,
>   the waters of the great deep,
> who made the depths of the sea a way
>   for the redeemed to pass over?

This passage alludes to the exodus from Egypt, by speaking of "days of old," "the generations of long ago," and by mentioning that God "dried up the sea." These evocations of the past can be used to convict the people of Israel of their ingratitude and faithlessness. But they can also be used as the basis for promising that God will act in the future in a mighty way. In fact, the opening words of Isaiah 51:9 call on God to act in the future: "Awake, awake, put on strength." The continuation of the passage in verse 11 then explicitly promises that God will bring redemption in a manner analogous to the exodus:

> And the ransomed of the LORD shall return
>   and come to Zion with singing;
> everlasting joy shall be upon their heads;
>   they shall obtain gladness and joy,
>   and sorrow and sighing shall flee away.

Theophanic acts of God in the past foreshadow further acts in the future. These acts of God lead up to God's climactic work of salvation in the first and second comings of Christ. The historical dynamics of salvation confirm what we have already observed about the dynamics of reflections, which is the dynamics of theophany (chapter 23). God's purposes become manifest in theophany, and continue to unfold even if the theophany itself is only temporary.

The Presence of God in Isaiah

We now consider the passages in the book of Isaiah that express an especially intense presence of God.

Isaiah Seeing the Prophecy (Isaiah 1:1)

The whole book of Isaiah is characterized as a *vision*: "The *vision* of Isaiah the son of Amoz, which he *saw* concerning Judah and Jerusalem in the days of Uzziah, Jotham, Ahaz, and Hezekiah, kings of Judah" (Isa. 1:1). This language is significant, because it places the whole book in the atmosphere of God showing himself and his plans to Isaiah in a visually oriented way. The introductory verses create a broad atmosphere of theophany for the whole book.[1]

---

1. I am aware that critical scholars divide the book among two, three, or more human authors. My view is that the whole book comes from Isaiah the son of Amoz. We cannot go into all the

God's Presence in His House (Isaiah 2:1–4)

Isaiah 2 prophesies that the nations will come to seek God:

> The word that Isaiah the son of Amoz *saw* concerning Judah and Jerusalem.
>
> It shall come to pass in the latter days
>   that the mountain of the *house* of the LORD
> shall be established as the highest of the mountains,
>   and shall be lifted up above the hills;
> and all the nations shall flow to it,
>   and many peoples shall come, and say:
> "Come, let us go up to the mountain of the LORD,
>   to the house of the God of Jacob,
> that he may teach us his ways
>   and that we may walk in his paths."
> For out of Zion shall go the law,
>   and the word of the LORD from Jerusalem.
> He shall judge between the nations,
>   and shall decide disputes for many peoples;
> and they shall beat their swords into plowshares,
>   and their spears into pruning hooks;
> nation shall not lift up sword against nation,
>   neither shall they learn war anymore. (Isa. 2:1–4)

The desire to seek God implies his special presence in his house. This presence is a grand fulfillment of the lesser presence of God about which Solomon prayed in his prayer of dedication for the temple (1 Kings 8:22–53). As the cloud filled the temple of Solomon (1 Kings 8:10–11), so in the future the glory of God will fill his house. That presence of God results in the going out of "the law" and "the word of the LORD" (Isa. 2:3). The law and the word themselves manifest the presence of God. It is implied that he is especially present in his house.

The fulfillment of this promise comes with Christ. It is Christ who is the final temple of God (John 2:21). In interpreting Isaiah, we must see the theological *meaning* of the house of God and the presence of God; we must not fixate on a structure of stone. Remember that the first site called "the house of God" was Bethel (Gen. 28:17). It was called that

---

arguments at this point. Even scholars with other views should admit that it is valuable to consider the book of Isaiah as a completed whole. That is what we are doing.

because of the presence of God, not because of a physical structure in the shape of a physical house.

The Commissioning of Isaiah (Isaiah 6:1–13)

The central, spectacular theophany in Isaiah comes in chapter 6. God appears in a vision to Isaiah and commissions him. It is a court theophany. It is suitable for underlining the solemnity and weight of the message that Isaiah is to bear and to communicate.

Commentators have debated as to whether this episode of commissioning is the *original* commissioning of Isaiah, or whether it comes later in his life. The vision takes place "in the year that King Uzziah died." But according to Isaiah 1:1, the span of Isaiah's ministry includes the reign of Uzziah as well as his successors, Jotham, Ahaz, and Hezekiah. It is possible that Isaiah's commission, described in Isaiah 6:1, took place *before* the death of Uzziah, but still within the final year of his reign. But, in view of the placing of the vision at a somewhat later point in the literary structure of the book, it seems more natural to see the whole account in 6:1–13 as falling at a point subsequent to the initial ministry of Isaiah. It nevertheless articulates powerfully the principle that is to be at work in the entire span of his ministry. He bears the word of God, and is to speak even though people do not have open ears.

The New Testament may contain a reference to Isaiah's vision in John 12:

> [39] Therefore they could not believe. For again Isaiah said,
>
> > [40] "He has blinded their eyes
> >   and hardened their heart,
> > lest they see with their eyes,
> >   and understand with their heart, and turn,
> >   and I would heal them."
>
> [41] Isaiah said these things because he *saw his glory* and spoke of him. (John 12:39–41)

John 12:39 quotes from Isaiah 6:10. So when John 12:41 says, "he saw his glory," it may have in mind the glory of the vision in Isaiah 6:1–4. (It is also possible that John is speaking more broadly of all that God revealed to Isaiah concerning the coming of the Messiah, including

Isa. 53:1, quoted in John 12:38.) Whether or not John is making a specific allusion, the glory of God in Isaiah 6:1–3 anticipates the glory of the incarnate Christ.

The Prophecy of Immanuel (Isaiah 7:14)

Isaiah 7:14 gives us the famous "Immanuel" prophecy:

> Therefore the Lord himself will give you a sign. Behold, the virgin shall conceive and bear a son, and shall call his name *Immanuel.*

As Matthew observes, the name *Immanuel* means "God with us":

> All this took place to fulfill what the Lord had spoken by the prophet:
>
>> "Behold, the virgin shall conceive and bear a son,
>>   and they shall call his name Immanuel"
>
> (which means, *God with us*). (Matt. 1:22–23)

For God to be "with us" expresses his presence—specifically, a presence in bringing salvation. And salvation itself comes through communion with God. So "God with us" is itself a summary of the meaning of salvation. Christ is "God with us."[2] He himself is God, the final theophany.

The Coming of the "Mighty God" in the Messiah (Isaiah 9:6)

The description of the Messiah as the "Mighty God" in Isaiah 9:6 implies that God appears in the person of the Messiah:

> For to us a child is born,
>   to us a son is given;
> and the government shall be upon his shoulder,
> and his name shall be called
> Wonderful Counselor, *Mighty God,*
>   Everlasting Father, Prince of Peace.

---

2. Bible interpreters debate as to whether Isaiah 7:14 is a *direct* prophecy of the coming of the Messiah, or whether during the time of Isaiah there is a preliminary fulfillment foreshadowing the coming of the Messiah. This debate need not concern us.

The Prophecy concerning Babylon (Isaiah 13:1)

The "oracle concerning Babylon" in Isaiah 13:1 is described as something that "Isaiah the son of Amoz *saw*." As in 1:1 and 2:1, the language of *seeing* evokes the atmosphere of theophany. In this case, the context is one of pronouncing judgment on Babylon. Judgment is one context in which theophany or an allusion to theophany is appropriate.

God's Punishment and Glory in Mount Zion

Isaiah 24:21–23 describes God's punishment in a passage linked to the appearance of his glory. The glory is the theophanic glory of his appearing:

> On that day the LORD will punish
>   the host of heaven, in heaven,
>   and the kings of the earth, on the earth.
> They will be gathered together
>   as prisoners in a pit;
> they will be shut up in a prison,
>   and after many days they will be punished.
> Then the moon will be confounded
>   and the sun ashamed,
> for the LORD of hosts reigns
>   on Mount Zion and in Jerusalem,
> and his *glory* will be before his elders.

A little earlier, the description includes the shaking of the earth, which is reminiscent of the earth shaking at Mount Sinai:

> The earth is utterly broken,
>   the earth is split apart,
>   the earth is violently shaken.
> The earth staggers like a drunken man;
>   it sways like a hut;
> its transgression lies heavy upon it,
>   and it falls, and will not rise again. (Isa. 24:19–20)

So the passage has several resonances with theophanic themes.

The Manifestation of God's Salvation

In the context of eschatological prophecy, Isaiah 25:9 describes the manifestation of God's salvation:

It will be said on that day,
> "Behold, this is our God; we have waited for him, that he
> might save us.
> This is the LORD; we have waited for him;
> let us be glad and rejoice in his salvation."

There is no explicit detail here that indicates that the coming of God includes a visual display. But God does come, and expresses his presence in salvation.

God's Triumph over Satanic Evil

In Isaiah 27:1 God vanquishes the forces of evil, concentrated in the figure of Leviathan: "In that day the LORD with his hard and great and strong sword will punish Leviathan the fleeing serpent, Leviathan the twisting serpent, and he will slay the dragon that is in the sea." This prophecy announces that God will utterly defeat Satan. The mention of the sword as the Lord's weapon shows a relation to warrior theophanies. The association of Leviathan with the sea calls to mind God's earlier triumph over Pharaoh in the waters of the Red Sea. Isaiah 27:1 speaks prophetically of a future day of salvation ("in that day"). This future salvation includes the powerful presence of God, and the warrior imagery suggests an appearance of God. The passage links itself naturally to other prophecies in Isaiah and elsewhere about the final act of salvation, which will include the manifestation of God and the destruction of all evil.

God's Triumph over Assyria

Isaiah 30:27–33 provides another passage with many features of theophany in the description:

> 27 Behold, the name of the LORD comes from afar,
> burning with his anger, and in thick rising *smoke*;
> his lips are full of fury,
> and his tongue is like a devouring *fire*;
> 28 his breath is like an overflowing stream
> that reaches up to the neck;
> to sift the nations with the sieve of destruction,
> and to place on the jaws of the peoples a bridle that leads astray.
>
> 29 You shall have a song as in the night when a holy feast is kept, and gladness of heart, as when one sets out to the sound of the flute to go

to the mountain of the Lord, to the Rock of Israel. [30] And the Lord will cause his majestic voice to be heard and the descending blow of his arm to be seen, in furious anger and a *flame* of devouring *fire*, with a *cloudburst* and *storm* and *hailstones*. [31] The Assyrians will be terror-stricken at the voice of the Lord, when he strikes with his rod. [32] And every stroke of the appointed staff that the Lord lays on them will be to the sound of tambourines and lyres. Battling with brandished arm, he will fight with them. [33] For a *burning* place has long been prepared; indeed, for the king it is made ready, its pyre made deep and wide, with *fire* and wood in abundance; the breath of the Lord, like a stream of sulfur, kindles it.

This passage mentions fire, smoke, the voice of the Lord, cloudburst, storm, and hailstones. There are reminiscences of Mount Sinai not only in the fire and thunderstorm imagery but in the references to the "arm" of the Lord (v. 30) and "the mountain of the Lord" (v. 29). God will make manifest his judgment as he did in the exodus. The passage manifests God's judgment on the Assyrians in the near future (v. 31), but it sits in a context that looks also to the far future and to consummate blessings (v. 26 pictures highly escalated blessings).

The Angel of the Lord Striking the Assyrian Camp

In an account parallel to 2 Kings 19:35, Isaiah 37:36 indicates that "the angel of the Lord went out and struck down 185,000 in the camp of the Assyrians. (See our discussion in chapter 38.)

The Glory of the Lord Revealed

Near the start of the large section of Isaiah 40–66 that proclaims God's salvation, the text speaks about the appearing of God's glory:

> "And the glory of the Lord shall be *revealed*,
>   and all flesh shall *see* it together,
>   for the mouth of the Lord has spoken." (Isa. 40:5)

Neighboring verses confirm the theme. The voice in verse 3, by telling people to prepare the way of the Lord, implies that *God* is coming. Also, in verses 9–10, God comes so as to be seen:

> [9] Go on up to a high mountain,
>   O Zion, herald of good news;

lift up your voice with strength,
  O Jerusalem, herald of good news;
  lift it up, fear not;
say to the cities of Judah,
  "*Behold* your God!"
¹⁰ Behold, the Lord GOD comes with might,
  and his arm rules for him;
behold, his reward is with him,
  and his recompense before him.

Verse 10 also includes some warrior language ("might"; "his arm"), connecting the coming of God with warrior theophanies.

Remembering the Exodus

As we indicated earlier in this chapter, Isaiah 51:9–11 reflects on God's work in the exodus, which included his appearing.

The "Servant Songs" in Isaiah

A number of specific prophecies tell of the coming of the Messiah. Against the background of the Immanuel prophecy in Isaiah 7:14 and the "Mighty God" prophecy of Isaiah 9:6, we see that these all point forward to the coming of a Messiah who is both God and man. As God, he is the final theophany.

God's Armor (Isaiah 59:16–18)

God is depicted in warrior terms, when he puts on armor to prepare to fight for his people and defeat their enemies:

He saw that there was no man,
  and wondered that there was no one to intercede;
then his own arm brought him salvation,
  and his righteousness upheld him.
He *put on righteousness as a breastplate*,
  and a *helmet of salvation* on his head;
he put on garments of vengeance for clothing,
  and wrapped himself in zeal as a cloak.
According to their deeds, so will he repay,
  wrath to his adversaries, repayment to his enemies;
  to the coastlands he will render repayment. (Isa. 59:16–18)

The Shining of God's Glory (Isaiah 60:1–3)

Isaiah 60:1–3 depicts the coming of God in terms of light and glory:

> Arise, shine, for your *light* has come,
>   and the *glory* of the LORD has risen upon you.
> For behold, darkness shall cover the earth,
>   and thick darkness the peoples;
> but the LORD will arise upon you,
>   and his *glory* will be seen upon you.
> And nations shall come to your *light*,
>   and kings to the brightness of your *rising*.

This language links itself to the theme of glory theophanies. It finds its fulfillment in two stages: the glory of Christ as seen in his transfiguration (Matt. 17:2) and in Revelation 1:12–16; and the glory of God displayed in the New Jerusalem (Rev. 21:23; 22:5).

Trampling in Edom (Isaiah 63:1–2)

God is depicted in man-like terms in his clothing and his might:

> Who is this who comes from Edom,
>   in crimsoned *garments* from Bozrah,
> he who is splendid in his *apparel*,
>   *marching* in the greatness of his *strength*?
> "It is I, speaking in righteousness,
>   *mighty* to save."
>
> Why is your *apparel* red,
>   and your *garments* like his who treads in the winepress?

The picture of might is reminiscent of a warrior theophany. But the specific visual picture is the imagery of a man treading a winepress. Fulfillment is found in Revelation 14:20 and 19:13, 15.

The Rending of the Heavens (Isaiah 64:1–3)

The voice of Isaiah or of the people pleads with God to come from heaven:

> [1] Oh that you would *rend* the heavens and *come* down,
>   that the mountains might *quake* at your *presence*—

² as when *fire* kindles brushwood
    and the *fire* causes water to boil—
to make your name known to your adversaries,
    and that the nations might tremble at your *presence*!
³ When you did awesome things that we did not look for,
    you *came down*, the mountains *quaked* at your *presence*.

Several points in the poetry evoke associations with theophany. We may begin with the expression "rend the heavens." It suggests a picture where the visual presence of God, usually confined to heaven, is revealed to the world. Then verse 1 speaks of God coming down and the mountains quaking, both of which are reminiscent of Mount Sinai. In Exodus 19 God "descended on it in fire," and "the whole mountain trembled greatly" (Ex. 19:18). Isaiah 64:2 mentions "fire," analogous to the fire on Mount Sinai. And verse 3 repeats the language about coming down.

Verse 3 appears to be about what God did at Mount Sinai, and possibly other occasions when he worked miracles: "When you did awesome things . . . " The earlier verses (vv. 1–2), however, ask God to work in the future in the manner in which he has worked in the past. The final act of God's salvation includes the appearing of God. And this intensive presence is fitting at the time when God does deeds even more spectacular than at Mount Sinai. The monumental change in history at the time of final salvation surpasses the changes set in motion by the theophany of Sinai.

Fiery Judgment (Isaiah 66:15–16)

Isaiah 66:15–16 depicts fiery judgment coming from the Lord:

"For behold, the LORD will come in *fire*,
    and his *chariots* like the *whirlwind*,
to render his anger in fury,
    and his rebuke with *flames of fire*.
For by *fire* will the LORD enter into judgment,
    and by his *sword*, with all flesh;
    and those slain by the LORD shall be many."

The depiction has similarities to chariot theophanies, fire theophanies, thunderstorm theophanies (the whirlwind), and warrior theophanies (the sword and the chariots). This theophanic description fits with a whole list of others that speak of judgment coming in a climactic way.

It is suitable within a passage that is giving a poetic picture of final salvation and judgment.

Hell as a Manifestation of God's Presence

The final scene in Isaiah depicts not only the enjoyment of salvation but also the weight of irreversible damnation:

> ²³ "From new moon to new moon,
>   and from Sabbath to Sabbath,
> all flesh shall come to worship *before me*,
>   declares the LORD.

> ²⁴ "And they shall go out and look on the dead bodies of the men who have rebelled against me. For their worm shall not die, their *fire* shall not be quenched, and they shall be an abhorrence to all flesh." (Isa. 66:23–24)

The description in verse 23 depicts people worshiping "before me," that is, before the presence of God. It is one among many sparse descriptions that point toward God's presence in theophany, and find their final fulfillment in the vision of God's face in Revelation 22:4: "they will see his face."

The next verse, Isaiah 66:24, depicts judgment. It will become one of the backgrounds for Jesus's teaching on hell. The judgment of damnation in one respect can be described as the *withdrawal* of God's presence in *blessing*. But God is still everywhere present in the universe. Damnation involves God being present to work in *wrath*. Damnation is a manifestation of God's justice in his anger against sin. It is one kind of manifestation of God. And it has thematic links with the theophanies that we have already seen. The unquenchable fire is the final manifestation of fire theophany, in its function of destroying evil. The horror of hell is not only in the fact that God withdraws his blessings, but that he does *not* withdraw himself. He is inescapably and unbearably present in the weight of his justice. Justice becomes a terrible thing for those who do not experience it in union with Christ's salvation.

The Whole of Isaiah

We have quickly surveyed some of the main passages in Isaiah that show intense language related to the themes of theophany, the appearing of

God, and the presence of God. But, as we have said before, the presence of God is pervasive. In the end, all parts of Scripture are related to theophany and to the presence of God, though for many passages the relation is more distant and less obvious.

Isaiah 1:1–9

We may illustrate this principle by considering Isaiah 1:1–9, verse by verse.
The vision (1:1):

> The vision of Isaiah the son of Amoz, which he saw concerning Judah and Jerusalem in the days of Uzziah, Jotham, Ahaz, and Hezekiah, kings of Judah.

As we observed earlier, the characterization of the book of Isaiah as a *vision* that Isaiah *saw* puts the book into relation to themes of theophany.
Invocation of heaven and earth (1:2a):

> Hear, O heavens, and give ear, O earth;
>   for the LORD has spoken:

Isaiah 1:2a calls on heaven and earth as witnesses against Israel. The invocation of heaven and earth puts us into a connection with creation as a reflection of God's presence (chapters 11, 21). Heaven and earth bear witness to the character of God (Ps. 19:1).

Here their function is somewhat different, namely to function, metaphorically speaking, as witnesses against the rebellion of the people of Israel. Their witness function connects the passage with the theme of the courtroom—and the ultimate courtroom is the divine courtroom, as depicted in court theophanies, and in Isaiah 6:1–13 in particular.
Rebellious children (1:2b):

> "Children have I reared and brought up,
>   but they have rebelled against me."

As we indicated earlier, God's fatherhood has a reflection in the human fatherhood of Adam and his descendants. The begetting of children is a reflection expressing the character of God, and reflecting the presence of God. But this reflection is twisted by rebellion, creating an anti-image of God. God is still manifested, even in the rebellion, because the rebellion does not escape dependence on God.

Knowledge from God (1:3):

"The ox knows its owner,
    and the donkey its master's crib,
but Israel does not know,
    my people do not understand."

Even animals reflect the glory and the knowledge of the Lord at a lower level. The tragedy of Israel and of all rebellion against God is the perversion of knowledge. Man made in the image of God should be reflecting the knowledge that God has. But this verse describes the failure of Israel properly to reflect God's knowledge. The glory of God is manifested in animals' knowledge, and is distorted in the twisted knowledge of human rebels.

Sin as a reflection of Satan (1:4):

Ah, sinful nation,
    a people laden with iniquity,
offspring of evildoers,
    children who deal corruptly!
They have forsaken the Lord,
    they have despised the Holy One of Israel,
    they are utterly estranged.

The people have become "offspring of evildoers," which has a subtle allusion to the offspring of the serpent in Genesis 3:15. Satanic offspring perverts the manifestation of the glory of God's fatherhood in human fatherhood.

The people are described as having "forsaken the Lord," and as being "utterly estranged." We see a thematic connection with the expulsion from the Garden in Genesis 3:23–24. In Genesis 3:24, Adam and Eve were cast out from the presence of God and from the theophanic manifestation of the cherubim. By analogy, Israel is now alienated from the theophanic presence of God.

Sickness and pollution (Isa. 1:5–6):

Why will you still be struck down?
    Why will you continue to rebel?
The whole head is sick,
    and the whole heart faint.
From the sole of the foot even to the head,
    there is no soundness in it,

but bruises and sores
    and raw wounds;
they are not pressed out or bound up
    or softened with oil.

Raw wounds disqualify a person from drawing near to God, according to Leviticus 15:1–12. That is, such a person cannot approach the special presence of God in the sanctuary, and this presence is associated with the theophany of God in the cloud.

More broadly, sores and bruises are a disorder in comparison with the original soundness of the human body. They contrast with the order of God and the order of his presence. The disqualification through physical uncleanness symbolizes the disqualification from the "uncleanness" of sin. Sin disqualifies us because it is antithetical to the holiness of God. At the same time, it is actually the presence of God in his holiness that provides the standard against the background of which the disqualification and the disorder are marked out for what they are.

Destruction from God (Isa. 1:7–8):

Your country lies desolate;
    your cities are burned with fire;
in your very presence
    foreigners devour your land;
    it is desolate, as overthrown by foreigners.
And the daughter of Zion is left
    like a booth in a vineyard,
like a lodge in a cucumber field,
    like a besieged city.

The proclamation of destruction has connections with the judgments of God described elsewhere in Scripture. All judgments take place by the presence of the power of God. And the final judgment takes place specifically by theophany (Rev. 20:11–15).

Judgment like Sodom and Gomorrah (Isa. 1:9):

If the Lord of hosts
    had not left us a few survivors,
we should have been like Sodom,
    and become like Gomorrah.

The text compares the desolation of Israel to the destruction of Sodom and Gomorrah, which has become an outstanding exemplar of judgment (chapter 34). The fire and sulfur raining on Sodom and Gomorrah and the completeness of their destruction foreshadow the judgment of the last day (Luke 17:29; 2 Pet. 2:6; Jude 7). The fire is like the fire of theophany. In Isaiah 1:9, God indicates that the judgment on the wickedness of Israel manifests the same justice and fiery anger of God's presence. His judgment on Israel is theophany-like. As Hebrews says, "our God is a consuming fire" (Heb. 12:29).

Extending the principles. Our walk through Isaiah 1:1–9 illustrates what might be done with the whole of Isaiah, and indeed the whole of the prophetic corpus. More than historical prose, poetic literature like the book of Isaiah invites us to consider possible allusions and thematic resonances with a larger body of literature. And in the case of Isaiah, the "literature" in question is preeminently the rest of the canon, particularly the Old Testament canon. When we follow out the tracks of thematic associations between Isaiah and the presence of God, we end up finding such connections virtually everywhere. Some connections are more distant and more indirect. Some are more obvious and more direct—as with the spectacular theophany in Isaiah 6:1–3. Appreciating Isaiah as a whole includes appreciating the near and distant allusions. And that implies appreciating the presence of God. We start with the passages like Isaiah 6:1–3 that express the presence of God at an intense level. But we can travel out from there to the rest of Isaiah.

40

God Appearing in the Prophets: Jeremiah and Others

By considering the book of Isaiah in more detail, we have illustrated what we may expect in all the prophetical books. We will be content to survey the rest of the prophets in a quicker way.

God Appearing in Jeremiah

The book of Jeremiah gives us the word of God, in which God is present. There are in addition a few special instances of God's presence.

The call of Jeremiah. God calls Jeremiah to his work of prophecy in Jeremiah 1:4–19. God draws near to Jeremiah in this call. We do not get any clear description of a theophany. But one verse is particularly suggestive: "Then the LORD *put out his hand* and *touched* my mouth. And the LORD said to me, 'Behold, I have put my words in your mouth'" (Jer. 1:9). The Lord "put out his hand." Is this expression a metaphorical description of the meaning of an invisible work toward Jeremiah? Or should we think of it as involving a visible and tactile aspect? God's commission to Isaiah in Isaiah 6 includes a physical touch: "And he [the seraph] touched my mouth and said: 'Behold, this has touched your lips; your guilt is taken away, and your sin atoned for'" (Isa. 6:7). We do not have this much detail in the case of Jeremiah. But we can say that the description is theophany-like and has similarities to a man theophany, as is suggested by the mention of the Lord's "hand."

Judgment and salvation in Jeremiah. The rest of Jeremiah has announcements of negative judgment and promises of salvation. Both involve the presence of God.

The new covenant. Climactic salvation comes when God makes "a new covenant" (Jer. 31:31). Jeremiah 31:32–33 indicates that this new covenant will be superior in efficacy to the covenant connected with Mount Sinai.

If the old covenant at Mount Sinai involved theophany, it seems logical that the new covenant would involve theophany again, and that God's appearing at the future climactic time would be superior even to what happened at Mount Sinai. The superiority includes greater intimacy between God and man, as is underlined by the fact that the people will have the law written "on their hearts," instead of the prominently external form of the law on stone that was given at Mount Sinai.

The promise of the new covenant is fulfilled in Christ. In Christ, God appears on earth in person. And Christ explicitly inaugurates the new covenant that Jeremiah promised: "And likewise the cup after they had eaten, saying, 'This cup that is poured out for you is the *new covenant* in my blood'" (Luke 22:20).

God's Presence in Ezekiel

God manifests his presence all through Ezekiel. But the outstanding manifestations of his presence come at the beginning and the end of the book.

God appearing in Ezekiel 1. God appears to Ezekiel in Ezekiel 1 in an elaborate and detailed theophany, which combines features of cloud theophany, fire theophany, court theophany (the living creatures), chariot theophany (the wheels), and man theophany (the man-like figure in vv. 26–28). This theophany is the most elaborate within the whole Old Testament.

God appears to Ezekiel in preparation for delivering the word of God to Ezekiel and calling him to his work as a prophet (chapters 2–3). God's appearing has at least three main functions. First, it underlines and authenticates the message that Ezekiel will bring to the people. Second, through his appearing God commissions and empowers Ezekiel, and assures Ezekiel of his presence while Ezekiel is carrying out God's commission and speaking to the people (note especially 2:2, 6–7; 3:3–4, 8–9). Third, the solemnity and awesome character of the theophany proclaim that God is a God who brings judgment. The first part of the book of Ezekiel is devoted almost entirely to material discussing negative judgment, which comes on the people of Israel (chapters 4–24) and also on surrounding nations (chapters 25–32).

God leaving the temple (Ezekiel 10). Because of the apostasy of the people, the glory of God, representing his presence in the temple, leaves the temple in Ezekiel 10:15–19. The process is completed in Ezekiel 11:23:

> Then the cherubim lifted up their wings, with the wheels beside them, and the glory of the God of Israel was over them. And the *glory* of the LORD *went up* from the midst of the city and stood on the mountain that is on the east side of the city. And the Spirit lifted me up and brought me in the vision by the Spirit of God into Chaldea, to the exiles. Then the vision that I had seen went up from me. And I told the exiles all the things that the LORD had shown me. (Ezek. 11:22–25)

The glory of the Lord moves toward "the east side of the city," in the direction of the location of the exiles. The implication is that, as the Lord abandons the house of his glory in Jerusalem, he will be present with his people in exile. A statement earlier in Ezekiel 11 confirms this idea: "Therefore say, 'Thus says the Lord GOD: Though I removed them far off among the nations, and though I scattered them among the countries, yet I have been a *sanctuary* to them for a while in the countries where they have gone'" (Ezek. 11:16). This decision of God to dwell among the exiles is symbolically manifested by the movement of the theophanic presence of God, a movement away from the temple.

God appearing in the new temple (Ezekiel 43). The wonderful theophany in Ezekiel 1 has a corresponding piece at the end of the book of Ezekiel. God gives Ezekiel a vision of a new temple (chapters 40–48), providing a remedy for the older temple of Solomon that Nebuchadnezzar destroyed. In connection with this vision, the glory of God comes to the new temple:

> And behold, the *glory* of the God of Israel was coming from the east. And the sound of his coming was like the sound of many waters, and the earth shone with his *glory*. And the vision I saw was just like the vision that I had seen when he came to destroy the city, and just like the vision that I had seen by the Chebar canal. And I fell on my

face. As the *glory* of the LORD entered the temple by the gate facing east, the Spirit lifted me up and brought me into the inner court; and behold, the *glory* of the LORD *filled the temple.* (Ezek. 43:2–5)

Some interpreters are inclined to treat this vision of the new temple as if it were a photographic description of a stony replacement for the Solomonic temple. But it is a vision, not a photograph. God gives Ezekiel a vision that uses the symbolism belonging to the Mosaic order of things, both the Mosaic tabernacle and the Solomonic temple. This whole order provides shadows of the final salvation that is to come, and the final presence of God that is to be manifested in the future. The use of such symbolism is fully appropriate to the times in which Ezekiel ministered and the people to whom God was speaking. The fulfillment comes in Christ. And when the fulfillment comes, it indicates more fully the symbolic meaning that God intended for the tabernacle and the Solomonic temple all along.[1]

At the end of the vision, Ezekiel sums up its theological significance: "And the name of the city from that time on shall be, The LORD *Is There*" (Ezek. 48:35). God brings his presence in a fuller and more emphatic way than was true of his earlier symbolic dwelling in the tabernacle and the Solomonic temple.

God Appearing in Daniel[2]

God speaks to Nebuchadnezzar through a dream (Daniel 2). In Daniel 2 Nebuchadnezzar receives from God a revelatory dream. But, in a manner parallel to the case of Joseph before Pharaoh, the dream is opaque to him as a pagan. God is present to Nebuchadnezzar, but in a strikingly veiled way. Daniel, as the representative of God, must interpret the king's dream. God is present in Daniel (Dan. 2:47), as Belshazzar later acknowledges in a parallel case: "I have heard of you that the *spirit of the gods* is in you, and that light and understanding and excellent wisdom are found in you" (Dan. 5:14).

The son of God appears in the fiery furnace (Daniel 3). In chap-

---

1. Discerning discussion can be found in Patrick Fairbairn, *An Exposition of Ezekiel* (reprint; n.l.: The National Foundation for Christian Education, 1969), 431–450; Iain Duguid, *Ezekiel* (Grand Rapids, MI: Zondervan, 1999), 478–486; G. K. Beale, *The Temple and the Church's Mission: A Biblical Theology of the Dwelling Place of God* (Downers Grove, IL: InterVarsity, 2004), 335–364.
2. For convenience, I am treating Daniel as one of the prophetic books, though the Jewish division of the Old Testament canon treats it as one of the Writings.

ter 3, Nebuchadnezzar sets up his fiery furnace. The fiery furnace is like a counterfeit of a divine fire theophany. It is a concrete expression of Nebuchadnezzar's idolatry in requiring people to bow to his idol (Dan. 3:6–7). It is fitting that, when God comes to rescue Daniel's three friends, he appears in a way that counters Nebuchadnezzar's idolatry. "He answered and said, 'But I see four men unbound, walking in the midst of the fire, and they are not hurt; and the *appearance* of the fourth is like a *son of the gods*'" (Dan. 3:25). This description indicates that Nebuchadnezzar saw a man theophany. But the human figure standing with the three others also stands out from the three others. He alone, among the four, has a god-like appearance. We are probably to think of a bright or fiery appearance, similar to Ezekiel 1:27–28. The description "like a son of the gods" comes from the mouth of Nebuchadnezzar, who is a polytheist. So he is thinking of a plurality of "gods." But when we reinterpret it in terms of the monotheism of Daniel and the rest of the Bible, we see a clear anticipation of Christ and his title, "Son of God."

The hand on the wall (Daniel 5). Next, we have an extraordinary case of a man's hand appearing: "Immediately the *fingers of a human hand appeared* and wrote on the plaster of the wall of the king's palace, opposite the lampstand. And the king saw the hand as it wrote" (Dan. 5:5). The hand is suggestive of a man-like theophany. But only the hand, not a full figure of a man, appears.

As in the case of Nebuchadnezzar's dream, Belshazzar and his wise men are unable to interpret the writing. God has given a revelatory sign, but it is opaque until it is interpreted by Daniel, who serves as the divine mediator. Belshazzar as a polytheist says that in Daniel is "the spirit of the gods," but the reader is given to understand that it is actually the presence of God in his Spirit.

The visible hand is doubtless a spectacular aspect of the scene with Belshazzar. But in a real sense God draws near to Belshazzar much more powerfully through the words that Daniel delivers—words of warning. Belshazzar hears the meanings of God and the judgment of God's court, in the form of a sentence of condemnation:

> "This is the interpretation of the matter: MENE, God has numbered the days of your kingdom and brought it to an end; TEKEL, you have been weighed in the balances and found wanting; PERES, your kingdom is divided and given to the Medes and Persians." (Dan. 5:26–28)

God is present in his word of condemnation to Belshazzar. He is also present in the subsequent act by which Belshazzar's rule comes to an end: "That very night Belshazzar the Chaldean king was killed. And Darius the Mede received the kingdom, being about sixty-two years old" (Dan. 5:30–31).

God on his throne (Dan. 7:9–10). Next, in Daniel 7:9–10, God appears on his throne to pronounce judgment against the kingdoms of the four beasts (7:2–8):

"As I looked,

> thrones were placed,
> > and *the Ancient of Days took his seat*;
> his clothing was white as snow,
> > and the hair of his head like pure wool;
> his throne was fiery flames;
> > its wheels were burning fire.
> A stream of fire issued
> > and came out from before him;
> a thousand thousands served him,
> > and ten thousand times ten thousand stood before him;
> the court sat in judgment,
> > and the books were opened." (Dan. 7:9–10)

As we observed earlier (in chapter 6), Daniel 7:9–10 is a court theophany. It also includes features associated with chariot theophanies and fire theophanies. The vision underlines the awesome character of God's judgment against the beasts, and the definitive character of the result.

The one like a son of man (Dan. 7:13–14). The vision in Daniel 7:13–14 of "one like a son of man" (v. 13) has features belonging to theophany:

"I saw in the night visions,

> and behold, with the *clouds of heaven*
> > there came one like a *son of man*,
> and he came to the Ancient of Days
> > and was presented before him.
> And to him was given dominion
> > and glory and a kingdom,

> that all peoples, nations, and languages
> should serve him;
> his dominion is an everlasting dominion,
> which shall not pass away,
> and his kingdom one
> that shall not be destroyed."

The presence of a cloud and the presence of "the Ancient of Days" show us a theophany (see chapter 4). The "one like a son of man" is a human-like figure, in pointed contrast to the bestial character of the four preceding kingdoms. He has the role of the last Adam, achieving the dominion that Adam lost. At the same time, he comes "with the clouds of heaven," clouds that belong to the appearing of God in theophany. The figure is both man and God.

Since the whole scene is visionary, it remains somewhat mysterious. But the mystery is fully revealed when Christ comes. At his trial he identifies himself as "the Son of Man" of Daniel 7:13: "Jesus said to him, 'You have said so. But I tell you, from now on you will see the Son of Man seated at the right hand of Power and coming on *the clouds of heaven*'" (Matt. 26:64). Jesus is God and man. As such, he fulfills both the human side and the theophanic side of the vision of Daniel 7:13–14.

The man clothed in linen (Dan. 10:5–21). The "man" who appears to Daniel in Daniel 10:5–21 has striking features:

> I lifted up my eyes and looked, and behold, a man clothed in linen, with a belt of fine gold from Uphaz around his waist. His body was like beryl, his face like the appearance of lightning, his eyes like flaming torches, his arms and legs like the gleam of burnished bronze, and the sound of his words like the sound of a multitude. (Dan. 10:5–6)

Some of these features are reminiscent of the theophany that came to Ezekiel in Ezekiel 1:26–28. There are also notable similarities to the description of Christ in Revelation 1:12–16. Finally, the reaction of the men around Daniel is similar to the reaction of those around the apostle Paul when Christ initially appears to him on the road to Damascus (Dan. 10:7; Acts 9:7).

Because of the similarities, it seems probable that the figure is a preincarnate appearance of Christ, anticipating his incarnation. But some interpreters think that we have an appearance of an angel. If so, this angel reflects on a creaturely level the glory of Christ. This appearance is comparable to a man-like theophany (chapter 7).

God Appearing in Hosea

Next, let us consider the book of Hosea. Hosea recalls the time when Jacob met God at Bethel, and when he wrestled with God:

> ³ In the womb he took his brother by the heel,
>   and in his manhood he *strove* with God.
> He *strove* with the angel and prevailed;
>   he wept and sought his favor.
> ⁴ He *met* God at Bethel,
>   and there God *spoke* with us—
> ⁵ the LORD, the God of hosts,
>   the LORD is his memorial name. (Hos. 12:3–5)

These reflections lay the foundation for God continuing to have communion with his people. Verse 4 says that "God spoke *with us*." He spoke with Jacob. But Jacob was a representative for the people of Israel who were his descendants. Hosea 12:6 therefore continues by making an application in the form of a call for repentance:

> "So you, by the help of your God, *return*,
>   hold fast to love and justice,
>   and *wait* continually for your God."

Repentance reaffirms communion with God, such as God has given in choosing Jacob and his descendants as his people.

God Appearing in Joel

The day of the Lord in Joel. The day of the Lord is the day when God appears in order to act in judgment and salvation. The description of the day of the Lord in Joel 2:1–11 is similar to a warrior theophany. The Lord comes with "his army" (2:11). Fire and war horses accompany him (vv. 3–4).

But the vision proceeds to unfold like a dream that turns into a nightmare. Instead of coming to save the people of Israel, the Lord comes with a fire that devours the land of Israel (v. 3). Instead of the wings of the living creatures and their noise, we have the wings of the locusts and a crackling like fire as they devour the vegetation.

There are some differences among interpreters about the detailed significance of the vision. In my view, the people of Israel have already experienced a locust plague, as described in Joel 1. Joel 2:1–11 may be a re-description of the same plague, but it appears to me that it is not *merely* a re-description. Rather, it builds on the crisis of the plague by layering on top of the literal locust plague an even more devastating judgment. This judgment comes in "the day of the LORD," and takes the form of the army of the Lord coming to destroy. The locust plague in Joel anticipates the vision of locusts in Revelation 9:1–11, which is part of the theophanic imagery pervading Revelation. God appears in judgment.

The presence of God pouring out his Spirit (Joel 2:28–32). God expresses his presence intensely in pouring out his Spirit, as prophesied in Joel 2:28–29. Accompanying this outpouring are signs affecting nature, reminiscent of theophany:

> "And I will show wonders in the heavens and on the earth, blood and fire and columns of smoke. The sun shall be turned to darkness, and the moon to blood, before the great and awesome day of the LORD comes." (Joel 2:30–31)

The presence of God in judging the nations (Joel 3:1–16). God expresses an intense presence in the promise that he will come to judge the nations. As part of this picture of God coming in judgment, we have a more specific picture of God sitting to judge: "Let the nations stir themselves up and come up to the Valley of Jehoshaphat; for there I will *sit to judge* all the surrounding nations" (Joel 3:12). The expression of "sitting" is reminiscent of a court theophany. And the coming of judgment is the expected time when God will manifest himself visibly.

God present in his house (Joel 3:18). The final section in Joel 3 announces salvation, in contrast to the negative judgments in the earlier part of Joel 3. Positive salvation comes in the environment of "the house of the LORD," which symbolizes his presence. The blessings are from God and manifest his goodness and grace.

God Appearing in Amos

Having seen how the descriptions of God's appearance work out in a number of prophetic books, we can be even briefer with the rest of the books of the Minor Prophets. Here is what we find in Amos:

- God comes to "meet" his people:

"Therefore thus I will do to you, O Israel;
    because I will do this to you,
    prepare to *meet your God*, O Israel!" (Amos 4:12)

- The day of the Lord is darkness:

Woe to you who desire the day of the Lord!
    Why would you have the day of the Lord?
It is *darkness*, and not light,
    as if a man fled from a lion,
    and a bear met him,
or went into the house and leaned his hand against the wall,
    and a serpent bit him.
Is not the day of the Lord *darkness*, and not light,
    and *gloom* with no brightness in it? (Amos 5:18–20)

The darkness is reminiscent of the darkness at Mount Sinai (Ex. 19:18; 20:21; Deut. 5:22).

- The Lord forms locusts as a judgment:

This is what the Lord God showed me: behold, he was forming locusts when the latter growth was just beginning to sprout, and behold, it was the latter growth after the king's mowings. (Amos 7:1)

The expression concerning the Lord "showing" Amos suggests a visible appearance. And what Amos sees is the Lord "forming locusts." Are we to think of a visible appearance of God here? The language is theophanic, but it may be only a way of describing the Lord's invisible involvement in forming the locusts.

- The Lord appears beside the altar:

I saw the Lord standing beside the altar, and he said:

"Strike the capitals until the thresholds shake,
    and shatter them on the heads of all the people;
and those who are left of them I will kill with the sword;
    not one of them shall flee away;
    not one of them shall escape." (Amos 9:1)

The Lord appears in judgment. Amos does not give visual details, but the brief description suggests a man theophany when it describes the Lord as "standing."

God Appearing in Jonah

In the book of Jonah, God shows himself through speech, providence, and miracle, rather than primarily through unusual visual displays. But his presence is manifest all through the book, not least in its ironies. The sailors give glory to the God of Israel after they have seen his presence made manifest in the storm and in the quieting of the storm (Jonah 1:16). Jonah experiences the mercy of God in God's provision of the great fish (1:17; cf. 2:1). Jonah's rescue from death prefigures the resurrection of Jesus Christ, which is a climactic manifestation of God's presence in the salvation of the world (Matt. 12:40). Jonah also experiences the continued persistence of God, compelling him to go to Nineveh in spite of his attempt to escape (Jonah 2:10–3:2).

The Ninevites themselves experience the presence of God through Jonah's preaching, and they repent (Jonah 3:5). It is indeed a manifestation of the presence of God, for why should they believe a mere word from Jonah? We can infer that God sent his Holy Spirit to them, and the Holy Spirit was present to bring about their repentance.

Jonah experiences further providential works of God, with the plant, the worm, and the blazing sun, which work together to bring him a lesson interpreted by God's word. God is present in the lesson of the whole book, concerning his mercy that extends even to the enemies of Israel.

God Appearing in Micah

- God's presence is expressed in the house of the Lord:

It shall come to pass in the latter days
    that the mountain of the *house of the* LORD
shall be established as the highest of the mountains,
    and it shall be lifted up above the hills;
and peoples shall flow to it. (Mic. 4:1)

God Appearing in Nahum

- God appears in storm:

The LORD is slow to anger and great in power,
    and the LORD will by no means clear the guilty.

His way is in *whirlwind and storm,*
  and the *clouds* are the dust of his feet. (Nah. 1:3)

His manifestation here is reminiscent of Mount Sinai. He comes for judgment: He "will by no means clear the guilty."

God Appearing in Habakkuk

God appears in Habakkuk in two special ways, in 3:3–5 and in 3:8–15.

- God appears in brightness:

God came from Teman,
  and the Holy One from Mount Paran. *Selah*
His splendor covered the heavens,
  and the earth was full of his praise.
His *brightness* was like the *light;*
  rays *flashed* from his hand;
  and there he veiled his power.
Before him went pestilence,
  and plague followed at his heels. (Hab. 3:3–5)

The last lines about "pestilence" and "plague" show that the context is again one of judgment.

- God appears as a warrior in brightness:

Was your wrath against the rivers, O LORD?
  Was your anger against the rivers,
  or your indignation against the sea,
when you *rode* on your horses,
  on your *chariot* of salvation?
You stripped the *sheath* from your *bow,*
  calling for many *arrows. Selah*
  You split the earth with rivers.
The mountains saw you and writhed;
  the raging waters swept on;
the deep gave forth its voice;
  it lifted its hands on high.
The sun and moon stood still in their place
  at the *light* of your *arrows* as they sped,
  at the *flash* of your glittering spear.
You marched through the earth in fury;

you threshed the nations in anger.
You went out for the salvation of your people,
    for the salvation of your anointed.
You crushed the head of the house of the wicked,
    laying him bare from thigh to neck. *Selah*
You pierced with his own arrows the heads of his warriors,
    who came like a whirlwind to scatter me,
    rejoicing as if to devour the poor in secret.
You trampled the sea with your *horses*,
    the surging of mighty waters. (Hab. 3:8–15)

We see here aspects belonging to warrior theophanies, chariot theophanies, and glory theophanies.

God Appearing in Zephaniah

- God appears in darkness:

A day of wrath is that day,
    a day of distress and anguish,
a day of ruin and devastation,
    a day of *darkness and gloom*,
a day of *clouds* and *thick darkness*. (Zeph. 1:15)

The darkness is reminiscent of Mount Sinai.

- The Lord is in the midst:

The LORD *within her* [Jerusalem, the oppressing city] is righteous;
    he does no injustice;
every morning he *shows forth* his justice;
    each dawn he does not fail;
    but the unjust knows no shame. (Zeph. 3:5)

The Lord is present in Jerusalem even amid injustice. But the prophecy later turns to a brighter day.

- The Lord is in the midst for salvation:

The LORD has taken away the judgments against you;
    he has cleared away your enemies.
The King of Israel, the LORD, *is in your midst*;
    you shall never again fear evil. (Zeph. 3:15)

"The Lord your God *is in your midst*,
  a mighty one who will save;
he will rejoice over you with gladness;
  he will quiet you by his love;
he will exult over you with loud singing." (v. 17)

God Appearing in Haggai

- God fills the latter house with glory:

"'And I will shake all nations, so that the treasures of all nations shall come in, and I will fill this house with *glory*, says the Lord of hosts. The silver is mine, and the gold is mine, declares the Lord of hosts. The latter *glory* of this house shall be greater than the former, says the Lord of hosts. And in this place I will give peace, declares the Lord of hosts.'" (Hag. 2:7–9)

This promise prophesies a grand fulfillment of the glory theophanies in the Old Testament.

Haggai is written in a situation in which the people have returned to the Promised Land after the exile. They have begun to build the temple, but it lacks the glory of Solomon's temple (Hag. 2:3). As we have seen, the theophanic glory of the Lord filled Solomon's temple when it was dedicated. There is no corresponding record of a theophany of glory that filled the postexilic temple. The coming of the Lord in a climactic manifestation of glory is still to come. All of this points forward to the coming of Christ.

God Appearing in Zechariah

- Zechariah sees "the angel of the Lord":

And they answered the *angel* of the Lord who was standing among the myrtle trees, and said, "We have patrolled the earth, and behold, all the earth remains at rest." (Zech. 1:11)

Zechariah also mentions "the angel who talked with me," who may be distinct from the angel of the Lord (1:13, 14, 19, etc.).

- God appears in glory and in fire in the renewed Jerusalem:

"'And I will be to her a wall of *fire* all around, declares the Lord, and I will be the *glory* in her midst.'" (Zech. 2:5)

The prophecy indicates that God will appear in the New Jerusalem in a manner resembling theophanies of fire and glory. G. K. Beale points out how Zechariah 2:5 prophesies the expansion of God's glory.[3] God's glory fills all of Jerusalem and encompasses it like a wall. The expansion anticipates the time when God's glory will fill the entire world: "For the earth will be filled with the knowledge of the glory of the Lord as the waters cover the sea" (Hab. 2:14; compare Isa. 11:9).

- God appears in confrontation with Satan:

  Then he showed me Joshua the high priest standing before the angel of the Lord, and Satan standing at his right hand to accuse him. And the Lord said to Satan, "The Lord rebuke you, O Satan! The Lord who has chosen Jerusalem rebuke you! Is not this a brand plucked from the fire?" (Zech. 3:1–2)

The confrontation has similarities to the court theophany in Job 1, in which Satan appears before the Lord. The context is one where the Lord vindicates the accused saint. Joshua the high priest is the principal representative for the entire people of God.

The passage has foreshadowings of Christ in two diverse respects. Joshua the high priest foreshadows Christ, who is the final high priest. In addition, the Lord himself rebukes Satan. This rebuke is a form of vindication for Joshua, and by implication a vindication for the people whom Joshua represents. The Lord dismisses Satan's accusation, and thereby acquits Joshua. This acquittal in Zechariah pictures beforehand the acquittal described in Romans 8:33–34:

  Who shall bring any *charge* against God's elect? It is God who *justi-fies*. Who is to *condemn*? Christ Jesus is the one who died—more than that, who was raised—who is at the right hand of God, who indeed is *interceding* for us.

God the Father as the judge and Christ as the intercessor are both involved in justifying us. The distinct roles of God the Father and Christ the Son are partially anticipated in Zechariah 3:2, where the Lord has two roles:

  And *the* Lord said to Satan, "*The* Lord rebuke you, O Satan!"

The Lord who addresses Satan is like Christ who intercedes; the Lord

---

3. Beale, *Temple and the Church's Mission*, 143.

who directly rebukes Satan is like God the Father, who sits as judge and rebukes Satan by pronouncing our justification. The court scene in Zechariah 3:1–2 thus anticipates the New Testament revelation of justification through Christ.

- The Lord appears as a warrior on behalf of his people:

> Then I will *encamp at my house* as a guard,
>   so that none shall march to and fro;
> no oppressor shall again march over them,
>   for now I see with my own eyes. (Zech. 9:8)

> Then the LORD will *appear* over them,
>   and his *arrow* will go forth like lightning;
> the Lord GOD will sound the trumpet
>   and will *march* forth in the whirlwinds of the south. (Zech. 9:14)

- The Lord appears through his Messiah in the famous prophecy fulfilled on Palm Sunday:

> Rejoice greatly, O daughter of Zion!
>   Shout aloud, O daughter of Jerusalem!
> Behold, your king is coming to you;
>   righteous and having salvation is he,
> humble and mounted on a donkey,
>   on a colt, the foal of a donkey. (Zech. 9:9)

- The house of David will be like God:

> On that day the LORD will protect the inhabitants of Jerusalem, so that the feeblest among them on that day shall be like David, and the house of David shall be *like God*, like the *angel of the LORD*, going before them. (Zech. 12:8)

In saying that the house of David will be "like God" and "like the angel of the LORD," the text virtually implies that "the house of David" will be a theophanic manifestation. To a casual reader, this claim might seem improbable. But it turns out to be perfectly true in the time of fulfillment. "The house of David" has its fulfillment in Christ, who is descended from David and sums up the whole line of kings. He *is* the climactic and permanent theophany, as John 1:14 and 14:9 say and Hebrews 1:3 confirms.

- The Lord appears as pierced:

> "And I will pour out on the house of David and the inhabitants of Jerusalem a spirit of grace and pleas for mercy, so that, when they look on *me*, on him whom they have *pierced*, they shall mourn for him, as one mourns for an only child, and weep bitterly over him, as one weeps over a firstborn." (Zech. 12:10)

We see the fulfillment when Christ is pierced on the cross:

> But one of the soldiers *pierced* his side with a spear, and at once there came out blood and water. He who saw it has borne witness—his testimony is true, and he knows that he is telling the truth—that you also may believe. For these things took place that the Scripture might be fulfilled: "Not one of his bones will be broken." And again another Scripture says, "They will look on him whom they have *pierced*." (John 19:34–37)

- The Lord appears as a warrior to fight for his people:

> Then the LORD will go out and *fight* against those nations as when he fights on a day of battle. On that day his *feet shall stand* on the Mount of Olives that lies before Jerusalem on the east, and the Mount of Olives shall be split in two from east to west by a very wide valley, so that one half of the Mount shall move northward, and the other half southward. (Zech. 14:3–4)

This prophecy is fulfilled by Christ as the divine warrior. He fights against sin and Satan and defeats them, both in his first coming and in his second coming.

God Appearing in Malachi

- The messenger of the covenant comes, and his coming is the coming of God:

> "Behold, I send my messenger, and he will prepare the way before *me*. And the Lord whom you seek will suddenly come to *his temple*; and the messenger of the covenant in whom you delight, behold, he is coming, says the LORD of hosts. But who can endure the day of his coming, and who can *stand* when he *appears*?" (Mal. 3:1–2)

The "messenger of the covenant" has to be distinguished from the first messenger, designated "my messenger," who prepares "the way before me." (The first messenger, "my messenger," describes prophetically the coming of John the Baptist [Matt. 11:10].) After him comes "the Lord whom you seek," who is further identified as "the messenger of the covenant."

Several indications combine to lead to the conclusion that the messenger of the covenant is himself God. First, "my messenger" (John the Baptist) prepares for "me," that is, for God. Second, the messenger of the covenant is called "the Lord." To be sure, the Hebrew word is the ordinary word for "lord," not the tetragrammaton ("Jehovah"), the special name of God (the "LORD," indicated by small capital letters in English). But this word *Lord* does indicate his exalted status. In addition, he is "the Lord whom you seek"—not an unknown entity, but a person whom the people already long for. Who ought they to long for most but God himself? Third, the Lord comes "to his temple." The temple is the temple of God, and its designation as "*his* temple" shows that the Lord, the owner, is God. Fourth, the question, "who can stand?" implies that the coming of the Lord is the coming of the one before whom none can stand—that is, the coming of God. Finally, the opening expression in Malachi 3:1 builds on Isaiah 40:3, where the prophetic voice prepares the way for the coming of *God*:

> A voice cries:
> "In the wilderness prepare the way of the LORD;
>   make straight in the desert a highway for our God."

These indications within the passage are confirmed by the fulfillment. Jesus is the one whom John the Baptist is preparing for. He is the *divine* messenger of the covenant.

- A book is written before the Lord:

> Then those who feared the LORD spoke with one another. The LORD paid attention and heard them, and a book of remembrance was written *before him* of those who feared the LORD and esteemed his name. (Mal. 3:16)

The picture of a book written "before him" suggests a whole theophanic courtroom scene, where a heavenly record is produced concerning those who fear the Lord. It is a short statement, but it alludes to God appearing in court.

- The sun of righteousness rises:

> "But for you who fear my name, the *sun* of righteousness shall *rise* with healing in its wings. You shall go out leaping like calves from the stall." (Mal. 4:2)

This prophecy comes in the context of the day of the Lord: "For behold, the day is coming" (v. 1). The day has theophanic fire: "burning like an oven" (v. 1). The picture of the sun of righteousness is an expression of God appearing in brightness, one kind of glory theophany (chapter 5). It is suitable as a contrast to the dark times in which Malachi prophesies, and the dark fate that awaits the wicked.

Other Parts of the Prophets

In surveying these verses from the prophets, we have skimmed the surface. Our earlier examination of Isaiah 1:1–9 shows that the prophets are full of the presence of God. We have selected only some of the prominent passages where his presence is most noteworthy and where it is more closely related to the language of theophany.

41

God Appearing in the
Poetical Books: Job

Now let us consider the presence of God in the book of Job.

Satan's Challenge

God appears prominently near the beginning of the book and near the end. Both cases describe theophanies in the narrow sense. The first appearance, in Job 1–2, involves two successive scenes of a similar nature:

> Now there was a day when the sons of God came to present themselves *before the LORD*, and Satan also came among them. (Job 1:6)

> Again there was a day when the sons of God came to present themselves *before the LORD*, and Satan also came among them to present himself before the LORD. (Job 2:1)

We have a court theophany (see chapter 6), though no details are given concerning the appearance of God. A deliberative council is conducted in the presence of God, similar to the council described in 1 Kings 22:19–22.

What we see and hear about the presence of God suits the context in Job. The council gives us insight into the determination and execution of God's will. Scripture can talk about the decrees of God within contexts where there is no reference to a theophany. But the scene in Job is appropriate, because the book of Job needs to indicate the way in which the accusations of Satan play a role. The text gives us a vision of the divine council so that Satan can be introduced in his antagonistic role, and yet we may also see the interaction between the plans of God and the purposes of Satan.

The two opening scenes (Job 1 and 2) play a key role in the whole book of Job. They allow the readers of the book to know crucial information about the heavenly sphere, while Job, Eliphaz, Bildad, Zophar, and Elihu remain firmly planted on earth. None of them has access to this crucial information. As a result, they enter into an extensive debate as to why Job is suffering. The debate partly involves a contest about wisdom. Who can access wisdom, and how? Who has the wisdom to interpret the meaning of Job's sufferings?

The theophanic scenes at the beginning of the book provide a sharp contrast between heaven and earth, and between the wisdom of the divine council and the limited vision of earthly inhabitants. One central concern in theophanies throughout the Bible is the theme of communion with God. Who has communion with God in such a way that he can act wisely on earth, and also interpret wisely the meaning of events?

Some theophanies also have a close connection with the judgment of God and with the manifestation of his justice. This concern also comes up in the book of Job. In Job 1, God in heaven has already definitively pronounced Job to be "a blameless and upright man, who fears God and turns away from evil" (v. 8).

God's Presence through the Book of Job

But as the story unfolds, Job's friends attack his integrity, and the circumstances themselves seem to testify against Job. So who is right? Who knows? Only God could give a definitive answer. And God remains concealed in heaven. The book of Job is about the presence of God in his heavenly manifestation, and it is also about his apparent absence or inaccessibility when human beings want answers to mysteries.

At times Job longs for a meeting with God—a definitive manifestation of God's presence. But Job knows that he as a mortal man is not adequate for such a meeting:

> "Truly I know that it is so:
>   But how can a man be in the right *before God*?
> If one wished to contend with him,
>   one could not answer him once in a thousand times.

He is wise in heart and mighty in strength
—who has hardened himself against him, and succeeded?"
(Job 9:2–4)

"Though he slay me, I will hope in him;
yet I will argue my ways *to his face*." (Job 13:15)

"Oh, that I knew where I might *find him*,
that I might come even to *his seat*!
I would lay my case *before him*
and fill my mouth with arguments.
I would know what he would answer me
and understand what he would say to me.
Would he contend with me in the greatness of his power?
No; he would pay attention to me.
There an upright man could argue with him,
and I would be *acquitted* forever by my *judge*." (Job 23:3–7)

Similar ideas are found elsewhere in Job—for instance, 9:14–20, 32–35.
Job also expresses confidence in a final manifestation of God:

"For I know that my Redeemer lives,
and at the last he will *stand* upon the earth.
And after my skin has been thus destroyed,
yet in my flesh I shall *see God*,
whom I shall *see* for myself,
and my eyes shall *behold*, and not another.
My heart faints within me!" (Job 19:25–27)

At the same time, while waiting, Job is worn out by the presence of God, a presence that allows the multiplication of his suffering. God will not leave him alone:

"What is man, that you make so much of him,
and that you set your heart on him,
visit him every morning
and test him every moment?
How long will you not look away from me,
nor leave me alone till I swallow my spit?
If I sin, what do I do to you, you watcher of mankind?
Why have you made me your mark?
Why have I become a burden to you?" (Job 7:17–20)

" . . . for the hand of God has touched me!
Why do you, like God, pursue me?
Why are you not satisfied with my flesh?" (Job 19:21–22)

God's climactic presence at the end of history brings deliverance, Job says. But God's presence in the present moment is a trial. God is present all through the book—too much present for Job. At the same time, at a crucial moment Job proclaims the inaccessibility of divine wisdom. It is beyond Job and beyond his friends (Job 28). That proclamation confirms the point made in the narrative about the divine council in Job 1–2. The reader of Job hears, but normally human beings do not hear.

God Appearing to Job

A second theophany occurs near the end of the book of Job, in chapters 38–41. It is remarkable in its elaboration. At its beginning, Job 38:1 mentions a visible side to the theophany: "Then the LORD answered Job out of *the whirlwind* and said: . . . "

The primary focus in the narrative clearly belongs not to the visible manifestation but to what God says. In what God says, he surveys remarkable works that he does in creation and in providence. This survey reminds us of what we saw earlier. In a broad sense, creation itself and God's rule in providence manifest his presence. They are, broadly speaking, like an "appearance" of God. They testify to his limitless wisdom. And as a result they also highlight the limitations that we find in human attempts at wisdom. Human beings like Job and his friends attempt to understand the purposes of God. But they fall short, and, in the case of Job's friends, they fall into sin:

> The LORD said to Eliphaz the Temanite: "My anger burns against you and against your two friends, for you have not spoken of me what is right, as my servant Job has. Now therefore take seven bulls and seven rams and go to my servant Job and offer up a burnt offering for yourselves. And my servant Job shall pray for you, for I will accept his prayer not to deal with you according to your folly. For you have not spoken of me what is right, as my servant Job has." (Job 42:7–8)

Remarkably, God never explains to Job or to the three friends why he afflicted Job. They never learn what we as readers learned in Job 1–2 about the heavenly council. Their lack of knowledge, even at the end of the narrative, underlines effectively one of the themes of theophany: God manifests himself and his character, but in this manifestation he remains God, whose knowledge and wisdom reach beyond human understanding (Isa. 40:28).

The book of Job looks forward to the coming of Christ. Christ suffered as a righteous sufferer. Indeed, he is the supreme righteous sufferer, far surpassing Job (Heb. 4:15). Through Christ's death and resurrection God's righteousness and justice are vindicated and displayed. They become manifest, through Christ's substitutionary work:

> It was to show his righteousness at the present time, so that he might be just and the justifier of the one who has faith in Jesus. (Rom. 3:26)

Jesus's entire life on earth is the supreme theophany, as we have said. But the climax to this lifelong theophany comes in his death and resurrection. Here God reveals himself:

> "Now is the Son of Man *glorified*, and God is *glorified* in him. If God is *glorified* in him, God will also *glorify* him in himself, and *glorify* him at once." (John 13:31–32)

God reveals his righteousness, because it is evident that he does not wink at sin or ignore it. Nor does he forgive it in violation of the standards of his righteousness. Simultaneously, he reveals his mercy: he is "the justifier of the one who has faith in Jesus" (Rom. 3:26).

The manifestation of God in the whirlwind in Job 38–41 foreshadows the climactic manifestation of God in the death and resurrection of Christ.

42

God Appearing in the Psalms

For the most part, the book of Psalms does not focus on visual phenomena that manifest the presence of God in a spectacular way. The Psalms focus on how the communion between God and his people impacts their experience. They express both highs and lows in the emotions—both joy and sorrow. These joys and sorrows are constantly intertwined with people's relation to God.

The Presence of God as a Theme in the Psalms

The whole book of Psalms can be seen as unfolding aspects of God's presence—it shows how God's presence is experienced by the people of God.

As a generality, we can say that psalms of joy show us the reality of God's presence in the form of blessing to his people. (Think, for example, of Ps. 16:11: "in your presence there is fullness of joy; at your right hand are pleasures forevermore.") Such blessing has many sides to it, but one side lies in the fact that blessing produces a response of joy, thanksgiving, and praise. God is present to bless. God is also present in the very act of singing and praying in thanksgiving. The words of joy and thanksgiving express and manifest God's worthiness to receive thanks. Thus they manifest God and his character.

The theme of God's worthiness runs through many psalms. But we may also try to appreciate each psalm in its unique texture. So there are as many forms and expressions of the presence of God as there are psalms.

God's presence is also expressed in psalms of lament and suffering. Psalms can express such experiences in more than one way. The psalmist may lament that God is distant. God has not yet come to his help. Where is God in these circumstances?

> Why, O Lord, do you stand *far away*?
>   Why do you *hide yourself* in times of trouble? (Ps. 10:1)

> Be not *far* from me,
>   for trouble is near,
>   and there is none to help. (Ps. 22:11)

> You have seen, O Lord; be not silent!
>   O Lord, be not *far* from me! (Ps. 35:22)

Or a lament may speak of God being present in the very experience of suffering, which is suffering under his wrath:

> Your *wrath* lies heavy upon me,
>   and you overwhelm me with all your waves. *Selah*
> You have caused my companions to shun me;
>   you have made me a horror to them.
> I am shut in so that I cannot escape. (Ps. 88:7–8)

> O Lord, rebuke me not in your *anger*,
>   nor discipline me in your *wrath*! (Ps. 38:1)

Sometimes a lament *combines* language about wrath and language about God being distant:

> How long, O Lord? Will you *hide yourself* forever?
>   How long will your *wrath burn* like fire? (Ps. 89:46)

This combination might seem paradoxical. But at a deeper level there is harmony. God "hides himself" when he withdraws his blessing. God "hides" his goodness. At the same time, he may manifest and reveal his anger. The *kind* of manifestation that God makes of himself varies from case to case. In this way, psalms of lament and distress are just as much about the presence of God, in a broad sense, as are the psalms of rejoicing.

We also have psalms of meditation, whose mood is quieter than either extreme of joy or sorrow. Psalms meditate on God's wisdom, or on the reward of the righteous, or on God's works in history. God manifests his character in wisdom, in rewards for the righteous, and in his works in history. So these psalms too are about the presence of God and the manifestation of his presence in the world.

With such a pervasive concern for God's presence in the book of Psalms, what role is there for theophany and spectacular visible manifestations of his presence? Such things play a minor role, because many psalms focus on the people of God and their response, rather than on visual manifestation of God as such.

Yet there are places in the Psalms where the language of visible manifestation comes more to the foreground. It is worth listing some of the main instances. But these main instances should not be isolated from the rest of the book of Psalms. The prominent instances fade off into less prominent ones, and these fade off into the many psalms that express God's presence in broader ways.

The Psalms are poetic songs. Poetry contains allusions. It invites us not merely to stay at an elementary level of one-dimensional meaning, but to think about further associations. At this level of allusion and association, the Psalms are full of the presence of God. And because his presence is associated with theophany elsewhere in the Bible, such theophanic associations belong to the Psalms as well. Modern readers are often not aware of them. It is just necessary to adjust to the way in which poetic allusion works in the Psalms.

We will list more instances of the presence of God from the first few psalms, to provide a better idea of the many patterns for the presence of God. Then we will include a few prominent instances from later psalms.

The Lord Manifesting Himself in the Righteous (Psalm 1)

The Lord's righteousness is manifested in the righteous man:

> Blessed is the *man*
> who walks not in the counsel of the wicked,
> nor stands in the way of sinners,
> nor sits in the seat of scoffers. (Ps. 1:1)

Through absorbing God's law, the righteous man reflects the character of God (v. 2). By implication, the righteous character of God is manifested and displayed in him. The picture of the ideal righteous man points forward to Christ, who is perfectly righteous and who alone fulfills the picture completely. In this fulfillment, Christ manifests the presence of God in his righteousness.

In addition, righteousness from God himself is manifested in the judgment, when the way of the righteous stands out and the wicked is swept away (v. 5–6). Psalm 1 does not include overtly theophanic language. But thematically it links itself to the judgment of God, which we know comes by theophany.

The Lord Manifesting Himself in the King (Psalm 2)

The Lord manifests himself through the rule of the Israelite king, ultimately the messianic king:

> As for me, I have set my King
>   on Zion, my holy hill. (Ps. 2:6)

The king manifests on earth the rule and power and justice of God.

The decree of judgment comes from God in heaven: "he who sits in the heavens laughs" (v. 4). In this verse we get a small glimpse of a theophany, suggestive of a court theophany. The effect on earth is manifested in the enthronement of God's messianic representative in verse 6.

In addition, the mention of "Zion, my holy hill" evokes the theme of God's presence in the place that he has chosen. This presence was demonstrated when the cloud of glory filled the completed Solomonic temple (1 Kings 8:10–11). The presence of God in the temple and with the Israelite king on his throne serves as a type and shadow pointing to a climactic presence of God, through his Messiah, through whom the nations are subdued (Ps. 2:8–10).

Psalm 2, which along with Psalm 1 serves as a kind of introduction to the Psalter, functions as a key example of the theme of God's presence. God's presence is focused on his king and on his temple. The later psalms that take up the theme of the king, or the theme of the temple, or the theme of Zion the holy mountain, or the holy city, continue to articulate the reality of the presence of God. They are forward-pointing pictures, looking toward a time of final salvation, when God will come in a more intensive and spectacular way than what he has done with the exodus from Egypt, the Mosaic tabernacle, the Solomonic temple, and the reigns of the judges and the kings.

The Lord as Protector and as Warrior (Psalm 3)

Psalm 3 contains one of many expressions of God's protection:

> But you, O LORD, are a *shield* about me,
>   my glory, and the lifter of my head. (Ps. 3:3)

The Lord is a shield, a fortress, a stronghold, a rock (Ps. 18:2). One may multiply expressions concerning his care and protection. All these express in a broad sense the character of God, his mercy toward his people, and his kindness in drawing near to them. These expressions have their consummate fulfillment in the safety of the new heaven and the new earth (Rev. 21:1). They have inaugurated fulfillment in the protection of Christ toward his sheep: "I give them eternal life, and they will never perish, and no one will snatch them out of my hand" (John 10:28).

One aspect of protection is in dealing with enemies. In Psalm 3, the Lord fights against the enemies of the psalmist:

> Arise, O LORD!
>   Save me, O my God!
> For you *strike* all my enemies on the cheek;
>   you *break* the teeth of the wicked. (Ps. 3:7)

Such language about fighting has resonances with warrior theophanies elsewhere in the Old Testament. The warrior language in the Psalms should be seen as an expression of the intensive presence of God, coming to judge his enemies and the enemies of his people.

God Manifesting His Goodness (Psalm 4)

Psalm 4 contains one of the many places that speak of God's display of goodness using the metaphor of light and the display of that light from his "face" or presence: "Lift up the *light* of your *face* upon us, O LORD!" (Ps. 4:6).

God's Presence in His House (Psalm 5)

God's presence is especially expressed in his house or temple:

> But I, through the abundance of your steadfast love,
>   will enter your *house*.
> I will bow down toward your *holy temple*
>   in the fear of you. (Ps. 5:7)

The experience of a special presence of God in the temple, and a special blessing as people commune with God, is a precious reality of Old Testament times. It foreshadows God's presence in Christ, who is the final meeting place of God and man:

> For there is one God, and there is one *mediator* between God and men, the man Christ Jesus, who gave himself as a ransom for all. (1 Tim. 2:5–6)

The Turning of God (Psalm 6)

Psalm 6 is a psalm of lament that pleads with God to "turn" to the psalmist:

> *Turn*, O LORD, deliver my life;
> save me for the sake of your steadfast love. (Ps. 6:4)

The language of turning evokes a picture of God's localized presence, and may suggest his appearing to the psalmist and working on his behalf.

Assembly before God (Psalm 7)

In Psalm 7 we have a brief picture of peoples assembling before God's presence:

> Arise, O LORD, in your anger;
> lift yourself up against the fury of my enemies;
> awake for me; you have appointed a *judgment*.
> Let the assembly of the peoples be *gathered about you*;
> over it return *on high*.
> The LORD *judges the peoples*;
> *judge* me, O LORD, according to my righteousness
> and according to the integrity that is in me. (Ps. 7:6–8)

The language evokes a picture of God appearing before the assembly of peoples. He pronounces judgment on behalf of the righteous and against the enemies. In this language we see similarities to court theophanies.

God's Glory Displayed in the World (Psalm 8)

God displays his glory in the natural world:

> O Lord, our Lord,
>> how majestic is your *name* in all the earth!
> You have set your *glory* above the heavens. (Ps. 8:1)

The language here is reminiscent of a glory theophany. The mention of God's name speaks of the manifestation of his character. It enjoys connections with the manifestation of God's name to Moses in the exalted encounter in Exodus 34:

> The Lord descended in the cloud and stood with him there, and proclaimed the *name* of the Lord. The Lord *passed before* him and proclaimed, "The Lord, the Lord, a God merciful and gracious, slow to anger, and abounding in steadfast love and faithfulness." (Ex. 34:5–6)

Man himself is a principal focus for the display of God's glory, because man has been given a God-like position of rule:

> Yet you have made him a little lower than the *heavenly beings*
>> [or *than God*; ESV footnote]
> and crowned him with *glory* and honor. (Ps. 8:5)

Enemies Perishing from God's Presence (Psalm 9)

The judgment on enemies comes from God's presence:

> When my enemies turn back,
>> they stumble and perish *before your presence.*
> For you have maintained my just cause;
>> you have *sat on the throne*, giving righteous *judgment*. (Ps. 9:3–4)

The poetry here presents the picture of a court theophany.

Later in the psalm, the picture is elaborated to underline God's comprehensive judgment:

> But the Lord sits *enthroned* forever;
>> he has established his *throne* for justice,
> and he *judges* the world with righteousness;
>> he *judges* the peoples with uprightness. (Ps. 9:7–8)

The psalm also indicates the *location* in Zion of God's special presence:

> Sing praises to the Lord, who *sits enthroned in Zion*! (Ps. 9:11)

The Lord Hiding (Psalm 10)

Psalm 10 begins with one of the instances concerning how people struggle over the absence of God's blessing, which is a kind of absence of God's presence:

> Why, O LORD, do you *stand far away?*
>   Why do you *hide yourself* in times of trouble? (Ps. 10:1)

We have already mentioned this theme, which extends through many psalms of suffering.

The Lord's Presence in His Temple (Psalm 11)

Psalm 11 contains one of many expressions of the Lord's presence in heaven, in his temple:

> The LORD is in his *holy temple;*
>   the LORD's *throne is in heaven;*
>   his eyes see, his eyelids test the children of man. (Ps. 11:4)

The language is reminiscent of court theophanies, with God's throne as the center of an angelic court. It is also reminiscent of cloud and glory theophanies that are associated with the tabernacle of Moses and the temple of Solomon.

In the parallel poetic lines in verse 4, God's "holy temple" is parallel to his "throne . . . in heaven." In view of this parallelism, the expression "holy temple" in the first line is probably pointing primarily to God's dwelling place in heaven, rather than the temple to be established on the earthly Zion. The earthly temple, of course, is a shadow and copy of the heavenly temple (1 Kings 8:27–30). The poetic language of the psalmist can move freely between a reference to the heavenly temple and an allusion to their earthly temple that symbolically manifests it. Both are to be associated with God's presence, and both become locations of theophanies.

Psalm 11:7 also speaks of the presence of God through "his face":

> the upright shall *behold his face.*

The final fulfillment of this promise is found in the theophany of Revelation 22:4: "they will see his *face.*" The inaugurated stage of fulfillment is found in our communion with Christ:

For God, who said, "Let light shine out of darkness," has *shone* in our hearts to give the *light* of the knowledge of the *glory* of God in the *face* of Jesus Christ. (2 Cor. 4:6)

The Lord's Presence in Connection with Hiding (Psalm 13)

In Psalm 13, the psalmist asks that God turn from hiding himself and give light:

> How long, O LORD? Will you forget me forever?
>> How long will you *hide your face* from me? (Ps. 13:1)

> Consider and answer me, O LORD my God;
>> *light* up my eyes, lest I sleep the sleep of death. (v. 3)

Both of these expressions have connections with theophany. The language of hiding is the opposite of the revealing that takes place in theophany. The language of giving light is reminiscent of glory theophanies.

We have looked at enough cases to see, in the book of Psalms, major themes expressive of God's presence. Now we content ourselves with mentioning a few more prominent cases in the rest of the Psalms.

Joy in the Consummation of God's Presence

Psalm 16:11 speaks of joy before God in a way that anticipates the presence of God in theophany at the consummation:

> You make known to me the path of life;
>> *in your presence* there is fullness of joy;
>> at your right hand are pleasures forevermore.

A similar picture is found in Psalm 17:15:

> As for me, I shall *behold your face* in righteousness;
>> when I awake, I shall be satisfied with your likeness.

Thunderstorm Appearance (Psalm 18)

Parallel to 2 Samuel 22:8–15, Psalm 18:7–14 has features of thunderstorm theophany (see chapter 2).

Revelation of God in the Heavens (Psalm 19)

Psalm 19 speaks of the glory of God revealed in what he has made:

> The heavens declare the *glory* of God,
>> and the sky above proclaims his handiwork.
> Day to day pours out speech,
>> and night to night reveals knowledge. (Ps. 19:1–2)

This language is reminiscent of glory theophanies and creation as a theophany-like manifestation of the presence of God.

The Coming of the King (Psalm 24)

Psalm 24 not only speaks about ascending to "the hill of the Lord," "his holy place" (v. 3); it also depicts the coming of "the King of glory" into his house:

> Lift up your heads, O gates!
>> And be lifted up, O ancient doors,
>>> that the King of *glory* may *come* in.
> Who is this King of glory?
>> The Lord, strong and mighty,
>>> the Lord, *mighty in battle*!
> Lift up your heads, O gates!
>> And lift them up, O ancient doors,
>>> that the King of glory may *come* in.
> Who is this King of glory?
>> The Lord of hosts,
>>> he is the King of glory! *Selah* (Ps. 24:7–10)

The sense of dramatic entrance conveys a picture of a physical appearance. The poetry also contains an expression about battle that draws a connection with warrior theophanies: "mighty in battle."

Beholding God (Psalm 27)

Psalm 27 contains lines exulting in the intimacy of fellowship with God:

> One thing have I asked of the Lord,
>> that will I seek after:
> that I may dwell in the house of the Lord
>> all the days of my life,

to *gaze upon* the beauty of the LORD
and to inquire in his temple. (Ps. 27:4)

The Voice of the Lord Thundering (Psalm 29)

Psalm 29 has resonances with thunderstorm theophanies:

The voice of the LORD is over the waters;
the God of glory *thunders*,
the LORD, over many waters.
The voice of the LORD is *powerful*;
the voice of the LORD is full of majesty. (Ps. 29:3–4)

God reveals his power and majesty in the thunder of his voice.

God in the Midst (Psalm 46)

God is in the *midst of* his holy city:

God is in the *midst of* her; she shall not be moved;
God will help her when morning dawns. (Ps. 46:5)

The presence of God in the city symbolizes more broadly his presence with his people. As a whole psalm, Psalm 48 also celebrates the presence of God in "the city of our God" (v. 1).

God Coming for Judgment (Psalm 50)

Psalm 50 describes a visible accompaniment when God comes in judgment:

The Mighty One, God the LORD,
speaks and summons the earth
from the rising of the sun to its setting.
Out of Zion, the perfection of beauty,
God *shines* forth.
Our God *comes*; he does not keep silence;
before him is a devouring *fire*,
around him a mighty *tempest*.
He calls to the heavens above
and to the earth, that he may *judge* his people. (Ps. 50:1–4)

The language has resonances with thunderstorm theophanies.

God Treading Down Foes (Psalm 60:12)

Psalm 60:12 contains a small piece alluding to warrior theophanies: "It is he who will *tread down* our foes." Similarly we have in Psalm 64:7, "But God *shoots his arrow* at them."

God Shining (Psalm 67)

Psalm 67 expresses the desire for God's face to shine:

> May God be gracious to us and bless us
>   and make his *face* to *shine* upon us, . . . *Selah* (Ps. 67:1)

The language about *shining* is reminiscent of glory theophanies. We may think also of Moses's face, which shone after he had seen the glory of God (Ex. 34:29). And the language of God's "face" strongly underlines the presence of God.

The Lord Coming at Sinai (Psalm 68)

Psalm 68 reflects on Mount Sinai and indicates that the once-for-all appearance on Sinai is related to later manifestations of the presence of God among his people:

> O God, when you went out *before* your people,
>   when you *marched* through the wilderness, *Selah*
> the *earth quaked*, the heavens poured down rain,
>   before God, the One of *Sinai*,
>   before God, the God of Israel.
> Rain in abundance, O God, you shed abroad;
>   you restored your inheritance as it languished. (Ps. 68:7–9)

The mention of rain, twice in these lines, links the thunderstorm at Mount Sinai with later provisions of rain for the land.

Later verses in the same psalm have the effect of connecting Mount Sinai with Mount Zion (v. 16), with warrior theophanies, and with temple theophanies:

> The *chariots* of God are twice ten thousand,
>   thousands upon thousands;
>   the Lord is among them; *Sinai* is now in the *sanctuary*.
> You ascended on *high*,
>   leading a host of captives in your train

> and receiving gifts among men,
>   even among the rebellious, that the LORD God may *dwell there*.
>   (Ps. 68:17–18)

This passage shows the way in which poetry may combine various aspects associated with God's presence, as expressed in theophany. What God has done in the past—particularly at Mount Sinai—serves as an encouragement for people to call on him now and to have hope for the future manifestation of his presence.

Glory Filling the Earth (Psalm 72)

In Psalm 72 the presence of God is expressed most vigorously through the vision of the rule of the great king established by God—the Messiah. But near the end of the psalm we also find a note associated with glory theophanies:

> Blessed be his *glorious* name forever;
>   may the whole earth be filled with his *glory*!
>   Amen and Amen! (Ps. 72:19)

God in the Exodus (Psalm 77)

Psalm 77 reflects on the thunderstorm theophany at Mount Sinai:

> When the waters saw you, O God,
>   when the waters saw you, they were afraid;
>   indeed, the deep trembled.
> The *clouds* poured out water;
>   the skies gave forth *thunder*;
>   your *arrows* flashed on every side.
> The crash of your *thunder* was in the *whirlwind*;
>   your *lightnings* lighted up the world;
>   the earth *trembled* and shook.
> Your way was through the sea,
>   your path through the great waters;
>   yet your footprints were unseen.
> You led your people like a flock
>   by the hand of Moses and Aaron. (Ps. 77:16–20)

The thunder, whirlwind, and lightning, which were the immediate accompaniments of the theophany at Mount Sinai, go together closely with God's acts before and afterward—dividing the Red Sea, and leading the people to the Promised Land. The poem links theophany in a narrow sense—Mount Sinai—with the presence and appearance of God in a broader way—in the exodus as a whole. The two go together as twin manifestations of the presence and power of God.

God with the Cherubim (Psalm 80)

God is described together with the cherubim:

> Give ear, O Shepherd of Israel,
>   you who lead Joseph like a flock.
> You who are *enthroned upon the cherubim*, shine forth. (Ps. 80:1)

This verse offers another instance that evokes the picture of a court theophany. It is interesting that the evocation comes without further explanation or preface, as the psalmist calls on God:

> stir up your might
>   and *come* to save us! (v. 2)

In fact, the reality of God's power and majesty, as displayed in court theophanies, should be a motivation for prayer at all times. God is the God who rules and who acts in power on behalf of his people.

A similar mention of God's presence occurs later in the same psalm:

> Turn again, O God of hosts!
>   *Look down from heaven*, and see;
> have regard for this vine. (Ps. 80:14)

The Divine Council (Psalm 82)

Psalm 82 speaks explicitly about the divine council:

> God has taken his place in the *divine council*;
>   in the midst of the *gods* he holds *judgment*:
> "How long will you judge unjustly
>   and show partiality to the wicked?" *Selah* (Ps. 82:1–2)

The picture is an interesting one, because the participants in the divine council are "the gods." In the context of the sole sovereignty of God Most High, the designation "the gods" is a supremely exalted title for human rulers, some of whom rule unjustly: "How long will you judge unjustly" (v. 2). Later verses continue the thought:

I said, "You are *gods*,
>   *sons* of the Most High, all of you;
nevertheless, like men you shall die,
>   and fall like any prince." (vv. 6–7)

The Most High has pronounced judgment against these unjust judges. He does so within a court theophany, "the divine council." This one case of judgment goes together with the general principle that God is judge of the whole earth:

Arise, O God, *judge* the earth;
>   for you shall inherit all the nations! (Ps. 82:8)

Earlier judgments foreshadow the final judgment of Revelation 20:11–15, which takes place in theophany.

God among the Heavenly Beings (Psalm 89)

Psalm 89 includes a scene where God is among the "heavenly beings":

Let the heavens praise your wonders, O Lord,
>   your faithfulness in the assembly of the holy ones!
For who in the *skies* can be compared to the Lord?
>   Who among the *heavenly beings* is like the Lord,
a God greatly to be feared in the *council of the holy ones*,
>   and awesome above all who are *around him*?
O Lord God of hosts,
>   who is mighty as you are, O Lord,
>   with your faithfulness all *around you*? (Ps. 89:5–8)

The psalm contains several expressions referring to angelic beings around God. We have language evoking the picture of a court theophany, "the council of the holy ones."

In the last line, rather than angels surrounding God's presence on his throne, it is *faithfulness* that surrounds him. The expression may at first look incongruous. But it matches what we have seen about the significance of theophany. Angels, though created beings, reflect the splendor and majesty of the uncreated God. In a certain respect, God creates reflections of himself in his angels. Theophany displays who God is and what is his character. His character is to be *faithful*. He also sustains faithfulness in his creatures—angels and faithful human beings. A display of faithfulness "around" God, whether in his angels, in his creation, or in his works of redemption, functions to reflect God. The function of the display of faithfulness is the same as the function of theophany. We see God.

The next verses in Psalm 89 reflect on God's rule over the sea:

> ⁹ You rule the raging of the sea;
>   when its waves rise, you still them.
> ¹⁰ You crushed Rahab like a carcass;
>   you *scattered* your enemies with your *mighty arm*. (Ps. 89:9–10)

These verses have theophanic overtones. Let us see how. "Rahab" (v. 10) is another name for Egypt. It occurs prominently in poetic passages where Egypt is the enemy of God and God's people. The language about crushing Rahab thus alludes to the exodus and the events at the Red Sea (cf. Isa. 51:9–10, discussed in chapter 39 above). In these events God manifested himself in visible form, in the cloud of fire and in the sea itself, which God used as a judgment against Egypt. The events at the Red Sea also include elements of warrior theophany. Verse 10, by speaking of God scattering his enemies, calls to mind the picture of a warrior theophany.

Psalm 89:9 speaks more generally: "You rule the raging of the sea." In the context of verse 10, verse 9 indicates that the particular events in crossing the Red Sea illustrate a broader principle. God rules over the sea in his providence. And the ultimate background for God's providential rule lies in the rule that he exerted in creating the world and bounding the sea. In God's providence he stills storms. In creation, he subdued the initially unformed waters (Gen. 1:2). A parallel idea is found in Job 26:12–13:

> By his power he stilled the sea;
>   by his understanding he *shattered* Rahab.
> By his wind the heavens were made fair;
>   his hand *pierced* the fleeing serpent.

The larger context of providence and creation in Job 26 suggests that these verses allude poetically to creation, to providence, and to the triumph of God at the Red Sea. The language of shattering and piercing pictures God as a warrior. So again the idea of a warrior theophany is in the background. The links between creation, providence, and redemption in Job 26:12–13 confirm that the same three should be seen as part of the background for Psalm 89:9–10.

After its wonderful reflections on God's majesty and faithfulness,

Psalm 89 wrestles with how to reconcile God's faithfulness with the apparent lapse in the covenant with David. And so we come finally to a verse, mentioned earlier, that combines God's "absence" in hiding with his "presence" in wrath:

> How long, O LORD? Will you *hide* yourself forever?
> > How long will your *wrath burn* like *fire*? (Ps. 89:46)

Clothing for God (Psalm 93)

Psalm 93 is among the passages that describe clothing for God:

> The LORD reigns; he is *robed in majesty*;
> > the LORD is *robed*; he has put on strength as his *belt*.
> Yes, the world is established; it shall never be moved.
> Your *throne* is established from of old;
> > you are from everlasting. (Ps. 93:1–2)

Clothing, as we observed, shows us the nature of the person clothed (chapter 22). So its presence functions in a manner parallel to the function of God's *throne*. God's nature is exhibited by his immediate environment, which reflects him.

Clouds around Him (Psalm 97)

Psalm 97 describes clouds around God:

> *Clouds* and *thick darkness* are all around him;
> > righteousness and justice are the foundation of his *throne*.
> *Fire* goes before him
> > and *burns* up his adversaries all around.
> His *lightnings light* up the world;
> > the earth sees and *trembles*.
> The mountains melt like wax *before* the LORD,
> > *before* the Lord of all the earth.
> The heavens proclaim his righteousness,
> > and all the peoples *see* his *glory*. (Ps. 97:2–6)

The mention of clouds introduces a larger complex of poetry with multiple associations with theophany: thick darkness, throne, fire, lightnings, trembling earth, glory. The peoples *see* his glory (v. 6).

The opening context is a broad context of God's rule:

The LORD *reigns*, let the earth rejoice;
    let the many coastlands be glad! (Ps. 97:1)

In later verses the psalm goes on to reflect on condemnation (v. 7) and salvation (vv. 8–12). The whole sweep of providence and history is included in the scope. This psalm is instructive about the way in which the specific and focused vision given in a theophany in the narrow sense throws light on the character of God and the character of his reign. Therefore, it serves as a window or perspective on the whole of God's rule and his kingdom, through all of history.

The Lord Enthroned (Psalm 99)

Psalm 99 makes a similar point:

The LORD reigns; let the peoples tremble!
    He *sits enthroned upon the cherubim*; let the earth *quake*!
The LORD is great in Zion;
    he is exalted over all the peoples.
Let them praise your great and awesome name!
    Holy is he!
The King in his *might* loves *justice*.
    You have established equity;
you have executed *justice*
    and righteousness in Jacob. (Ps. 99:1–4)

Justice comes from the throne of God, the one who "sits enthroned upon the cherubim" (v. 1). We have here the language of court theophany.

Creation as Theophany (Psalm 104)

We saw earlier (chapter 11) that Psalm 104:1–4 applies theophanic imagery to God's work in creating the world. Creation displays the character of God; it manifests him, and so is related to theophany in the narrow sense.

The Right Hand of God (Psalm 110)

The Messiah ("the Lord") sits at God's right hand:

The LORD says to my Lord:
    "Sit at *my right hand*,
until I make your enemies your footstool." (Ps. 110:1)

The position at God's right hand evokes the larger picture of a court theophany. In this theophanic picture, the Messiah takes the chief and honored position of power. Similar language occurs in verse 5: "The Lord is at your right hand." The effect of this position is to execute judgment on all opposition: "until I make your enemies your footstool" (v. 1).

This prophetic psalm anticipates the rule of Christ, beginning at his exaltation to heaven and culminating in the new heaven and new earth: "For he must reign until he has put all his enemies under his feet. The last enemy to be destroyed is death" (1 Cor. 15:25–26).

The Lord's Sight from Heaven (Psalm 113)

Psalm 113 has a brief description of the Lord's work from heaven:

> The LORD is *high above* all nations,
>   and his *glory* above the heavens!
> Who is like the LORD our God,
>   who is *seated on high*,
> who looks far down
>   on the heavens and the earth?
> He raises the poor from the dust
>   and lifts the needy from the ash heap. (Ps. 113:4–7)

The language evokes a picture of God on his throne, which would come in the context of a court theophany. He sits on his throne for the purpose of caring for the poor and needy.

Trembling at God's Presence (Psalm 114)

The earth trembles when God appears:

> *Tremble*, O earth, at the *presence* of the Lord,
>   at the *presence* of the God of Jacob,
> who turns the rock into a pool of water,
>   the flint into a spring of water. (Ps. 114:7–8)

The context is reflecting on God's work in the exodus from Egypt. Like Psalm 68, this psalm relates the specific theophanic phenomena at Mount Sinai to the larger work of God in miracle and providence, putting his works in a cosmic setting:

The sea looked and fled;
  Jordan turned back.
The mountains skipped like rams,
  the hills like lambs.
What ails you, O sea, that you flee?
  O Jordan, that you turn back?
O mountains, that you skip like rams?
  O hills, like lambs? (Ps. 114:3–6)

The Lord Enthroned (Psalm 123)

Psalm 123 speaks of the Lord enthroned:

To you I lift up my eyes,
  O you who are *enthroned* in the heavens! (Ps. 123:1)

The language is reminiscent of a court theophany. The reflection about God's enthronement encourages prayer (v. 2).

The Lord's Presence with an Individual Saint (Psalm 139)

The whole of Psalm 139 is noteworthy because of its emphasis on the presence of God. There is explicit mention of his presence:

Where shall I go from your *Spirit*?
  Or where shall I flee from *your presence*?
If I ascend to heaven, you *are there*!
  If I make my bed in Sheol, you *are there*! (Ps. 139:7–8)

Praising the Lord as a Prelude to Final Presence (Psalm 150)

The book of Psalms finds a fitting conclusion in Psalm 150, a magnificent song of praise. The psalm explicitly refers to God's presence in heaven:

Praise the LORD!
  Praise God in his *sanctuary*;
  praise him in his mighty *heavens*! (Ps. 150:1)

By heaping up and multiplying praises, the psalm points naturally to a future when praise will be consummated. It points to the worship of God in the new heaven and new earth: "his servants will *worship* him. They will see his *face*, and his name will be on their foreheads" (Rev. 22:3–4). Seeing the face of God is the final form of worship.

43

God Appearing in the
Solomonic Books

Now let us consider the presence of God in the Solomonic books: Proverbs, Ecclesiastes, and the Song of Solomon.

Covenant, Wisdom, and Presence

Special visual appearances of God—theophanies in a narrow sense—do not occur in Proverbs, Ecclesiastes, or the Song of Solomon. But God is present. To begin with, he is present in verbal communication, in the same way that he is present in the rest of the Bible, because every part of the Bible is the word of God. God is present with his word. In addition, God is present in the contents of the *Wisdom* books, because the wisdom in the books has its source in God. God manifests his wisdom in these books. ("Men spoke from God as they were carried along by the Holy Spirit"; 2 Pet. 1:21.)

The presence of God in wisdom is an important theme in the Wisdom books. For that reason, at least one scholar has argued that the theme of God's presence deals more adequately with the whole scope of Old Testament writings than does the theme of covenant.[1] The theme of

---

1. Samuel Terrien, *The Elusive Presence: Toward a New Biblical Theology* (San Francisco: Harper & Row, 1978), 3, 42; on pages 36–37, Terrien cites G. Fohrer as a predecessor (Georg Fohrer, *Theologische Grundstrukturen des Alten Testaments* [Berlin/New York: de Gruyter, 1972], 95–112). Both of these scholars do not accept the divine authorship of the Bible, but they have made useful observations about the importance of the theme of God's presence.

covenant leads us naturally to think about God's historical covenants with the people of Israel, beginning with Abraham and continuing through the covenant at Mount Sinai. But the Wisdom Literature in the Old Testament, including Job as well as Proverbs and Ecclesiastes, does not give a prominent role to a discussion of these historical covenants. Wisdom is more closely related to creation, as we can see from Proverbs 8:22–31, where wisdom is involved in God's creation of the world.

In fact, the two strands of covenant and wisdom are in harmony. They come together in the figure of Solomon, as seen in 1 Kings 4:29–34. Earlier, 1 Kings gives an account of Solomon asking the Lord for wisdom (3:3–14). The context includes the fact that Solomon is in the line of the covenant with David (2 Sam. 7:4–17). In addition, Solomon offers covenantal sacrifices at Gibeon (1 Kings 3:4). God already has an established covenantal relation to Solomon. He grants Solomon wisdom through this covenantal relation. At the same time, 1 Kings 4:29–34 compares Solomon's wisdom to the wisdom that is found in other nations:

> . . . so that Solomon's wisdom surpassed the wisdom of all the people of the *east* and all the wisdom of *Egypt*. For he was wiser than all other men, wiser than Ethan the Ezrahite, and Heman, Calcol, and Darda, the sons of Mahol, and his fame was in all the surrounding *nations*. (1 Kings 4:30–31)

So wisdom does have an international scope, extending beyond God's covenant with Israel. Proverbs and Ecclesiastes discuss wisdom without explicit references to historical covenants with Israel. Yet the connection with Solomon still offers a covenantal context. And Proverbs repeatedly refers to God by his covenantal name, "the LORD" (Jehovah; cf. Ex. 6:2). Both covenant and wisdom are expressions of God's presence, so we should see harmony rather than tension between the different themes.

God's Presence in the Book of Proverbs

God is present in the book of Proverbs, all through the book, as "the LORD," who is the source of wisdom:

> The fear of the LORD is the *beginning* of knowledge;
>   fools despise wisdom and instruction. (Prov. 1:7)

In the first nine chapters of Proverbs, a father instructs his son in the ways of wisdom. The father in view is a human father, but he imitates God as divine father:

> My son, do not despise the LORD's discipline
> > or be weary of his reproof,
> for the LORD reproves him whom he loves,
> > as a *father the son* in whom he delights. (Prov. 3:11–12)

Some individual proverbs also speak of the Lord as the judge who rewards the righteous and destroys the wicked. Here are some instances:

> The LORD does not let the righteous go hungry,
> > but he thwarts the craving of the wicked. (Prov. 10:3)

> The way of the LORD is a stronghold to the blameless,
> > but destruction to evildoers. (v. 29)

> The eyes of the LORD keep watch over knowledge,
> > but he overthrows the words of the traitor. (Prov. 22:12)

God's Presence in Ecclesiastes

God's presence is an issue all the way through Ecclesiastes, because Ecclesiastes attempts to understand events observed on earth by using wisdom. It is largely a confession of the *limitations* of human wisdom. There is much "under the sun" that we do not understand:

> When I applied my heart to know wisdom, and to see the business that is done on earth, how neither day nor night do one's eyes see sleep, then I saw all the work of God, that man cannot find out the work that is done under the sun. However much man may toil in seeking, he will not find it out. Even though a *wise* man claims to know, he *cannot find it out*. (Eccles. 8:16–17)

Ecclesiastes recognizes God as the ultimate source and foundation for wisdom, and recognizes that he gives a measure of wisdom to human beings. But it is largely occupied with the limitations of our access to the meaning of his ways.

God's Presence in the Song of Solomon

God is present in the Song of Solomon through the manifestation of his goodness in human romantic love. It is God who created man male and female (Gen. 1:27) and who established marriage with Adam and Eve (Gen. 2:24).

Beyond this level of understanding, much depends on how we interpret the Song of Solomon. The ancient fathers of the church saw in the book an allegorical picture of Christ's love for the church. But they were not willing to see a direct reference to human sexual love. Scholarly interpreters in the twentieth and twenty-first centuries have mostly gone to the other extreme: they find love poems but no second dimension in which the poetry alludes to Christ's love for the church.

In fact, both levels are there. The starting level is undeniably found in references to romantic sexual love. God created human sexuality, and it is among the things that God pronounced "very good" at the end of the sixth day of creation (Gen. 1:31). So we should not be squeamish about acknowledging God's goodness to us in sexuality. At the same time, within a fallen world, marred by human sin, who is equal to the ideal of love that the Song of Solomon raises for us? The failures in human love lead us inexorably to asking about divine love, of which the best human love is only an imitation.

Moreover, the Song of Solomon refers to Solomon (Song 1:1; 3:11), who is a covenantal figure. Song of Solomon 3:11 refers to the day of Solomon's wedding:

> Go out, O daughters of Zion,
>   and look upon *King Solomon*,
> with the crown with which his mother crowned him
>   on the day of his *wedding*,
>   on the day of the gladness of his heart.

The allusion to the wedding of the Israelite *king* puts us in the context of God's covenantal promises to David and the celebration of the wedding of the king in Psalm 45:

> My heart overflows with a pleasing theme;
>   I address my verses to *the king*;
>   my tongue is like the pen of a ready scribe. (Ps. 45:1)

We know from the Old Testament that God as king of Israel is also husband to his people (Jer. 31:32). God's relation of love to Israel has its fulfillment in the even more intimate relation that the church now enjoys with Christ:

Husbands, love your wives, *as* Christ *loved* the church and gave himself up for her, that he might sanctify her, having cleansed her by the washing of water with the word, so that he might present the church to himself in splendor, without spot or wrinkle or any such thing, that she might be holy and without blemish. (Eph. 5:25–27)

I feel a divine jealousy for you, since I betrothed you to one *husband*, to present you as a pure virgin to Christ. (2 Cor. 11:2)

So the Song of Solomon has allusive connections to the New Testament fulfillment in intimacy with Christ. This fulfillment in the time of the New Testament is an *inaugurated* fulfillment, still awaiting consummation in the time of climactic intimacy at the marriage supper of the Lamb: "Let us rejoice and exult and give him the glory, for the *marriage* of the Lamb has come, and his Bride has made herself ready" (Rev. 19:7; cf. v. 9). The poetic allusiveness of the Song of Solomon, the sinful contaminations of human love, and the context of the full canon all invite us to see in the Song an expression of Christ's love for his church.

If so, the Song of Solomon is about the presence of God. The presence of God expresses itself in the presence of Christ with his church, a presence with deep love and affection. That presence also provides a foretaste of the consummate presence, yet to come in the new heaven and the new earth (Rev. 22:4).

44

God Appearing in Postexilic History (Ezra–Esther)

Now consider the presence of God in the postexilic historical books of Ezra, Nehemiah, and Esther.

Return from Exile

Ezra, Nehemiah, and Esther cover a remarkable series of events in which God again and again shows favor to his people. The events are remarkable because, from a merely human point of view, it might have seemed to the Israelites as well as to the surrounding nations that the Lord's special relation to his people Israel had terminated with the exile. God drove them out of the land that he had promised them. Seemingly, he had repudiated them. An onlooker might easily have concluded that the God of Israel was not a God of real power at all—or if he was, that he had abandoned his people forever.

It might seem also that there was little prospect that the people who were exiled would ever return. When they did return, it took place in fulfillment of prophecies such as Isaiah 44:26–28; 45:1, 13; Jeremiah 29:10; and earlier, Deuteronomy 30:3–5.

God's Presence in the Events of Return

The return from exile seemed remarkable, even "miraculous" in a loose sense. God was in it, as Ezra 1 illustrates by explicitly mentioning God's work in Cyrus and in the exiles who returned:

The LORD *stirred up* the spirit of Cyrus king of Persia, so that he made a proclamation throughout all his kingdom and also put it in writing:

"Thus says Cyrus king of Persia: The LORD, the God of heaven, has given me all the kingdoms of the earth, and *he has charged* me to build him a house at Jerusalem, which is in Judah. Whoever is among you of all his people, may his God *be with* him, . . . "

Then rose up the heads of the fathers' houses of Judah and Benjamin, and the priests and the Levites, everyone whose spirit God had *stirred* to go up to rebuild the house of the LORD that is in Jerusalem. (Ezra 1:1–5)

This decree from Cyrus is only the beginning of a whole series of events in which God shows favor to his people, sometimes amid opposition. So the whole account in Ezra and Nehemiah is filled with the presence of God.

But the events belong to what we might call "ordinary providence." We do not hear of extraordinary miraculous works. And, significantly, we do not hear of any instance where God appeared in an extraordinary visible display.

The Prayer in Nehemiah 9: God's Presence in Past History

The closest we come to an instance of God appearing is found in the prayer in Nehemiah 9, which rehearses some of the "signs and wonders" that God did in the exodus:

"And you saw the affliction of our fathers in Egypt and heard their cry at the Red Sea, and performed *signs and wonders* against Pharaoh and all his servants and all the people of his land, for you knew that they acted arrogantly against our fathers. And you made a name for yourself, as it is to this day. And you divided the sea before them, so that they went through the midst of the sea on dry land, and you cast their pursuers into the depths, as a stone into mighty waters. By a *pillar of cloud* you led them in the day, and by a *pillar of fire* in the night to light for them the way in which they should go. You *came down* on Mount Sinai and spoke with them from heaven and gave them right rules and true laws, good statutes and commandments." (Neh. 9:9–13)

The signs and wonders all declare God's special presence. He is dramatically present especially in the pillar of cloud and fire.

Nehemiah 9 mentions the pillar of cloud and fire a second time, in a context that shows God's mercy to Israel after the incident with the golden calf:

> "you in your great mercies did not forsake them in the wilderness. The *pillar of cloud* to lead them in the way did not depart from them by day, nor the *pillar of fire* by night to light for them the way by which they should go." (Neh. 9:19)

The prayer in Nehemiah 9 calls on God to continue to be faithful to his covenant and continue to show mercy. It asks God to continue to be *present*.

The Expectation for the Glory of God

But in all of Ezra and Nehemiah, there is no record of a special visible appearance of God to the people who have returned. Especially noteworthy is that we do not hear about God appearing in the cloud of glory to consecrate the postexilic temple. Haggai 2 seems to promise it:

> "'and I will fill this house with *glory*, says the LORD of hosts.'" (Hag. 2:7)

> "'The latter *glory* of this house shall be greater than the former, says the LORD of hosts.'" (v. 9)

But it does not happen within the time frame of Ezra and Nehemiah. Instead, we have a record that includes disappointment:

> But many of the priests and Levites and heads of fathers' houses, old men who had seen the first house, *wept* with a loud voice when they saw the foundation of this house being laid, though many shouted aloud for joy. (Ezra 3:12)

> And Nehemiah, who was the governor, and Ezra the priest and scribe, and the Levites who taught the people said to all the people, "This day is holy to the LORD your God; do not mourn or *weep*." For all the people *wept* as they heard the words of the Law. (Neh. 8:9)

> "'Who is left among you who saw this house in its former glory? How do you see it now? Is it not as *nothing* in your eyes?'" (Hag. 2:3)

God is present among the returned exiles, but his presence has a kind of subdued form. This subdued manner of presence has the effect of keeping the people aware that the promises of the coming of God's glory remain for the future. As we now know, they point forward to the coming of Christ.

God's Presence in Esther

The same patterns about the presence of God hold for the book of Esther. As many commentators have pointed out, Esther is remarkable in that the name of God appears nowhere in the Hebrew text. But God is everywhere in the narrative in his secret working in providence. Among other things, the book of Esther teaches us to try to understand that God is present and that he works on behalf of his people even when we see no miraculous effects.

Commentators sometimes point out the large number of events that are crucial for rescuing the Jews from the danger of annihilation. Vashti is rejected. Esther is chosen and taken into the harem. Esther is favored and made queen. Mordecai reports the plot against the king. The king cannot sleep (Est. 6:1). The person reading to the king comes to the passage about Mordecai revealing the plot. And so on. We recognize that God is present in all these events, and more, once we understand the story as a whole.

PART IV

A HISTORY OF
GOD APPEARING:
THE NEW TESTAMENT

45

God Appearing in the Earthly Life of Christ (Gospels)

The Gospels give us records of the life of Christ on earth. His life brings to fulfillment the entire spectrum of theophanies and appearances of God in the Old Testament. Temporary appearances give way to the climactic, permanent appearance. God became man in the incarnation. The presence of God that people experience throughout Old Testament times comes to fulfillment in the presence of God in Christ. Christ is "Immanuel," "God *with us*" (Matt. 1:23), manifesting God's presence at the climax of history.

Because the New Testament has its center in Christ, everything in the New Testament is connected to the theme of God's presence. It is difficult to choose just some passages amid this richness. For the sake of brevity, we will be selective. But the passages we select illustrate the broader theme, that God comes to us in Christ.[1]

Some Passages Indicating God's Climactic Presence

The book of Hebrews describes the climactic character of God's appearing:

> Long ago, at many times and in many ways, God spoke to our fa-
> thers by the prophets, but in *these last days* he has spoken to us by
> his *Son*, whom he appointed the heir of all things, through whom

---

1. See also Vern S. Poythress, *The Miracles of Jesus: How the Savior's Mighty Acts Serve as Signs of Redemption* (Wheaton, IL: Crossway, 2016).

also he created the world. He is the *radiance* of the glory of God and the *exact imprint* of his nature, and he upholds the universe by the word of his power. After making purification for sins, he sat down at the right hand of the Majesty on high. (Heb. 1:1–3)

Hebrews labels the time of Christ's coming "these last days," because in them, "by his Son," God has brought to fulfillment the plans articulated and foreshadowed throughout the Old Testament. "For *all* the promises of God find their *Yes* in him" (2 Cor. 1:20).

So, in a broad sense, the entirety of the record in the Gospels constitutes a theophany. More than the other Gospels, John explicitly uses language linked to theophanic themes: "And the Word became flesh and *dwelt* among us, and we have seen his *glory*, *glory* as of the only Son from the Father, full of grace and truth" (John 1:14). The Greek word for *dwell* in this verse (*skēnoō*) is not the most common one, but one linked to the Old Testament tabernacle. The word for *glory* has links with the glory of God that appears in the cloud, the cloud that settles on the tabernacle (Ex. 40:34–38).

John also indicates what it means to *see* Jesus:

Jesus said to him, "Have I been with you so long, and you still do not know me, Philip? Whoever has *seen* me has *seen* the Father. (John 14:9)

But what John says explicitly holds true implicitly for the other Gospels. When Jesus comes, God appears. Jesus is the final form of God's presence among human beings. He is the one *mediator*:

For there is one God, and there is one *mediator* between God and men, the man Christ Jesus. (1 Tim. 2:5)

Intensive Manifestations of God's Appearing

Granted that God is present throughout the Gospels, we can still take note of the fact that God brings about a few special times in which his presence is manifested in particularly striking ways. We explore these in the rest of this chapter.

Angels Connected with Jesus's Conception and Birth

The first cluster of special manifestations of God's presence has to do with angels. Angels are not a theophany in the narrow sense, but they manifest the presence of God, whom they represent. And they are representatives belonging to God's heavenly court, so they have a close association with court theophanies.

Angels appear in a number of contexts related to Jesus's birth. The angel Gabriel announces the birth of John the Baptist to Zechariah (Luke 1:11). Gabriel later appears to Mary to announce the coming conception of Jesus (v. 28). Angels appear and announce Jesus's birth to the shepherds (2:9, 13).

An angel appears to Joseph more than once to give guidance. He appears to Joseph while Mary is pregnant, indicating what is happening and telling Joseph to proceed with the marriage (Matt. 1:20–21). An angel appears more than once giving Joseph guidance to protect Jesus (2:13, 19). A third time Joseph is given guidance in a dream, but this time the text does not say whether an angel appears (v. 22).

Why do we have this remarkable cluster of angelic appearances? God was pleased to do it. We may not know all the reasons, but some seem evident. Angels instructed Joseph so that he would know what to do at a number of points that affected the infant Jesus. More broadly, through the messages of angels, God drew near to Mary and Joseph and guided them.

Miracles Connected with the Birth of Jesus

We also see miracles taking place in connection with the birth of Jesus. The central miracle is the miracle of the incarnation itself. God came to us and became man ("Immanuel"). It is fitting that a number of other miracles cluster around this central event. They underline the importance of the incarnation.

Miraculously, Zechariah becomes unable to speak (Luke 1:22), then his speech is restored (v. 64) and he prophesies concerning his son John and the Messiah (vv. 67–79). In this context, these miracles serve as a special manifestation of the presence of God, causing the people to be in expectation concerning John (vv. 65–66).

The star that appears to the wise men anticipates the rising of the glory of God in the person of Christ (Isa. 60:1).

The miracles associated with Christ's birth are only the beginning. All the miracles recorded in the Gospels highlight the presence of God in various ways.[2]

---

2. Ibid.

The Baptism of Jesus

The baptism of Jesus contains phenomena associated with a theophany:

> And when Jesus was baptized, immediately he went up from the water, and behold, the heavens were opened to him, and he saw the Spirit of God descending like a dove and coming to rest on him; and behold, a voice from heaven said, "This is my beloved Son, with whom I am well pleased." (Matt. 3:16–17)

"The heavens were opened," implying that there was a vision of God's special presence in heaven. The Spirit of God appeared, "descending like a dove." And there came a voice—the divine voice.

Such a theophany is fitting to prepare the way for the beginning of Jesus's public ministry. The Father authenticates the Son in his role as messianic Savior. The Spirit comes to be with him and empower him. The voice, by picking up on themes from Psalm 2:7 and Isaiah 42:1, indicates that Jesus brings the messianic fulfillment of Old Testament prophecies. These events set the stage for understanding that the Father is present in the Son through the Holy Spirit in all of Jesus's ministry.

The Sermon on the Mount

The Sermon on the Mount, taking place on a mountain (Matt. 5:1), takes up themes belonging to the giving of the law on Mount Sinai. So the whole scene has a rich association with the theophany on Mount Sinai. But there are noteworthy differences. The voice comes in the context of Jesus's humanity. It is a voice of blessing and salvation, in contrast to the terrifying experience at Mount Sinai.

Walking on Water

When Jesus walks on water, the experience should remind the disciples of the Old Testament passages that indicate God's control over the sea (Ex. 15:8; Pss. 29:10; 107:23–32). Jesus's appearance is like a theophany of God in which he appears over the sea:

> And the Spirit of God was *hovering over* the face of the *waters*. (Gen. 1:2)

> " . . . who alone stretched out the heavens
>   and *trampled* the *waves* of the sea." (Job 9:8)

You *trampled the sea* with your horses,
    the surging of mighty waters. (Hab. 3:15)

Similar patterns are found elsewhere in the Old Testament (Pss. 77:19; 107:25–30). Against the Old Testament background, the fact that Jesus walks on water underlines Jesus's divine identity and his divine power to subdue all chaos and opposition.

The Transfiguration

An account of the transfiguration occurs in all three Synoptic Gospels: Matthew 17:1–8; Mark 9:2–8; Luke 9:28–36. At the center of the accounts in all three Gospels are two events with theophanic overtones. First, Jesus appears in radiant white:

> And he was transfigured before them, and his face *shone* like the sun, and his clothes became *white as light*. (Matt. 17:2)

This appearance is reminiscent of the glory theophanies in the Old Testament. This bright appearance within the context of the transfiguration indicates the glory that intrinsically belongs to Jesus as the preexistent Son, and which belongs also to his exalted state, after his resurrection. The transfiguration is a kind of preview of his exaltation. But during his earthly life, in the state of humiliation, this kind of revelation of his glory is an exception.

Second, a cloud comes, and a voice comes out of the cloud:

> Behold, a *bright cloud* overshadowed them, and a *voice* from the *cloud* said, "This is my beloved Son, with whom I am well pleased; listen to him." (Matt. 17:5)

This cluster of events obviously alludes to the cloud and the divine voice at Mount Sinai. Or, since Christ is at the center of God's purposes, we can say that Mount Sinai is designed by God to be an anticipation and foreshadowing of the coming of Christ and his transfiguration. Entering the cloud in Luke 9:34 is similar to Moses entering the cloud in Exodus 24:18. But, unlike at Mount Sinai, the heavenly voice at the transfiguration does not continue to speak, and does not deliver an extended message, parallel to the Ten Commandments at Mount Sinai. Instead, the voice directs the disciples' attention to Jesus and his speech: "listen to him!"

The result of this directive is to imply at the very least that Jesus is analogous to Moses. But, since there is no delivery of an extended message, we may go a step further and conclude that Jesus's teaching is the fulfillment of the heavenly voice at Mount Sinai. So the words of Jesus are the voice *of God*, not merely the voice of Moses. His exalted status goes together with his title, "my beloved Son." In the light of the rest of Matthew (Matt. 28:19), this status includes the fact that he is divine. So his appearance in brightness is a more intensive manifestation of what he always is: he is God. His appearance on earth is the final theophany.

The Crucifixion as Theophanic

The crucifixion shows theophanic motifs in two contrasting ways.

First, there is darkness. Matthew records the coming of darkness while Jesus was on the cross: "Now from the sixth hour there was *darkness* over all the land until the ninth hour" (Matt. 27:45; cf. Mark 15:33; Luke 23:44). The darkness is parallel to the darkness at Mount Sinai (Ex. 20:21; Deut. 4:11; 5:22–23). It is suitable for expressing the judgment of God against sin, and therefore also against Jesus as the sin-bearer. Matthew and Mark both link the darkness to Jesus's cry of being forsaken (Matt. 27:46; Mark 15:34). He was forsaken, because God's wrath came on him for the sake of our sin (1 Pet. 2:24). This judgment of God was ultimate in nature. Jesus's sacrifice fully paid for sin, in contrast to the inadequacy of the animal sacrifices of the Old Testament (Heb. 10:1–14).

Second, the Gospel of John takes a complementary approach by putting the emphasis on the revelation of the glory of God in the cross. That is, we see God's glory in the cross, once we understand its theological significance. The glory of the Father and of the Son is revealed, because God shows his wisdom, his justice, his mercy, and the wonder of his salvation through and in the midst of the suffering and shame of the cross. John prepares us for this understanding by indicating that the cross is a revelation of glory:

> "Father, *glorify* your name." Then a voice came from heaven: "I have glorified it, and I will *glorify* it again." . . . "Now is the judgment of this world; now will the ruler of this world be cast out. And I, when I am *lifted up* from the earth, will draw all people to myself." He said this to show by what kind of *death* he was going to die. (John 12:28–33)

The Father is glorified when Christ is "lifted up from the earth." He is "lifted up" *both* in the crucifixion (his *death*; v. 33) and in his ascension (cf. John 14:2–3). The meaning of Christ's victory and his ascension are reflected backwards, illuminating the significance of the crucifixion, so that in the end we see it also is glorious: God works salvation through death itself.

Angels Proclaiming the Resurrection of Jesus

Angels appear at the tomb to announce Christ's resurrection. A spectacular appearance of God through his messengers is fitting, because of the importance of Christ's resurrection.

The account in Matthew 28:1–10 is noteworthy, because there seem to be resonances with the banning of mankind from the garden of Eden in Genesis 3:23–24. In Genesis 3, heavenly beings in the form of cherubim guard the way to the tree of life. Adam and Eve are banished. In Matthew 28:1–10 we have a kind of reversal of the banishing. The angel who appears does not bar the way to the tomb, but on the contrary invites the women, "Come, see the place where he lay" (v. 6). The guard of soldiers had the job of barring the way to the tomb. Now they tremble in fear (v. 4). The tomb has become, not the location of death, but the location testifying to new life: "He is not here, for he has risen, as he said" (v. 6).

Jesus in His Resurrection as Theophany

After the account of the tomb in Matthew, Jesus himself appears (v. 9). He is like the tree of life in Eden, because he is himself resurrection life, and provides that life to those who are his. Unlike the tree of life in Eden, he is accessible: "And they came up and took hold of his feet and worshiped him" (v. 9). Through his death and resurrection he has opened the way to God, the way to the tree of life.

46

God Appearing in Acts

Now let us consider the presence of God in the book of Acts.

The Pattern in Acts

A major thrust in the book of Acts concerns how the gospel spreads through the world of the Roman Empire by the power of the Holy Spirit. The Holy Spirit is continually present in this process, so God is present. He is sometimes present spectacularly, through signs and wonders. These miracles underline the reality of his presence through the Holy Spirit, who indwells the people of God. In addition, God is present in the Christians who bring the word of the gospel. In reading Acts, it is easy to concentrate on the most noteworthy demonstrations of God's presence. But we should not miss the fact that these noteworthy cases serve the larger purpose of God, and that the presence of God is manifested all through the book of Acts in the people of God and in their spread of the gospel.

The pattern for the spread of the gospel is laid out by Jesus in Acts 1: "But you will receive *power* when the Holy Spirit has *come upon* you, and you will be my *witnesses* in Jerusalem and in all Judea and Samaria, and to the end of the earth" (Acts 1:8).

The witness in Jerusalem begins when Peter proclaims the gospel on the day of Pentecost (Acts 2). The gospel comes to Judea and Samaria beginning in Acts 8:

> And there arose on that day a great persecution against the church
> in Jerusalem, and they were all scattered throughout the regions of

Judea and Samaria, except the apostles. . . . Now those who were scattered went about *preaching the word*. (Acts 8:1–4)

Acts 8:5–25 gives special attention to Samaria.

The spread of the gospel to the "end of the earth" includes several phases. First, Jews, "devout men from every nation under heaven," hear the gospel in their own languages on the day of Pentecost (Acts 2:5–6). Second, the Ethiopian eunuch hears the gospel from Philip (Acts 8:26–39). Third, Christ appears to Paul and appoints him to be an apostle to the Gentiles (Acts 9:15; cf. Acts 22:21; 26:17–18).

But the spread of the gospel to the end of the earth takes a more definite step forward with the conversion of Cornelius and his relatives and friends (Acts 10). At first, the converts are mainly God-fearing Gentiles. But raw pagan Gentiles also come (e.g., Acts 16:31–32; 1 Thess. 1:9). The apostle Paul, as the apostle to the Gentiles, is a principal agent in the process. His conversion, recounted in Acts 9, is an important turning point.

We should understand, then, that throughout Acts God shows his presence through the Holy Spirit, through the preaching of the gospel, and through miracles that confirm this preaching. Having understood that, we may still note the most prominent events where God shows his presence, in connection with themes associated with theophany.

The Ascension of Jesus (Acts 1)

God has been present with the disciples because Jesus was present: "He presented himself alive to them after his suffering by many proofs, *appearing* to them during *forty days* and speaking about the kingdom of God" (Acts 1:3). At the end of a period of forty days, Jesus is taken up from them: "And when he had said these things, as they were *looking on*, he was *lifted up*, and a *cloud* took him out of their sight" (v. 9).

The events of the ascension have connections with themes from Old Testament theophanies. The most obvious of these is the *cloud*: "a *cloud* took him out of their sight." The cloud in Acts 1:9 reminds us of the cloud theophanies in the Old Testament.

But in this case in Acts, there are some reversals. In the Old Testament, we find instances where God comes by descending in a cloud. Here, God, in the person of Jesus, *ascends*. In Old Testament theophanies, God appears in a cloud. Here, he *disappears* in a cloud. In Ezekiel 1, the theophany progressively reveals to Ezekiel a cloud, living creatures, and then a human figure in the center. Here, Jesus is the human figure in the center, but the movement of events and of textual focus goes from Jesus to the cloud, and finally to angelic figures: "And while they were gazing into heaven as he went, behold, *two men* stood by them in white robes" (Acts 1:10). These similarities and differences make sense, given the special nature of Jesus's ascension. He is going away, rather than coming, and his going is a kind of mirror image of his future coming: "Men of Galilee, why do you stand looking into heaven? This Jesus, who was taken up from you into heaven, will *come* in the *same way* as you saw him *go* into heaven" (Acts 1:11). The second coming of Jesus is the beginning of the final theophany in history. So his ascension is a mirror image of theophany. It still *is* a theophany, but with some reversals of normal sequences.

The Descent of the Spirit on Pentecost (Acts 2)

We also find a theophany taking place on the day of Pentecost, when the Holy Spirit descends:

> When the day of Pentecost arrived, they were all together in one place. And suddenly there came from *heaven* a *sound* like a mighty rushing *wind*, and it filled the entire house where they were sitting. And divided tongues as of *fire* appeared to them and rested on each one of them. (Acts 2:1–3)

The fire symbolizes and manifests the presence of the Holy Spirit. This phenomenon can be classified as a fire theophany.

As is usual with Old Testament theophanies, the extraordinary visual phenomena come only for a short time. But they indicate the inauguration of a permanent relationship. The Mosaic covenant was inaugurated with the theophany at Mount Sinai. It continued as a deposit in the form of the two tablets of stone. Here the Holy Spirit is the blessing of God's presence in the new covenant. The inauguration through extraordinary visible appearances signifies that the Holy Spirit has come. But it also implies that he remains: "And they were all *filled with* the Holy Spirit and began to speak in other tongues as the Spirit gave them utterance" (Acts 2:4).

The corporate body of the people of God has become the new temple. They are filled with the Holy Spirit in a manner that fulfills the earlier cases where the cloud of glory filled the tabernacle or temple (1 Kings 8:10–11). This reality extends throughout the book of Acts.

We also see special instances of filling with the Holy Spirit: "Then Peter, *filled* with the Holy Spirit, said to them, 'Rulers of the people and elders, . . . '" (Acts 4:8). Paul is filled with the Spirit when he is initially commissioned: "Brother Saul, the Lord Jesus who appeared to you on the road by which you came has sent me so that you may regain your sight and be *filled* with the Holy Spirit" (Acts 9:17).

Jesus's Appearance to Paul

It is interesting that the giving of the Spirit to Paul follows a theophany, where Jesus appears to Paul: "Brother Saul, the Lord Jesus who *appeared to you* on the road by which you came has sent me . . . " (Acts 9:17). Earlier, we have an account of this appearance:

> Now as he [Saul] went on his way, he approached Damascus, and suddenly a *light* from *heaven* shone around him. And falling to the ground, he heard a voice saying to him, "Saul, Saul, why are you persecuting me?" And he said, "Who are you, Lord?" And he said, "I am Jesus, whom you are persecuting." (Acts 9:3–5)

The language about a light from heaven shows that we have an instance of theophany—in fact, Christophany. Saul as a rabbi knows from the Old Testament what a theophany is. He knows that he is experiencing one. What he does not know is the personal identity of the human figure: "I am Jesus." This appearance revolutionizes Paul, because it brings together two sides that he thought were utterly at odds: the God of Israel (who can appear in theophany) and Jesus of Nazareth.

As in other cases, the theophany is momentary, but the effects are permanent. This moment is the starting point for Paul being an apostle to the Gentiles:

> But when he who had set me apart before I was born, and who called me by his grace, was pleased to *reveal his Son* to me, in order that I might *preach* him among the Gentiles, I did not immediately consult with anyone; . . . (Gal. 1:15–16)

The Vision to Peter (Acts 10)

In Acts 10 Peter sees a vision and hears a voice. The voice is the voice of God. But is the vision a theophany? Not in the narrowest sense. Peter does not see a direct visible manifestation of God himself. But he does *meet* God in a broader sense. The vision is a significant turning point in Acts, because it opens the door for Peter to overcome his prejudices and proclaim the gospel to the Gentiles in Cornelius's house. This episode clearly has an important place in the entire plan of the spread of the gospel in the book of Acts.

Light to the Gentiles (Acts 13:47)

A small connection with theophany can be found in Acts 13:47. Paul and Barnabas say,

> For so the Lord has commanded us, saying,
>
> > "I have made you a *light* for the Gentiles,
> > that you may bring salvation to the ends of the earth."

The quote is from Isaiah 49:6. The word *light* recalls the glory theophanies of the Old Testament. According to the prophecy in Isaiah 49:6, the light of God in these theophanies will come to be manifested and seen and received by "the Gentiles." It will lead to "salvation to the ends of the earth."

The light in Isaiah 49:6 is ascribed to the messianic servant of Isaiah 42:1 and 49:5. He is the servant who brings back Jacob and gathers Israel, which means that he is not simply identical with historical Israel. On the contrary, he is *ideal* Israel, the messianic representative who does the will of God in contrast to the failure of historical Israel.

Now in Acts 13:47, the key verse, Paul and Barnabas declare that, in preaching the gospel to the Gentiles, they are instruments in fulfilling the prophecy in Isaiah. Interestingly, the two occurrences of "you" in Acts 13:47 are singular (Greek *se*), not plural. The singular corresponds to the singular in Isaiah 49:6, which refers to the messianic servant. Paul and Barnabas are representatives acting in the name of the Messiah, and with the power of the Holy Spirit sent from the Messiah, and with the indwelling of the Spirit who is the Spirit of the Messiah. So their work is one aspect of fulfilling the prophecy.

The apostles bring "light." The light of the truth of the gospel is an expression of the truth of God, who communicates himself and his plan for salvation in the light of the gospel. The coming of this light can be compared to a theophanic communication of theophanic light.

Light from Christ in Acts 26

We find another mention of this theme of light in Acts 26. Acts 26:2–23 provides a long speech by Paul. It contains three direct references to light:

(1) The light of Christ appearing to Paul:

"At midday, O king, I saw on the way a *light* from heaven, *brighter* than the *sun*, that *shone* around me and those who journeyed with me." (Acts 26:13)

(2) The commission to Paul to turn Gentiles to the light:

" . . . to open their eyes, so that they may turn from darkness to *light* and from the power of Satan to God, that they may receive forgiveness of sins and a place among those who are sanctified by faith in me." (v. 18)

(3) Paul's description of the work of Christ:

" . . . that the Christ must suffer and that, by being the first to rise from the dead, he would proclaim *light* both to our people and to the Gentiles." (v. 23)

The passage also contains mention of *other* appearances of Christ, beyond the initial appearance at Paul's conversion: "But rise and stand upon your feet, for I have *appeared* to you for this purpose, to appoint you as a servant and witness to the things in which you have seen me and to those in which I *will appear* to you . . . " (v. 16). The mention of other appearances naturally leads us toward the next chapter in our discussion, where we consider the New Testament letters.

The Gospel at Rome

But first, let us consider one final passage in Acts, namely Acts 28:30–31:

He [Paul] lived there [in a house in Rome] two whole years at his own expense, and welcomed all who came to him, *proclaiming* the kingdom of God and *teaching* about the Lord Jesus Christ with all boldness and without hindrance.

This passage shows that the light of the gospel has come to Rome, the heart of the empire and the representative, ruling city of the empire. It has come in the form of the proclamation and teaching of the apostle Paul.

The preceding passage draws an explicit connection with light by talking about resistance to *seeing*:

> . . . "'Go to this people, and say,
> "You will indeed hear but never understand,
>   and you will indeed *see* but never *perceive*."
> For this people's heart has grown dull,
>   and with their ears they can barely hear,
>   and their *eyes* they have closed;
> lest they should *see* with their eyes
>   and hear with their ears
> and understand with their heart
> and turn, and I would heal them.'

> Therefore let it be known to you that this salvation of God has been sent to the Gentiles; they will *listen*." (Acts 28:26–28)

When the Gentiles "listen," as Paul says, they also "see" in the spiritual sense.

In sum, in Acts 28:30–31 Paul bears the light of Christ, who is the image of God:

> In their case the god of this world has blinded the minds of the unbelievers, to keep them from seeing the *light* of the gospel of the *glory* of Christ, who is the *image* of God. For what we proclaim is not ourselves, but Jesus Christ as Lord, with ourselves as your servants for Jesus' sake. For God, who said, "Let *light shine* out of darkness," has *shone* in our hearts to give the *light* of the knowledge of the *glory* of God in the *face* of Jesus Christ. (2 Cor. 4:4–6)

Through the presence of Paul and his preaching, light has come to reside in Rome. This metaphorical light of the gospel can be compared to the light of Old Testament theophanies. The city and the empire can never be the same again!

47

God Appearing in the Letters
of the New Testament

Now let us consider the New Testament letters (Romans–Jude).

The Broad Scope of God's Presence in the Letters

God is present at every point in the New Testament letters. As we indicated in discussing Acts, the Holy Spirit dwells in Christian believers. This indwelling includes the authors of the New Testament letters. Moreover, the authors write under the inspiration of the Holy Spirit, which is distinct from the indwelling of the Holy Spirit in all believers (2 Pet. 1:21). For example, Paul introduces himself as "a servant of Christ Jesus, called to be an *apostle*, set apart for the gospel of God" (Rom. 1:1). The label *apostle* indicates that he is sent by Christ. He is a certified messenger of Christ. And in this respect he is analogous to an angelic messenger. The Old Testament angelic messengers in turn reflect the *great* and unique messenger, the divine messenger who is the Lord himself. We are thinking of the "angel of the Lord" in those passages that indicate that the figure in question is divine. If we allow a broad form of relationship to theophany, Paul's function as divine messenger has theophanic resonances.

In addition, the Holy Spirit is present in his work of inspiration to guide the writing of the letters, and in his work of illumination to guide those who read.

In addition to this general principle, we may note places in the letters that specifically discuss theophanies or that use language with theophanic resonances. That is what we will do. Since the *degree* and *intensity* of such resonances varies over a spectrum, we must confine ourselves to some of the main cases.

The Summary of the Gospel as Revelation of Christ (Romans 1:4)

In Romans 1:4, Christ's resurrection displays who he is. By displaying who he is, his resurrection functions like a theophany: "[he] was *declared* to be the Son of God in power according to the Spirit of holiness *by his resurrection* from the dead, Jesus Christ our Lord."

The Appearing of God in the Gospel (Romans 1:17)

Subordinate to the manifestation of Christ in his resurrection, the gospel proclamation of his resurrection displays who he is. It is a *revelation*: "For in it [the gospel] the righteousness of God is *revealed* from faith for faith, as it is written, 'The righteous shall live by faith'" (Rom. 1:17). In contrast to this display of salvation comes a display of wrath: "For the wrath of God is *revealed* from heaven against all ungodliness and unrighteousness of men, who by their unrighteousness suppress the truth" (v. 18). This revelation of wrath is reminiscent of the revelation of wrath in some of the theophanies of judgment in the Old Testament.

The Appearing of God in Creation (Romans 1:19–20)

In harmony with what we have said earlier about the creation as a manifestation in which God displays his character, Romans 1:19–20 expounds how God is seen through creation:

> For what can be known about God is *plain* to them, because God has *shown* it to them. For his invisible *attributes*, namely, his eternal power and divine nature, have been clearly *perceived*, ever since the creation of the world, in the things that have been made. So they are without excuse.

Manifestation of the Judgment of God and the Gospel of God (Romans 2–3)

Romans 2–3 continues to develop the theme of revelation introduced in Romans 1. The passage shows a strong interest in the theme of revelation and the contrast between what is open and what is secret. In Romans 2:5, judgment will be revealed. The *secrets* of human hearts will be revealed (Rom. 2:16). Romans 2:28–29 discusses the distinction between what is true inwardly (in part, secretly) and what is true outwardly. Romans 3:6 mentions the future, open judgment of the world. According to Romans 3:21, "the righteousness of God has been *manifested*"—openly disclosed or revealed. What is revealed in Christ *shows* "his righteousness at the present time" (Rom. 3:25–26).[1] All of this language shows analogies with the intense forms of theophany that we have met in the Old Testament.

Manifestation in Paul's Ministry (Romans 15)

Later in Romans, Paul picks up the language of *seeing* in describing the effects of his own ministry of the gospel: "Those who have never been told of him will *see*" (Rom. 15:21). The power of the gospel that Paul brings is demonstrated also "by the power of signs and wonders, by the power of the Spirit of God" (15:19). As we have seen from Acts, the apostle Paul is bringing light to the Gentiles. This light functions to reveal God, and so is analogous to theophanic light.

Revelation of Mystery (Romans 16:25–27)

The book of Romans closes with a return to the theme of revelation, revelation of mystery formerly hidden:

> Now to him who is able to strengthen you according to my gospel and the preaching of Jesus Christ, according to the *revelation* of the *mystery* that was kept *secret* for long ages but has now been *disclosed* and through the prophetic writings has been made known to all nations, according to the command of the eternal God, to bring about the obedience of faith—to the only wise God be glory forevermore through Jesus Christ! Amen. (Rom. 16:25–27)

Revelation and mystery recall to mind the nature of Old Testament theophanies. Theophanies reveal what was formerly hidden about God. Of course, every Old Testament theophany belongs to the larger history

---

1. Marcus Mininger has written a dissertation on revelation in Romans 1–3, and I am grateful to him for alerting me to the prominence of this theme (Mininger, "What Is Revealed, Where, and How: Uncovering the Theme of Revelation and Discovering a New Approach to Reading Romans 1:16–3:26" [PhD diss., Westminster Theological Seminary, 2016]).

of *progressive revelation*. Not all is revealed at an early point. What is revealed is a foretaste of the climactic revelation in Christ.

The Glory of God's Presence in the Church (1 Corinthians 3:10–17)

First Corinthians 3:10–17 describes the church as the dwelling place of God in the Spirit: "Do you not know that you are God's *temple* and that God's Spirit *dwells in* you?" (v. 16). The church is described here as the fulfillment of Old Testament glory theophanies when God came to dwell in the tabernacle and in Solomon's temple, to be present among his people.

The Glory Revealed in the Resurrection of the Body (1 Corinthians 15)

In 1 Corinthians 15 Paul discusses at more than one point the glory associated with the resurrection body. This glory reflects the glory of God in theophany. More specifically, our resurrection bodies follow the pattern of Christ's resurrection, and so they reflect the theophany-like manifestation that takes place in Christ's exaltation:

> It is sown in dishonor; it is raised in *glory*. It is sown in weakness; it is raised in power. (1 Cor. 15:43)

> Just as we have borne the image of the man of dust, we shall also bear the *image* of the man of *heaven*. (v. 49)

The Glory in Moses and in the New Covenant (2 Corinthians 3)

Second Corinthians 3 compares and contrasts the old covenant and the new:

> Now if the ministry of death, carved in letters on stone, came with such *glory* that the Israelites could not gaze at Moses' face because of its *glory*, which was being brought to an end, will not the ministry of the Spirit have even more *glory*? (2 Cor. 3:7–8)

Moses's face shone in response to theophany. The glory belonging to the new covenant surpasses this glory. We shine as we more and more reflect the glory of Christ:

And we all, with unveiled face, *beholding* the *glory* of the Lord, are being transformed into the same *image* from one degree of *glory* to another. For this comes from the Lord who is the Spirit. (2 Cor. 3:18)

Such description of the reception of the gospel presupposes that Christ's presence is like a glory theophany. And as we behold Christ in the gospel, we reflect that same glory in becoming Christlike, "transformed into the same *image*."

The Revelation of the Glory of Christ in the Gospel (2 Corinthians 4:4–6)

In discussing 2 Corinthians 4:4–6 earlier, we already indicated that it presents language akin to a glory theophany:

In their case the god of this world has blinded the minds of the unbelievers, to keep them from seeing the *light* of the gospel of the *glory* of Christ, who is the *image* of God. For what we proclaim is not ourselves, but Jesus Christ as Lord, with ourselves as your servants for Jesus' sake. For God, who said, "Let *light shine* out of darkness," has *shone* in our hearts to give the *light* of the knowledge of the *glory* of God in the *face* of Jesus Christ.

This light and glory from God is then *manifested* in "jars of clay" (2 Cor. 4:7), "so that the life of Jesus may also be *manifested* in our mortal flesh" (v. 11).

Special Revelations to Paul (2 Corinthians 12:1–4)

In 2 Corinthians Paul mentions, in passing, further revelations that he has received:

I must go on boasting. Though there is nothing to be gained by it, I will go on to *visions and revelations* of the Lord. I know a man in Christ who fourteen years ago was caught up to the third *heaven*—whether in the body or out of the body I do not know, God knows. And I know that this man was caught up into *paradise*—whether in the body or out of the body I do not know, God knows—and he heard things that cannot be told, which man may not utter. (2 Cor. 12:1–4)

These further visions are distinct from the vision of Christ at Paul's conversion. Did he see Christ in them? Acts 26:16 indicates that Paul would be given further visions of Christ: "those in which I *will* appear to you." But in 2 Corinthians 12 Paul—in accord with his intention to shame the Corinthians—refuses to give details. They do not need to know. Indeed, to a large extent they cannot know: "things that cannot be told, which man may not utter" (v. 4). This mystery underlines a principle that we have seen repeatedly: Theophany involves mystery. God reveals himself, but not fully. And he conceals many things until the consummation.

Paul's Conversion

In Galatians Paul talks about Christ appearing at the time of his conversion:

> But when he who had set me apart before I was born, and who called me by his grace, was pleased to *reveal* his Son to me, in order that I might preach him among the Gentiles, I did not immediately consult with anyone . . . (Gal. 1:15–16; cf. 1:12)

This appearance is a glory theophany and a man theophany, as we already observed in talking about the accounts in Acts (chapter 46). It confirms the authenticity of Paul's message, including his unique role as an apostle to the Gentiles. His authority is not merely derivative from the other apostles, but comes from Christ himself.

The Deity of Christ in Colossians

Colossians emphasizes the full deity of Christ, and uses this emphasis to refute the false teachers, who allege that they have secret knowledge. God is fully revealed in Christ:

> For in him the whole fullness of deity *dwells bodily*, and you have been filled in him, who is the head of all rule and authority. (Col. 2:9–10)

The language of filling and dwelling picks up on themes from temple theophanies in the Old Testament. Since the "fullness of deity dwells" in Christ bodily, he is himself the final, permanent theophany.

Seeing Christ in Heaven (Colossians 3:1–4)

Spiritually speaking, we are to look on the reality of Christ's rule in heaven:

> If then you have been raised with Christ, seek the things that are above, where Christ is, *seated at the right hand* of God. *Set* your minds on things that are above, not on things that are on earth. (Col. 3:1–2)

By the Spirit we see heavenly realities. The eyes of our heart are opened to know Christ (Eph. 1:18). In a broad sense, this kind of experience of sight is like the human experience of a theophany, but it takes place spiritually rather than by physical sight.

The mind that spiritually understands heavenly reality receives its consummate form of understanding when Christ appears openly:

> When Christ who is your life *appears*, then you also will *appear* with him in *glory*. (Col. 3:4)

In the consummation, we ourselves will reflect the glory associated with glory theophanies, such as the appearance of glory on the Mount of Transfiguration.

Christ's Coming (1 Thessalonians 4–5)

First Thessalonians describes the second coming of Christ, and this coming is a climactic theophany:

> For the Lord himself will *descend from heaven* with a cry of command, with the voice of an *archangel*, and with the sound of the trumpet of God. And the dead in Christ will rise first. Then we who are alive, who are left, will be caught up together with them in the *clouds* to *meet* the Lord in the air, and so we will always *be with* the Lord. (1 Thess. 4:16–17)

Though the description is spectacular, the purpose is practical—to comfort and encourage believers: "Therefore encourage one another with these words" (1 Thess. 4:18).

The Appearing of Christ in 2 Thessalonians

Second Thessalonians also has a description of Christ's coming, with associated glory:

> . . . when the Lord Jesus is *revealed from heaven* with his mighty *angels* in *flaming fire*, inflicting vengeance on those who do not know

God and on those who do not obey the gospel of our Lord Jesus. They will suffer the punishment of eternal destruction, *away from the presence* of the Lord and from the *glory* of his might, when he *comes* on that day to be *glorified* in his saints, and to be marveled at among all who have believed, because our testimony to you was believed. (2 Thess. 1:7–10)

Angels, fire, glory, and coming from heaven all belong in the context of the coming of God to earth, which here takes place in the coming of Christ. It is the fulfillment of earlier Old Testament comings in theophany.

Once again, the purpose of giving this picture of the second coming is practical:

To this *end* we always pray for you, that our God may make you worthy of his calling and may fulfill every resolve for good and every work of faith by his power, so that the name of our Lord Jesus may be *glorified* in you, and you in him, according to the grace of our God and the Lord Jesus Christ. (vv. 11–12)

The Destruction of the Man of Lawlessness (2 Thessalonians 2)

We also find theophanic elements in connection with the judgment of the man of lawlessness in 2 Thessalonians 2: "And then the lawless one will be *revealed*, whom the Lord Jesus will kill with the breath of his mouth and bring to nothing by the *appearance* of his *coming*" (2 Thess. 2:8).

The passage also speaks about the "coming" of the lawless one, a coming that is a kind of counterfeit opposite to the coming of Christ:

The *coming* of the lawless one is by the activity of Satan with all *power* and false *signs and wonders*, and with all wicked *deception* for those who are perishing, because they refused to love the truth and so be saved. (2 Thess. 2:9–10)

The coming of the lawless one is opposite to the coming of Christ. The power and signs and wonders in this lawless coming are opposite to the miracles that sometimes accompany theophany—think, for example, of the exodus from Egypt. Satan counterfeits the power of God when he sends the lawless one. The result of theophany is a revelation of the truth of God. The result of this Satanic counterfeit is a revelation of deception.

Christ Manifested in the Flesh (1 Timothy 3:16)

First Timothy 3:16 contains an instance of language concerning God's presence that is similar to descriptions of theophany: "Great indeed, we confess, is the *mystery* of godliness: He was *manifested* in the flesh, vindicated by the Spirit, *seen* by angels, proclaimed among the nations, believed on in the world, taken up in *glory*." Christ's "manifestation" in the flesh is a theophany, as we have observed.

Appearing of Grace (Titus 2:11)

In Titus 2:11 the grace of God appears, in a way reminiscent of theophany: "For the grace of God has *appeared*, bringing salvation for all people." The mention of *grace* has ties with the emphasis on God's mercy and grace in the theophany to Moses in Exodus 34:6–7. Grace and truth have appeared climactically in Christ, who enables us not only to know about the grace and truth of God but also to receive God's goodness (John 1:17).

Similar language comes up again in Titus 3:

> But when the goodness and loving kindness of God our Savior *appeared*, he saved us, not because of works done by us in righteousness, but according to his own mercy, by the washing of regeneration and renewal of the Holy Spirit. (Titus 3:4–5)

"The goodness and loving kindness of God" are seen in Christ.

The Second Coming as Christian Hope (Titus 2:13)

Christians hope for the theophany in the second coming of Christ: " . . . waiting for our blessed hope, the *appearing* of the *glory* of our great *God* and Savior Jesus Christ."

Throne Theophany (Hebrews 1:13)

Hebrews 1:13, quoting from Psalm 110:1, contains another picture related to theophany:

> And to which of the angels has he ever said,
>
>> "Sit at *my right hand*
>> until I make your enemies a footstool for your feet"?

The expression "sit at my right hand" evokes the larger picture of God on his throne (see the discussion in chapter 42).

Jesus Has Opened the Way to Heaven (Hebrews 10:19-20)

Jesus has opened the way into the presence of God in heaven:

> Therefore, brothers, since we have confidence to *enter* the holy places by the blood of Jesus, by the new and living way that he *opened* for us through the curtain, that is, through his flesh, . . . (Heb. 10:19–20)

Recalling Mount Sinai and Now Mount Zion (Hebrews 12:18-24)

Hebrews 12:18–21 recalls the theophany at Mount Sinai with all its terror:

> For you have not come to what may be touched, a *blazing fire* and *darkness* and *gloom* and a *tempest* and the sound of a trumpet and a voice whose words made the hearers beg that no further messages be spoken to them. For they could not endure the order that was given, "If even a beast touches the mountain, it shall be stoned." Indeed, so terrifying was the *sight* that Moses said, "I tremble with fear."

Hebrews 12 then contrasts this older theophany with the new experience of the greater presence of God in the heavenly Zion:

> But you have come to *Mount Zion* and to the city of the living *God*, the *heavenly* Jerusalem, and to innumerable *angels* in festal gathering, and to the assembly of the firstborn who are enrolled in heaven, and to *God*, the *judge* of all, and to the spirits of the righteous made perfect, and to *Jesus*, the mediator of a new covenant, and to the sprinkled blood that speaks a better word than the blood of Abel. (Heb. 12:22–24)

A final warning in this passage takes up the language of fire theophany: "For our God is a consuming *fire*" (Heb. 12:29). The character of God as "consuming fire" is the source explaining the meaning of fire theophanies.

The Second Coming as Glorious (1 Peter 1:7)

First Peter speaks of the *revelation* of Christ at his second coming: ". . . so that the tested genuineness of your faith—more precious than gold that perishes though it is tested by fire—may be found to result in *praise* and *glory* and honor at the *revelation* of Jesus Christ" (1 Pet. 1:7). The revelation of Jesus Christ is the revelation of his glory. But glory comes to him partly because the tested faith of the saints is seen to honor him.

The Transfiguration Described by Peter (2 Peter 1:16–18)

Second Peter 1:16–18 contains Peter's reflection on the transfiguration:

> For we did not follow cleverly devised myths when we made known to you the *power* and *coming* of our Lord Jesus Christ, but we were eyewitnesses of his majesty. For when he received honor and *glory* from God the Father, and the voice was borne to him by the Majestic *Glory*, "This is my beloved Son, with whom I am well pleased," we ourselves heard this very voice borne from *heaven*, for we were with him on the *holy mountain*.

As we observed in discussing the Gospels, the transfiguration is a form of theophany, reminiscent of Mount Sinai (chapter 45). At the same time, it is superior to Mount Sinai—it is the fulfillment, while the theophany at Mount Sinai is only the anticipation.

Eyewitness Experience (1 John 1:1–3)

First John reflects on the manifestation of God in the earthly life of Christ:

> That which was from the beginning, which we have heard, which we have *seen* with our *eyes*, which we *looked upon* and have touched with our hands, concerning the word of life—the life was made *manifest*, and we have *seen* it, and testify to it and proclaim to you the eternal life, which was *with the Father* and was made *manifest* to us—that which we have *seen* and heard we proclaim also to you, so that you too may have fellowship with us; and indeed our fellowship is with the Father and with his Son Jesus Christ. (1 John 1:1–3)

This passage picks up on themes from theophany, by speaking of seeing the manifestation of God. Here too, Christ is the climax, greater than the Old Testament theophanies.

The Coming of the Lord (Jude 14–15)

Jude describes the coming of the Lord with angels:

Behold, the Lord *comes* with ten thousands of his *holy ones*, to execute *judgment* on all and to *convict* all the ungodly of all their deeds of ungodliness that they have committed in such an ungodly way, and of all the harsh things that ungodly sinners have spoken against him.

The description has similarities to Old Testament instances of court theophanies for judgment. But this instance of final judgment takes place through the very activity of the Lord coming. The final judgment is similar in character to the judgment of the lawless one in 2 Thessalonians 2:8, a man whom the Lord will "bring to nothing by the appearance of his coming." The very appearing of the Lord destroys all resistance.

48

God Appearing in Revelation

Finally, we come to the book of Revelation. How does God appear in Revelation?

We have already discussed the book of Revelation, in chapters 18 and 19. I would refer readers back to those chapters for extensive discussion. But in drawing our study to a conclusion, we can review some of the principal points about the theme of God's presence and appearing in Revelation.

The High Points in Revelation

The high points in God's appearing in Revelation occur in four places: (1) the appearing of Christ in Revelation 1:12–16; (2) the appearance of God on his throne in Revelation 4, and the Lamb in Revelation 5; (3) the appearance of Christ on a white horse in Revelation 19:11–21; and (4) the appearance of God and the Lamb in the new heaven and new earth (Rev. 21:1–22:5).

We could add a fifth and a sixth place if we want, or more than that. In chapters 18 and 19 we indicated that, in an expansive sense, the whole central visionary section of Revelation, from 1:12 to 22:5, is a gigantic theophany. The whole of it is one long exposition of the presence of God in his appearing.

But it is also true that there are high points. It is important to appreciate their key roles. The intensive appearances in Revelation 1:12–16, 4:1–5:14, 19:11–21, and 21:1–22:5 each make an important contribution. They come at appropriate points in the unfolding of the revelation from God.

Christ Appearing among the Churches (Revelation 1:12–16)

Revelation 1:12–16 comes at the beginning of the visionary section. Christ is the mediator for the entire book, as Revelation 1:1 indicates: "The *revelation* of Jesus Christ, which God *gave him* to *show* to his servants the things that must soon take place. He made it known by sending his angel to his servant John." Revelation 1:12–16 also introduces Revelation 2–3, where Christ—the same Christ described in 1:12–16—gives the messages to each of the seven churches. It is suitable, then, that we have in Revelation 1:12–16 a vision proclaiming in vivid terms the glory of Christ.

The Rule of God in History (Revelation 4–5)

Revelation 4–5 has a central role because it depicts the universal rule of God in his majesty, power, and worthiness. It also depicts the Lamb as the one who is "worthy" (5:9). He is worthy to open the scroll, signifying that he has the unique mediatorial role in the working out of God's plan for history, a plan unfolded in more detail in the rest of the cycle of seven seals (6:1–8:1) and in the other cycles of judgment (8:2–22:5).

Christ's Triumph (Revelation 19:11–21)

Next we come to Revelation 19:11–21. At the second coming, Christ appears. The second coming is the central Christian hope in Revelation. So the actual appearance of Christ in Revelation 19:11 provides a climax. His appearance is also the occasion for his destruction of all opposition (vv. 20–21). His triumph is complete. Praise the Lord!

The Consummate Appearance of God (Revelation 21:1–22:5)

Revelation 21:1–22:5 has the key role of serving as the final resolution of the struggles of history. "Behold, the *dwelling* place of God is *with* man" (21:3). The announcement constitutes the consummate fulfillment of the Immanuel principle, "God with us" (Matt. 1:23). God is present in a consummate way. This presence includes a vision of God:

> No longer will there be anything accursed, but the throne of God and of the Lamb will be *in it*, and his servants will worship him. They will *see his face*, and his name will be on their foreheads. (Rev. 22:3–4)

The presence of God is also described in the language of glory theophany:

> And I saw no temple in the city, for its temple is the Lord God the Almighty and the Lamb. And the city has no need of sun or moon to shine on it, for the *glory* of God gives it *light*, and its *lamp* is the Lamb. (Rev. 21:22–23)

It is fitting that the consummate manifestation of the presence of God should include a consummating theophanic description. Not only do his servants "see his face" (22:4), but the entirety of the New Jerusalem is filled with the glory of God (21:22–23). The New Jerusalem has a cubical shape (21:16), like the shape of the Most Holy Place in the Old Testament. The Most Holy Place symbolized beforehand the holiness of God's presence, which now resides in the people of God with consummate intensity.

Unity of Revelation

These passages that provide high points fit harmoniously and wonderfully into the picture of the entire book of Revelation. God the king comes, for judgment and salvation. He comes to consummate the achievement already accomplished in the first coming of Christ, which was the inauguration of the time of the end and the fulfillment of Old Testament prophecies of the last days. "He who testifies to these things says, 'Surely I am coming soon.' Amen. Come, Lord Jesus!" (Rev. 22:20).

The Relation of Theophany to Other Themes

In all these passages in Revelation we have an interlocking of multiple themes—the themes of covenant and of kingdom as well as the theme of presence. The manifestations of God in Revelation confirm his faithfulness to his covenant promises and underline the power and scope of his kingship. The final vision of God in Revelation 21:1–22:5 includes all these elements. The final dwelling of God with man is the final expression of his *presence*. It is also the realization of the commitments made in his *covenant*. And it is the supreme manifestation of his *kingship*: "the throne of God and of the Lamb will be in it" (Rev. 22:3). Amen.

Conclusion

The theme of God's presence travels all the way through the Bible. It goes from the beginning of history to the end, from the creation of the world to the consummation of all things. This theme takes particularly emphatic form with passages that speak of God appearing.

As we have seen, some of these passages are metaphorical. In some passages, there may be no literal visual phenomena of a spectacular kind. But the passages invite us to see and understand the work of God, whether it be in miracles, in ordinary providence, or in the mysteries of his work of salvation and its application to us. Other passages describe visible phenomena in which God made visual contact with his people. Other passages reflect on appearances of God in past history.

The theme of God's presence is a rich one. Other books delve into other aspects and implications.[1]

Functions of Theophanic Imagery

All of these passages function simultaneously in three ways. First, they reveal who God is. They manifest his character and his glory. Second, they reinforce the biblical teaching that God in his kindness and grace draws near to his people—he is "God with us" (Matt. 1:23). Third, they stir up the expectation for that final coming and appearance of God, which will take place in the second coming of Christ and the consummate victory that his coming will bring.

---

1. Ryan J. Lister, *The Presence of God: Its Place in the Storyline of Scripture and the Story of Our Lives* (Wheaton, IL: Crossway, 2014); John M. Frame, *The Doctrine of God* (Phillipsburg, NJ: P&R, 2002); G. K. Beale, *The Temple and the Church's Mission: A Biblical Theology of the Dwelling Place of God* (Leicester, UK: Apollos; Downers Grove, IL: InterVarsity, 2004).

Roots in God

In Christ, God comes to be "with us." Matthew 1:23 makes it clear that Christ has as one of his names "Immanuel (which means, God with us)." Our fellowship with God has a creational basis in the fact that we as human beings were made in the image of God (Gen. 1:26–27). But the communion of God with man, the presence of God in blessing, was broken by Adam in the fall into sin. Only in Christ is there a way back: "Jesus said to him, 'I am the way, and the truth, and the life. No one comes to the Father except through me'" (John 14:6). Communion is the gift of God, because we are redeemed by the blood of the Lamb (Rev. 1:5–6).

But this human communion with God has an even deeper analogue in the communion that God has with himself. Before there ever was a world, God *is*. And this God has communion in the three persons of the Trinity:

> In the *beginning* was the Word, and the Word was *with* God, and the Word was God. He was in the beginning *with* God. (John 1:1–2)

God is present first of all and eternally to himself. The Father is present with the Son, the Word, and the Word with the Father, and the Father and the Son with the Holy Spirit. This communion is intimate. Mysteriously, it is an eternal indwelling among the persons, the Father in the Son and the Son in the Father, and the Holy Spirit in both. This primary indwelling is the ultimate and only foundation for God's communion with human beings:

> " . . . that they may all be one, just as you, Father, *are in* me, and I *in* you, that they also may *be in* us, so that the world may believe that you have sent me. The *glory* that you have given me I have given to them, that they may be one even as we are one." (John 17:21–22)

Because God is God, in the communion and indwelling of the persons of the Trinity, he is pleased to present himself to us in his manifestation and his appearing. Glory be to the Father, and to the Son, and to the Holy Spirit, world without end!

May the reality of our communion with God stimulate us to serve God in the hope of the fuller communion to come:

> He who testifies to these things says, "Surely I am coming soon." Amen. Come, Lord Jesus! (Rev. 22:20)

APPENDICES

Appendix A

"The Angel of the Lord"

What is the meaning of the expression "the angel of the Lord"? The expression "the angel of the Lord" and analogous expressions occur in various contexts in both the Old and New Testament. As indicated in chapter 7, the Hebrew Old Testament uses the key word *mal'ak* (מַלְאָךְ), which is sometimes translated "angel." It is also sometimes translated "messenger," and that is what the word consistently means. The personage so designated functions to bring a message from someone. Thus, "the angel of the Lord" brings a message from the Lord. In itself, the Hebrew word for "messenger" does not give information about what *kind* of personage is being designated. It could be a created angel; it could be God himself; or it could be a prophet (Hag. 1:13) or a priest (Mal. 2:7). In the case of a messenger of the Lord, the focus is on the fact that the Lord has commissioned the being in question, so that he brings a message with the Lord's authority. Sometimes the context allows us to see that the being is himself divine. But in other cases he is human or angelic. Or we may not be sure, because in some cases there is not enough information.

When the messenger is divine, he is God. At the same time, he is *sent* by God. The idea of sending indicates that there is a differentiation between the sender and the sent one. This differentiation foreshadows the fuller revelation in the New Testament, where we see that Christ is sent by the Father in the power of the Holy Spirit. When Christ comes, he shows us the Father and the Spirit who dwell in him. In the Old Testament, the appearances of God in human form foreshadow the incarnation of Christ. This much may suffice to summarize key points from the fuller discussion given in the body of this book.

Discussions by Others

In discussing divine appearances, we have chosen in this book to pay attention primarily to the Bible itself. But there is considerable scholarly discussion of the meaning of the angel of the Lord and other Old Testament appearances. For the sake of brevity, we will focus on a recent contribution by Andrew Malone, *Knowing Jesus in the Old Testament?*,[1] which in turn interacts with many preceding works. Early in his book, Malone distinguishes three possible approaches to the idea of Christ's presence in divine appearances: appearances of God in Jesus (such as John 14:9), appearances involving all three persons of the Trinity, and appearances "of the Son alone" (p. 18). Malone argues that there is not enough evidence for the last of these three.

But Malone's three formulations are inadequate for discussing the Trinity. In view of the indwelling of persons of the Trinity, what could it mean for the Son to appear "alone"? In the ordinary sense, the Son is never "alone."[2] It is true that the Son alone became incarnate. He has a unique role in redemption. But all three persons of the Trinity are always involved in the work of God in creation, providence, and redemption. And, as John 14:9 indicates, we see the Father in the Son.

The mutual indwelling of the persons of the Trinity goes together with the distinctions between the persons. The persons of the Trinity have subtly distinguishable roles when God acts in creation, providence, and redemption. The visible manifestations of God in the Old Testament, especially in the case of a human form, foreshadow the incarna-

---

1. Andrew Malone, *Knowing Jesus in the Old Testament? A Fresh Look at Christophanies* (Nottingham, UK: Inter-Varsity, 2015). All page numbers in the body of this appendix are from Malone's book.

2. In fairness to Malone, he formulates his alternative of the Son appearing "alone" because he thinks it is the theory offered by some earlier works (which he rejects). A prime example is found in James A. Borland, *Christ in the Old Testament* (Chicago: Moody, 1978). Borland summarizes his own view and that of a number of other writers as "the view that Christ *alone* appeared in the human-form theophanies" and that "Christ was the *sole* agent of the Christophanies" (ibid., 67, 70, italics mine). What does Borland actually mean? Does he mean that the Son can be "alone" in an absolute sense? The Son alone became incarnate. But in his incarnation he is indwelt by the Father and the Spirit. So he is not alone in that sense. Borland himself explicitly mentions the doctrine of the Trinity in the middle of his discussion (ibid., 68–69), perhaps without realizing that it might be in tension with his wording about Christ's "sole" agency. If we were to take seriously his affirmation of the Trinity, and use it to qualify his other statements, to what extent would he still disagree with Malone? So the disagreement between Malone and earlier works may not be as sharp as it seems.

tion. The connection forward to the incarnation is validated by the fact that the New Testament has theophanic themes that also occur in the Old Testament. For example, we can see similarities between the appearance of Christ in Revelation 1:12–16 and the features in the theophanies in Ezekiel 1:27, Daniel 7:9–10, 13, and 10:5–6. Or consider the connections between the transfiguration in Matthew 17:1–8, Mark 9:2–8, and Luke 9:28–36 and the appearance of God on Mount Sinai in Exodus 24 (and also Exodus 19–20). These connections mean that Christ is the climactic fulfillment of Old Testament theophanies.

So we may describe Old Testament theophanies as appearances of the preincarnate Christ, the second person of the Trinity. But Christ appears in the context of the indwelling of the Father and the Spirit. Moreover, we need a qualification: the earlier appearances are not "temporary incarnations." There is only *one* incarnation, the one through the Virgin Mary. The Old Testament appearances foreshadow and anticipate the incarnation as a once-for-all event that takes place in the fullness of time (Gal. 4:4). Some Old Testament appearances involve a temporary human *form*. Only from the time of the incarnation onward does the Son of God take to himself a human *nature*.

The *Meaning* of "the Angel of the Lord"

Now let us look at a detailed proposal concerning the expression "the angel of the Lord." Andrew Malone argues at one point that the expression "the angel of the Lord" means "the angel the Lord," that is, "the angel who is the Lord."[3] What he is saying is not merely that in some cases the "angel" is divine (which is true), but that the *meaning* of the key Hebrew expression is "the angel the Lord" (not "the messenger sent by the Lord"). But this interpretation does not work. Several points are relevant.

(1) The meaning *messenger* is built into the key Hebrew word *mal'āk* (sometimes translated "angel"). The presence of that meaning naturally leads to an expectation that, if there is a modifying word, it may well identify the sender of the message. And indeed we find such modifying words a number of times. Haggai 1:13 speaks of "Haggai, the *messenger* of the Lord," who "spoke to the people with the Lord's message." This verse alone is decisive. There is no internal linguistic difference between

---

3. Malone, *Knowing Jesus in the Old Testament?* 98–102, 109; the expressions in quotes are my summary, not Malone's exact wording.

the Hebrew expression in Haggai 1:13 and the other expressions about "the messenger [angel] of the Lord" on which Malone focuses.

Similarly, the priest in Malachi 2:7 is described as "the *messenger* of the LORD of hosts," in a context where he brings "instruction." The instruction should be understood as instruction in the law (Lev. 10:11). So the message he brings is from the Lord. Another example occurs in Malachi 3:1. "My messenger" in this verse has the modifying item "my" identifying the one who sent the messenger. Other examples include "the messengers of God" in 2 Chronicles 36:16, and "his messengers" in 2 Chronicles 36:15. Both expressions refer to the prophets sent with God's message to the people.

There are also examples of using the word for "messengers" when there are human senders: "the *messengers* of Ben-hadad" (1 Kings 20:9), "the *messengers* of the king of Samaria" (2 Kings 1:3), and "his *envoys*" (Isa. 30:4). Finally, 2 Samuel 24:16 has an instance where Malone himself admits that "the angel of the LORD" is in some fashion distinct from "the LORD" who speaks to him (p. 112). Malone attempts to evade the force of this evidence by saying that this "angel" might not be the same as the "angel" in other Old Testament verses. We freely grant that the expression "the angel of the Lord" may have more than one *referent* (see Luke 1:11 as well as Hag. 1:13). But through his own observations on 2 Samuel 24:16 Malone has undermined his theory that the *meaning* of the expression is "the angel [who is] the Lord."

(2) The proposed meaning "the messenger who is the Lord" is awkward because it leaves no motivation for calling the Lord "the messenger." If the personage is simply the Lord, with no sense of differentiation[4] from a second personage who sent him, how is he still a messenger? He has a message, to be sure, but it is simply his own. In that case, he speaks on his own behalf, not as a "messenger."

(3) In the course of his argument, Malone appeals to various possible parallels like "the songs of Michael Jackson" or "the river Euphrates" or "the daughter of Zion" (pp. 98–100), to show that the meaning "the angel the Lord" is possible. But these parallels are not convincing. Words like "songs" and "river" differ from the word "messenger" because they do not automatically suggest a sender or author. "Daughter of Zion" is a closer parallel, but Malone does not discuss the fact that

---

4. We distinguish here carefully between meaning and referent. The meaning of the key expression is "the messenger of [sent by] the Lord." The referent, the person to whom the expression refers, may still be the divine Son as the messenger sent by the Father.

the context is metaphorical and that there may still be a subtle differentiation: Zion is the location (or the city), and the "daughter" is the *populace* in that location. In the case of the word "messenger," there is a natural differentiation between the messenger and the source for his message and commission.

(4) The issue is not whether the word "of" in English or the analogous constructions in Hebrew can have a wide range of meaning. They certainly can. The issue concerns the natural meaning of a particular collocation of words—"the messenger of the Lord"—based on parallel passages and the immediate context. The mere theoretical possibility of another meaning matters little, when there is an obvious meaning available for this particular expression, namely the sense "the messenger from the Lord," a meaning confirmed by parallels (Hag. 1:13; Mal. 2:7).

(5) Malone claims that "we do not actually find corresponding examples such as 'an envoy of Solomon' or 'an ambassador of Hezekiah' using the word *mal'āk*" (p. 102). He later qualifies this by saying, "We never meet a *singular* 'messenger of Nebuchadnezzar'" (p. 109, italics mine). But the Old Testament includes plural examples ("messengers"), as we saw in point (1) above. The plural examples are relevant because they indicate that a modifying word typically indicates the sender. It is special pleading to exclude these examples.

In addition, we are still left with Haggai 1:13 and Malachi 2:7, where the singular term "messenger" occurs. These verses offer clear counterexamples to Malone's idea. What does Malone say about these verses? Malone cites Haggai 1:13 more than once in the course of his book to point out that the expression "the messenger of the Lord" does not always designate a supernatural figure. Malone is correct: we must not naively assume that the expression has the same referent in every context. But Malone fails to observe that Haggai 1:13 is quite relevant in showing the normal *meaning* of the expression ("messenger from the Lord, i.e., sent by the Lord"). The meaning remains the same even though the person to whom it may *refer* varies from one context to another. Malone also leaves out 2 Samuel 24:16 when considering evidence for the meaning.

Malone attempts at one point to put the postexilic verses in a separate category, by postulating that they may represent a late and different development (p. 115). Yes, a distinctive development is theoretically possible. But there is no solid *positive* evidence for it. The postulation of development makes sense only if one has *already* decided that Malone's theory is correct. In that case, the contrary evidence has to be explained another way. The most convenient way is to postulate that the contrary evidence shows the existence of an earlier contrary meaning.

(6) Malone also claims that we never find expressions about God's sending: "If the Angel were God's envoy, . . . we might expect mention of God's sending the Sent One of the Lord" (p. 111). This claim, like the case in (5) above, is an argument from silence rather than from evidence. And it is weak, for at least two reasons. First, "sending the Sent One" is redundant, and that redundancy might be one reason why we do not find more instances. Second, there are at least two cases that come near to providing what Malone claims is not there in the Old Testament. In 2 Chronicles 36:15, "the LORD, the God of their fathers, *sent* persistently to them by his messengers." The next verse, 2 Chronicles 36:16, further defines the "his messengers" as "the messengers of God." Haggai 1:13, as we observed, uses the expression "the messenger of the LORD," and in the same verse defines his role: he "spoke to the people with the LORD's message." The preceding verse (v. 12) says that Haggai was *sent*: "the words of Haggai the prophet, as the LORD their God had *sent* him." The surrounding verses also contain similar information about Haggai's role: "the word of the LORD came by the hand of Haggai the prophet" (1:1; cf. 1:3; 2:1, 10).

(7) Malone's discussion of "the angel of the Lord" on page 112, like his initial formulation of options on page 18, is troubled by failure to reckon fully with the mystery of the indwelling of persons in the Trinity. He discusses whether the "angel" is "entirely disjoint" from God who sends him, and whether God and the angel are "two completely separate individuals." The discussion appears to be framed so that either they are "entirely disjoint" or they are completely identical. Malone gives no space at this point to consider whether there is a third, deeper alternative: there is mystery here, a mystery further unveiled in the New Testament, where we see both the distinction of persons in the Trinity and the reality of each being fully God and indwelling the others. In effect, Malone's discussion misses options that are not within the bounds of his simple (but unclear) formulations.

Do We Isolate the Instances of Divine Messengers?

There is an obvious way of responding to my points, and making a further defense of the view that the meaning is "the angel [who is] the

Lord." A person could do it by stressing the special nature of the cases where the Old Testament speaks about a messenger who is divine. The argument would go as follows. When the messenger is divine, there can be no differentiation between God and the messenger, because the Old Testament clearly teaches that there is only one God. The messenger simply *must* be identical with God. And so appeals to analogous normal usages with human and angelic messengers are not relevant.

Such an argument would be appealing if a person held to a monadic or unitarian kind of monotheism, and was committed beforehand to permitting no differentiation within God. But in fact God is the Trinitarian God. So it is false to assume that the unity of God precludes any revelation of differentiation. Moreover, we must allow in principle that such a revelation could take place even at a fairly early stage in history (for example, the plural "us" in Gen. 1:26 or 3:22; or, less obviously, the differentiation between God and his word in divine speeches in Genesis 1, or the differentiation between God and his Spirit in Gen. 1:2, or between God and his breath in Gen. 2:7).

Even though a person concedes that the New Testament teaches a differentiation of persons within one God, he could still claim that this is irrelevant for the Old Testament, because finding differentiation in the Old Testament involves an anachronistic reading of the New Testament back into the Old Testament. There are two extremes here. On one extreme lies the view that everything in the New Testament can be "read back," with no attention to the fact that the Old Testament represents an earlier stage in progressive revelation. On the other extreme lies the view that the Old Testament is essentially disconnected from the later New Testament revelation (at least until the New Testament "creates" fresh connections). Neither extreme does justice to progressive revelation.

So is there a third alternative? Yes. What is foreshadowed in the Old Testament is more clearly revealed in the New. Old Testament revelation is revelation of God, and God is always Trinitarian. So the revelation itself is intrinsically Trinitarian, even though it takes the later revelation in the New Testament to throw more light on its intrinsic nature. On this basis, we understand that appearances of God in human form in the Old Testament anticipate the fuller revelation of the Trinity that takes place when the Son becomes incarnate and takes to himself human nature.

Finally, let us observe a deeper issue. The texts that speak about a *divine* messenger cannot in fact be isolated from the texts that speak about human and angelic messengers. Many instances of language about God operate by analogy with human actions. God plans, speaks, loves, and brings about effects in the world. God is a great king and a warrior and a savior. God uses "anthropomorphic language" to describe himself. We understand what is meant in these expressions because we see analogies between God and the human actions of planning, speaking, loving, and bringing about effects. Likewise we see analogies between God on the one hand and human kings and warriors and saviors on the other hand. The language about God makes sense because of analogies. If we isolate certain texts just because they refer to God, and we give them radically different meanings from the corresponding usages with human beings, we undermine the pattern for divine revelation in general. That is unacceptable.

Consequently, the expression "the messenger of the Lord" needs to be treated by analogy with instances of human messengers. And then the passages about human messengers, mentioned in point (1) above, remain relevant. They show that for both human messengers and divine messengers, added information like "of Ben-hadad" or "of the Lord" indicates the source for the commission and the message.

Final Trinitarian Focus

On the final page of the body of his book, Malone returns to affirm briefly the idea that Christ could appear in the Old Testament in a Trinitarian context rather than in "the exclusive sense" (p. 198). Yes, indeed. But this final affirmation is in tension with most of the rest of the book, which appears to focus on only three options: an appearance that allows no differentiation *at all* ("the angel who is the Lord"), an appearance of a created angel, or an appearance of Christ "alone."

Appendix B

A Theophany in Genesis 1:2?

Genesis 1:2 says, "the Spirit of God was hovering over the face of the waters." What is the significance of this description? Do we have here a theophany, a visible appearance of the Spirit of God? Meredith G. Kline has vigorously argued that we do.[1] Kline draws attention to the use of the unusual term "hover" or "flutter" (Hebrew *rḥp*, רחף), which in the Hebrew Old Testament occurs with this meaning only in Genesis 1:2 and Deuteronomy 32:11. In addition, the expression "without form" in Genesis 1:2 and the expression "waste" in Deuteronomy 32:10 both translate the same Hebrew word (*tōhû*, תהו). Deuteronomy 32:10–11 has picked up key vocabulary from Genesis 1:2. By doing so, it draws an analogy between God's care in the unformed condition of creation and his care in the "unformed" wilderness that Israel crossed on the way to the Promised Land. Largely on the basis of this correlation of texts, Kline concludes that the Spirit in Genesis 1:2 is an appearance of the "Glory-cloud" that later accompanied the exodus from Egypt.

Kline has helpfully drawn attention to a significant correlation between texts: Genesis 1:2 and Deuteronomy 32:10–11 are indeed topically connected. Both speak of the care of God, and both use the same special term for "hovering." But a correlation is not always an identity. The care of God is manifested in more than one way—theophany is an intensive form of a larger pattern for God's actions. Genesis 1:2 might

---

1. Meredith G. Kline, *Images of the Spirit* (Grand Rapids, MI: Baker, 1980), 13–15; Meredith G. Kline, *Kingdom Prologue: Genesis Foundations for a Covenantal Worldview* (Overland Park, KS: Two Age, 2000), 42–43.

be speaking of the larger pattern, without directly describing a special visual appearance. Hence, in my opinion, Kline has overestimated the confidence with which we may speak of a *theophany* in Genesis 1:2, in the narrow sense of the word *theophany*. Moreover, the language in Genesis 1:2 suggests an association with the fluttering of the wind (the Hebrew word *ruach* [רוּחַ] for "spirit" in Gen. 1:2 can also mean *wind*). Note that Ezekiel 37:9, John 3:8, and Acts 2:2 all associate the Holy Spirit with *wind*. If in fact Genesis 1:2 enjoys associations *both* with the "eagles' wings" of Deuteronomy 32:11 *and* with the fluttering of the wind, it dissolves the sense of pure identity between Genesis 1:2 and Deuteronomy 32:11.[2]

Kline has also gone beyond the evidence in concluding that the theophany is an appearance of the "Glory-cloud" rather than another kind of theophany.[3] Let us suppose for the sake of argument that Genesis 1:2 does refer to a special theophany of a visible kind. If so, why not a *fire* theophany, as in Acts 2:3–4 and Revelation 4:5? Or why not a thunderstorm theophany, which may include *wind* (Ps. 18:10; Ezek. 1:4)? Or why not a human appearance, in accordance with the later creation of man "in the image of God" in Genesis 1:26–27 (which Kline himself believes is connected to Gen. 1:2)? Fire and thunderstorm are both associated with the appearance of God in "a thick cloud" at Mount Sinai (Ex. 19:9). And a human appearance is suggested in Exodus 24:10. But then we have *multiple* rich associations with multiple aspects of theophany, not *just* an identification of Genesis 1:2 with the cloud. Moreover, we can see that fire also occurs apart from a cloud, as in Exodus 3:2, Acts 2:3, and Revelation 4:5. Wind appears apart from a

---

2. The word "howling" in Deuteronomy 32:10 ("the howling waste of the wilderness") probably designates the howling of wild beasts in the wilderness, not the howling of the wind (Francis Brown, S. R. Driver, and Charles A. Briggs, *A Hebrew and English Lexicon of the Old Testament with an Appendix Containing the Biblical Aramaic* [Oxford: Oxford University Press, 1953], 410). If, on the other hand, the reference should turn out to be to the howling of the wind, it would strengthen the association with the wind, and undermine the theory that Genesis 1:2 refers exclusively to a glory-cloud theophany.

3. Kline, *Images of the Spirit*, 15. To his credit, Kline recognizes a thematic association with wind as well as with cloud. He speaks of "this theophanic cloud-and-wind form of the Spirit" (ibid.). But this manner of combining terms for cloud and wind can easily lead to neglecting the specific character of individual theophanies, some of which may include a cloud but not wind, or wind but not a cloud. Other theophanies, of course, like 2 Samuel 22:11–12, include both. In the end, all kinds of theophanies are integrally related, but that observation also is in tension with the attempt to identify Genesis 1:2 as one specific form.

Similar observations could be made about Kline's term "Glory-cloud" (ibid.). In a fair number of instances, cloud and glory come together in a theophany. But there are also theophanies with dark clouds, and there are theophanies of glory that suggest brightness and comparisons with the sun rather than an association with a cloud. So cloud and glory are not interchangeable.

cloud in 2 Kings 2:11 and Acts 2:2. A human figure appears apart from a cloud in Genesis 18:2 and Joshua 5:13. All in all, there are many *kinds* of appearance in theophanies. Genesis 1:2 does not indicate clearly that we should think solely of a cloud theophany.

Nevertheless, in a loose sense all theophanies are correlated to each other and are correlated to other expressions that speak of the presence of God. With this qualification, Kline's observations are a most useful contribution to the study of theophany. In fact, his whole book *Images of the Spirit* offers an important discussion on the theme of theophany.[4]

---

4. See also Jeffrey Jay Niehaus's book, which builds on Kline's work (Niehaus, *God at Sinai: Covenant and Theophany in the Bible and the Ancient Near East* [Grand Rapids, MI: Zondervan, 1995]). Niehaus's book points out that the ancient Near Eastern use of the icon of a winged sun disk establishes a correlation between bird-like wings and a glory theophany (150–153).

Appendix C

Understanding Genesis 3:8

Genesis 3:8 says, "And they [Adam and Eve] heard the sound of the LORD God walking in the garden in the cool of the day." As we indicated briefly in chapter 30, Meredith Kline finds in this verse a reference to the appearing of the Holy Spirit, and advocates translating the Hebrew expression behind "the cool of the day" as "the Spirit of the Day [of the Lord]."[1] Let us consider this interpretation.

An Appearance of the Cloud?

First, was there a theophany? The text does not say *explicitly* that there was a special visual appearance. But Adam and Eve hid themselves from "the presence of the LORD God," indicating that the Lord was intensely present in a specific location. The information is sparse. The special presence is theophany-like. It is a theophany in a *broad* sense. But we need not conclude more.

Second, if there was a special visual appearance, what form did it take? Kline thinks that it took the form of the Spirit manifesting his presence in a cloud. If so, the verb *walking* is not the most transparent way of describing the appearance. The word *walking* hints, of course, at the possibility of theophany, and Kline appropriately cites other passages where God says that he walks in the midst of his people. But does this

---

1. Meredith G. Kline, "Primal Parousia," *Westminster Theological Journal* 40 (1978): 245–280; Meredith G. Kline, *Images of the Spirit* (Grand Rapids, MI: Baker, 1980), 97–131; also Jeffrey Jay Niehaus, *God at Sinai: Covenant and Theophany in the Bible and the Ancient Near East* (Grand Rapids, MI: Zondervan, 1995), 155–159.

language evoke a picture of the movement of wind or a cloud, or rather the movement of a man-like figure?

Kline himself observes that "this verb is used to describe the movement of agents of the divine council, which is found within the Glory-cloud, . . . "[2] Precisely: it is human-like or angelic figures belonging to "the divine council," not the cloud, that characteristically "walk." If we have a cloud of glory, and not a human figure, should we not expect a different wording, such as, "the cloud of glory was moving in/descending on/standing in the garden on the day of the Lord"? Obviously, that is not what Genesis 3:8 has.

"The Spirit of the Day"

In addition, we should consider Kline's proposed translation, "the Spirit of the Day." This translation has difficulties. The Hebrew word for "spirit" may also mean *wind* or *breath*. It is not obvious that it means *spirit* in Genesis 3:8. In effect, Kline must infer some words that are not there: he thinks that the meaning is "the Spirit [of the Lord] of the Day [of the Lord]." Without the extra words, the Hebrew is fully capable of being interpreted as meaning, "in the breeze [wind] of the day," or, more interpretively, "in the cool of the day." Most translations take this route. Without the extra words "of the Lord," the word translated "Spirit" can just as easily mean "wind," and the word for "day" need not mean "the Day of the Lord." It can just mean "day," that is, the same day on which Adam and Eve sinned.

In addition, Kline's translation does not explain well the key preposition introducing the phrase "cool of the day." In Hebrew there is a preposition *le* (לְ), represented in the ESV and other English translations by "in." Kline construes the Hebrew preposition *le* as indicating *role* or *purpose*.[3] We would then have, "the Lord God walking in the garden *as/in the role of* the Spirit [of God in cloud theophany] of [belonging to] the day [of the Lord]."

In the Old Testament, the language concerning the Spirit of God implies the presence of God, and the designation "Spirit" anticipates the doctrine of the Trinity developed in the New Testament. Ultimately we are dealing with the mystery of one God in three persons. But for God to function *as* the Spirit of God is an awkward expression, especially

---

2. Kline, *Images of the Spirit*, 102.
3. Ibid., 105–106.

within the Old Testament, and a comparatively early part of Old Testament revelation at that.

The Storm of the Day

Jeffrey Jay Niehaus offers an alternate hypothesis.[4] He appeals to an Akkadian word, *ūmu*, which seems to be a cognate to the Hebrew word for day (*yôm*, יוֹם). The Akkadian word can mean either "day" or "storm." Reasoning from the Akkadian word, the Koehler-Baumgartner Hebrew lexicon indicates that the Hebrew word (*yôm*) may also have both meanings (Ludwig Koehler and Walter Baumgartner, *The Hebrew and Aramaic Lexicon of the Old Testament* [Leiden-New York-Köln: Brill, 1995], 2:401); but the second meaning "storm" is explicitly marked as doubtful. Following this possible lead, Niehaus postulates that the key phrase "cool of the day" should be translated "wind of the storm" (but Koehler-Baumgartner itself does not list Genesis 3:8 as a possible instance of the meaning "storm").

Niehaus's evidence is thin and doubtful, and capable of other interpretations. Moreover, the immediate context in Genesis 3:8 does not give a clear indication that there is a different meaning for the key Hebrew word *yôm*. The word *yôm* has the meaning "day" in its repeated uses in Genesis 1–2. There is no indication that it suddenly has a new and (at best) rare meaning in Genesis 3:8. Even if we suppose that the word for "day" can also mean "storm" in Hebrew, the human and divine authors of Genesis would know that such an introduction of a new meaning would not be clear, given the context. If they wished to talk about a storm, they would therefore have used one of several Hebrew words that unambiguously means "storm." So Niehaus's hypothesis fails to be convincing.

Conclusion

In sum, Genesis 3:8 is far too sparse in information to support Kline's interpretation. He must read in a lot by means of associations with other passages that become explicit about the day of the Lord. All these passages are of course related by various thematic associations. But association does not necessarily imply pure identity. And we are still left with the awkwardness of the Lord God functioning "as" the Spirit

---

4. Niehaus, *God at Sinai*, 156–157.

(not fully parallel to Isa. 28:6, where a spirit of justice is provided to a human judge).

The prominent evangelical commentaries by Wenham, Hamilton, Waltke, and Collins, written after the appearance of Kline's view in 1978 and 1980, would be aware of Kline, but none of them mentions his view of Genesis 3:8 or supports it. Collins briefly mentions two articles that interpret the "wind" of Genesis 3:8 as a violent storm wind, only to reject these as implausible in the context.[5] "In the cool of the day" fits the context.

---

5. C. John Collins, *Genesis 1–4: A Linguistic, Literary, and Theological Commentary* (Phillipsburg, NJ: P&R, 2006), 151n8. See also the discussions of Genesis 3:8 in Victor P. Hamilton, *The Book of Genesis Chapters 1–17* (Grand Rapids, MI: Eerdmans, 1990); Bruce K. Waltke with Cathi J. Fredricks, *Genesis: A Commentary* (Grand Rapids, MI: Zondervan, 2001); and Gordon J. Wenham, *Genesis 1–15*, Word Biblical Commentary, vol. 1 (Waco, TX: Word, 1987).

Bibliography

Alexander, T. Desmond, and Simon J. Gathercole. *Heaven on Earth: The Temple in Biblical Theology*. Exeter, UK: Paternoster, 2004.

Beale, G. K. *The Book of Revelation: A Commentary on the Greek Text*. Grand Rapids, MI: Eerdmans, 1999.

———. *The Temple and the Church's Mission: A Biblical Theology of the Dwelling Place of God*. Leicester, UK: Apollos; Downers Grove, IL: InterVarsity, 2004.

Beale, G. K., and Mitchell Kim. *God Dwells among Us: Expanding Eden to the Ends of the Earth*. Downers Grove, IL: InterVarsity, 2014.

Beasley-Murray, G. R. *The Book of Revelation*. Greenwood, SC: Attic; London: Marshall, Morgan, & Scott, 1974.

Borland, James A. *Christ in the Old Testament: Old Testament Appearances of Christ in Human Form*. 2nd ed. Ross-shire, UK. Mentor, 1999.

Brown, Francis, S. R. Driver, and Charles A. Briggs. *A Hebrew and English Lexicon of the Old Testament with an Appendix Containing the Biblical Aramaic*. Oxford: Oxford University Press, 1953.

Collins, C. John. *Genesis 1–4: A Linguistic, Literary, and Theological Commentary*. Phillipsburg, NJ: P&R, 2006.

Cornelius, Emmitt. "'Being Going to Be Born to Mary': An Overview and Appraisal of Robert W. Jenson's View of the Incarnation as an OT Phenomenon," *Journal of the Evangelical Theological Society* 58/2 (2015): 353–366.

Duguid, Iain. *Ezekiel*. Grand Rapids, MI: Zondervan, 1999.

Fairbairn, Patrick. *An Exposition of Ezekiel*. Reprint. n.l.: The National Foundation for Christian Education, 1969.

Fohrer, Georg. *Theologische Grundstrukturen des Alten Testaments*. Berlin/New York: de Gruyter, 1972.

Frame, John M. *The Doctrine of God*. Phillipsburg, NJ: P&R, 2002.

———. *The Doctrine of the Knowledge of God*. Phillipsburg, NJ: P&R, 1987.

Futato, Mark D. *Creation: A Witness to the Wonder of God.* Phillipsburg, NJ: P&R, 2000.

Hamilton, Victor P. *The Book of Genesis Chapters 1–17.* Grand Rapids, MI: Eerdmans, 1990.

Heidelberg Catechism, The. http://reformed.org/documents/index.html ?mainframe=http://reformed.org/documents/heidelberg.html, accessed June 24, 2016.

Hendriksen, William. *More Than Conquerors: An Interpretation of the Book of Revelation.* Grand Rapids, MI: Baker, 1939.

Jastrow, Marcus. *A Dictionary of the Targumim, the Talmud Babli and Yerushalmi, and the Midrashic Literature.* 2 vols. New York: Pardes, 1950.

Johnson, Dennis E. *Triumph of the Lamb: A Commentary on Revelation.* Phillipsburg, NJ: P&R, 2001.

Johnston, Robert K. *God's Wider Presence: Reconsidering General Revelation.* Grand Rapids, MI: Baker, 2014.

Kidner, Derek. *Genesis: An Introduction and Commentary.* London/Downers Grove, IL: InterVarsity, 1967.

Kline, Meredith G. *Glory in Our Midst: A Biblical-Theological Reading of Zechariah's Night Visions.* Overland Park, KS: Two Age, 2001.

———. *Images of the Spirit.* Grand Rapids, MI: Baker, 1980.

———. *Kingdom Prologue: Genesis Foundations for a Covenantal Worldview.* Overland Park, KS: Two Age, 2000.

———. "Primal Parousia," *Westminster Theological Journal* 40 (1978): 245–280.

Kline, Meredith M. "The Holy Spirit as Covenant Witness." ThM thesis, Westminster Theological Seminary, 1972.

Koehler, Ludwig, and Walter Baumgartner. *The Hebrew and Aramaic Lexicon of the Old Testament.* 5 vols. Leiden-New York-Köln: Brill, 1995.

Kreider, Glenn R. *God with Us: Exploring God's Personal Interactions with His People throughout the Bible.* Phillipsburg, NJ: P&R, 2015.

Lister, J. Ryan. *The Presence of God: Its Place in the Storyline of Scripture and the Story of Our Lives.* Wheaton, IL: Crossway, 2014.

Malone, Andrew S. *Knowing Jesus in the Old Testament? A Fresh Look at Christophanies.* Nottingham, UK: Inter-Varsity, 2015.

Mininger, Marcus. "What Is Revealed, Where, and How: Uncovering the Theme of Revelation and Discovering a New Approach to Reading Romans 1:16–3:26." PhD diss., Westminster Theological Seminary, 2016.

Murray, John. "The Attestation of Scripture." In *The Infallible Word: A Symposium by Members of the Faculty of Westminster Theological*

Seminary. Edited by N. B. Stonehouse and Paul Woolley. 3rd rev. ed.. Philadelphia: P&R, 1967. 1–54.

Niehaus, Jeffrey Jay. *God at Sinai: Covenant and Theophany in the Bible and the Ancient Near East*. Grand Rapids, MI: Zondervan, 1995.

Poythress, Vern S. "Counterfeiting in the Book of Revelation as a Perspective on Non-Christian Culture," *Journal of the Evangelical Theological Society* 40/3 (1997): 411–418, http://www.frame-poythress .org/counterfeiting-in-the-book-of-revelation-as-a-perspective-on-non -christian-culture/.

———. "The Holy Ones of the Most High in Daniel VII," *Vetus Testamentum* 26/2 (April 1976): 208–213.

———. *The Miracles of Jesus: How the Savior's Mighty Acts Serve as Signs of Redemption*. Wheaton, IL: Crossway, 2016.

———. *Reading the Word of God in the Presence of God: A Handbook for Biblical Interpretation*. Wheaton, IL: Crossway, 2016.

———. *Redeeming Science: A God-Centered Approach*. Wheaton, IL: Crossway, 2006.

———. *The Returning King: A Guide to the Book of Revelation*. Phillipsburg, NJ: P&R, 2000.

———. *The Shadow of Christ in the Law of Moses*. Reprint. Phillipsburg, NJ: P&R, 1995.

Rhodes, Ron. *Christ before the Manger: The Life and Times of the Preincarnate Christ*. Grand Rapids, MI: Baker, 1992.

Savran, George W. *Encountering the Divine: Theophany in Biblical Narrative*. London/New York: T&T Clark, 2005.

Terrien, Samuel L. *The Elusive Presence: Toward a New Biblical Theology*. San Francisco: Harper & Row, 1978.

Van Til, Cornelius. *An Introduction to Systematic Theology: Prolegomena and the Doctrines of Revelation, Scripture, and God*. Edited by William Edgar. Phillipsburg, NJ: P&R, 2007.

Waltke, Bruce K., with Cathi J. Fredricks. *Genesis: A Commentary*. Grand Rapids, MI: Zondervan, 2001.

Wenham, Gordon J. *Genesis 1–15*. Word Biblical Commentary. Vol. 1. Waco, TX: Word, 1987.

Westminster Confession of Faith, 1646.

General Index

Scripture Index

Also Available from Vern Poythress

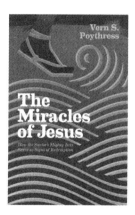
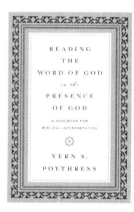
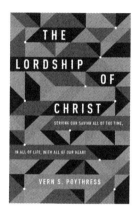

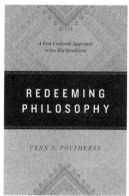
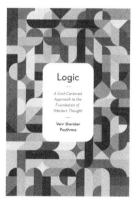

For more information, visit crossway.org